Map of Chipping Ongar showing the main historic sites.

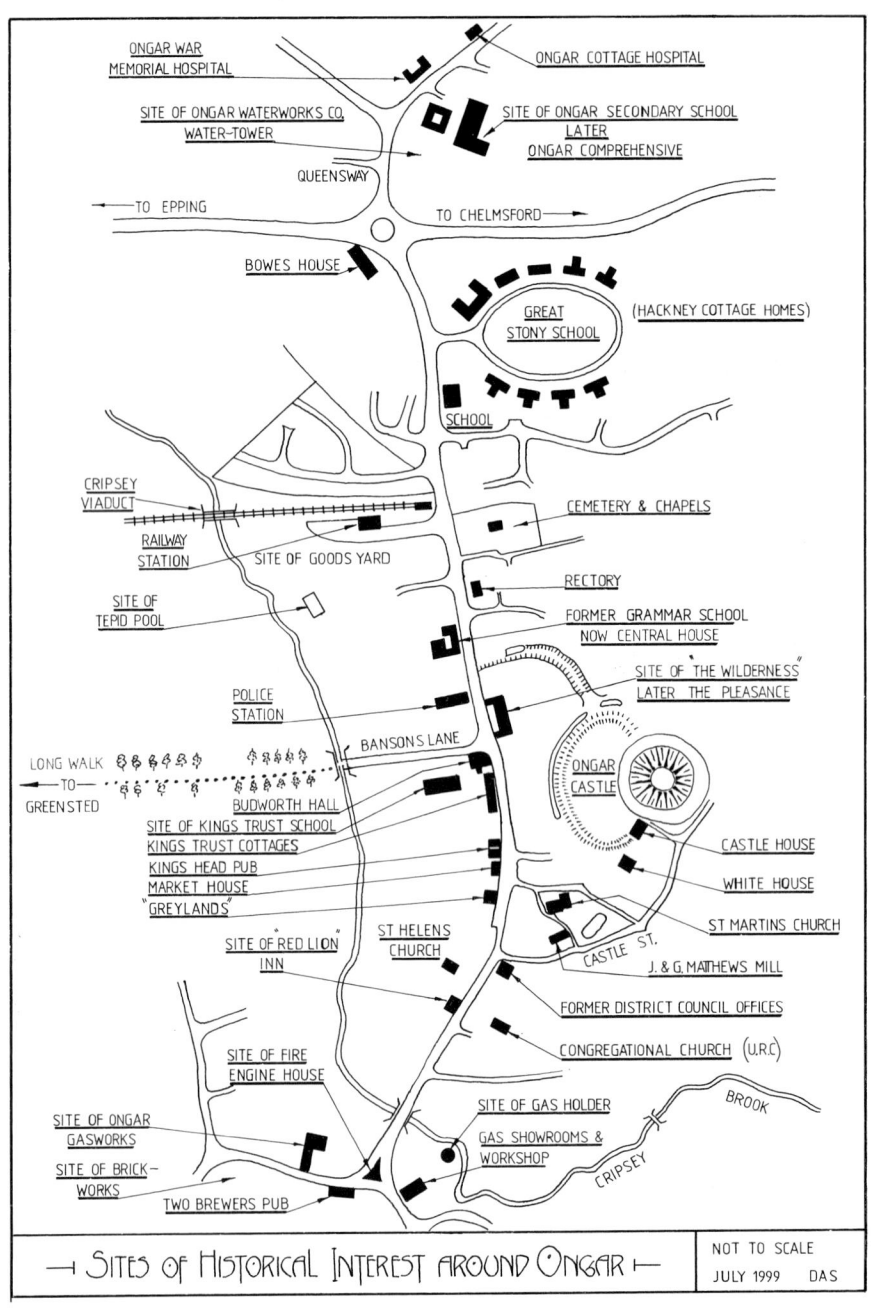

Aspects of the History of Ongar

by

Ongar Millennium History Group

published 1999

Published by the Ongar Millennium History Project
2 Landview Gardens Ongar Essex CM5 9EQ

copyright Ongar Millennium History Project

ISBN 0 9535048 0 8

All rights reserved. No part of this publication
may be reproduced, in any form, in whole or in part,
without prior permission in writing
from the publisher.

First published 1999
reprinted 2000

Printed and bound by The Lavenham Press Limited
Water Street Lavenham Suffolk CO10 9RN

FOREWORD

I was delighted to be asked to write a foreword for this book. It is an impressive community project and all those involved should be proud of what they have produced.

Local history has not always been valued. For many people it is easy to assume that history happened somewhere else, normally in a school textbook rather than around us.

This book proves that history happened in Ongar. Learning about local history grounds us in our community, and helps us to place ourselves in a long and continuing story. Learning how the Budworth Hall in Ongar got its name brings the past into our everyday lives. History is about grand events, as well as everyday lives, and this book records both, from tales of Tudor courtiers living in Ongar to accounts of more mundane, but equally important, matters such as health care and poor relief in the area.

Besides recording the people and the events which make up Ongar's rich history, this book is a celebration of the town. It is clear that all the chapters have been written by people who love Ongar. Where a community cherishes its past, they also care about its future. This book indicates that Ongar will have a vibrant future.

Sue Davies

Museums Officer, Epping Forest District Museum

April 1999

EDITOR'S PREFACE

The inspiration for the Ongar Millennium History Project came from two people – Marion Slade and Felicitie Barnes. Both had worked together on a history of the Budworth Hall as part of its centenary celebrations in 1996 and had agreed that it would be good to tackle a similar project when they had more time.

Later that year Marion approached a number of people whom she thought might be interested. I think that she had a very clear idea of her objectives from the outset. These were to produce a new history of the civil parish of Ongar and to establish a town walk. She also had more general plans to increase awareness of the richness and fascination of local history.

It is particularly sad that Marion died in the summer of 1997 when the project was barely hatched. However, her thorough preparations gave the group the momentum that it needed. She herself had intended to write the chapter on local government. Her meticulous notes on the subject have been invaluable to both Jenny Main and myself. We have tried to follow her example.

Marion often referred to a "definitive" history of Ongar. That, of course, cannot be written because history never stands still. There are always errors to be corrected and new sources to be found. Attitudes to history change too, and the earlier accounts of Ongar reflect the particular interests of their time. One of my priorities as editor was to attempt to ensure that all articles were referenced to enable future historians to return to our sources. As it has not always been possible to do this as thoroughly as I had hoped, I apologise in advance!

There is a precedent for collaborative research in Ongar. In 1951 the WEA undertook an ambitious study now deposited in the Essex Record Office. A glance through the footnotes in the relevant volume of the Victoria County History shows how useful it was to the author, and is a reminder of the important contribution that amateur historians can make to local history.

I am not a historian by training, but listening to people has been a large part of my working life. I have spoken to people who remember the regular traffic of hay carts through Ongar to London, and to a soldier who fought in the Boer War. Memories are an irreplaceable archive, lost without trace on the death of the individual. One purpose of this book is to weave these vivid accounts into the factual text.

Ongar has had surprisingly few historians. William Holman made notes for a county history (never published) in the early eighteenth century. Philip Morant's *History of Essex,* published in 1768, was an enormous undertaking and is still much referred to. Inevitably he relied in part on other writers and we suspect – on the evidence of his account of the castle – that he never visited Ongar. Nevertheless he looked at a prodigious number of documents at a time when they were largely unappreciated, uncatalogued and in private hands. His enthusiasm for these sources is not disguised by his clear and elegant prose.

Many subsequent accounts drew heavily on the earlier writers, but three Victorians made original contributions, Isaac Jennings in 1862, Phillip Budworth in

1876 and the rector of Chipping Ongar, R. I. Porter, in the following year. These authors had their own motives for writing, but they all recognised the value of looking at, and quoting from original documents, rather than repeating the familiar texts of earlier historians. In this century the WEA survey in 1951 and the relevant volume of the Victoria County History in 1956, are both still invaluable sources for historians. Several pictorial histories have been published in the last decade, showing vivid visual images of the last hundred years. They emphasise the popularity of old photographs and the importance of preserving these images. But they cannot tell us what people thought, or what motivated their actions. I hope that this history will begin to answer some of these questions.

Inevitably this book will contain errors of fact and interpretation. Often it has had to rely on other printed sources, and will inevitably reproduce some of their mistakes. However it does contain much new material which should provide a useful starting point for future researchers. A great deal of work has gone into its production, and I am grateful to everyone who has given practical and financial help. My committee has been extremely supportive. Ongar Parish Council and *The Ongar Observer* have backed us unstintingly from the outset. Our thanks are particularly due to our major commercial sponsor, Printed Forms Equipment International Ltd of Loughton and owner of Mulberry House. Without my contributors, who include four local artists and a calligrapher, there would have been no book. My daughter Kathy, with endless patience, has wrestled with computer demons and turned my amateur typescript into an acceptable form. I am extremely grateful to them all.

Copies of material, which it has not been possible to include in this book, have been deposited at Ongar Library and the Essex Record Office. Archaic units of measurement and currency, and a list of abbreviations used in the text, are defined in the Appendix. The list of subscribers, who demonstrated their confidence in this book by buying copies in advance, is printed on the next page.

Michael Leach

September 1999

The Millennium Logo. The striking logo on the title page of this book was designed by Margaret Abbess, a local artist. She has initiated and overseen several other community projects, including the wall hanging in the Ongar Health Centre, and we are extremely grateful for her contribution to this project. The repeating radiating motifs represent the Norman motte of Ongar castle and the clock tower of the Budworth Hall, symbolising the enormous changes, from a feudal to an egalitarian society, which have taken place over the last 1000 years.

LIST OF SUBSCRIBERS

Margaret **Abbess**
Neil Humphrey & Josephine **Allen**
John & Mona **Amor**
The **Armes** Family

Professor Stanley & Mrs Jean **Ball**
Joyce & Walter **Barnard**
Felicitie & Ron **Barnes**, Nicola,
    Kerry, Tracy & Ashley
Elisabeth **Barrett**
Dr David **Bewley-Taylor**
Mrs Olive **Billett**
D.L. & Mrs M.I. **Bird**
Richard, Beverley,**Bowring**
    Rebecca & Charlotte
Bertram **Brighty**
Mrs Eileen E. **Brodie**
Philip **Brooke**
Marie **Brown**, Roy Smith,
    Brian Green & Ann Marrett
Paul & Margaret **Buxton**

The **Cassingham** Family
Mr & Mrs W.D. **Charnley**
Mr & Mrs Neil **Clayton**
Jenny **Cole**
Jill **Coward**
Jon **Coward**
Tim **Coward**
Les & Florrie **Cracknell**

Eve & Peter **Davis**
Paul, Viv, Clare & Karen **Davis**
Stephen **Davis** & Charity Green
Edna **Dawkins** (née Truscott)
Tim **Dealhoy**
Nicola **Deller**
The late Ernest Sidney **Dimon**
Angela **Duncan** & Lesley Adams

Mr Tony & Mrs Noreen **Earl**,
    Sarah & Nicholas
Jean & Antony **Easter**
The **Eastland** Family
Gillian **Eastman**
Denise, Bill, Katie & Peter **Evans**
Margaret & Peter **Evans**

Sally **Facey**
Julia E. **French**
Raymond J. & the late Gwenda A. **French**

Graham W. **Gassor**
The late William J. & E. Eveline **Gassor**
    (née Spearman)
Graham F. **Getgood**
Robin Taylor **Gilbert**
Peter & Brenda **Gildersleve**
Edwyn & Dorreen **Gilmour**
Peter John **Gold**
Pauline & Dudley **Goldsworthy**

Daphne & Frank **Hart**
Ted & Sylvia **Hatfield**
Anne **Hills**
Peter & Sylvia **Hills**
Angela & Ged **Hocter**
Dr & Mrs James **Hodsdon**
John **Holness**
Olive **Hopkins**
Hedley Connock **Hoskin**
Geoff & Marlene **Hunt**

Elaine **Jacobs**
Mr R.N. & Mrs J.A. **Jenkins**

Jean & Ernest **Kendrick**
Charles & Ingrid **Kellam**
Sandra **Kerr**
Derek M.J. **King**
Rodney **Kinzett**
Mrs Betty D. & the late Mr George A. **Kirk**
Harry **Knight**

Elizabeth **Lamb**
Philip **Lane**
Michael **Leach**
John H. **Leatherland**
Zoe E.L. **Lee**
The late Enid **Linney**
Martin **Longcroft**
Alys Alane Christina **Lunn**

Robert **MacDonald**
Matthew **Maher**
Benjamin **Main**
Jenny & Nigel **Main**
Kim, Derek & Stuart **Main**
Mr D.J. **Manning**
A.E. **Matters**
Mr A.W. **Morrison** FRCS
Colin & Jill **Morrison**
Harry **Myles**

Bruce **Neville**
Paul **Newman**

Catherine Louise **O'Mahony**
Charles Alexander Olin **O'Mahony**
James Lawrence Olin **O'Mahony**
Mrs Veronica **O'Neal**

Steve, Julie, Josie & Ella **Pinder**
Marion **Pfister**
Brian **Platten**

Dr I.Z. & Mrs S. **Qazi**, Arif & Omar

Richard & Brenda **Ray**
Elizabeth **Ray**
James **Ray**
Stephanie **Ray**
Daphne & Norman **Roberts**
Roy & Betty **Rogers**
Roger & Mary **Roles**
John R. **Root**

Walter & Daphne **Samuel**
Gillian **Sheldrick**
Mrs Phyl **Sirkett**
Stanley **Slade**
Joan M. **Smith**
William Edwin **Smith**
Mr & Mrs D. **Spring**
Miss Christina Duff **Stewart**
Ann T. **Sweeney**
Barrie & Anne **Sydenham**

Keith & Rosemary **Tait**
Mr David **Taylor**
Geoffrey **Tebbot**
Amanda & David **Tester**
David & Wendy **Thomas**
Maureen & Richard **Thompson**
Alan & Christina **Thornton**
Joyce & John **Titmarsh**
Eleanor E. **Turner**
Malcolm T. F. **Turner**
Derek L. **Turnidge**

Michael Anthony & Maura
    Patricia **Urwin**

John & Brenda **Ward**
S.G. **Welch**
David & Tanya **Welford**
Hazel & Stuart F. **Weston**, Josie & Robbie
John **Whaler**
Harold & Dee **Wieland**
Mrs I.L. **Williams**
Leonard & Mary **Williams**
Ronald & Annie **Wingar**, Julie, Ian & Sally
John **Winslow**
The late Ethel **Winslow**
Michael **Wood**
Keith & Jean **Wright**

Lilian **Yardley**

Ongar & District Healthcare League of
    Friends
Ongar Flower Club
Ongar United Reformed Church
Theatre Resource
Willingale Women's Institute

CONTENTS

Foreword iv
Editor's preface v
List of illustrations xi
Chapter 1 1
   Ongar Castle
      by Marion Pfister
Chapter 2 6
   Ongar Great Park
      by Sandra Kerr
Chapter 3 8
   St Andrew's church, Greensted
      by David Tester
Chapter 4 13
   St Martin's church
      by Frank Hart
Chapter 5 23
   Religious dissent in Ongar from 1662 to 1810
      by Michael Leach
Chapter 6 30
   St Helen's church
      by Helen Nyman
Chapter 7 34
   Chipping Ongar and the Morices
      by Margaret Buxton
Chapter 8 50
   The Taylor family of Ongar and their houses there
      by Robin Taylor Gilbert
Chapter 9 104
   Local government in Ongar
      by Jenny Main
Chapter 10 127
   Poor relief in Chipping Ongar
      by Martyn Lockwood
Chapter 11 138
   Law and order in Chipping Ongar
      by Martyn Lockwood
Chapter 12 144
   The Joseph King Trust
      by Gillian Sheldrick
Chapter 13 149
   The history of Ongar Grammar School
   Part one: 1811–1859
      by I. L. Williams
Chapter 14 158
   The history of Ongar Grammar School
   Part two: 1860–1940
      by John Whaler
Chapter 15 169
   Secondary education in Ongar 1936–1989
      by John Harrop
      & John Swallow on the closure saga
Chapter 16 179
   A home for the homeless: From Ongar Cottage Homes to Great Stony School
      by Ron Barnes

Chapter 17	188

    A history of trade and commerce in Chipping Ongar
        by Elisabeth Barrett

Chapter 18	205

    Ongar's pubs and inns
        by Ron Walker and Elisabeth Barrett

Chapter 19	214

    Pharmacy in Ongar
        by Elisabeth Barrett

Chapter 20	219

    Health care and the local hospitals
        by Michael Leach

Chapter 21	230

    The railways of Ongar
        by Edwyn Gilmour

Chapter 22	249

    The utilities
        by Harry Myles

Chapter 23	255

    Henry Childs of Ongar
        by Philip Brooke

Chapter 24	260

    Captain Budworth and the Budworth Hall
        by Michael Leach

Chapter 25	270

    Primrose McConnell and Ongar Park Farm
        by Sandra Kerr

Chapter 26	275

    Ongar Cricket Club
        by Bernard Shuttleworth

Chapter 27	280

    Scouting in Ongar
        by Peter Evans

Chapter 28	290

    Ongar and District Horticultural and Allotments Society
        by Tanya Welford

Chapter 29	293

    The development of Cloverley Road
        by Wendy Thomas
    with illustrations by Jane Whaler

Chapter 30	302

    Living history – eye witness accounts
        by Felicitie Barnes & Christina Thornton

Chapter 31	313

    Landmark trees
        by Bob MacDonald

Appendix	320
Index	321

LIST OF ILLUSTRATIONS

Church Lane, Chipping Ongar in 1913 from a watercolour by Annie Gilbert .... front cover
Map of Chipping Ongar, showing the main historic sites .... frontispiece

1.	Roman roads in south west Essex .... page	0
2.	Plan of the Saxon and Norman earthworks .... page	2
3.	Greensted church in 1849 .... page	9
4.	St Martin's church in 1796 .... page	15
5.	Castle House in about 1850 .... page	37
6.	The martyrdom of Ralph Jackson of Chipping Ongar in 1556 .... page	42
7.	The Rev. Isaac Taylor .... page	61
8.	Castle House drawn by Jane Taylor .... page	75
9.	The Peaked Farm by the Rev. Isaac Taylor .... page	82
10.	No. 10, Castle Street by Isaac Taylor .... page	86
11.	Descendants of the Rev. Isaac Taylor .... page	102
12.	Descendants of Isaac Taylor of Stanford Rivers .... page	103
13.	The Old Town Hall in 1818 .... page	105
14.	Ongar Grammar School about 1875 .... page	154
15.	Ongar Grammar School in 1905 .... page	163
16.	The architect's drawing of the Ongar Cottage Homes .... page	182
17.	Early Victorian view of Ongar High Street .... page	189
18.	Gradient profile of the Loughton to Ongar railway .... page	232
19.	London Transport timetable of 1965 .... page	243
20.	Ongar Waterworks share certificate .... page	250
21.	The Wilderness in about 1850 .... page	260
22.	The architect's drawing of the Budworth Hall .... page	263
23.	No. 65, Cloverley Road .... page	295
24.	No 53, Cloverley Road .... page	296
25.	Mr Frederick Dicker, undertaker and builder .... page	298
26.	Nos. 35 & 37, Cloverley Road .... page	299

Acknowledgements: We are very grateful to the following for their permission to reproduce the illustrations used in this book.

Margaret Abbess: Ongar Millennium Logo.
Philip Brooke: 20.
Essex Record Office: 4.
Robin Taylor Gilbert: 7.
Michael Leach: 13, 14, 17 & 22.
London Transport: 19.
David and Ann Manners: drawings in chapter 32.
Osborne Collection, Toronto: 8, 9 & 10.

David Silverstone: frontispiece, 1 & 2.
The Architects' Journal: 16.
The Builders' Group: 3.
The Railway Magazine: 18.
The Syndics of Cambridge University Library: 6.
Derek Turnidge: 5, 15 & 21.
Jane Whaler: 23, 24, 25 & 26.
Clare Wilson: front cover.

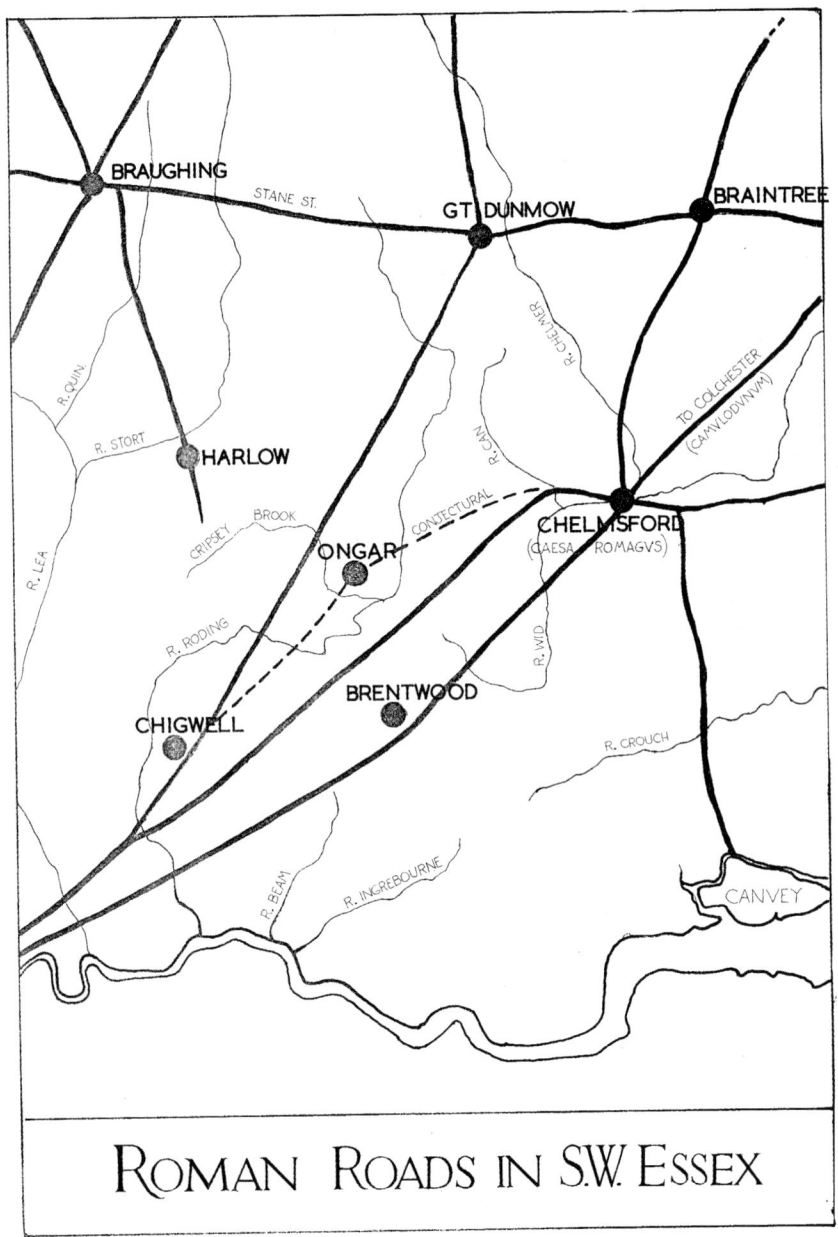

Figure 1 The main Roman roads in south west Essex

chapter 1

Ongar Castle

by Marion Pfister

Ongar Castle lies on a promontory of land which juts out between two rivers, the Roding, and its tributary, the Cripsey Brook. In the past it could have been relatively easily defended, as the river valleys were probably very marshy and only the north side open to attack.

In Roman times Ongar was not on any direct route to anywhere. There were two long distance roads nearby, one running from London to Dunmow through Ongar Park Wood, the other via Navestock and Doddinghurst towards Chelmsford. Recently a stretch of Roman road has been identified between Ongar and Chelmsford[1] which could tie up with the possible local route from Chigwell via Ongar suggested by Drury and Rodwell.[2]

The only evidence that the castle site was occupied in Roman times is from 1767 when Peter Muilman stated that '*several Roman foundations have been discovered in this parish, particularly in the church and churchyard.*'[3] It has always been assumed that Roman bricks were used in the construction of St Martin's church. If so, these are unlikely to come from very far away and, if not local, then possibly from the proven villa site at Greensted.[4] However a recent study suggests that brick making was re-established as early as the mid twelfth century, and that the walls of St Martin's may contain the mediaeval great brick, as well as re-used Roman material.[5]

The name Ongar is from the Saxon "angra" meaning grassland, which indicates that Ongar was less thickly wooded than the surrounding district.[6] There are two Ongars, High Ongar on the east side of the river Roding, and Chipping Ongar on the west.

Ongar is also the name given to the hundred, which was a territorial division which was formed for '*the adjustment of taxation, the maintenance of peace and order, and the settlement of local pleas.*'[7] So Ongar must have been a town of some importance to give its name to the hundred, which lies along the river Roding from Loughton in the south to Leaden Roding in the north.

Tradition ascribes the creation of hundreds to King Alfred the Great or his son Edward the Elder, as a defence against the Danes. It is possible that Chipping Ongar was set up as a burgh, a defensive site with a small fort. The possible line is shown on a plan of Ongar Castle drawn by Josiah Gilbert[8]. I have not found any trace of his northerly ditch; however, the southern bank and ditch can still be seen running downhill through the allotments south of Castle Street. An excavation through this bank and ditch was carried out in 1981 by Mike Eddy for ECC. This

ASPECTS OF THE HISTORY OF ONGAR

showed that it formed part of an enclosure, pre-dating the castle, running southwards to the edge of the floodplain and west along Bushey Lea. A late Saxon date was tentatively proposed.[9]

We know from the Domesday Book that Ongar at the time of the Norman conquest was in the hands of *'Ailida as 1 hide and 1 manor – now the Count [holds it] in demesne.'*[10] This means that the land was not let out to a tenant but kept for the Count's own use. The Count in question was Eustace, Count of Boulogne, a very important man and very close to William the Conqueror. Although he acquired many pieces of land in the area, this was the only manor he had from Ailida, as all the rest of her estate went to Ralf Barnard. Ongar was a special case: *'From her the manor seems to have passed on to Ingelric the priest; for in 1068 William the Conquerer confirmed the gift of Ongar by Ingelric to the house of St Martin-le-Grande, London. In spite of the gift, however, Ongar was held in 1068 by Ingelric's successor Eustace, Count of Boulogne.'*[11]

It seems that the Lady Ailida was very anxious to get rid of the manor of Ongar, for within two years of the conquest she had transferred ownership to Ingelric. If there was a small fort of some kind it would seem logical not to want to be in possession of it. The fact that Ongar was passed on to such a powerful man as Eustace suggests the possibility that it might have posed a threat to the rulers.

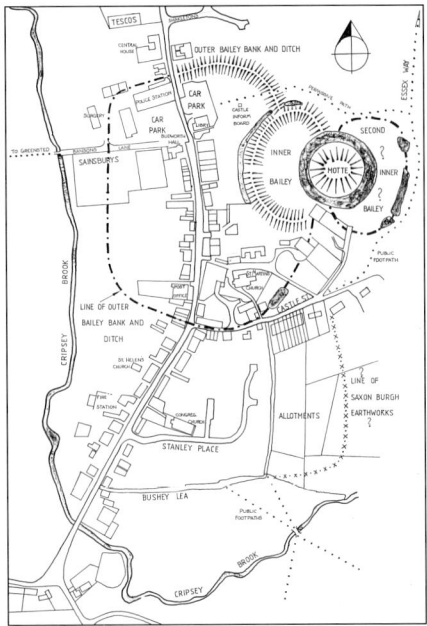

Figure 2   The Norman castle earthworks (and the possible Saxon burgh) shown in relation to the modern town of Chipping Ongar.

ONGAR CASTLE

Ongar Castle is basically a "motte", a mound with a moat around it, and a "bailey", a courtyard with another moat around it. When I was a child I could never understand why people on the beach dug big mounds of sand with a ditch round and called it a sandcastle, for it never looked like a castle to me. In fact, these were examples of mottes.

The motte and bailey did not exist in Normandy before 1066. The idea was developed in England to meet the demands of the individual situation at the time, and one is shown being built in the Bayeaux Tapestry. They could be constructed more quickly than a stone castle, though it has been calculated that the building of the Ongar motte would have taken about 24,000 man hours.[12] Often they were built on previously fortified sites where there was a water supply. At South Mimms, Herts[13] and Farnham, Surrey[14] the foundations of towers were incorporated within the motte. Earth from the moat was piled up, levelled off and reinforced with layers of rock or beaten earth. A tower was built on the top with a palisade round the edge and a crust of clay put on the outside to prevent uneven settlement. The ditch around the motte may originally have been dry as at Pleshey today, though it is now full of water suggesting that it may have been lined with clay to overcome the porosity of the local glacial gravel. The wooden tower on the motte was reached by a flying bridge or gangway which could be raised if necessary.

The inner bailey was a courtyard which housed all the main buildings, hall, kitchen, sleeping quarters, stables, storerooms and workshops. It was surrounded by an internal bank with palisade, a moat around the outside and a gateway. The principal bailey in Ongar Castle has the gateway on the west side facing towards Greensted; there are still traces of Roman bricks and flints there. The bailey moat can be seen at the back of the library car park.

The motte and bailey castle acted as a suitable headquarters, a base from which a small body of men under a leader could range over an area and retire if attacked. In dire need the defenders could retreat to the tower on the motte and pull up the drawbridge or gangway.

Ongar Castle has a second or outer bailey which surrounded the small town and incorporated the church. The large bank and ditch ran on the line of what is now Castle Street, probably with a gateway at the narrow part of the High Street. It went round the west side of the town and back with another gateway near the police station. The substantial remains of the bank and ditch can be seen on the north side of the library car park. A section to the west of the High Street was excavated by Mike Eddy for the ECC in 1981. He came to the conclusion that this defence was most likely to date from the civil war of 1135–1152 AD, and was therefore later than the original motte.[15]

When the town defence was built, St Martin's church, or at least part of it, was already there. The roof frames at the western end of the chancel have been dated by Cecil A. Hewett to between c.1080 and c.1100, the two nearest the nave being the oldest.[16] The church is outside the inner bailey and would have been used by the local population, who would not have been welcome in the inner sanctum. There may have been a third bailey on the east side of the motte at some time, with its moat marked by a line of duck ponds and depressions which can be seen from the public footpath.

When was the castle built? Although many books claim that it was built by Richard de Lucy in 1153, I agree with J. H. Round that it was 'thrown up' by Count Eustace and was the caput of the count's Essex fief (i.e. the headquarters of his estates in Essex) in about 1080.[17] This is approximately the same time that the chancel roof of St Martin's, Chipping Ongar, was put in place. Eustace is reputed to have built another castle at Ansty in Hertfordshire. After the death of Eustace, Chipping Ongar passed to his daughter or granddaughter Maud and her husband King Stephen, as part of the honour and estates of Boulogne.

Then followed a civil war between King Stephen and his cousin Matilda, daughter of Henry I. During this period, our town bank and ditch were probably constructed. The war came to an end on the death of King Stephen when Matilda's son, Henry II, came to the throne. Between December 1153 and October 1154 the manor was granted by William, son of Maud and Stephen, to Richard de Lucy, later the justicar (i.e. chief justice) to Henry II. Ongar Castle became the caput of Richard's honour of Ongar.

The new king Henry II is reputed to have pulled down more than eleven hundred castles,[18] but Ongar survived. It was most probably Richard de Lucy who expanded the church, procured a fair and a market, added the name Chipping (meaning market) and after the neglect of the previous 50 years, made Ongar a place for a king to visit, which Henry II did in 1157. Since then, the castle has been put to no apparent military use (or indeed any use other than as an amenity, see Chapter 7) except for some practice trench digging on the motte by the Army during the First World War.[19]

References

1. Going, C.J. 'The Roman Countryside' in Bedwin. O. (ed) *The Archaeology of Essex* (1996) ECC
2. Drury, P.J. & Rodwell, W. 'Settlement in the later Iron Age and Roman periods', *Archaeology in Essex to AD 1500*, CBA Research Report 34 (1980)
3. Muilman, P. *A Gentleman's New and Complete History of Essex*, (1770)
4. ERO Sites and Monuments Record, No. 86
5. Rodwell, W. J. "Holy Trinity Church, Bradwell-juxta-Coggeshall" in *Essex Archaeology and History*, 3rd series, vol 29 (1998) p.105
6. VCH Essex vol 4 (1956) p. 155
7. Stenton, Sir F. *Anglo-Saxon England*, (1971) OUP p.292
8. Gilbert, J. 'Ongar', in *The Essex Review*, (1904)
9. *Essex Archaeology and History*, 3rd series, vol 15, (1983) p. 165
10. VCH Essex vol 1 (1903)
11. VCH Essex vol 4 (1956)
12. Pounds, N. J. G. *The Mediaeval Castle in England and Wales* (1994) CUP
13. Renn, D. *Norman Castles in Britain*, (1973) London, p.31

14 Thompson, M.W. 'Recent excavations in the keep of Farnham Castle' in *Mediaeval Archaeology*, vol vi, (1960)
15 *Essex Archaeology and History*, 3rd series, vol 14, (1982) p. 136
16 Hewett, C. *Church Carpentry*, (1982), Phillimore p. 3
17 Round, J.H. 'The Honour of Ongar', in *Trans. Essex Arch. Soc.* n.s. vol vii 142–52
18 Meiklejohn, J.M.D. *A new history of England and Great Britain* (1899) A.M. Holden
19 inf from Paul Buxton

chapter 2

Ongar Great Park

by Sandra Kerr

An Anglo Saxon will of 1045 refers to *'the wood outside the deerhay (deerhage)'* in the very place where Domesday records a "parcus", so the existence of at least one park before the conquest seems established.[1] Ongar Great Park is named in the Close Rolls for 1215 when King John ordered the keeper of the Forest of Essex to allow Richard Rivers to have *'two leaps in his great park of Aungr.'* A deerleap is a one-way valve letting deer into the park from outside, and permission for this was needed as the park abutted onto a royal forest. This document shows that the park was in existence in 1215. It is mentioned in the Close Rolls twice in 1243 in connection with the disposal of the property of the late owner, Matilda de Lucy. It contained timber trees, which the king gives permission to be felled. In 1244 Ongar Great Park is described as adjacent to *'10 acres of woodland which the king gives permission to be grubbed out.'* On all three occasions it is called the great park of Ongar.[2] The park was still active with deer in it in 1294, and subsequently gave its name to the manor of Ongar Park in Stanford Rivers.[3] The line of the park boundary can still be seen on a modern map as field and parish boundaries.[4] It has the characteristic shape of early parks – a rectangle with rounded corners – and two features which point to its being very early. The parish boundaries have been laid out or adapted to fit the shape of the park – this would date the park before about 1170 when parish boundaries were no longer altered to fit the shape of new parks.[5] The other feature is the exceptionally large size of the park, about 1200 acres – some five times the area of the average park. It was rightly called the Great Park – the probable reason for this is that the park was intended to keep red deer, rather than the usual fallow deer which are easier to keep on a small area of land.

Deer parks were areas of land, usually enclosed, set aside and equipped for the management and hunting of deer and other animals. They were generally located in open countryside on marginal land or adjacent to a manor house, castle or palace. They varied considerably in size (from 7 acres to 3900 acres), and usually comprised a combination of woodland and grassland, providing the essential mixture of both cover and grazing for deer. Parks could contain a number of features, including hunting lodges (often moated), rabbit warrens, fish ponds and enclosures for game and were usually surrounded by a park pale, a massive fenced or hedged bank often with an internal ditch. The park was supervised by "parkers" from one or more buildings called lodges, usually set on a high point to command a view of whatever was not hidden by trees. It was the Norman aristocracy's taste for hunting that led to the majority of parks being constructed. The peak time for the laying-out of parks between 1200 and 1350 coincided with a period of considerable prosperity amongst the nobility. From the fifteenth century onwards,

ONGAR GREAT PARK

few parks were constructed and, by the end of the seventeenth century, the deer park in its original form had largely disappeared.

The chief expense of a park was the pale. Fallow deer are as strong as pigs and more agile than goats and it is not easy to fence them in. A mediaeval pale was made of cleft oak stakes, individually set in the ground and nailed to a rail. The pales rotted and repairs were costly in labour and good timber. Sometimes there was a wall instead. Ongar's park pale was set on a substantial bank with a ditch each side. Ongar Great Park had ceased to be a functional park by about 1640.[1]

The map of c.1800 shows that land around Ongar Park Hall had been landscaped, with straight rides cut through the woodland and a tree-lined drive leading towards the house from the west.[6] Many of the field names indicated on the map are descriptive, for example, Long Meadow and Barn Field. Others derive from the names of former tenants, for example, Penningtons Meadow is named from a tenant of that name in the late seventeenth century.[7] Stanford Gate, which now lies beneath the railway line near Blake Hall station, was one of the gates to the mediaeval park. Coney Heath may indicate the position of a rabbit warren and Great Plasto and Little Plasto derive from Old English pleg-stow – *'a sport place, a place where people gathered for play.'*[8] Park Wood in the south largely survived until the destructive times after the Second World War and subsequent agricultural changes. The railway line from Epping to Ongar also bisects the park.

Deer parks were a long-lived and widespread monument type. Today they serve to illustrate an important aspect of the activities of mediaeval nobility and still exert a powerful influence on the pattern of the modern landscape. Where a deer park survives well and is well-documented, or associated with other significant remains, its principle features are normally identified as nationally important.[9]

The surviving park pale is described in the Schedule under Section 1 of the Ancient Monuments and Archaeological Areas Act 1979:

> *'The park pale north west of Collier's Hatch survives particularly well as an upstanding earthwork bank with partly buried ditches. The bank, buried landsurface and ditch fills contain artefactual and environmental information relating to the construction and use of the park pale, and thus of the deer park as a whole. Ongar Park is a particularly early, and a well documented, example of an English deer park and is the earliest known park in Essex.'*[9]

References

1. Rackham, O. *Ancient Woodland* (1980) London
2. Calendar of Close Rolls (1242–1247)
3. VCH Essex vol 4, p.211
4. Hunter, J. *Ancient Landscapes – Ongar Great Park* (1994) ECC
5. Rackham, O. *Trees and Woodland in the British Landscape* (1976) p. 153
6. map (A Reduced Plan of the Manor of Onger Park): ERO T/M 212
7. ERO D/DCcT27
8. Smith, A. H. *English Place-Name Elements* (1956) Cambridge UP
9. Section 1, Ancient Monuments and Archaeological Area Act (1979)

chapter 3

St Andrew's church, Greensted

by David Tester

No history of Ongar would be complete without mention of St Andrew's church, Greensted-juxta-Ongar. Despite recent dendrochronological analysis of the wooded plank walls which indicate that they date from around 1063 AD (rather than the 845 AD date given by an earlier test), it is still acknowledged as the oldest wooden stave built church in the world. In all probability, it was built by Hamo Dapifer, the new Norman lord of the manor recorded in the Domesday Book.

The 51 plank walls that you see today are split oak logs, and stand side by side connected by fillet of wood slotted into a groove in the side of each plank. These wooden tongues are clearly visible on the north wall. The planks were originally set directly into the ground, with the bevelled upper end let into a wall plate. A part of the original wall plate can be seen in the north wall where the entrance door of the church was once positioned. The roof would have been thatched.

The dwarf brick walls which now support the upright timbers were inserted in the restoration of 1848. What is believed to be the only full length plank is to be found in the corner of the north wall, adjacent to the tower. The inside of the timber walls, finished with an adze, would have been plastered. In common with other churches in pre-literate times, it would have been painted with biblical scenes. It is recorded that during the 1848 restoration plaster was still to be found on the inside of the plank walls, and some traces were still evident in 1995. Since its initial construction, the church has undergone many changes. The Normans built the chancel walls in flint, which can still be seen today. Their other legacy was the piscina in the south east corner of the chancel, where the communion vessels and the priest's hands were washed. The Tudors rebuilt the chancel, using the Norman flint as well as their own small bricks, with a priest's door and adjacent window in the south wall, as well as a new east window. The only remaining Tudor glass is set in the quatrefoil window of the tower, and is believed to depict St Edmund. The thatched roof was replaced with clay tiles at this time.

At the archdeacon's visitation on 19 September 1683, it was noted that repairs were in progress to deal with cracking on either side of the chancel window, by placing new beams inside. The writer was sceptical about how effective this would be.

In 1848–49, the nave underwent major refurbishment, as the unsupported walls were found to be sinking into the Essex clay. The wall planks were lifted and the decayed timber at the lower ends removed, thereby shortening the timbers.

ST ANDREWS' CHURCH, GREENSTED

Figure 3   Greensted church in 1849 from *The Builder* of 1849. Note the nave buttresses which were removed during restoration.

They were then replaced (but, it is thought, not in their original positions) in sills laid on the new dwarf brick walls. The timber wall plates were also renewed. The roof was rebuilt in fir, covered with boarding and lathed and tiled. The tiles were bedded in mortar. The western gable had survived intact up to this date but part of it was removed to form a vestry door. It is not known if these timbers were destroyed or used elsewhere, and no records were made of the original roof construction which was destroyed at this time. A new timber porch, a copy of fifteenth century work, replaced a small weather boarded structure.

A detailed report of this refurbishment in *The Builder* in 1849 records that there were 25 planks on the north side and 21 on the south side, those on the north being the least decayed. They were about 6 ft high, including the sill and plate, formed of rough half trees about 12 ins wide and 6 ins thick. The uprights were set into oak sills, 8 ins square, tenoned into a $1^{1}/_{2}$ ins groove and secured with oak pins. The sill on the south was laid on the actual earth, but in two places on the north side rough flints had been driven in underneath. The wall plates averaged 7 ins square, and the wall planks were tenoned and pinned into a groove in the same way as on the sill. Decay necessitated the shortening of the planks on the south by an average of 5 ins, those on the north by about 1 ins. When re-erected, the south walls were 4 ft 4 ins high, those on the north 4 ft 8 ins. The report also mentions that the interior was plastered, and that the uprights were so effectively tenoned together that there was no evidence of wet being driven in at the feather edge junction of the uprights. The original roof was heavy, consisting of a tie beam, less that 6 feet above floor level, with struts, but the details of its construction were not recorded.

William White, in his 1848 *Directory of the County of Essex* stated that *'the primitive part of the fabric is about to be repaired'* and described the nave as 29 ft

ASPECTS OF THE HISTORY OF ONGAR

9 ins long, 14 ft wide and $5^1/_2$ ft high at the sides. The Rev. P. W. Ray was the incumbent.

By 1891, the roof had decayed to such a state that it was replaced by a new one in oak, designed by the Chelmsford architect Fred Chancellor. The new roof was similar to the 1848 one, although this time leaving a 2 inch gap between the boarding and the lathes. A brick buttress, set against the timbers of the north wall, was also removed as *'it was not assisting in the maintenance of the fabric.'* The cost of these works was paid for by public subscription, liberally started by the churchwarden William Hewitt Esq. who was residing at Greensted Hall. In 1902, settlement of the chancel arch was noted. This was corrected by removing part of the lower arch, inserting wrought iron ribs, and remaking the arch in cement.

In 1990, following structural movement of the walls, steelwork was inserted to brace the roof and make it act as a beam spanning from one end of the church to the other. The church was closed for a time while this work was in progress. The latest addition to the church is a new font, made in 1987 by Russell Thomas. It is in oak, shaped with a hand adze in keeping with the construction of the wall timbers. It was designed by Sir Hugh Casson R.A.

What stood on this site before the present building? Excavations in June 1960 established that there had been an earlier small wooden chancel built of earth fast upright logs which had been replaced by a second larger timber chancel with a wooden sill, similar to the existing nave. The earlier building was thought to date from the late sixth or early seventh century. Monks from St Aidan's abbey in Lindisfarne travelled south in the seventh century with St Cedd taking Christian teaching to the pagan populations of the east Saxons in about 654 AD. St Andrew was their patron saint, whose relics were said to have been brought to this country. Did the Lindisfarne monks travel through the Essex forest to reach Greensted (which means a clearing in a forest) to find a shrine dedicated by our pagan ancestors to the spirits and gods of the forest? Could this explain why the church is dedicated to this saint, rather than to the rather more obvious choice of St Edmund?

The church today, whilst small, has a thriving congregation of all ages, and welcomes many thousands of visitors each year.

The legend of St Edmund

Although dedicated to St Andrew, Greensted is probably better known for its association with England's first patron saint, St Edmund. Legend and fact have become inextricably entwined, and what follows is probably a mixture of both.

He was born in Nuremburg in 840 AD, son of Alkmund of Saxony. Offa, king of East Anglia, met the boy at his father's court while on a pilgrimage, and was so impressed by him that he named him as his successor. Following Offa's early death, Edmund came to this country, landing at Hunstanton. He travelled to Attleborough where, it is said, he spent a year in a monastery preparing himself for his duties as king. He was crowned in Bures on Christmas Day 855 AD by Bishop Humbert.

Very little is known of the years between then and his martyrdom, although his reign was peaceful and he was highly regarded as an honest and pious ruler. However this peace was shattered in 869 AD when an army of invading Danes, under their chief Ivar the Boneless, left their camp in York and travelled south to East Anglia, settling in for the winter at Thetford, some 20 miles from Hoxne. An ultimatum was delivered by the Danes to Edmund, requiring him to surrender his wealth and his kingship, and to renounce the Christian faith. In return, they would allow him to live as a vassal under the rule of Ivar. This he refused to do and the Anglo-Saxon Chronicle records that King Edmund fought against them, and that the Danes gained a victory and slew the king.

Details of his capture vary somewhat. Some say that he was captured after the battle, others that he surrendered to the Danes to avoid further bloodshed. Another story says that he was betrayed by a bride and groom, having hidden beneath a bridge which they crossed on the way to their wedding. What is agreed, however, is that he was beaten by the Danes after capture, presumably in an attempt to get him to agree to the terms of their ultimatum. Still refusing to denounce his Christian faith, he was tied to a tree, shot to death with arrows and beheaded. The martyrdom is depicted in St Andrew's in the window in the north wall of the chancel, and in a painting hanging on the north side of the nave. Legend has it that his head was thrown into a wood, and that when friends came to recover the body, they found it being guarded by a wolf (perhaps one of Edmund's hunting hounds). When the head was placed with the body, they became miraculously united. This legend is depicted, with the St Edmund crown, on the west spandrel in the church.

Controversy still surrounds the place of his death. Some believe it to be Haeglesdune or Haegelisdun (now known as Hellsdon), whilst others believe it to be Hoxne. Edmund's body was buried in a chapel erected on the site of his martyrdom and there it remained for some 30 years, after which it was suitably enshrined at Beodericsworth (now known as Bury St Edmunds). The relics were removed to London for safe keeping in 1010 by the monk Ailwyn, when East Anglia was invaded by the Vikings, and kept at the church of St Gregory. In 1013, they were returned to Bury St Edmunds, and rested overnight at Greensted on the journey back. As if the legends surrounding this saint were not mysterious enough, the *Bury Post* of 11 October 1848 records that, in September of that year, an ancient oak fell in the village of Hoxne, and that an arrow head was found embedded within it. The annual growth rings were said to have shown that it was more than a thousand years old. A stave cross, with two crossed arrows and a simple inscription, now stands on the spot.

His feast day is kept on 20 November – the day of his death – and is celebrated in the dioceses of Northampton and Westminster, and by the monks of the Benedictine order.

ASPECTS OF THE HISTORY OF ONGAR

Sources

1. Tyers, I. *Tree ring analysis of timbers from the stave church at Greensted, Essex* (1996) Historic Buildings and Monuments Commission for England
2. Christie, H., Olsen, O., Taylor, H. M. 'The Wooden Church of St Andrew, Greensted' in *The Antiquaries Journal* (1979) vol. lix part 1
3. Morris, J. (ed) *Domesday Book – Essex* (1983) Phillimore.
4. Pressey, Rev. W. J. 'Visitations held in the Archdeaconry of Essex in 1683' in *Trans. Essex Arch Society* n.s. vol. xix p. 268 (1929)
5. Hewitt, C. A. *English Historic Carpentry* (1980) Phillimore
6. *'The Builder'* 13 January 1849 and March 1849
7. Winper, T. *The County of Essex* (1879) Cambridge
8. *Essex Review* (1892) vol. 1 p. 139
9. White, W. *History, Gazeteer & Directory of the County of Essex* (1848)
10. Chancellor, F. ms, Church of St Edmund Greensted ERO: D/F 8.251 and W 162
11. Scarfe, N., 'The Body of St Edmund – a Study in Necrobiography' in *Suffolk Institute of Archaeology* vol. xxxi (1970)
12. Jones, R. L. 'Greensted Log Church & St Edmund' in *The Essex Countryside* (April 1964)
13. VCH Essex vol. 4 (1956) p. 60
14. Evans, M. C. & Rogers, B. 'The Search for a Saint' in *Sunday Telegraph Review* 24 October 1993
15. Sell, Wade, Postins (architects and conservation consultants) 'St Andrew's Greensted, Essex - Specification and Schedule of Works' (1990)
16. Morant, P. *History of Essex* (1768) vol. 1 p. 152
17. Letter of J. Lethieullier 21 January 1751: Stowe MS 752
19. Dearmer, Rev. P. *Everyman's History of the English Church*

chapter 4

St Martin's church

by Frank Hart

The construction

The original building, consisting of nave and chancel, has usually been attributed to the latter part of the eleventh century. The walls are constructed of coursed flint rubble, with quoins and horizontal courses of red brick and tiles, believed to be Roman as it was generally assumed that brickmaking was not resumed until later in the middle ages. There is a definite Roman villa site at Greensted and possibly other nearby sites as well. This suggests that there would have been sources of brick and tile close at hand. The majority of the surviving mediaeval flint churches in Essex contain Roman brick,[1] an early example of recycling building materials. However a recent study by Rodwell suggests that the large bricks used in St Martin's are not Roman but mediaeval "great" brick, dating from the re-introduction of brick making in the mid twelfth century. This means that the present church may have been built in the mid twelfth century, possibly in association with building work at the adjoining Ongar castle by Richard de Lucy.[2] The surviving flint walls of the church clearly show the position of many of the original putlog holes, through which timbers passed to support the internal and external scaffolding during construction. Flint masonry was built in stages, each stage needing to harden within its shuttering before the next was added. The clear demarcation between these stages, or "lifts," can still be seen in many areas of the external wall surface.

The chancel

The chancel roof is a complex structure with its trusses dating from at least three phases of construction up to the thirteenth century. The truss immediately to the east of the chancel arch is thought to be the earliest. The whole roof was strengthened in the seventeenth century by the addition of three arched braces, dated 1643.[3] In the 1950s, the then rector, Canon John Vaughan Jones, invited college friends from Oxford to carbon date the earliest timbers, a technique which they were perfecting. The results suggested a date of 1080 to 1100.[4] The chancel arch and nave roof were rebuilt about the middle of the fourteenth century. At some point, the east and west gables of the church were lowered, perhaps in connection with the replacement of the nave roof, or the insertion of the enlarged east window. Lowering the west gable necessitated blocking up two of the Norman lancet windows in this wall.[5]

The east chancel window is modern, but has been reconstructed within the splays of the fourteenth century window. Removal of plaster in the nineteenth century revealed traces of four single light windows, confirming that the original Norman east window consisted of six narrow openings, arranged in two rows of three under a higher gable.[6] The stained glass in this window was made by Leonard Walker R.I., a talented artist with worldwide recognition. The colours of the glass, together with the thickness of the individual pieces varying from 4 to 30mms, produce a dramatic effect when seen against the early morning sun.

There are two windows in the north wall. The one nearest the altar is an original round headed Norman light, the other is an early sixteenth century three light window with brick splays and mullions. The three stained glass panels in the latter were fitted in 1934 in memory of Colonel Richard Lionel Walter. Between these windows, and at a lower level near the altar rail, is a small pointed hatch, with a small door, opening into a cavity in the thickness of the wall. When the rendering was removed from the external surface of this wall at this point in 1887, a large defect and a possible hole for the roof beam of a lean-to structure was found. It was suggested that this was an ankerhold or hermit's cell, with the small internal lancet providing him with a view of the high altar. The external wall was rebuilt after the defect was photographed, and is marked now only by a low Victorian round headed doorway.[7]

At the west end of the north wall of the chancel an arched opening leads up four steps into the vestry. The short passage, together with the sink cupboard to the right, formed the original vestry added to the church in the nineteenth century. This small building was extended in 1917 to form the present vestry and choir room.

In the sanctuary, the four riddel posts and bar were erected in 1925 as a memorial to W. E. Holt, parish clerk from 1899 to 1924. The sanctuary area was re-ordered in 1953. The wooden Holy Table was replaced by one in stone; and a new credence table, bishop's chair and servers' stools were provided.

On the south side of the chancel, below an original round headed Norman light, there is a piscina for cleaning communion vessels, probably dating from the late thirteenth century. The larger window in this wall is thirteenth century, made up of three grouped graduated lancet lights,[8] and in the south west corner, there is a blocked priest's doorway only visible from the outside. This originally opened directly into the priest's stall, an arrangement perpetuated today by the position of the modern stall for the rector. Externally the remains of a sundial (or "mass dial") can be seen on the door jamb, positioned to enable the priest to check the time for holding services.

Between the two south chancel windows is a monument to Sarah Mitford (died 1776) by the famous sculptor Joseph Nollekens.[9] On the south side of the altar is a black marble slab marking the grave of Jane Pallavicini (died 1637), daughter of Sir Oliver Cromwell, who fought on the Royalist side in the Civil War against his better known nephew Oliver Cromwell. Jane Pallavicini's son, Horatio (died 1648), rests beside her. The Pallavicinis were Italian bankers who thrived under Elizabeth I and came to live in Ongar. There is a monument in the south west corner of the chancel to Nicholas Alexander (died 1714), possibly by the sculptor Edward Stanton.[10] Other memorial slabs in the chancel record Robert Hill (died 1648), Ann

ST MARTIN'S CHURCH

(formerly King), his second wife (died 1668), Ann Greatherd his daughter (died 1683) and Thomas, son of the rector John Campe (died 1719).

The nave

The pulpit in the nave is late sixteenth century, made of oak, hexagonal with a moulded top, and two panels carved with jewel ornament and arabesques.[11] The stained glass in the two adjoining windows in the nave is in memory of Walter Fenn and his wife May, and their son and daughter John and Gertrude Fenn. Made by Francis Stephens and installed in 1963, both have a missionary theme with links to David Livingstone who lived in Ongar for six months in 1838 to receive instruction from the Rev. Richard Cecil, the Ongar Congregational minister, while training for the ministry. The window nearest the pulpit is of the worship of the Magi with the two bottom panels depicting the Slaughter of the Innocents and the Flight to Egypt. The second window shows St Philip and the Ethiopians, with the bottom left panel showing Livingstone meeting Stanley amidst African huts. The right hand panel shows African converts being baptised. The north wall of the nave has another original Norman window. Memorial slabs in the floor of the nave (now covered by carpet) record John King (died 1657), Elizabeth his wife (died 1651) and Joseph King, their son (died 1679). The terms of the will of the latter set up the Joseph King trust (see chapter 12).

Figure 4 St Martin's church in 1796 from an engraving in *The Gentleman's Magazine*, showing the north porch. There is a ladder hanging under the eaves of the chancel.

The original entrance to the nave was by a door in the north wall, which was blocked in 1814.[12] The position of this doorway can be seen clearly both on the outside and on the inside. There is a holy water stoup on the inside to the right of the opening. When this doorway was closed, a new entrance, with a small porch, was made at the west end. There were originally three Norman windows side by side in the west gable but the outer two were filled in when the nave roof was lowered. It is difficult to see the position of these blocked windows externally, but the reveals are clearly visible on the inside. The large window below the surviving Norman opening has wooden tracery (painted to resemble stone), and was probably inserted in the nineteenth century to light the well at the back of the gallery, possibly when the new entrance was formed in this wall in 1814. The fourteenth century nave roof timbers,[13] which greatly enhance the appearance of the church today, were hidden behind a lathe and plaster ceiling which was removed under a faculty granted on 24 March 1935. The white painted board infill was replaced by a thermal acoustic boarding fixed to the upper surface of the roof timbers when the nave and chancel were re-tiled in 1995.

The south aisle

By the late 1870s, the church was getting too small for the population, a problem aggravated by the increasing number of pupils at Ongar Grammar School. At the same time the general condition of the church – particularly the fabric – was causing concern, and in November 1880 a parish meeting was called to discuss these issues, resulting in proposals to carry out a "reconstruction" of the church.[14] These included a new south aisle, and the replacement of the west porch built earlier in the century. The architect, Clapton Rolfe of Oxford, was commissioned, but the plan to add a south aisle to this "unusually complete" Norman church was to prove controversial. The recently formed Society for the Protection of Ancient Buildings (SPAB) sent two members (G. P. Boyer and Philip Webb) to make a detailed survey of the church in January 1883. A somewhat acrimonious correspondence ensued between the SPAB, the architect and the rector, the Rev. James Tanner. The SPAB favoured building a second church in order to preserve St Martin's unaltered. Both the architect and the rector vigorously opposed this on the grounds of historical precedent, as well as the cost to a parish with limited financial resources. Perhaps as a sop to the SPAB, the architect stated that he intended to reuse a window from the old south wall if feasible, and to incorporate other salvaged material from the old building in the core of the new wall. There is no visible evidence that this was done. The SPAB also tried, without success, to obtain the support of Captain Budworth.[15]

Permission to construct the south aisle (and to remove certain named graves in the churchyard on the site of this extension) was given in a faculty issued on 3 May 1883 and the construction was completed during 1884. Features included Norman style windows in the new south wall (some of which took stained glass from the original south nave windows) and an oak board ceiling supported by eleven cross beams. Five of these bear carved wooden angels with shields showing the symbols of the Crucifixion. While some aspects of the south aisle are typically Victorian in style, the roof blends in well with the earlier work in the body of the church, and was admired by Cecil Hewett.[16] Clapton Rolfe also designed a new west porch in 1885. Frederick Noble, the local builder, produced the working drawings in 1887 and the actual reconstruction took place in 1888.

ST MARTIN'S CHURCH

The font

The font has had several different positions in the nave, the earliest known being on a plinth just inside the west door in front of the war memorial. It was moved to its present position either during the reconstruction in the 1880s, or when the war memorial was installed after the First World War. In April 1960, a faculty was obtained to move it back to its earlier position, but this was not done. At this time a font bowl was found in a High Street garden near the inner bailey moat, dating from the fifteenth century and presumably originally from St Martin's. This was restored and erected on a new base in its present position in 1963.

The pews

The earliest reference to pews is found in the vestry minutes of 12 September 1749 when it was decided to install an additional pew on the left side of the nave, and to create double sized family pews. At the same time two additional pews were built at the front of the gallery. Thereafter, various measures were taken to increase the seating capacity of the church. A committee, set up to advise on *'the state of the church, and to consider what future accommodation be made for the inhabitants,'* reported to the vestry on 7 April 1812. One proposal (which was implemented) was to close the south door of the nave and to build a pew in the area thus freed. The north door immediately opposite was closed in 1814, and two more pews added. The pressure on accommodation continued, and on 8 August 1832 the vestry considered the re-ordering of the pew layout, and the mixture of 20 single and double (family) pews was replaced by 36 single pews, 18 on each side of the nave. It appears that the pews were still of the high box type, as the specification of the work included run numbers being fixed to the pew doors. The cost was estimated at £100.[17]

It is not clear when the present pews were installed. At a vestry meeting on 31 May 1855 *'it was proposed by Mr Potter, and seconded by Mr Hancock, that it would be an advantage to the church to have the pews made lower.'* An amendment that *'it is the opinion of the parishioners that the pews are better as they are'* was carried by 20 votes for, to two against.[18] The south aisle pews installed in 1884 were to be the same height as those in the nave, so the latter must have been replaced with lower pews some time in the previous 30 years – probably in 1860, when the SPAB report noted that *'the church underwent very harsh and ignorant treatment resulting in lasting injury to the building.'* [19]

The earliest form of heating was a circular finned boiler in the centre of the nave. Its position can still be identified by the cut back of the pews on either side. An early form of central heating with pipes and radiators was installed in 1919, when a boiler room was built under the newly extended vestry. The unusual feature of this system (still in use today) is that large diameter pipes and heat fins are located just under the roof on each side of the nave. Before the recent provision of thermal barrier roof boards, most of the available heat would have been lost through the roof and only the organist, high in the gallery, might have had some benefit in winter!

ASPECTS OF THE HISTORY OF ONGAR

The organ

The first organ was erected and in use by May 1835. Voluntary subscriptions were called for and 71 individuals contributed £122 3s 6d. This covered the initial cost of £50 and an organ fund was set up. All outgoings for repairs, tuning, organist's salary and payments to boys to blow the organ (one shilling per year!) were recorded. The first organist, Mrs Champness, was paid £3 15s 0d a quarter between 1843 and 1850. In 1876 it was decided to repair the organ and to move it from the gallery to the chancel and there was a special service to mark the completion of this on 18 October 1877. The cost of this work (and the installation of pews in the vacated area of the gallery) was defrayed by another subscription, which operated in 1878. It appears that the organ was giving further trouble in 1879 as there was much correspondence with the organ builder in Rose Street, Soho, London.[20] There is no record of the outcome.

Miss Hall was appointed organist in 1876 at a salary of £20 per annum. In 1880 she applied for, and was granted, an increase of £5 per annum, so presumably her performance was satisfactory up to this point. However, on 29 December 1880 she was sent a letter (signed by the rector, Mr Tanner, and the churchwarden, Mr F. Rose) which stated *'Your complete unfitness for the discharge of your duties on the evening of Sunday last the 26 December, coupled with the fact that this is by no means the first time that it has occurred, oblige us to ask you to tender your resignation of your appointment as organist of St Martin's church.'* A short reply was soon sent as follows: *'Rev J Tanner, Mr F Rose, I resign the Organ. E. P. Hall.'* There is no further background to this intriguing episode but the vestry appointed a new organist on 21 April 1881 at a salary of £35 per annum.[21]

However, it seems that the instrument itself continued to be unsatisfactory. The vestry was informed on 18 April 1895 that £250 had been raised towards the purchase of a new one. Authority to proceed was given and the new organ was installed in the chancel in 1896. In March 1919, it was agreed to reconstruct the organ and to move it back to the gallery which was cut back by 7 feet and provided with a new oak front as seen today.[22] In 1945 there was a proposal to remove the gallery and to rebuild the organ on a platform supported by four columns astride the nave. This plan was subsequently abandoned.

The gallery

It is not clear from the vestry records when the gallery was built, but it was certainly in existence in 1749 when the vestry authorised two additional pews in the gallery. The construction of the gallery had involved cutting away part of the supporting timbers of the fifteenth century belfry, possibly contributing to structural problems in the south west corner of the building, necessitating the rebuilding of the upper part of the gable when the south aisle was built in 1884.

The rectors

A list of the rectors of St Martin's will be found in the church, the first listed being Stephen Bolton in 1350. From about 1254, the patronage, or the right to appoint

ST MARTIN'S CHURCH

priests to the living, was vested in the lords of the manor who are listed in the Victoria County History, and (apart from a few breaks) this continued up to the cessation of the manor on the death of Lady Swinburne in 1896. The most notable break occurred in 1548 when the parish of Chipping Ongar was amalgamated with Greensted, an event fully described in chapter 7. The patronage was acquired by the Guild of All Souls in 1905.[23]

Little is known about many of the rectors. Richard Vaughan (1578 to 1580) left to become Bishop of Bangor, subsequently becoming Bishop of Chester and finally Bishop of London.[24] John Lorkin (1659/60 to 1662) was ejected for refusing to conform to the Act of Uniformity (see chapter 5). George Alsop (1670 to 1673) was appointed by the bishop in 1670 to read divine service at the Quaker meeting house in Gracechurch Street. Presumably this was an attempt to impose conformity on what was seen at that time as a rebellious sect, but he was violently opposed and had to make his escape.[25] Two of his published books suggest that he may have travelled – *A Character of the Province of Maryland* in 1668, and *A Sermon Preached at Sea* in 1678.[26] Joseph Beadle (1680 to 1692), also vicar of Great Burstead, was one of Charles II's Royal chaplains.[27] Not surprisingly, St Martin's had a succession of curates at this time and problems arose, leading to the sequestration of the fruits of the living by the churchwardens in 1690. This move was opposed by Mr Beadle in the Court of Arches, but the outcome is unknown.[28] In 1770, the rector, Thomas Wayte, surrendered his traditional right to graze his animals in the churchyard in return for an annual payment of 7s 6d.[29] Richard Porter (1869 to 1878) had a keen interest in local history and published the invaluable *A few Notes on the Town and Parish of Chipping Ongar* in 1877. James Tanner (1878 to 1915) was very active in the parish and was involved in many local organisations, such as the Horticultural Society of which he was chairman in 1896. His niece, Miss L.W. Tanner, left the residue of her state in a trust which (after the death of her aunt) was to be used for *'the beautification of the church.'*[30]

The first reference to a rectory was in 1254 when it was valued at 4 marks. By 1535 the building was valued at £6.[31] Up to 1723 the building (later described as two cottages and outhouses) was immediately to the north of the church, on the site of the present houses in St Martin's Mews. In that year, the property now known as the Old Rectory was purchased, with 5 acres of glebe land (sold for building in the 1960s and now occupied by the Shakletons estate). This purchase was made possible by donations of £109 2s by the rector of Bobbingworth, £100 from Edward Colston and £200 from Queen Anne's Bounty[32] and the building served as the rectors' home for the next 250 years. On the retirement of Canon John Vaughan Jones in 1982, the Diocese of Chelmsford, pursuing its policy of replacing expensive old buildings with new ones, sold the property but retained the southern half of the garden on which to build the present rectory.

The former rectory buildings adjoining the church were rented out until 1785, by which time they had become very dilapidated and the church sought, and obtained, a faculty to demolish them. The proceeds from the sale of building materials were used to improve the rectory, but a terrier shows that the site was still owned by the church in 1810.[33] By 1837 this land had passed into the ownership of Brook Hurlock of the White House,[34] and the churchyard had been narrowed to provide coach access to his house. In his book, R. I. Porter wryly noted that the church had no record of this transaction.

In 1928 a proposal was tabled to unite the benefices of Greensted, Chipping Ongar, Bobbingworth and Shelley but this was abandoned the following year.[35] Finally, in August 1986, the Queen's Privy Council authorised the union of the benefices of Chipping Ongar and Shelley into the single parish of Chipping Ongar with Shelley.

Parish officials and their responsibilities

The office of churchwarden was already in existence by the time St Martin's was built and had full legal recognition by the thirteenth century. They acted as trustees of the church building and its contents and were responsible for the congregation, as well as for law and order in the parish. They were chosen annually by the community and had extensive powers within the parish, in the vestry and in the appointment of other parish officers. Government legislation steadily added to their areas of responsibility, particularly under the numerous poor law acts. They personally had power to keep order in the church and would have been responsible, in 1608, for William Small's appearance in court for fighting in the churchyard. He claimed that George Harris had struck him with a dagger, *'wounding him in divers places'*, and explained that he had *'wrong'* the dagger from his assailant and *'stroke him therewith'* outside the churchyard. He was acquitted.[36]

From the seventeenth to the nineteenth centuries, churchwardens were responsible for a variety of financial matters, from the levying of the poor rate to providing funds for the upkeep of the church and its ministry. It was the churchwardens who petitioned the vestry for authority to carry out alterations to the church, and they were responsible for the approved action. There were occasional clashes with the vestry, as on 1 April 1771 when Richard White wrote in his own hand *'I Richard White late Church Warden of the parish of Chipping Ongar did very imprudently and by ill advice spend money in ornamenting the Church contrary to the Consent of the Vestry and as I cannot be reimbursed without the Indulgence of the Parishioners I hope an Acknowledgement of my Fault will procure it.'*[37] There is no record of what he had done, or whether he was reimbursed.

They were also responsible for church discipline through the church courts. Failure to attend church was an offence from 1593, and, in March 1683, 29 parishioners were presented at the Archdeacon's court at Romford for failing to receive the sacrament at Easter.[38] It is not clear why nearly one in ten of the adult population refused to attend church, but it may have been dissatisfaction with the absentee rector, Mr Beadle, or a group of nonconformists taking a stand against the established church. This is discussed further in chapter 5.

Up to about 1878, the cost of maintaining the church and its services was through the parish rate, or by subscription for specific projects. Many attempts were made to start voluntary collections at services (the first recorded was authorised by the vestry in 1755, when £4 16s was collected in four weeks) but most ceased after a time. Between 1826 and the abolition of church rates in 1868, the vestry authorised an annual parish rate varying between 3d and 1s in the pound on all *'occupiers of lands, tenements and hereditaments'* in the parish. This was understandably unpopular with nonconformists who did not see why they should support a church that they did not attend.

In 1869, the rector and churchwardens, responding to the loss of revenue from the abolition of church rates, called a meeting of the vestry on 19 May. However there was still opposition to collections in church, and a further proposal for a quarterly collection in the church was lost by one vote in the vestry of 21 July 1871. Finally, on 9 April 1874, the vestry unanimously approved the proposal, but it seems that this did not solve the church's financial problems arising from the loss of the parish rate.[39] The churchwardens called a public meeting on 22 July 1878 *'to take into consideration the best means of providing funds for the expenses of the Parish Church. The present voluntary subscription being insufficient, it will be proposed that they be supplemented by monthly offerings in the church.'* The vestry abolished voluntary subscriptions in 1908, and collections were to be taken in the church every Sunday.[40] However it seems that there were some doubts about this course of action, for in 1910 it was reduced to a fortnightly interval.

Churchwardens always had the support of other parish officials, such as the parish clerk whose post had been in existence since the eleventh century. The first reference at St Martin's was a fatal one. John the Clerke was killed by a falling bell clapper in 1285 while ringing the bell.[41] By the eighteenth century his duties were less dangerous, for the vestry on 7 August agreed to allow *'John Lawrence the Church Clerk a salary of 40 shillings a year from Easter last in consideration whereof he is to find mopps and broomes and at all times to keep the church and churchyard clean and decent and do all the duties belonging to the office of Church Clerk'*[42] In 1805 his salary was increased to five guineas a year and, apart from the established responsibility for cleaning, he was instructed to *'open the windows several times in the week when the weather is fine and dry in order to keep the Church well aired.'*[43]

Another official was the beadle who acted as an usher and kept order in church. In 1805 the vestry allowed him a salary of two guineas per annum, and a *'lace blue coat and hat every four years.'* In 1807 he was instructed to *'remain in the Aisle of the Church on Sundays until the Litany Service is over, for the purpose of shewing Strangers to convenient seats in the Church, and that he occasionally attend to the observance of decorum in the Gallery.'*[43] Clearly those at the back of the church were not always paying full attention to the service! This office has now disappeared and the duties are undertaken by a sidesperson on a voluntary basis.

Before the churchyard closed on 31 December 1866, the sexton acted as church caretaker and gravedigger and received fixed fees. In 1814, for example, the vestry resolved that he *'be allowed to receive five shillings for every brick grave that is and in the churchyard the same being dug by the parties requiring it, and that for opening a brick grave he shall also have five shillings.'*[43] Though the churchyard

ASPECTS OF THE HISTORY OF ONGAR

was closed in 1866 when Ongar cemetery was completed (see chapter 9), a schedule was produced in 1867 listing 45 existing graves in which interments could still take place, so presumably the sexton had a continuing, if dwindling, role for some time after this date.

References

1. Ryan, P. *Brick in Essex* (1996) published privately, p.14
2. Rodwell, W. R. "Holy Trinity Church, Bradwell juxta Coggeshall – a survey of the fabric" in *Essex Archaeology and History* vol 29 (1998) p.105
3. Hewett, C. *Church Carpentry* (1982) Phillimore p.31
4. inf from Canon John Vaughan Jones
5. RCHME, *Inventory of the Historical Monuments in Essex* vol 2 (1921) p.52
6. ibid
7. *Archeological Journal* (1888) p.284
8. RCHME, op cit p.52
9. Pevsner, N. *The Buildings of England – Essex* (1979) Penguin p.125
10. ibid
11. RCHME op cit
12. vestry minutes ERO: D/P 124/8/2
13. RCHME op cit
14. vestry minutes ERO: D/P 124/8/5
15. plans and correspondence at the Society for the Protection of Ancient Buildings: SPAB archives
16. Hewett, C. op cit p.101
17. vestry minutes ERO: D/P 124/8/3
18. ibid
19. SPAB survey report dated 19 January 1883: SPAB archives
20. ERO: D/P 124/6/2
21. ibid
22. vestry minutes ERO: D/D 124/8/5
23. VCH (Essex) vol 4 (1956) p.162
24. ibid p.163
25. ibid
26. Wing, D. *Short-Title Catalogue 1641–1700* (1992) Modern Language Association of America
27. Craze, M. *History of Felsted School 1564–1947* (1955) Ipswich
28. Houston, J. (ed) *Index of Cases in the Court of Arches* (1972) British Record Society
29. vestry minutes D/P 124/8/1A
30. VCH op cit p.164
31. ibid p.163
32. Porter, R. I. *A few Notes on the Town and Parish of Chipping Ongar* (1877) Ongar
33. VCH op cit p. 163
34. Chipping Ongar tithe award ERO: D/CT 262A
35. ERO: D/P 124/3/8
36. note in records held by parish
37. vestry minutes D/P 124/8/1A
38. archdeacon's visitation book ERO: D/AEA 44
39. vestry minutes ERO: D/P 124/8/4
40. notice of meeting
41. for full account see: *Essex Archeological Society Transactions* n.s. vol vii p. 188
42. vestry minutes ERO: D/P 124/8/1A
43. vestry minutes ERO: D/P 124/8/2

chapter 5

Religious dissent in Ongar from 1662 to 1810

by Michael Leach

There is no evidence to show how Chipping Ongar responded to the religious turmoils of the later sixteenth and early seventeenth century. Successive monarchs had a strong desire to retain overall control of the church through the bishops, while puritans felt that the work of the Reformation was only half done and that bishops and church rituals were Romish relics that should be swept away. There were very real fears of a return to Catholicism by invasion or conversion. However it is clear that Ongar had a puritan ministry for nearly a century before the Restoration of Charles II. Hugh (or Hugo) Ince, rector from 1582 to 1617, was described by the "Puritan List" of 1604 as '*a sufficient and diligent preacher.*' His successor, Thomas Graves, rector from 1617 to 1635, showed his puritan credentials (and risked Bishop Laud's displeasure) by signing the petition in favour of Thomas Hooker, the Chelmsford preacher who had to flee to Holland to escape persecution. Daniel Joyner, rector from 1635 to 1643, signed the intolerant and sternly puritan "Essex Testimony" in 1648.[1] Of the next six rectors before the Restoration, five refused to conform with the re-established Church of England in 1662, and were ejected from their livings. One of them, Elias Pledger, was described in 1650 as '*an able and godly minister.*'[2] There seems little doubt that Ongar had fervent puritan and resident clergy over this period, and that there would have been little need to form a separate congregation.

On 24 August 1662, John Lorkin, rector of Chipping Ongar, was ejected from his living for refusing to subscribe to the Act of Uniformity.[1] Amongst other provisions, the Act required the use of the Book of Common Prayer, and the avoidance of extemporare prayer which was central to puritan worship. Not only did the Restoration bring to an end at least 60 years of puritan worship in Ongar, but it also removed the Ongar Classis. This local committee may have met in the parish church, or in the Crown Inn, Chipping Ongar, which was the meeting place chosen by the Parochial Inquisition on 9 September 1650.[2] Lay members outnumbered clergy on the classis which was responsible for the administration of the parishes in the Ongar Hundred. After 1660, control was returned to the Bishop of London and local people largely lost their influence over church affairs. It is difficult to assess the quality of the post-Restoration clergy. However, Jacob Crook, rector from 1664 to 1670, was in the archdeacon's court in 1668 for '*not residing upon his living.*'[3] Joseph Beadle, rector from 1680 to 1691, was a non-resident minister who had another parish at Great Burstead and left this parish in the hands of a succession of curates.[4] In a defamation case in the Court of Arches, it was suggested that he was '*a frequenter of alehouses.*'[5] Most puritans would have disapproved very strongly of such a habit. So there is some evidence to show why local people might have been dissatisfied with their minister, and made moves to form a separate congregation outside the established church.

Edmund Calamy, whose father was ejected from the neighbouring parish of Moreton in 1662, wrote of John Lorkin '*at his church, several of his brethren carried on a weekly lecture. He was an infirm but solid person, and had a good estate which he lived upon, being very ready to entertain his brethren.*'[1] Repressive legislation followed soon after. The First Conventicle Act of 1664 made nonconformist meetings of more than five people illegal and punishable by fines and transportation. It was not even safe to express an opinion. George Sparkes, sexton of Chipping Ongar, was presented at the Archdeacon's court in Brentwood in February 1664 for '*saying that the Common Prayer [Book] is a meene Calling.*'[3] It is not clear where John Lorkin lived after his ejection, but the Five Mile Act of 1665 would have made it difficult for him to live or preach in the immediate area. It has been claimed by many that he was the first minister of the dissenting congregation, but the only evidence for this is the ambiguous statement by Calamy above. Unfortunately attempts to trace John Lorkin's will (if he ever made one) have been unsuccessful.

There was a brief respite from persecution in 1672 with Charles II's Declaration of Indulgence which suspended all repressive religious legislation. Nonconformists in North Weald, Stapleford Abbots, High Ongar and High Laver took the opportunity to license houses for worship.[6] Other meetings may have considered it too risky to advertise their presence – with justification, in view of the repressive legislation that followed Parliament's revocation of the Declaration of Indulgence in the following year. So Chipping Ongar's failure to register a meeting does not necessarily exclude the presence of a dissenting congregation in the town.

Nonconformity returned to being an illegal organisation, and has left few records. Bishop Compton's survey of 1676 was an attempt to establish the strength of nonconformity in the country. It is reckoned that it underestimated numbers, and that it probably excluded those dissenters who were "occasional conformers" and attended their parish church a few times a year to keep out of trouble. The survey showed only one nonconformist in Chipping Ongar, and only 33 in the whole Ongar Hundred.[7] This must have been a very unrealistic figure, but would probably have pleased the ecclesiastical authorities who were hoping to demonstrate to Charles II that nonconformity was not a threat to the country!

In 1683, during a period of widespread persecution of nonconformity, 29 Chipping Ongar parishioners were presented at the Archdeacon's court '*for not receiving the Sacramt of the Lord's Supper in that parish at Easter or Whitsuntide last.*'[8] They were mainly small farmers and tradesmen and their wives, but did include Thomas Velley. He would have been a figure of some importance in the community, being the steward of the manorial court and (later) a justice of the peace, as well as the father of a future rector. At least one of the offenders was not intimidated by the ecclesiastical authorities – John Mead, a glover, told the court that '*they mought all goe to the Devell for money.*'[8] It is not clear if these individuals were non-conformists, or whether their quarrel was with an unpopular absentee rector.

The Glorious Revolution of 1688 re-established religious tolerance of dissenters (apart from anti-Trinitarians and Roman Catholics), although a licence to use a building for nonconformist worship remained obligatory until the nineteenth century. The Presbyterian and Independent (or Congregational) churches were briefly united in 1690 (the "Happy Union"), and set up a general fund to provide, amongst other things, adequate remuneration for ministers. The resulting survey is somewhat confusing, as Ongar appears twice. One section reports a meeting of 200 hearers, with a minister Mr Tyro, '*a worthy man but poor,*' who received £20 per annum in subscriptions from his congregation. Another section lists places which formerly had had a congregation, or where there might be an opportunity for establishing a new one, and notes '*Onger. A dark corner. Mr Paget through Mr Rowes means was prevailed with to come among them, whose labours are well approved, they promised him £30 per annum but ye performance less than £20.*'[9] Possibly Mr Paget was an earlier minister who had left after receiving a smaller income than expected. But there clearly was, or had been, a nonconformist congregation at that time. Another indication of difficulties comes in a letter from Walter Cross, author and dissenting divine, dated about 1698, '*to enquire iff you have any message to Angure – our errand is the setting that church in order & officers as far as our assistance can.*'[10]

Fifteen years later, there are 23 entries in the Chipping Ongar parish church register headed '*A Register of those said to be bap. by ye Teacher of ye separate Congregation.*'[9] The baptisms are not in chronological order, and some are not properly dated but they appear to span January 1705 to March 1709. Looking through the parish register, it is clear that some of these infants returned later to the parish church for burial. This could be explained by the lack of a suitable burial ground for nonconformists. Also, subsequent children of some of these parents were baptised in the established church.[11] It would seem that there was free movement between the two churches, though it is very surprising to find the Ongar nonconformist minister John Nettleton having his daughter baptised in the parish church on 9 May 1740! This would have normally been grounds for excluding a member from the congregation.

There is other evidence of nonconformist activity at this time. A licence for the use of Walter Buchanan's house in Chipping Ongar as a place of worship for "presbitarians" was granted in July 1706,[12] and another for the house of Samuel Clarke of Chipping Ongar for "protestant dissenters" in July 1707.[13] Both these men had children baptised by the "teacher of the separate congregation" mentioned above. Houses for nonconformist worship were also registered in Writtle, North Weald and Navestock at this time.[14]

Dr John Evans, secretary to the "Committee of the Three Denominations", compiled a list of nonconformist congregations in England and Wales, with the aid of county agents. The list was made between 1715 and 1718, but he continued to make additions and amendments up to the end of his life in 1729. It shows that the minister at Chipping Ongar was Simon Weaver and that there were 200 hearers, of whom four were gentlemen and eight had votes for the county. Simon Weaver was "removed" in 1724, and was followed by John Tren in 1725 and John Nettleton in 1726.[15] All three ministers were ordained (this was not mandatory in the Independent church at the time). John Tren's ordination took place in the meeting house at Chipping Ongar on 7 May 1725 and was commemorated by a sermon, later published under the title of *'The Nature of Pastoral Office or the Apostle Peter's Exhortation to the Elders of the church, briefly considered.'*[16] John Tren moved on to the St Helen's Lane meeting house in Colchester.[17] Dr Evan's list shows congregations in all the adjoining towns (Epping, Brentwood, Harlow, Romford, Chelmsford) as well as in the hamlet of Pilgrim's Hatch (200 hearers) and Abbess Roding with 500 hearers. Though these figures seem astonishingly large, recent research claims that they are broadly accurate.[18] Clearly these large congregations could no longer continue to meet in private houses, and many chapels or meeting houses were built at this time.

Amongst the archives of the Ongar United Reformed Church are a series of copyhold deeds. Each time a manorial property changed hands, a new deed was issued by the manor court, describing the property, the owner and the tenants. It appears that the present site of the chapel and the cottages in front was originally in two parts. One was an apple orchard in 1685, but by 1720 it consisted of *'Messuage or Tenement withall and singular the Barns Stables Orchards Gardens and backsides thereunto belonging together with one building called the Meeting House thereupon lately erected.'* The deeds for the other part dated 1705 refer to Nathaniel Lacey, "clericus", as copyholder in 1699 – this may be the rector of Greensted who died in 1700. The property is described in a similar style (obviously without the meeting house), appended with the description *'over against the sign of the Lion,'* which was the inn on the opposite side of the High Street. One occupant was Thomas Ross, father of one of the children baptised by the teacher of the separate congregation.[19]

Simon Weaver, *'clerk of High Ongar,'* acquired the copyhold of the part with the meeting house in 1720, adding the ownership of the other part in 1724, the year he ceased to be minister. He then owned both parts until his death in 1737.[19] He is noted on 27 July 1712 as *'the Revd. Mr Simon Weaver of Onger'* when he baptised the daughter of Lachlan Ross, pastor of the Abbess Roding congregation. This suggests that he was the nonconformist minister at that time. It seems that the first chapel had been erected by September 1714, when Lachlan Ross noted that James Ives was *'baptised by me at Onger Meeting House.'* [20]

Nothing is known of the building of the first chapel, or how it was financed (probably by subscription). An undated print (dating from after the death of the Rev. Isaac Taylor, as his tombstone is shown) by C. Ingrey shows a modest building with two tiers of windows on the south side, and a hipped tiled roof.[21] The west front is not typical of an early meeting house and was probably a late eighteenth or early nineteenth century addition. It has pilasters and a pediment, with a parapet to conceal the roof. There was a small single storey building attached to the rear which was probably a vestry. An internal gallery of some sort is suggested by a reference in the burial register,[22] and the original internal seating arrangements would have separated men from women. It was also quite usual at this time, even in nonconformist churches, for the best pews to be sold to wealthier members of the congregation.[23] A *'map of the burying ground'* drawn up by the Rev. Isaac Taylor in 1824 shows that the building was roughly 18 feet by 36 feet, and the rear extension was about 10 feet by 12 feet.[22]

The Rev. John Nettleton, minister from 1726, was married to Elizabeth, older sister of Phillip Doddridge of Northampton. The letters of this famous nonconformist divine have been published. From these, it is clear that the Nettletons were living in Hampstead up to June 1726 when Doddridge wrote to his sister *'I do most seriously desire to know how you go on in your new settlement and whether my brother's school begins to fill. I would wish myself one of his scholars, as I am sensible that it might be much for my improvement.'* It is not clear where this school was, but it may have been in Ongar, as this was the year of John Nettleton's move. By 1734, Elizabeth was seriously ill, and Doddridge wrote on 13 June, *'I fear there is no hope for my poor dear sister's life. She declines and consumes daily and now lives on three Savoy biscuits a day. I am very much troubled by this melancholy news and have some thoughts of going directly to Ongar.'* Five days later, he wrote *'I returned yesterday from Ongar, where I preached once only on Lord's Day. My poor sister is in a deep consumption.'* He referred to a fishing expedition with his brother-in-law, ironically describing his *'extraordinary success'* in landing a minnow, whereas John Nettleton landed a *'very large and fine chub.'*[24] Elizabeth was buried at the parish church on 6 September 1734.[10] On 12 July 1735, Doddridge noted without comment that John Nettleton was *'to be married again in a few days.'*[25] The first two children of this second marriage were baptised at Abbess Roding meeting house by Lachlan Ross,[20] but their third child was baptised at the parish church, as noted above.[11]

It is not clear when John Nettleton became minister at Epping, or whether he looked after both congregations. But on 22 July 1747, Philip Doddridge was at Epping with other ministers (including John Green of Chipping Ongar) for the "setting apart" (i.e. exclusion from the church) of his brother-in-law. No reasons are given. After this his health declined and, in August 1749, Doddridge wrote, *'to Epping to visit my poor brother Nettleton – he is a piteous spectacle, much disabled both in mind and body.'*[25]

One of the copyhold deeds dated 1740 refers to part of the property as a *'tenement in the occupation of John Green and used as a boarding school.'* Was this the successor to John Nettleton's school? He was the steward of the manorial court, and probably the John Green of Chipping Ongar who, in 1740, loaned £410 to Theophilus Green, apothecary of Chelmsford, a member of the nonconformist meeting in that town.[26] If they are the same person, the size of the loan suggests that he was well-off. It is not clear when he became minister at Chipping Ongar, but he served for a number of years and was remembered by an old lady living in

1825.[27] By 1764, the date of the earliest surviving baptism register, the Rev. John Somerset was minister.[22]

There is little evidence to show the nature of the congregation or the form of its religious practices at this time. The licence for worship of 1706 stated '*presbitarian*,'[12] but this might have been used as a global term for nonconformity. The Evans list of 1716–18 showed the Rev. Simon Weaver as Presbyterian.[15] As mentioned above, the Scottish Presbyterian minister from Abbess Roding, Lachlan Ross, had links with the Ongar congregation. Also, the surviving fragment of his "almanack," dating from July 1723 to August 1725, shows that he preached four sermons at Ongar during that period.[20] John Tren, ordained at Ongar in 1725, also appears to have been Presbyterian when he moved to Colchester.[17] But the next minister, John Nettleton, had links with the Independent divine Philip Doddridge, as described above. This would seem to indicate a shift to the Independent (later called Congregational) church. Modern authorities suggest that there was no clear cut distinction between the two in rural areas.[23] In 1765, the congregation was described by its minister, John Somerset, as '*the Congregation of Protestant Dissenters at Chipping Ongar.*'[22]

The register of baptisms from September 1764 begins with the names of 17 subscribers and 12 members.[22] Only four names occur on both lists, suggesting that most of those who supported the church financially had not been, or did not wish to be admitted as members. By this time, the Independent churches were noted for their strict discipline, and their readiness to expel (or refuse to admit) those whose faith or life style was not exemplary.[23] However, many of those bringing infants for baptism up to 1774 were not on the updated list of members. Was the Ongar chapel more tolerant than most? What is clear is that the majority came from Chipping Ongar and the surrounding parishes, although a few were from much further afield – Tillingham, Cheshunt and London, for example. The Londoners, Thomas and Sarah Lambert, may have had Ongar connections, as a note by their daughter's baptism on 4 November 1774 states '*died at Ongar 14th May 1778.*'

According to later writers,[21&27] who largely based their accounts on some notes written by the Rev. Isaac Taylor in 1811, '*the church had dwindled to nothing*' by 1782. In that year the Rev. Thomas Bingham from Dedham came to preach and baptise, apparently on an honorary basis for several years. By 1784, the chapel building had fallen into serious disrepair, necessitating the sale of the cottages south of the entranceway to meet the costs. The purchaser was Mr Bingham himself. In 1786, '*a few of the serious people*' re-formed the church and chose him as their minister.

In spite of the perilous state of the congregation, recorded baptisms only fell to just under four per annum at this time. The Rev. Thomas Hutchins preached for two years from 1794, but '*his sentiments having undergone a change on the subject of baptism, he left Ongar, and went to London.*'[27] By the late 1790s and early 1800s, baptisms were down to just over two per annum, and did not rise significantly until the ministry of the Rev. Isaac Taylor from 1811. In common with most nonconformist churches, the Ongar congregation had dwindled from the heady days of the late seventeenth century and needed a revitalising force. This it found in Isaac Taylor, whose achievements are described in Chapter 8.

References

1. Davids, T. *Annals of Evangelical Nonconformity* (1863) London
2. Smith, H. *Ecclesiastical History of Essex* (1934) Colchester
3. Archdeacon's Act Book, ERO: D/AEA 43
4. Archdeacon's Act Book ERO: D/AEV 11
5. Court of Arches Deposition Book. Lambeth Palace Library: Eee 6
6. VCH Essex vol 4 (1956)
7. Whiteman, A. *The Compton Census of 1676 – A Critical Edition* (1987) OUP
8. Archdeacon's Visitation Book, ERO: D/AEV 13
9. Gordon, A. *Freedom after Ejection* (1917) Manchester UP
10. Letter from Walter Cross, ERO: T/B 156
11. Chipping Ongar parish register, ERO: T/R 76
12. Meeting house licence, ERO: Q/SBb 35
13. ibid: Q/SBb 38–39
14. ibid: Q/SBb 41–41a
15. Evans, J. *Dissenting Congregations in England and Wales* (MS in Dr William's Library)
16. Harris, W. *A Sermon Preach'd at Onger at the Publick Ordination of Mr John Tren* (1725) London
17. VCH Essex vol 9 (1994)
18. Spufford, M. (ed) *The World of Rural Dissenters* (1995) Cambridge
19. Copyhold deeds, ERO: T/R 168/14
20. Abbess Roding non-conformist registers, ERO: RG4/486
21. Pinchback, H. *Ongar Congregational Church – A Short History* (1937) Ongar
22. Chipping Ongar non-conformist registers, ERO: RGA 791
23. Watts, M.R. *The Dissenters from the Reformation to the French Revolution* (1978) Clarendon Press
24. Humphreys, J. *The Correspondence and Diary of Philip Doddridge* (1829–1831) in Dr William's Library
25. Nuttall, G.F. *Calendar of Correspondence of Philip Doddridge* (1979) Hist. Manuscripts Comm.
26. Grieve, H. *The Sleepers and the Shadows* (1994) Essex County Council
27. Jennings, I. *The Origins and History of Nonconformity in Chipping Ongar* (1862) Ongar

chapter 6

St Helen's church

by Helen Nyman

Restrictive legislation against Roman Catholics persisted for a century after dissenters had obtained their religious freedom. It was not until the Catholic Relief Act of 1791 that Catholics could worship in their own churches, and only after 1850 did the law allow the creation of a Catholic church hierarchy. Immigration from Ireland in the middle of the nineteenth century, stimulated by the potato famine and the prospects of work on railway construction, increased the need for Catholic places of worship. Missions were established in many towns, helped by the greater freedom of movement provided by the railways. As with dissenters, any suitable barn or private house might be used. Occasionally, the private chapel of a country house provided a more convenient place for worship, and an 1854 enquiry into Catholics in the area showed that a group led by Thomas Reynolds, a furniture broker of Chipping Ongar, '*comes regularly to Kelvedon Hall to do his duties with all his family.*'[1] The Wright family of Kelvedon Hall had been Catholics for several generations.

For some years there had been attempts to supply priests for Ongar, and the Rev. Father Kyne of Brentwood wrote in 1859 '*I have made a beginning in Chipping Ongar.*' With financial assistance from Lord Petre and Miss Tasker, he rented a house for a year in the town centre. However, this did not appear to succeed, as two years later he wrote '*I wish there could be some beginning made in Chipping Ongar.*'[2]

The arrival of the railway in Ongar in 1865 appears to have provided the stimulus or the means to establish the mission. The Servite friars, newly arrived from Italy, travelled by train from their house in Chelsea to Epping every Saturday. They heard confessions there until 10pm and then rose early on Sunday to celebrate Mass. Then they travelled on to Ongar to hear confessions and celebrate Mass in a barn behind the King's Head. After lunch, they returned to London. By 1867, it was served by priests from Barnet, with Sunday Mass at 11.30am, and Benediction at 6.30pm.[1&2] From 1865 to 1869 the mission was known as the Mission of St Mary and St Joseph, Ongar.[2]

The mission was successful, and by 1869 plans for a permanent building were in hand. Countess Helen Tasker of Middleton Hall, Brentwood and the 12th Lord Petre were the chief benefactors. The church was opened on 21 April 1870[3] and consecrated by Archbishop Manning and came under the Archdiocese of Westminster. The dedication was altered to St Helen in honour of its benefactress. The Rev. Henry James Pare was appointed parish priest and he also served the Epping and Ongar Union workhouses. By 1874, he was serving a new mass

ST HELEN'S CHURCH

centre in Dunmow[2] and one of his successors in 1888 celebrated Mass once a month in Saffron Walden, Epping and Great Dunmow.[2] The Ongar priest continued to serve the Epping Union workhouse until the formation of a separate parish in 1923.[4]

Significant improvements were made in 1897. A contemporary reported:

> 'the interior of the Roman Catholic church has undergone quite a transformation. A beautiful stained glass window depicting St Jacobus the Pilgrim surrounded by exquisite flowers and foliage has been placed in the south side of the church beside the altar of St Joseph...the appearance of this church is now equal to any of its size in England, and testifies to the energy of the priest who is beloved by his flock.'[5]

In 1904, Father Schaeffer opened a Catholic orphanage in Chipping Ongar, as a branch of St Joseph's Home, Bow, East London. It was not successful, and was closed the following year.[3] In 1905 Father Thomas Byles, a diocesan missionary priest, was appointed. He was a learned man, and a good preacher and a caring pastor to his people. Some Ongar boys, wanting to learn to box, had reason to remember him for the rest of their lives. He took on their instruction, using a large shed behind the church. In 1912 he was invited to assist at his brother's marriage in New York, and booked his ill-fated passage on the "Titanic," leaving Southampton on Easter Wednesday. The three priests on board (the other two being an Austrian and a Lithuanian) celebrated Mass the following Sunday, using Father Byles's portable altar and accessories. The sermon was given by Father Byles in English and French.[6]

After the sinking of the "Titanic," a lady survivor stated *'after the Titanic was struck, Father Byles was active in getting women and children into the lifeboats. He then returned to the other passengers who had become excited. He went about giving absolutions and blessings which calmed the people. He then began the recitation of the Rosary and, regardless of creed, the responses were loud and strong. More women and children were helped into a boat, a sailor pleaded several times for Father Byles to board as well but he refused.'* As the last boat left, a passenger said that she could still hear distinctly the voices of the priest and the responses to the prayers. Then came the faint singing of "Nearer my God to Thee."[6]

The congregation of St Helen's were deeply distressed at the loss of their greatly loved pastor. Many were at the requiem Mass addressed by Monsignor Watson who said of him *'he was a man of great learning, great zeal, and had a love for the poor and great humility.'*[6] A beautiful stained glass window was dedicated to him, the three lights showing St Patrick, the Good Shepherd and St Thomas Aquinas.

On the opposite side of the church is another stained glass window showing St Thomas the Apostle. The round window at the back of the church was provided by the daughter and son of Henry Jump, in his memory. It shows the Virgin Mary and Child with three doves on each side. The Holy Spirit is depicted by a dove at the top of the window, surrounded by various saints including St Anne, and St

ASPECTS OF THE HISTORY OF ONGAR

Helen who found the True Cross. The beautiful Stations of the Cross were donated by the Baugh family, former pharmacists in the town, in about 1964.[7]

Parochial duties were increased by serving a new mission at Epping in 1912, putting a severe strain on church funds.[8] During the First World War, there were additional responsibilities with two military hospitals in the area, and there was further financial anxiety in 1918 when it was noted that the Duke de Moro would in future be unable to make his customary generous annual donation to the parish.[9]

In July 1917, due to the growth of the population of Essex and the number of new churches, the new diocese of Brentwood was formed with Bishop Bernard Ward as its first bishop. By 1923, the boundaries of the Ongar parish had been established and Father O'Sullivan no longer had to travel to Epping by train every Sunday to celebrate Mass.[4] However, it is clear that what was still a large scattered rural parish, with an inadequate stipend, required very hard work and considerable dedication from the parish priest.[10]

Father Loveland, shortly after his arrival in the parish in 1955, wrote to the Bishop of Brentwood about his proposals to extend the church. A fund was established soon afterwards.[10] By 1970 plans had been drawn up by a Catholic architect, Mr Birchall-Scott.[11] In order to enlarge the church on its restricted site it became necessary for the congregation to turn about. The wall at the west end was opened up, and the new extension was built towards the garden at the rear. A stone altar was placed at the west end of the new building, with tiled steps up to the Sanctuary. A new entrance porch at the east end with double doors and a window completed the work.

Clergy of the Mission of St Mary and St Joseph, Ongar [2&12]

1865	Henry Fox
1866	Michael Gualco

Dedication changed to **St Helen** in 1870

1867–76	Henry James Pare (missionary apostolic)
1877	William Rayleigh (missionary apostolic)
1877–79	H. Maria Jouanneau (missionary apostolic)
1880–92	David Charles Nicols (missionary apostolic & missionary coadjutor)
1893–?	Cornelius Ryan (missionary apostolic)
?	Michael Moloney (missionary rector)
1894–95	James J. Hazel (temporarily assigned)
1896–97	William Smullen
1897–99	Under the care of various Dominican Friars
1900	Charles Collingridge (missionary rector)
1900–02	Adrian Forti Scuto (priest)
1903–04	Patrick William Lorkin (missionary apostolic)
1905–12	Thomas R. D. Byles (missionary apostolic and missionary rector)
1912	James Connor (missionary coadjutor)
1912–14	John J. Caulfield (missionary rector)
1914–16	John Boyland (priest)
1917–50	Michael O'Sullivan (priest and rector)

ST HELEN'S CHURCH

1959–55 Stephen A. Keane (priest)
1955–73 William J. Loveland (parish priest)
1973–84 Brian W. Drea (parish priest)
1984–94 Brian K. Galvin (parish priest)
1994   Andrew Hurley (priest in charge)

References

1   *Essex Recusant*, vol 13 (1971)
2   VCH Essex vol 4 (1956)
3   *Essex Recusant* vol 14 (1972)
4   Diocese of Brentwood Archives: Visitation Returns and Boundary Commission correspondence
5   *Essex Review* (1897) vol 6, p.67
6   *Essex Recusant* vol 17 (1975)
7   Diocese of Brentwood Archives: Visitation Return of 1967
8   Diocese of Brentwood Archives: mission accounts for quarter ending 31/12/1912
9   Diocese of Brentwood Archives: Visitation Return of 1918
10 Diocese of Brentwood Archives: correspondence file
11 Diocese of Brentwood Archives: Visitation Return of 1970
12 St Helen's register of baptisms 1865–1922 and Diocese of Brentwood Archives: Visitation Returns 1905–1970

chapter 7

Chipping Ongar and the Morices

by Margaret Buxton

The Morices were the most important family in sixteenth-century Ongar. Three generations of the family earned lasting distinction through their services in the Tudor court from the time of Henry VII to Elizabeth I, and by making Chipping Ongar their home they helped to put it on the national map. The addition of a sizable gentleman's dwelling-house to the earthwork of Ongar Castle effectively put '*Onger ad castrum*' otherwise '*Chepinge Onger*'[1] back in the position it had held when the castle mound was erected; it became a place worth a royal visit. But the Morice contribution to the history of Chipping Ongar was not all positive, since it was thanks to them that the town nearly lost its church, as well as gaining a house capable of receiving Queen Elizabeth.

The first member of the family to reach distinction, and to plant it firmly on Essex soil, was James Morice, whose career started in the late fifteenth century. He held several offices in the household of Henry VII's mother, Lady Margaret Beaufort, most importantly that of clerk of the works. In this capacity he played a leading role in the building programme of this devout patron of learning, both on her own residences, and in the planning and supervision of her Cambridge foundations, Christ's College and St John's College. These responsibilities continued after Lady Margaret's death in 1509, when work was still in progress on both colleges, and in 1510 James was summoned back to Cambridge from Essex by the bishop of Rochester, John Fisher, to see to the chapel at St John's. Sixteen years later Morice was still involved in his old mistress's affairs, this time the endowment of her school and chantry at Wimborne in Dorset. From about the time of the countess's death, Morice was probably living on the Essex manor which came to him through his service to her. She bought Roydon Hall and gave it to Christ's College in 1505–6, and it was from the college that James obtained his 99 year lease of the estate. To this, thirty-five years later, he was able to add a long lease of the adjacent Temple Roydon.[2]

In the second part of his life James Morice's career moved to the king's household, where he became a gentleman usher and joint receiver-general in the court of general surveyors. Through the connections formed in royal service and the territorial acquisition which went with it, he was admirably placed to promote his sons. William, the eldest, was able to start his career in the household of Richard Pace, dean of St Paul's, and Ralph (who became the most distinguished) was a scholasticus at Christ's College in 1522, while a third son, Philip, entered the service of Thomas Cromwell, having attempted to become secretary of the Duke of Richmond.[3] James Morice was more than a builder and administrator. He shared the interests of his royal patron, and owned a significant collection of devotional books.[4] When he died towards the end of 1557, he had lived long enough to see much of England's traditional devotions swept away, and Mary Tudor's efforts to restore them. Perhaps James had begun to change his own religious views; he might have been influenced by his own aspiring sons, whose commitment to Protestant beliefs had long been clear. Certainly the terminology of his will, with its lack of traditional reference to the saints, leaving his soul simply *'unto thandes of allmighty god the father of heaven'* suggests he had moved far from the piety of Lady Margaret.[5]

William Morice, with whom the family's Ongar connection started, was born about 1500. He was probably well over halfway through his life before he became seriously committed to interests in Essex, and his earliest activities were centred in London and the royal administration. At the end of 1530 William was working alongside his father in the court of general surveyors of crown lands, and six years later they were joint recipients of a profitable crown office which dealt with the recovery of debts. James Morice was active in easing his eldest son into valuable positions. William was a yeoman of the chamber when, also in 1530, he was granted in reversion the offices of surveyor and general receiver of the estate of the late Lady Margaret, the king's grandmother, which had previously been handled by his father and an associate.[6] He went on to become gentleman usher of Henry VIII's chamber. By 1536, when he sent a new year's token to Thomas Cromwell (with thanks for kindness to his brother Philip who had been robbed at sea), William Morice had his own connections in the highest quarters.[6] Perhaps most important for William at this stage of his career were the links forged through his younger brother Ralph, who in 1528 became secretary to Thomas Cranmer (four years before his surprising elevation to Canterbury), a position which he held for over twenty years, and which proved influential both at the time and later.

In 1543, when Archbishop Cranmer was under attack, Ralph had his own counter-plot, and was active in lobbying court supporters to counter the king's anger. Ralph Morice was imprisoned in Mary's reign, but managed to escape and spent the later part of his life in Kent at Bekesbourne, where Cranmer himself had a residence (and where the archbishop's arms, initials and motto are still to be seen in the stone plaques of his gatehouse).[7] The reminiscences of the archbishop penned by this close associate who knew him so well, proved to be a main source (and one that is still valuable) for estimates of him. Ralph Morice was both a committed evangelical and a man of persuasive powers, and at an important stage of both their lives he was close enough to his elder brother William to influence the latter's religious commitments as well as his marriage.

Ralph's vivid anecdotes of Cranmer (they tell us for instance that he was short-sighted and that he had a habit of biting his lip at moments of tension) refer to two conversations in which William (*'myne eldeste brother'*) took part. William emerges as a man who was not afraid to speak his mind in the royal circles of Henry VIII's chamber in which he held office. Sir Thomas Seymour, according to the tale, was trying to discredit Cranmer (and attack episcopal possessions in general) by spreading reports of the archbishop's neglect of the traditional hospitality expected of one in his position for the sake of accumulating properties for his family. William Morice, when this was '*blastid…abrode in the courte,*' broke in to declare the rumour manifestly false, with the result that the king was persuaded some time later to call Seymour to account and he had to eat his words, and (according to Ralph) plans for curtailing episcopal endowments were stopped.[8]

Another incident recounted by Ralph involved Cranmer himself and offers an illuminating example of reforming differences. The archbishop had been arguing the virtues of tolerance towards papists, '*using them frendlie and charitablie,*' with a readiness to forgive their offences, as the means to win them over to the gospel. William Morice, perhaps with a youngish man's fervour and impulsive enthusiasm, thought otherwise. This '*fervently evangelical courtier*' (as Cranmer's recent biographer calls him) took on the archbishop for his advocacy of concord through persuasion, which took the form of always bearing '*a good face and countenance unto the papistes*;' he was '*ernest with hym for the admendment of this his qualitie*' – which tells us something about Cranmer's character, as well as Morice's. Ralph, in recording this event in later years, after William's death, added that '*Mr Isaac, yett lyvyng, ys a witness of the mattier.*' This was Edward Isaac of Well in Kent, an evangelical who was a long-standing friend of Ralph Morice, and who was working for Thomas Cranmer in the 1530s.[9]

In 1532 this close-knit group (William and Ralph and Edward Isaac) took it on themselves to visit in prison ('*the deap dungen in Newgate*') a man who was about to be burned as a relapsed heretic. James Bainham was a Middle Temple lawyer who, having been examined by Thomas More and the bishop of London, had recanted and then gone back on his abjuration. Reportedly the three men were anxious to discover more about the reasons for Bainham's condemnation, and enlisted Hugh Latimer, the celebrated preacher (a friend of Isaac's) to accompany them. The occasion is odd, and was perhaps not without risk. The conversation that has come down to us gives all the exchanges to Latimer, who found one of the stated reasons for Bainham's obduracy quite lacking in any substance worth dying for, though he supported the denial of purgatory. Did the others learn something worth knowing? If they did, they kept it to themselves, and it was too late to do more than try to comfort Bainham who went to the stake next day (30 April 1532). The affair is certainly suggestive of a dangerous readiness to play with fire, given the growth of heresy in England at this time, and the fact that Latimer had himself recently been under examination before five or six bishops. William Morice, like Ralph (who wrote to support Latimer when he was again in trouble for his preaching in Bristol the following year), had certainly put his reforming commitment on display.[10]

By 1539 William had sealed the friendship of this evangelical triumvirate by marrying Edward Isaac's sister, Anne. It is not known where the Morices began their married life. William was on the lookout for a new home, and before long he found one in Chipping Ongar. The manor that went with Ongar Castle had belonged to the Stafford family since the mid-fourteenth century, and passed into royal hands when Edward Stafford, Duke of Buckingham, was executed for treason in 1521. At that time the castle estate was held by Thomas Maple, yeoman of Chipping

Ongar, whose family was farming the manor ten years before Buckingham's death. He was granted a 21 year lease running to 1545. In 1537, on the point of leaving for the west country, William Morice wrote to Thomas Cromwell reminding him about his suit for a lease in Essex, the renewal of which had been promised to the existing tenant by the chancellor of the court of augmentations, Sir Richard Rich. This promise called for urgent action. It seems to have been forthcoming. For in September 1537 William Morice obtained an eighty year lease of the Ongar manor, to start when Maple's ended, which mean twaiting another eight years before he gained possession.[11] With his foothold in the court William was well placed to push his interests in this territorial base, and the date of the lease may have coincided with his marriage. He was able to improve his position in short order and to gain outright possession in May 1542 of the manor and advowson of Chipping Ongar, thanks to the king granting it to an intermediary who transferred his interest to Morice.[12] It was here, on a site immediately adjacent to the castle mound, where there is no evidence to suggest the existence of an earlier house, that he began building – perhaps with the benefit of his father's expert advice.

Figure 5   Castle House in about 1850, a pencil sketch by C. Mott junior.

A fair amount of nonsense has been written about William Morice's Castle House, the bones of which (truncated on either side) remain today much as they were when he built it. Morant gives the following description of the castle:

> *It was situated on the top of a very high round artificial hill,...and surrounded by a large moat; which, with several other moats, composed the old fortification...This castle being grown much ruinous and decayed, was taken down in Qu. Elizabeth's reign by the then owner William Morice Esq; who, in the room of it, erected a very strong, handsom brick building, three stories high: and by reason of its lofty situation, prospects, beauty, and pleasant walks exceeded any place in this county. But this building was demolished by Edward Alexander Esq; who in 1744 erected, instead of it, a large and handsom summer-house.'*[13]

ASPECTS OF THE HISTORY OF ONGAR

Apart from the sheer improbability of a three-storey Tudor residence (not Elizabethan, since William Morice died well before Elizabeth's accession) on the top of a fifty-foot mound, Morant fails to account for the existence of precisely such a building standing on adjacent flat ground long after Alexander built his folly. Philip Morant cannot have visited Ongar. His account is taken, almost verbatim, from an earlier eighteenth-century one by Richard Newcourt, and that in turn seems to have derived from the notice written by the topographer John Norden for his late sixteenth-century *Speculum Britanniae*. At Chipping Ongar, Norden reported, '*Jeames Morrys, Esq. hath ther erected a very proper house of pleasure upon the topp of a Mount, wher was somtyme a castle: it is seene farr of, and hath most large and pleasant perspect.*'[14] The "house of pleasure" (replaced by the later summer house) seems to have confused the topographers. Its eighteenth-century existence is well authenticated, both in a print and in the assorted dressed stones which over the years have descended from the top of the mound into the moat, leaving behind only a single brick corner.

What if anything William Morice (or his son James) thought fit to do with his castle mound awaits the judgement of an archaeologist. But we know enough about his house from the contemporary record of it in the inventory taken at his death, as well as from the building itself, remodelled in the last century. The inventory lists the contents of the rooms in Castle House in April 1554 – we have to guess which floor they were on. The hall and kitchen must have been downstairs, but it sounds as if all the best rooms were above. They included the '*greate parler*,' which had some of the best furnishings, including '*the kynges armes in a table*,' two '*tables of pictures one of kynge henry theight, the other of the frenche kynge*,' needlework carpets and cushions. (The picture of the French king perhaps owed something to Morice having been on Henry VIII's campaign in France in 1544). The great chamber with its hangings of blue and yellow say, was less formal (and its contents worth half the value), and housed '*a chamber potte*.' Like the great parlour this room had an inner chamber with a bed, and the best bed in the house was in the chamber that opened out of the little parlour. It seems likely that some of these subsidiary rooms were in the narrow wings taken down in the nineteenth century. The '*study chambre*' had a humble '*falde bedstead*,' and there was also a chamber over the kitchen, with a trussing bed, and '*the galery*' held a press for '*wrytinges*,' four other chests, '*a feilde tente veray olde*' and '*a bathinge tubbe*.' The servants' chambers (which included six bedsteads, four feather-beds, four pairs of blankets and two mattresses) were no doubt on the top floor. All told William Morice's house sounds like a fairly typical residence for a Tudor country gentleman who had a house in London as well as his place in the shires, a man who sported his arms in silver on his own basin and ewer, and who could entertain on a respectable scale with the comforts of the day, even if without very much to show in the way of cultural distinction. William Morice certainly died well-to-do, whatever headaches he left for his heirs in Chipping Ongar, and the total of his inventoried goods in 1554 was £292 3s.[15]

Despite his advances in the reign of Henry VIII, William Morice and his evangelical friends had every reason to rejoice at the accession of Edward VI – the young king who was confidently expected to carry forward England's reform as another Old Testament Josiah. Morice himself spent the last six month of Henry's reign in custody. On 15 May 1546 the Privy Council was pursuing him '*for thies matiers of Crome.*'[16] Morice had apparently (shades of 1532 and the visit to Bainham) been interesting himself suspiciously in the affairs of Dr Edward Crome. Crome was a reformist preacher whom Ralph could have heard when he was in Cambridge in 1522, and who was now the talk of the town in London. Crome had been in trouble twice before for preaching advanced views, and on Passion Sunday 1546 repeated his challenge by a sermon in the Mercers' Chapel that attacked the accepted doctrine of the Mass by representing it as a commemoration of Christ's death. He was ordered to recant but instead defiantly delivered yet another risky sermon on 9 May, with the result that he was called to account and his allies and suspected sympathisers were rounded up. Among them was Latimer who was examined by the council the day before William Morice. It was a time of considerable danger for reformers, and the investigations that followed the Crome affair led to about sixty evangelicals fleeing abroad. Morice was not alone, but that was small comfort when he found himself placed under house arrest in Richard Southwell's house by the Charterhouse, subject to a recognisance of 50 marks as warranty of his readiness to reappear before the council, if summoned, during the coming year. Also under a cloud in this establishment was one John Louth, who more than thirty years later, near the end of quite a successful career in the Elizabethan church, wrote up his reminiscences for the benefit of John Foxe, the martyrologist. His memory may not have infallible after that passage of time, although his rather smug recollection of how Morice was '*but symply lodged, and I* [as tutor to Southwell's son] *lay nyghtly in my sylke bedd*' rings true. More interesting is the comment that '*mr. W. Moryshe*' was '*there kepte in pryson…by commandement of the lorde Rych and others, who wold fayne have hadd hym bornte, for his lordshyppe of Chyppyn Onger.*' [17]

Was Sir Richard Rich really out to damn Morice as a heretic? The story might not have seemed incredible during the last months of Henry VIII's reign, as the inherent ambiguity of England's religious position bore hard on advanced believers. In mid-May 1546 Rich was one of the commissioners who were sent orders for the burning of three heretics at Colchester '*for the example and terrour of others.*'[18] Rich, although a professional turncoat, notorious for his role in the trial of Thomas More and (as Emmison put it) '*one of the most powerful and obnoxious of the king's ministers,*' was conservative at heart and nothing if not greedy for land. He had seized every opportunity offered by the reformation land market to build up a huge landed estate in Essex.[19] It included holdings in and around Chipping Ongar in Shelley, Fyfield, Blackmore and Stondon, and we have seen that he was interested in the lease of the castle estate. George Harper, from whom William Morice finally acquired this property, had the previous month alienated to Sir Richard Paslow Hall in High Ongar, which had belonged to Waltham Abbey.[20] At Morice's death the lands which he held in High Ongar adjacent to his own included, as well as the four-acre '*Rye meade,*' '*Tuftes feilde*' of thirty acres, which was rented from Lord Rich.[21] The historian John Strype (1643–1737) was certainly in no doubt as to the territorial rivalries that mired the position of that *person of good quality,* William Morice, whom Rich and others would have been ready to see burned *out of the desire they had of enjoying his fair manor.* He was writing much later, but his closeness to Roger Morice may have given him personal knowledge of the family history of this time.[22] But if Rich and Morice were in competition for Chipping Ongar, they soon came to terms with each other, and found advantages in cooperation – for shared benefits.

As soon as Edward VI succeeded, the opportunities for Protestant advance seemed assured. According to John Foxe, who drew on Ralph Morice's recollections of Cranmer in his great Book of Martyrs, the archbishop's busy secretary advised his master to seize this chance to initiate previously frustrated church reforms: *'now your grace may go forward in those matters, the opportunity of the time much better serving thereunto than in king Henry's days.'* [23] Proposed reforms were pushed ahead, bringing new openings for church spoliation – this time of parish churches. It is interesting to speculate (and we can do no more, since the records for what happened at St Martin's do not survive)[24] about the building materials that might have found their way from the church into William Morice's new house. We do not know how far he had got with its construction by the time that Archbishop Cranmer and Edward's government were seeing to the clearance from parish churches throughout the land of objects of *'superstition and idolatry,'* which included, besides sculptures of the saints and altarpieces, the imagery of Christ on the great rood beam that spanned the chancel arch. Much stone and timber, as well as church vestments and vessels, passed into private hands, and the government kept its check on parish sales as it undertook the confiscation of a gigantic treasure trove of parochial plate (silver-gilt crosses, chalices, patens, candlesticks and so on) in the course of altering churches for Protestant worship. Local commissioners were called on to make reports about alienations of church goods from the beginning of the reign. William Morice, together with his brother-in-law Edward Isaac, and Francis Wyatt featured in the return from Tillingham in October 1552, for failing to pay the church 40 shillings which they owed as executors of the will of Thomas Isaac, gentleman of Little Baddow.[25] Two years before this William and Edward had clubbed together to buy for over £1,000 the grant of a large package of lands of recently dissolved chantries and colleges scattered across eight counties from Suffolk to Somerset.[26] They were investing in the future – religious and material.

It is peculiar – and surely revealing – that the returns relating to church goods for which Richard Rich was responsible, unlike those surviving from the rest of Essex, seem effectively to have not bothered to make the required record of alienations. This high-handedness looks both suspicious, and in character. Such sales and alienations must have occurred in the hundreds of Ongar and Dunmow as well as elsewhere. It is tempting to suppose that this grasping man of means found it advantageous to turn a blind eye to embezzlement.[27] And we can suppose that William Morice, dogmatically disposed as he was to welcome the advent of radical reform, was himself not averse to participating in its iconoclastic inauguration.

That supposition is corroborated by what now seems like an extraordinarily shabby deal fixed up between Morice and Rich. Acting as patrons respectively of St Martin's, Chipping Ongar and St Andrew's, Greensted, they embarked on a scheme which could be represented as both legal and desirable from a reforming perspective, but which seemed utterly cavalier to local parishioners. It was an idea of beautiful simplicity – to make one church do instead of two. William Morice became an MP for the first time in Edward VI's first parliament. He did not, however, represent an Essex constituency, but the borough of Downton in Wiltshire, which was usually the preserve of Bishop Gardiner of Winchester (no conceivable ally), in whose absence abroad other patronage came into operation – and William as we know did not lack friends on high, including Cranmer. Sir Richard Rich, who owed to the new regime his new title of Baron Rich of Leez, was an old parliamentary hand and now, as chancellor, had a key role in the legislation of the new government. It cannot have been too difficult to get through a private act '*for the unytyng of the churches of Ongar and Grenested in Essex*,' by which the church and churchyard of Chipping Ongar passed into the hands of Morice, while the advowson of Greensted, to be the place of the worship of the enlarged single parish, was vested in Rich.[28]

The union of depopulated or uneconomic churches was not uncommon at this time, and had been legislated for by a statute of Henry VIII's last parliament. This allowed the consolidation of poor churches separated by less than a mile, provided the church authorities, the incumbents and those with an interest in the patronage all agreed. (No word here about the views of parishioners!)[29] However, things did not run smoothly for these patrons. Certain suspicions hang over the text of their act, in which Rich's rights to the Greensted advowson are written over an erasure, and in a hand (not that of the rest of the text) which also added at the end Morice's grant of Ongar church.[30] Certainly the parishioners of St Martin's did not take kindly to this arrangement. Luckily for them Edward's reign only lasted six and a half years, and Mary Tudor's accession gave the opportunity, which they took at once, to set matters to rights.

William Morice was in no position to resist. He sat in both parliaments of 1553, Edward's last and Mary's first (now for Cornish constituencies), and was among those who received a general pardon in December 1553.[31] But he was not one to do an about-turn in favour of Queen Mary, unlike his sometime associate Rich, who having supported Queen Jane rapidly made his peace with Mary and became a privy councillor. It is worth noticing that the name of Rich does not feature in the act repealing the parish union. The future looked distinctly unpromising for the Morice family, but William (unlike his brother Ralph) did not live to see the persecution of the following years, in which his own parish contributed to the harvest of '*godly martyrs*' that gave Essex preeminence in the eyes of John Foxe. Ralph Jackson, a 34 year-old serving-man of Chipping Ongar was one of thirteen individuals (two of them women) who were burned at Stratford on 26 June 1556.[32] Morice died in January 1554, when the new catholic regime was less than six months old, and it was left to his wife and son to face the music

ASPECTS OF THE HISTORY OF ONGAR

This included the local hostilities that resulted from the parochial rearrangement. The union was repealed by a statute in the spring parliament of 1554 which met ten weeks after William's death. The parishioners of both parishes were presented as *'lamentablie complayning'* about the *'sinister labour and procurement'* of William Morice Esquire, deceased, in effecting the union, *'inordinately seking his private lucre and profitt.'* He had acted (as he was of course entitled to) without their con-

Figure 6   The martyrdom of Ralph Jackson, serving man of Chipping Ongar with 12 others at Stratford on 27 June 1556. From Foxe's Book of Martyrs.

sent, had misrepresented the facts, including the distances involved and the ability of the parishes to maintain their churches. Greensted church was more than three quarters of a mile from Chipping Ongar, and too small to hold half the parishioners, added to which the curate could not cross the Cripsey brook in winter time, so that people had died without the last rites. Morice is portrayed as a ruthless profiteer, who had not only taken possession of the church, chancel and churchyard, with various other pieces of land belonging to the church, but had impounded all the ornaments, bells, vestments and chalices. He had (it was said) removed for his own use the valuable lead and reroofed the church with tiles, though it is not clear to what extent he had started to convert the building to secular use; the act refers to *'the place and house whiche was the churche chauncell and churcheyarde....'* (It is interesting to find that his possessions at his death included two fothers of lead worth £15.) The parishioners got their way, and the position was restored to what it had been before 1548, with the right of presentation to St Martin's reverting to William's son and heir James Morice.[33]

Even then the affair was not over. Local stirs apparently continued, to the extent that the fabric of Chipping Ongar's church was not yet secure. Early in June 1554,

William's widow Anne was cited to appear with other inhabitants of Chipping Ongar before the privy council's commissioners, to answer a charge '*that without auctoritie, of their oune heddes [they] attempted latelie to pluck downe the churche walles there.*' Order had to be restored among these parishioners '*for their good quyet and staye of their frendes doing therein*', and to this end the Lords also sent a letter to the inhabitants of Ongar.[34] It must have been a very divided parish. What exactly did the Morices have in mind for the church? Had it already by 1554 been turned over to some domestic use? Was it planned to annex church and churchyard to the new house? One wonders, too, about the position of Lord Rich in this very public besmirching of the recently deceased owner of the Ongar Castle estate. Strype, for whom William Morice was '*an old and great professor of religion*', thought vengefulness was behind the act. '*This was done, I am apt to think, in displeasure to William Morice.*'[35] There are a lot of unknowns in an imbroglio which has the flavour of an unholy Protestant alliance, with Morice too readily aping the ways of his much more powerful neighbour, Lord Rich, who lived on until 1567.

When William Morice died on 17 January 1554, his wife Anne was the main beneficiary of his estate, since his son and heir James (born in September 1538) was only fifteen.[36] William's father, the earlier James, was still alive in 1554, and the fact that he made his will (still sound in body and mind) in March 1555 owed much to the situation created by the death of his eldest son. He needed to provide for the succession of his Roydon estate, which was to pass to his grandson James '*to thintent the said James may be brought up in lerning.*' James was placed under the obligation to make yearly payments to his uncles Philip and Henry Morice who, with Ralph Morice (given a house called Fosters), were executors of this will. The old James Morice lived on another two and a half years and by the time his will was proved in November 1557 it seems that Ralph was the only survivor of his five sons.[37] It is doubtful how much the Ongar household could have seen of the head of the family after William's death, since grandfather James must have been very old, probably nearer eighty than seventy and very likely none too mobile. But his provision for young James's education must have helped the young man's studies at the Middle Temple.

William made his own short will the day before his death, when he was mortally ill but clear-headed. Six weeks earlier, he had received his royal pardon, but the will, brief though it is, amply demonstrates that the testator's sympathies were far removed from those of the new Marian regime.[38] Morice's three executors (left £10 apiece) shared his Protestant commitment, and as such were in no position to offer aid to his widow, though they were all closely connected to her. Sir Thomas Wyatt, provoked into rebellion by the announcement of the Queen's Spanish marriage on 15 January 1554 – the day before Morice drew up his will – went to the block on Tower Hill less than three months later, on 11 April. Sir Thomas Wroth and Edward Isaac (Anne's uncle and brother, the former married to Rich's daughter Mary) both realised early on that Queen Mary's England was no place for them; indeed Wroth had spent the early days of the new reign in custody in the Tower. Administration of the will was committed to them on 9 June 1554, but Wroth must have left the country soon after, since he was in Padua in July, and Isaac may have found his way to Frankfurt not long after.[39] Things were unravelling for the Morices, with their dedication to the Protestant cause, though it seems unlikely that, had he lived, William would have left his new house for foreign parts. Even Ralph did not do that, though he suffered for it and, *'declyned unto age'* and impoverishment, appealed to Queen Elizabeth to help the plight of his four unmarried daughters.[40]

James Morice, who gained possession of his inheritance in 1560, was by then a student at the Middle Temple, launched into the start of a successful legal career. He was married in his early twenties to Elizabeth Medley, daughter of George Medley of Tilty Abbey, which lies between Great Dunmow and Thaxted, not a long ride away.[41] James's father-in-law died soon after this family alliance but it seems likely that the ties remained close; the church at Tilty houses alongside the brass commemorating George Medley and his wife, that of James's sister Margaret, who married George Tuke (heir of Brian Tuke of Layer Marney), and died seven years before her brother in 1590.[42]

As a trained lawyer of the Middle Temple, James had a long and active career in Essex affairs, busying himself as JP from about 1573, and serving Colchester as town clerk by 1578. He also represented the borough in parliament in 1584, 1586, 1588 and 1593, and made a name for himself as both lawyer and a leading light among the godly puritans of the town, where the recorder, Sir Francis Walsingham, was a like-minded ally. One might have assumed that his Puritan objectives were pursued in his own parish by the incumbents he presented to the living, though that is not exactly borne out by the first of them, Robert Rowland, who was already rector of Greensted. In the 1570s proceedings were taken against John Weldon of Chipping Ongar for having *'kept play in hys house at tables...and syr Rowland parson of Grensted dyd play at tables ther the same day.'*[43] The rector who succeeded Rowland at Ongar in 1576, Thomas Morrys, seems likely to have been James's brother, specially as he had been vicar of Layer Marney, with which there were such close family connections. It was at the very end of his life that James Morice – evincing the readiness for plain speech that his father had displayed in his youth – employed his learning and convictions in a cause that earned him a niche in parliamentary history, and which took him (again like his father) into custody.

Some of James's official correspondence at Colchester survives from the 1580s, including a legal opinion delivered in the year of the Armada, as to what constituted a felony (was it or was it not a felony for a servant to take 30 shillings from a coffer of the kind usual in shops, with a hole in it, of which his master kept the key?).[44] Rubbing shoulders with neighbouring gentry as JP also kept up family connections, and Morice sometimes found himself acting alongside Henry Medley, his brother-in-law. One affair in which they both became involved one summer might have been funny had it not made the law seem an ass. On 5 August 1577, when he was aged thirty-eight, a married man with a growing family, James Morice with the sheriff and another justice was called out to deal with an all-female riot in Brentwood. Thirty women (all *'spinsters'* of the town) had turned out in force in the churchyard and *'steeple'* (tower) of Brentwood chapel. Richard Brooke, schoolmaster of the local grammar school, was attacked by these amazons. They pulled him out of the chapel and then shut themselves in, and the unfortunate justices found themselves frustrated by other locals, including a labourer called Dalley Day, who tried to rescue the ringleader, Thomasine Tyler (widow of the owner of the Swan and Bells Inns) from custody. The women were armed with an assortment of domestic artillery; five pitchforks, bills, a piked staff, three bows and nine arrows, a hatchet and a great hammer, two '*hott spittes*' and hot water in two kettles, and a great sharp stone. Morice and his co-justices imposed fines all round (4d on each woman, 2s on each man), but though they recorded the names of all the offenders seventeen managed to make their getaway before they could be committed to gaol. The justices might well have gone home red-faced, and the affair was specially galling for Morice who received a direct snub from a yeoman called John Mynto, refusing point-blank his request to come to the assistance of the justices.[45]

In the parliament of 1593, the last in which he sat, James Morice caused quite a stir by the strong line he took on a matter of ecclesiastical practice: the *ex officio* oath used in the ecclesiastical courts. In taking up this issue (on which this same year his anonymous book *A briefe treatise of Oathes* was published) Morice inevitably spoke not only as a lawyer but a Puritan layman deeply worried about the unreformed forms and practices of the English church. While his book demonstrated the legal objections to the use of an oath which could be seen as tantamount to forcing a defendant to accuse himself, it also argued a historical case (based largely on John Foxe's *Book of Martyrs*) that challenged episcopal authority, by stressing the infamous use of this procedure in the persecutions by earlier '*bloudie Bishops.*' He regarded the bishops' '*extorted oaths and examinations*' as props of '*a Romish hierarchy,*' and hoped to introduce bills against both the *ex officio* oath and unlawful imprisonment.[46] As attorney of the court of wards, Morice was a royal official, and he risked a good deal in combining his attack on the oath with criticism of Archbishop Whitgift's 1583 articles and other forms of subscription imposed by the church. He placed himself, in effect, on a collision course with Queen Elizabeth.

In 1593 James Morice, at fifty-four was (in contemporary terms) old and experienced, to be counted among the '*old, discreet, grave parliament-men.*' Yet he was ready to take risks for the cause he believed in, casting aside the caution advocated in his book; '*the holy ghost by the preacher well adviseth everie man not to be rashe with his mouth.*' James paid for his rashness, although he did not lack support of the kind that reflected respect for his person, as well as his views. Sir Francis Knollys was ready to defend Morice's good intentions, and his bill, and Lord Burghley told him he was '*a gentleman whose good fortune he had always wished,*' though on this occasion the attorney was unyielding to the extent that Burghley was forced to indicate that '*some little submission, Mr. Morice, would do well.*' None of this assistance could undo royal displeasure, which ordained that the offender '*should be sharply chidden, yea, and committed also.*'[47] So, family history repeating itself, James Morice found himself committed to house arrest for eight weeks – probably more comfortably than William had been in 1546.

James Morice was clearly a man of independent spirit, respected for his learning, as well as his zeal. He had friends in high places, and Burghley's friendliness may have owed something to a long-standing family association. In 1593 Burghley, at seventy-three, was perhaps about the age that Morice's grandfather (that earlier James) had been forty years earlier, when – feeling his age – he had sent a letter from Roydon to Cecil, offering to hand over various books and papers, and thanking Sir William for his '*great gentleness*' towards himself and his son Philip. Even after the reception of his proposals in 1593, there were those who hoped that Morice could advance the puritan cause in high places. Robert Cecil was approached that year by Lady Elizabeth Russell, on behalf of '*my cousin, Morrice,*' who '*hath been with me this afternoon, poor man.*' She was ready to resort to hyperbole in pressing James Morice's qualifications for public office, in particular that he should be made Master of the Rolls as some recompense for two months' detention without right of answer. '*Oh good nephew,*' Robert Cecil was told, '*the gravity, wisdom, care of maintaining law of the land, earning and piety of the man*' was such that, were he to become a councillor and master of the rolls, the supplicant might herself be well content to live on bread and water.[48]

James Morice, still attorney of the court of wards, made his will on 7 March 1596 and died the following February. Lawyer-like, he wrote his testament '*wholly with myne owne hande*' subscribing his name on every page. As was to be expected it documents his various interests, religious, intellectual, territorial and domestic. His wife Elizabeth and his eldest son John inherited his chattels, plate and household stuff, and the manor of Chipping Ongar with its appurtenances was entailed on John at Elizabeth's death. John was given '*all my bookes of the lawes of England, my Latyne greeke and Frenche bookes, with all my armour and weapons,*' with a prayer that came from an earnest Protestant heart that John, and the rest of the testator's children, '*may spende and passe the time of this their shorte and miserable life in all vertuose and godlie conversation and behaviour, studuyng and endevoring by the grace of god to be profitable members of Christes church and good subjects in the comon wealthe.*' Beneficiaries named in the will included '*my loving brother William Medley esquier*' (Elizabeth's brother) who was given a gold ring, Isaac Morice (a nephew) and Richard Morice ('*lovinge servante and kinsman*'). The Tukes appear in an obligation that James had as executor of his brother-in-law, to look after the interests of the latter's daughters, and Morice stipulated that (though it was to his own loss) a sum of £40 which he could have claimed should be paid over to them. There was also a legacy to four of the worthiest men inhabitants of Chipping Ongar.[49]

Was William Morice's new house ever honoured by a royal visit? A traditional belief that Queen Elizabeth stayed at Castle House in 1579 found its way into local publications, including a report in 1877 that '*some relics of Ongar Castle, in the form of some stained glass with the date on it, of Queen Elizabeth's visit to Mr. Morice, are yet extant, at Boxford Rectory, Suffolk.*'[50] This belief, stated as fact in the notes on Ongar in St Martin's church in 1979, roused the present inhabitants of Castle House to think about a quatrecentenary celebration. Unfortunately, although the queen passed by this way on her summer progresses, there seems to be no evidence that her party was accommodated in Chipping Ongar. But it was planned in 1579: '*xvi Julii 1579. From Grenewyche to Haveringe, from thence to Mr. Morrisse's at Onger: from thence to lord Rytche's.*' And over in Colchester letters were sent to Mr Morice '*to prepare himself to make oraysion*' at the queen's coming. The oration was duly delivered, but the reception at Castle House was aborted as the Morice children had measles.[51]

Castle House and its lands remained in the hands of James Morice's descendants well into the seventeenth century, though by then, after an advantageous match with another Essex family, they had turned themselves into Poyntzes, and were no longer doing much to spread the name of their locality in the wider world. John Morice (Poyntz), 1568–1618, seems to have been more interested in the good life of a country gentleman than in politics and the defence of principles. But like his father he was educated in the Middle Temple and the books and armour that he left to be preserved as a family heirloom may well have been those that had come to him from James. The Morice property was not yet free of the law. In 1647, John Morice, a collateral descendant, was arraigned in the House of Lords on charges of forging documents to support his title to Chipping Ongar and other estates. It was exactly a century since William Morice had built Castle House and unsuccessfully staked his claim to Chipping Ongar church.[52]

References

1. PRO, C142/100/32
2. Jones, M.K. & Underwood, M.G. *The King's Mother: Lady Margaret Beaufort, Countess of Richmond and Derby.* (1992), p.154, 201, 221, 234, 279; Willis, R. & Clark, J.W. *Architectural History of the University of Cambridge*, 3 vols. (1886), ii, pp.193–5, 199; VCH Essex, vol 8, pp.232, 234, 238; DNB, s.n. Beaufort.
3. Jones & Underwood *King's Mother*, p.279; MacCulloch, D. *Thomas Cranmer*, (1996), p.18. On William's five sons, two of whom (William and Oliver) had died before 21 March 1555, and two more (Philip and Henry) seemingly before 17 November 1557. See below n. 37.
4. Keiser, G.R. 'The Mystics and the Early English Printers: The Economics of Devotionalism', in Glasscoe, M. (ed.) *The Medieval Mystical Tradition in England* (1987), p.23.
5. PRO, PROB 11/39 (48 Wrastley)
6. *Letter and Papers...of Henry VIII*, (1862–1932), IV, iii, p.3078 (no.6083: 31); X, p.1 (no. 3)
7. MacCulloch, *Cranmer*, pp.303–5, 308, 311, 314, 517–19.
8. *Narratives of the Reformation*, ed. J.G. Nichols (Camden Soc., lxxvii, 1859), pp.260–3; DNB, s.n. Morice, Ralph.
9. *Narratives of the Reformation*, pp.246–7; MacCulloch, D., 'Archbishop Cranmer: concord and tolerance in a changing Church', in Grell, O.P. & Scribner, B. *Tolerance and intolerance in the European Reformation*, (1996), pp. 208–9; MacCulloch, *Cranmer*, p.203.
10. *Sermons and Remains of Hugh Latimer*, ed. G.E. Corrie (Parker Society, 1845), pp.221–4, 357–66; *The Acts and Monuments of John Foxe*, ed. J. Pratt (1877), iv, pp.770–72, vii, pp.473–7; *Actes and Monuments* (1563), pp.492–5, 1314 ff.
11. VCH Essex, iv, pp.160–1; ERO, D/DP M588; Bindoff, S.T. (ed.), *The History of Parliament; The House of Commons 1509–1558.* 3 vols (1982), ii, p.632; *Letters and Papers of Henry VIII*, XII, ii, p.281 (no. 796).
12. VCH, Essex, iv, p.61. George Harper, who obtained the Ongar estate by royal grant and alienated it shortly afterwards, was an esquire of the body to Henry VIII, and this was just one of numerous transactions of this kind at the time, which suggest he was something of a land broker. *Letters and Papers*, XVII, pp.161, 163, 166, 215, 163, 633.

ASPECTS OF THE HISTORY OF ONGAR

13 Morant, P. *History and honour Antiquities of Essex*, 2 vols (1768), i, pt.ii, p.128; for de Lucy's acquisition of the honor of Ongar in the 1150s see VCH Essex, iv, pp.159–60.
14 Newcourt, R. *Repertorium Ecclesiasticum Parochiale Londinense*, 2 vols. (1708–10), ii, p.450; John Norden, *Speculi Brittanniae Pars*, ed. H. Ellis (Camden Society, 1840), p.23.
15 PRO, PROB 2/255, a long narrow parchment roll of six membranes. Morice's debtors included Francis Wyatt (who owed £12 6s 8d), a member of the cadet branch of the Wyatts, recorded as living at Bobbingworth. *The Visitations of Essex*, ed. W.C. Metcalfe (Harleian Society, 13–14, 1878–9), i, p.331 (1612). "Say" was a fine-textured cloth; "falde" = folding.
16 *Acts of the Privy Council of England*, ed. J.R. Dasent et al (1890–1964), i, p.417.
17 *Acts of the Privy Council*, i, pp.458, 490; *Narratives of the Reformation*, p.45; MacCulloch, *Cranmer*, p.353; Wabuda, S. 'Equivocation and Recantation During the English Reformation: The "Subtle Shadows" of Dr Edward Crome', *Journ. Eccles. Hist.*, 44 (1993), pp.224–42; Brigden, S. *London and the Reformation* (1989), pp.362–77.
18 *Acts of the Privy Council*, i, p.418; VCH Essex, ix, p.122
19 Emmison, F.G. *Tudor Secretary: Sir William Petre at Court and Home* (1961), pp.44, 268, echoing A.F. Pollard in *DNB*; Bindoff (ed.), *History of Parliament*, iii, pp.192–5.
20 VCH Essex, iv, pp.47, 181. Rich bought his Fyfield estate in 1537, and it (and Paslow Hall) followed the same descent thereafter until 1863.
21 PRO, C142/100/32.
22 Strype, J. *Ecclesiastical Memorials*, 3 vols, (1882), I, i, p.596; idem, *Annals of the Reformation* (Oxford, 1824), I, i, pp.xii–xiii, 174. (My thanks to Dr Thomas Freeman for the Roger Morice reference.)
23 Foxe, J. *Acts and Monuments*, v, p.563. For Ralph's letter to Foxe's printer, John Day, with corrections and information for the Book of Martyrs, see Ellis, H. (ed.), *Original Letter of Eminent Literary Men*, (Camden Society, OS 23, 1843), pp.24–7.
24 There are no churchwardens' accounts for the parish in this period, nor do the Edwardian inventories – mentioned below – survive for Ongar.
25 King, H.W. 'Inventories of Church Goods, 6th Edw. VI', *Trans. Essex Arch. Soc.*, v, (1873), p.231. Presumably Thomas was a relative of Edward, whose branch of the family was based in Kent. On Francis Wyatt see above n.15.
26 *Calender of Patent Rolls, Edward VI*, iii, 1549–51, pp.273–4; Strype, *Ecclesiastical Memorials*, III, i, p.368.
27 King, 'Inventories of Church Goods, 6th Edward VI', *Trans. Essex Arch. Soc.*, New Series, ii, (1884), pp.223–250.
28 *Statutes of the Realm*, iv, p.ix, 55; House of Lords Record Office, Original Acts, 2 and 3 Edward, no.55; Bindoff (ed.), *History of Parliament*, ii, p.632. The only incumbent to be presented by Rich to the united parish was James Scott, rector of Greensted in 1548 and in 1552 of Chipping Ongar in addition; Newcourt, *Repertorium*, ii, pp.289, 451. Scott's predecessor at St Martin's was Richard Turner, presented by William Morice in February 1545; not to be confused with the vehement reformer who was close to Cranmer and Ralph Morice, though like this namesake he may have become an exile in Mary's reign. Emden, A.B. *A Biographical Register of the University of Oxford 1501–1540* (Oxford, 1974), p.581.
29 *Statutes of the Realm*, iii, pp.1013–14, 37 Henry VIII, cap.xxi.
30 Bindoff (ed.) *History of Parliament*, ii, p.632.
31 *Calendar of Patent Rolls, 1553–54*, p.412 (1 Dec. 1553)
32 Foxe, *Actes and Monuments* (1563), pp.1523–7 (with a woodcut of the event). Lord Rich was instrumental in some of these proceedings.
33 *Statutes of the Realm*, iv, pp.234–5, 1 Mary, Stat. 3, cap.x; PRO, PROB 2/255.
34 *Acts of the Privy Council*, v, p.34.
35 Strype, *Ecclesiastical Memorials*, III, i, p.181.
36 PRO, C142/100/32; Prob. 11/37 (3 More); inquisition *post mortem* and will of William Morice. Anne was given two thirds of the properties until James came of age. William is on record as having a younger son, Thomas, and a daughter, Margaret, who married George Tuke (son of Brian) and died in 1590, her monumental brass being at Tilty, the home of her brother James's wife's family, the Medleys. *Visitations of Essex*, i, p.256; Pevnser, *Essex*, p.392.

37 PRO, PROB 11/39 (48 Wrastley). Fosters might possibly be identified with Foster's Farm in Little Parndon (Reaney, P.H., *Place-Names of Essex*, (1935), p.49). Young James's payments of 40s per annum were to be made after the deaths of Philip and Henry to their sons (his cousins) Morgan and Richard Morice, and to Philip (another cousin, son of Oliver who had died before 1555).

38 PRO, PROB 11/37 (3 More). Anne was to enjoy two thirds of the estate during her lifetime, and the remaining third, allocated to meet the testator's debts, was to become James's when he was twenty-one.

39 For Anne Isaac/Morice's connections with Wroth (her uncle) and Wyatt (through her stepfather) see the biography of William Morice in Bindoff (ed.), *History of Parliament*, ii, pp.631–3.(Opinions have differed as to whether the Margaret Isaac who married Wroth was sister or aunt of William Morice's wife Anne). For Isaac's exile see Garrett, C.H., *The Marian Exiles*, (1938), pp.195–6; and on Wroth, who had lands in Theydon Bois and Chigwell (as well as elsewhere), see Bindoff (ed.), *History of Parliament*, iii, pp.667–8; VCH Essex, iv, pp.25, 74, 252.

40 Strype, J. *Memorials of Cranmer*, 2 vols, (1840), i, p.614, ii, pp.1018–20; *DNB*.

41 The biography in Hasler, P.W. (ed.) *The History of Parliament: The House of Commons 1558–1603*, 3 vols (1981), iii, pp.98–100 says he was married by 1560; cf. VCH Essex, iv, p.161 which suggests 1561 as more likely.

42 Pevsner, *Essex*, p.392; *Visitations of Essex*, i, p.256, ii, pp.595–6, 609–10.

43 ERO, Q/SR 48/32. Newcourt, *Repertorium*, ii, pp.289, 451 lists Robert Rowland as rector of Greensted (presented by Richard Rich) from 1561 to his death in 1593, and rector of Chipping Ongar (James Morice's first presentation) from 1571 to 1576, when (having looked after both parishes for five years) he was succeeded by Thomas Morrys.

44 ERO (Colchester), D/7 2/8, p.345.

45 ERO, Q/SR 64/46; Emmison, F.G., *Elizabethan Life: Disorder*, (1970), p.106.

46 *A briefe treatise of Oathes exacted by Ordinaries and Ecclesiasticall Iudges*, (Middelburg, R. Schilders, 1590?), Anon (STC, 18106), pp.10–11; Neale, J.E., *Elizabeth I and her Parliaments 1584–1601*, (1957), p.268; Collinson, P. *The Elizabethan Puritan Movement*, (1967), pp.256–7.

47 Neale, *Parliaments*, pp.258, 275; Morice, *Brefe treatise*, p.6; Hasler (ed.), *History of Parliament*, iii, p.99.

48 HMC, *Salisbury MSS at Hatfield House*, i, p.122; iv, pp.460–1; Collinson, *Puritan Movement*, p.443. In May 1553 James Morice felt unable, because of his age, to search through these documents.

49 ERO, D/AER 17/231. Unusually James gives his own age in the will ('*the lviiith yeare of myne age*', i.e. he was 57).

50 Porter, *A Few Notes…on…Chipping Ongar* (1877), p.4. The glass is stated to have come through the Morice family, the wife of the Boxford rector, John Byng, having received it from her father, the Rev. Henry Morice. Attempts to trace this glass have so far failed, as there is nothing fitting the description in the stained glass in today's Boxford House, all of which seems to be contemporaneous with the building, erected in 1819–20. (Information kindly sent by Conrad Swan, Esq., Garter Principal King of Arms.)

51 Nichols, J. *The Progresses, and Public Processions, of Queen Elizabeth*, 3 vols (1788–1805), ii, pp.110, 112, cf. pp.183, 195, 285–7; Christy, M., 'The Progresses of Queen Elizabeth through Essex and the Houses in which she stayed', *Essex Review*, xxvi (1917), pp.115–29, 181–95; Hasler (ed.), *History of Parliament*, iii, p.98.

52 Hasler (ed.), *History of Parliament*, iii, pp.100–101; VCH Essex, iv, p.161.

chapter 8

The Taylor family of Ongar and their houses there

by Robin Taylor Gilbert

Dramatis Personae

One of the most distinguished and interesting families to have been closely associated with Ongar was known in the first half of the nineteenth century as the Taylors of Ongar.[1] Its head was the Rev. Isaac Taylor (1759–1829), a man of many parts and of considerable and varied achievements, who was for eighteen years minister of the Independent Congregation at Ongar, which met for worship in the meeting house which once stood where the United Reformed Church now is. When Isaac Taylor arrived in Ongar in 1811, the Independent Congregation had been without a minister for some time and had just nineteen members. Less than twenty years later, membership had grown to such an extent that the small meeting house, built in the early eighteenth century, could no longer adequately hold the congregation.

On 17 February 1831, a fund was established for its repair and enlargement or rebuilding. On 24 April 1833, the first brick of the foundation of a new Meeting House or Chapel was laid on the same site. '*On the 24th of September following the Chapel was opened for Divine Worship when the Rev. James Stratten of Paddington preached in the morning and the Rev. John Clayton Jnr of London in the afternoon. The collection after the Services amounted to £73 7s 6d.*'

The Rev. Isaac Taylor himself had died in 1829, but it was entirely fitting that the foundation stone of the new chapel should have been laid by his four-year-old grandson, later Canon Isaac Taylor (1829–1901), a prominent Alpinist and a philologist of international reputation. This young Isaac Taylor was the second child and eldest son of yet another Isaac Taylor (1787–1865), generally known as Isaac Taylor of Stanford Rivers (where he lived, at Stanford Rivers House, for the last forty years of his life), scholar, theologian, philosopher, author, miniaturist, artistic designer, engraver, mechanical inventor and one of the most learned men of his day. Perhaps his most famous work, published anonymously in 1829, was *The Natural History of Enthusiasm*, as the *DNB* rather dauntingly has it, '*a historico-philosophical disquisition on the perversions of religious imagination*'. His (expurgated) translation of Herodotus was highly praised by the late Enoch Powell (Professor of Greek at the formidable age of 25, an authority on the Greek historians and no mean prose stylist himself), while his translation of Pascal was last reprinted as recently as 1995. Dr Murray, the editor of the *Oxford English Dictionary*, is alleged to have said in the 1870s that Isaac Taylor had coined more new words in the English language than any other modern writer. In 1824, on a more practical level, he patented a beer-tap which was for many years the standard model throughout Britain and, in 1848, an ingenious mechanical device for engraving upon copper. This was initially a financial disaster, but later (chiefly thanks to the greater business acumen of his nephew James Montgomery Gilbert) used on a large scale in the printing of calico in Manchester. Isaac Taylor was brought up as a dissenter and was for some years a deacon of the Independent Congregation at Ongar, but in about 1850 (out of conviction formed partly through his own study of Church history) he joined the Established Church, remaining close, however, to his many dissenting friends. He is buried in the churchyard of St Margaret, Stanford Rivers; the inscription on his tomb was composed by his sister Ann.

Isaac Taylor of Stanford Rivers was the younger brother of Ann Taylor (later Ann Gilbert) (1782–1866) and of Jane Taylor (1783–1824), both writers of minor distinction. They are best known as pioneers of verse for children. For instance, Ann wrote the once celebrated *My Mother* and *Meddlesome Matty* and Jane *Twinkle, Twinkle, Little Star*, still known the world over.[2] These were, however, the work of their adolescence and very early maturity; though praised in their day by such eminent men of letters as Walter Scott, Robert Southey and Robert Browning (and parodied by Robert Louis Stevenson, Lewis Carroll and many others) they should not be taken as the touchstone of the sisters' reputations.

In terms of literary merit, Jane's most impressive achievements were her novel *Display* (which has been not unfavourably compared with the work of her contemporary Jane Austen) and her verse satires published as *Essays in Rhyme*.[3] Though her work achieved acclamation in her own lifetime, the compliment of parody after her death and immortality in the nurseries of the world, Jane Taylor's literary talent was more potential than realised. Her promise was frustrated less by her illness and early death than by her unwillingness, once she reached maturity, to give rein to the undoubted sparkle in her nature, '*her natural propensity for joy and humour.*' Almost everything that she wrote as an adult was tinged with the sorrow of man's fallen nature, and with apprehension regarding her own salvation. Not, of course, that she would have had it otherwise, or regarded literary greatness as anything other than insignificant when compared with her responsibility to follow where her Saviour called. And, for all her genuine anguish about her own spiritual worth, there can be no more doubt for us than there was for her own family that she lived and died true to her principles and to her faith.

At the time when her literary career was cut short by her marriage in 1813, Ann was an astringent and respected literary critic of growing reputation. (It was the estimation of her character formed by reading her reviews that led her future husband, the Rev. Joseph Gilbert (1779–1852),[4] to propose marriage to her before he had even met her.) As a creative writer, although initially she received more critical acclaim than Jane, her memory was soon eclipsed by that of her more famous younger sister. Indeed, many of her own poems came to be ascribed to Jane, a borrowing which, she ruefully remarked, she could ill afford and which

Jane certainly did not require. She deserves better of posterity. In particular, her *Autobiography* and her letters, several of which are quoted below, are well worth reading, not only for the interest of the events they relate and of the people they portray, but for the masterly use of language they command. The poet James Montgomery rightly praised her prose style as *'perspicuous and beautiful'* and commented that it was the more remarkable in that she had not had the benefit of a classical education. A modern reader is likely to be as forcefully struck by the vividness and energy of writing shot through by a sparkling vein of wit.

Jane Taylor died quite young, of cancer, and her grave now lies, with those of both her parents, beneath the floor of the vestry of the United Reformed Church in Ongar. Ann lies, with her husband, beneath a vast Gothic sarcophagus, now sadly dilapidated, in the General Cemetery of the City of Nottingham, where she spent the last forty years of her life.

There were two further brothers and one sister who survived infancy. Martin (1788–1867) followed his uncle Josiah into the book-trade. The lame Jefferys (1792–1853), a *'wayward genius'*, became a successful children's author and illustrator and an inventor, living for several years at Pilgrim's Hatch. Jemima (1798–1886), the only one of the children to live in Ongar throughout the period of her father's ministry there, later married a prominent lace-manufacturer and Alderman of Nottingham, Thomas Herbert. Martin is buried in the churchyard in Navestock, though no trace of the grave remains, Jefferys at St Peter's, Broadstairs, and Jemima, like her sister Ann, in the General Cemetery in Nottingham.

Nor should the Rev. Isaac Taylor's wife Ann (1757–1830) be forgotten. Not only, although that is the memorial that she herself would have desired, was she a remarkable mother and a major influence on her talented children; as a Yorkshire visitor in 1824 had it, *'I never met with a person so truly great and yet so affectionately tender as Mrs Taylor.'*[5] As a child and as a young woman before her marriage, she had been a prolific writer of acerbic verse, none of which, alas, survives.[6] Late in life, she published a series of very popular manuals for young people and two novels (*The Family Mansion* and *Retrospection*). She also wrote, in collaboration with her daughter Jane, *Correspondence between a mother and her daughter at school*, a book of instruction for adolescent girls in the form of a fictional exchange of letters.

In 1865, a Sunday School was added at the rear of the chapel built in 1833. The architect, who made no charge for his services, was Isaac Charles Gilbert of Nottingham,[7] a grandson of the Rev. Isaac Taylor. The architect's older brother was Josiah Gilbert (1814–1892) of Marden Ash, painter, author, Alpinist and for many years Deacon of the (by then) Congregational Church in Ongar. Josiah Gilbert, for reasons which are not entirely clear, spent much of his childhood, from the ages of four to fifteen, living with his grandparents in Ongar. On the death of his grandfather, he lived briefly with his parents in Nottingham before moving to London to learn his trade as a portrait painter, in due course at the Royal Academy, where he subsequently exhibited on many occasions. In the autumn of 1843, he accepted an invitation to collaborate with his uncle Isaac Taylor on the development of the latter's mechanical engraving device. With his first wife Susan, Josiah moved from London to Marden Ash, where he rented (and later bought) the large house, known now and in previous centuries, but not apparently in Josiah's day, as Dyers. Here he lived for almost fifty years, a successful portrait painter and, later in his life, the author and illustrator of well-received books on art and on the Dolomite mountains (which he was largely responsible for introducing to the British public). He was a major benefactor of the Congregational church in Ongar, providing for the repurchase of the Livingstone Cottages in the High Street, which are still an important source of income to the present United Reformed Church. He was a member of the committee for the building of the Budworth Hall. At its opening, he gave an address on the history of Ongar, the notes for which were posthumously published in the *Essex Review*. The three portraits that he presented to the Budworth Hall still hung there in living memory, but at least one was sold in the early 1960s and all are now lost. And in Marden Ash he died on 15 August 1892. He is buried, however, close to his first wife in the Nottingham General Cemetery. His widow and second wife, Mary,[8] continued to live in Marden Ash until her death in 1925. She is well remembered by at least one inhabitant of Ongar still alive today, the remarkable Miss Korf, organist of the United Reformed church for the past seventy-five years. For many years of her widowhood her companion was Edith Haddon Herbert,[9] granddaughter of the Rev. Isaac Taylor's youngest daughter Jemima. Mary Gilbert is buried in the Ongar Cemetery, the grave marked by a vast slab, close to the twin chapels completed in 1867 to the design of her brother-in-law, Charles Gilbert.

All five houses in the immediate vicinity of Ongar in which the members of this remarkable family once lived are still standing today. This chapter seeks to bring together contemporary descriptions of some of these houses by members of the family, as well as briefly sketching the history of the family and the character and achievements of its head, the Rev. Isaac Taylor, and of his wife Ann. Appendices at the end of this chapter list the sources of information on the Taylor family, the whereabouts of portraits accessible to the public, and simplified family trees of the Taylors and Gilberts.

Who were the Taylors?

The Taylors were an Essex family only by adoption. Of the immediate family of the Rev. Isaac Taylor, only the youngest child, Jemima, was born in the county, in Colchester, though the elder Isaac himself had been brought up in Shenfield (where his maternal grandfather had property) and was educated at Brentwood Grammar School.

William Taylor of Worcester

The distant origins of the family are obscure. Little is known about William Taylor, a brassfounder and freeman of Worcester, grandfather of the Rev. Isaac Taylor. The place and date of his birth are uncertain, and even the date of his death is unknown, though there is evidence that he was still alive in the early 1750s. His wife's Christian name was Anne, but she cannot as yet be further identified. They appear to have had at least six children.

The primary source of information about him is the obituary of his son Isaac (which was almost certainly written by Isaac's son Charles, the Rev. Isaac Taylor's elder brother). William Taylor's business extended to the engraving of '*card plates, for tradesmen, book plates for the gentry, but especially to mark silver plate with coats of arms, &c.*' His son Isaac showed a particular aptitude for this work, thereby laying the foundation of the family's subsequent preeminence in the art of engraving. William's own *magnum opus* was reckoned to be one of a pair of chandeliers cast for the town hall in Worcester, a prestigious contract which he shared with a firm from Birmingham.

It is known that his sympathies lay with the Whigs against the Tories. In 1747, there was an election in Worcester, violently contested between the "Georgians" and the "Jacobites" and won by the former. The victors proceeded to antagonise their opponents still further by erecting a triumphal arch across the main street of Worcester, an engraving of which was '*spiritually undertaken by the Taylors.*' The backlash from the defeated "Jacobites" was such as '*to render the situation of the Taylor family rather unpleasant.*' (There is one other tantalising glimpse of political activity by the Taylors in the eighteenth century. William Taylor's great-granddaughter Ann Gilbert in her autobiography wrote of her grandfather, the first Isaac Taylor, '*He had been of some note not only in art but in politics, for he had taken an active part in Wilkes's election, and had lost considerably more than £1000 in doing so.*')[10] There is no direct evidence about William Taylor's religious affiliation, but there seems to be no reason to believe that he was a dissenter

Isaac Taylor (1730–1807)

William Taylor's son Isaac (the first of numerous members of the family to bear that name over the following two centuries) was the first member of the family to achieve a national reputation. He became an accomplished engraver and painter and a Fellow of – and in due course Secretary to – the Incorporated Society of Artists of Great Britain, a precursor of the Royal Academy.[11] He was a friend of Garrick, Goldsmith, Bartolozzi, Robert Smirke and Fuseli and employer and patron of Thomas Bewick, who mentions him in his *Memoir* with affection and respect.[12]

Isaac, born on 13 December 1730, showed an early interest in natural objects such as stones, plants, bark and leaves and, more particularly, in drawing them. In 1739, he was apprenticed to his father and soon made a speciality of engraving bookplates and silverware, which took him frequently to the houses of local landowners. In the early 1750s, a breach occured between Isaac and his father, and Isaac decided to move to London, where an uncle of his had already settled. Early in 1752, he set off, walking '*by the side of the waggon*' '*fired with the ambition of distinguishing himself as an artist.*' On arrival, as Cobbett was to do twenty-five years later, he spent a significant part of his capital (the sum of four pence!) on a work of art, a print by Audran after Le Brun of Moses delivering the daughters of Jethro. He then had the problem of finding work, at a time when the influence of the City Guilds upon the skilled labour market was still strong in London. His first employer was Francis Garden, a silversmith, an engagement which he owed to the connivance of another employee *at the introduction of a " foreigner" on cityground.'*

Shortly, however, Isaac Taylor began his association with the Jefferys family. He found work with Thomas Jefferys (d. 1771), an engraver of maps,[13] who later became Geographer to George III. In due course, he was entrusted with the engraving of a number of plates for the *Gentleman's Magazine* and for *Owen's Dictionary*. It was through this connection that Isaac Taylor met Thomas Jefferys's niece, Sarah Hackshaw Jefferys (1733–1809), whom he married on 9 May 1754 at Shenfield in Essex, where his father-in-law (Josiah Jefferys, a successful cutler employing sixty or seventy men) had property.

Although the Jefferys brothers became successful and prosperous businessmen, it seems that their origins were more humble.[14] Josiah Gilbert tells the romantic story that, at the age of eighteen, Josiah Jefferys *'married a Miss Hackshaw* [Jane Hackshaw (1710–1780)], *aged sixteen, as she was on her way to market.'* Her father, Robert Hackshaw (1675–1738) – a wealthy man with an estate at Rayleigh in Essex worth £1000 a year – was furious and virtually imprisoned her in his house for two years on pain of completely disowning her if ever she left it. Eventually, her brother persuaded their father to relent and to set up Josiah as a cutler. The marriage was then celebrated a second time. Subsequently, Robert Hackshaw's fortunes declined, chiefly, it seems, owing to lingering litigation over the provisions of his father's will, and, having mortgaged his estate, he was said to have died of grief. He was buried in Bunhill Fields burial ground, the first occupant of a family vault which later contained the mortal remains of several members of the Taylor family, including Isaac's obituarist, his son Charles. It was marked by a striking tomb-stone, of which there is now no trace.[15]

Robert Hackshaw's father, also named Robert (d. 1722), had been an adherent of William of Orange, came with him to England when he took the throne in 1688 and was appointed Purveyor to the King. Josiah Gilbert suggests that he was *'either of Dutch extraction or belonged to the Puritan emigration in Holland.'* He was apparently known as *'the "Orange Skipper", from having been employed, before the Revolution, to carry despatches backwards and forwards, concealed in his walking-cane.'* Jane Hackshaw, as a child, sat on the knee of Dr Watts, the hymn-writer, who gave her a copy of his *Divine Songs for Children*, which was passed down in the Taylor family as an heirloom. Jane Hackshaw's great-grandchildren, Ann and Jane Taylor, were, of course, to follow in Watts's footsteps and to produce verse for children of a religious nature. This was as popular in its day as that of Watts, although, in contrast to their secular work, ultimately less enduring.

There can be no doubt that Isaac Taylor fulfilled his ambition to distinguish himself as an artist and, in particular, as an engraver. Engraving was at this time the only means of producing in any quantity worthwhile reproductions of works of art.

ASPECTS OF THE HISTORY OF ONGAR

It met the growing demand of those who hungered for art, or for the status which went with it, but could not afford to hang their walls with the originals. Although engravers sometimes created original designs, they as often copied the works of other artists. (Charles Taylor indeed thought that it was preferable that the functions of design and of engraving should not be undertaken by the same artist.) However, engraving not only required a very high degree of skill, but was an art-form in its own right. Before about 1750, distinguished examples of such work had been a virtual monopoly of French and other continental engravers, but during Taylor's working lifetime (owing in part to his own achievements) that preeminence passed decisively to England. This transition was helped by immigrants, such as the Florentine Francesco Bartolozzi (of whom Isaac Taylor's sons were pupils) attracted by the lucrative patronage to be had in the richest city in the world. For a period of some twenty-five years prior to the French Wars of the mid-1790s, English engraving was the height of fashion and found a ready market not only at home, but also on the Continent.

Although Isaac Taylor did produce full-scale engravings of paintings and exhibited them regularly at the Incorporated Society of Artists between 1765 and 1780, his speciality was book illustration. In this field, he almost always engraved to his own designs. After the death of Anthony Walker in 1765, he could lay claim to be the preeminent living illustrator. Among his finest works were the vignettes to the *Poetical Works* of John Langhorne (1766) and to Goldsmith's *Deserted Village* (1770) and the illustrations for Samuel Richardson's *Sir Charles Grandison* (1778) – though, in the last case, Charles Taylor, while praising the engraving, is critical of the design. Plates engraved by Isaac Taylor were said to wear better at the press than those of any other engraver of his time.

Engraving made his reputation and his fortune, but painting was perhaps nearer to his heart. He retired early when he was little more than fifty and moved from London, where he had lived and worked at several addresses in and around Holborn, to what was then the village of Edmonton. At the time of his death, his address was given as Church Street. Here he amused himself by painting in oils. Although his withdrawal from society caused him to be quickly forgotten by the world of artistic fashion, he unobtrusively kept in touch with its developments for the rest of his life.

Shortly after his marriage in 1754, he had painted a fine pair of portraits in oils of his wife and of himself, which now hang in the Taylor Room in the Guildhall in Lavenham. Another portrait, a pencil drawing of Isaac Taylor in late middle age probably by his son Isaac, is in the possession of the author of this chapter. Several other portraits by Isaac Taylor, including two of Garrick, are in the British Museum collection.

Isaac Taylor died on 17 October 1807 and is buried in the churchyard of the parish church of All Saints, Edmonton, where his monument, now unidentifiable, stood not far from that of the essayist Charles Lamb. Isaac and Sarah Taylor had five children: Charles (1756–1823), Isaac (1759–1829), Josiah (1761–1834), Sarah (1763–1845) and Ann (1765–1832). Ann married an Oxford clergyman James

Hinton; one of their children was John Howard Hinton, who became a Baptist minister, Secretary of the Baptist Union and author of many works, celebrated in their day, on theology and education. Sarah married one Daniel Hooper, who came from a well-to-do landed family, owned a sail-making business and was buried in the Hackshaw/Taylor family vault in Bunhill Fields, being described on the tombstone as "Gent". Josiah became a successful bookseller and publisher, especially of works on architecture. Isaac, of course, was to become the Rev. Isaac Taylor.

Charles Taylor (1756–1823)

Charles Taylor (rivalled in learning in a learned family only by his nephew, Isaac Taylor of Stanford Rivers) was born on 1 February 1756 at Shenfield, where his grandfather Josiah Jefferys had property. His father Isaac had briefly, and apparently unsuccessfully, practised here as a land surveyor before returning to London to resume his career as an engraver. The evidence for Charles's schooling is contradictory, but he may, like his brother Isaac, have attended Brentwood Grammar School, before a brief stay at a school in the City.[16] At the age of fifteen or sixteen, Charles was articled to his father as an engraver, studying under Bartolozzi. He built for himself upon the meagre foundations acquired at school, mastering not only Latin and Greek, but also Hebrew and *'two or three modern languages;' 'moreover, as the son of an artist, and himself an artist by profession, at least, he had acquainted himself with numismatic lore, and with antiquarian art generally,'* making a particular study of the marbles in the collection of the Duke of Richmond. On 27 May 1777, he married Mary Forrest, niece of the chaplain of the Tower of London, Cornelius Humphreys. The couple immediately left for Paris, still then regarded as the principal school of engraving, where they spent a year and where Charles '*was industriously employed among the treasures of the King's library.*'

Charles Taylor returned to London, having only recently reached his majority. Largely by his own unaided efforts, he had attained a level of learning seldom matched at such an age by those boasting a university education. As an engraver, he had been scrupulously taught by his talented father; as a scholar, where his chief talent lay, he had no known mentor beyond his own reading.

He first set up home and business in High Holborn, producing engravings after pictures by Robert Smirke and Angelica Kauffmann. Early in 1780, he moved to No 8, Dyers Buildings, Holborn, where his first child, also called Charles, was born on 11 April. A few weeks later, Mrs Taylor was forced to flee with her baby son when Landell's Distillery nearby was set on fire during the Gordon Riots and Dyers Buildings were threatened. However, the threat passed unfulfilled, and the family was able to return. In 1785, the Taylors moved to 10, Holborn '*near Castle Street and Castle Yard*' and finally, in 1796, to 108, Hatton Garden, where Charles Taylor remained until his death in 1823.

This was the background to his life's work. However, although his income came initially from engraving (and later also from publishing), in each of these fields he was surpassed, respectively, by his brother Isaac and by his brother Josiah. His renown was founded, if for a long time anonymously, upon a quite different accomplishment. When he was thirteen, his father had purchased the premises and stock of a bookseller in High Holborn, and Charles was thereafter able to use the stock as a private library. He became an avid reader and, in his seventeenth year, he came upon a copy of Calmet's *Dictionnaire Historique et Critique de la Bible*. This massive work of scholarship fired his imagination. The perhaps unexceptional notion quickly grew that he would one day translate it into English and produce a learned commentary upon it. Such fits of enthusiasm for a Herculean task not infrequently seize the minds of individuals of a certain disposition, especially when they are young, and the enthusiasm is no doubt entirely sincere. What is unusual is for the resolve to last, and what is more unusual still is that it should be triumphantly carried out.

Presumably, it was not until he had achieved a measure of independence after his return from Paris that Charles Taylor was in a position to embark in earnest upon his great project. It was a further twenty years, in 1797, before he felt ready to begin to publish the results of his labours, which he did anonymously. The reception by the learned world of this first sample of his translation and commentary (illustrated by himself) was enthusiastic and was enhanced no doubt by the mystery surrounding the identity of the author. (Even the Archbishop of Canterbury enquired diligently who he might be.) Not that this was Charles Taylor's motive for seeking anonymity, or for continuing to seek it until his death. His nephew Isaac Taylor of Stanford Rivers speculated that the work itself was too important to Charles Taylor to allow him to risk its being discounted by the academic establishment through association with himself – '*an indictment against such a one as he was, would contain several counts:*- first count*, a layman:* second count*, a Nonconformist:* third count*, a member of no university.*' Thereafter, as further instalments and then further editions appeared, a natural modesty and an aversion to the distractions of publicity led him to refuse to acknowledge any connection with the work, beyond that of having engraved the illustrations. Taylor's *Calmet* remained a model for Biblical scholarship for many years.

Charles Taylor also edited two periodicals, *The Literary Annual Register* and its successor *The Literary Panorama*, and served for some years as an honorary librarian to the forerunner of the London Library, the London Library Society founded in 1785. Indeed, in 1801, the library itself was moved to his premises at 108 Hatton Garden, where it remained '*for several years*' before being transferred to a building in Finsbury. Isaac Taylor of Stanford Rivers wrote a memorable description of the interior of the house and of its master:

> '*It must have been at sundry times, during these years, and while the house in Hatton Garden was crammed with books – up-stairs, down-stairs, and in the hall and passages – that in my visits to the family, I saw my learned uncle; and not very seldom, when charged with some message from home, I was admitted into his study. Alas that photography was not practised fifty years ago! The man – his deshabillé, and*

his surroundings, would indeed have furnished a carte de visite not of the most ordinary sort. The scene! The tables – the library counters – the cheffoniers – the shelves and the floor (who shall say if the floor had a carpet?), all heaped with books: – books of all sizes and sorts: – books open, one upon another – books with a handful of leaves doubled in to keep the place – books in piles, that had slid down from chairs or stools, and had rested unmoved until a deep deposit of dust had got a lodgement upon them! Quires of proof sheets and revises – here and there, folded and unfolded. On the table usually occupied by the writer there was just room for an inkstand, and for a folded sheet of demy or foolscap.... [In appearance he was] no pale, sallow, nervous, midnight-lamp-looking recluse, or ghost. Not at all so, but a man – then just past mid-life – powerful in bony and muscular framework – singularly hirsute – well limbed, well filled out, erect in walk, prominent and aquiline in feature – teeming, as one should say, with repressed energy'.

It is interesting that Charles Taylor's brother Isaac (by no means an envious or ungenerous man) *'never regarded him as learned,'* attributing his achievements rather to a facility for epigraphy, the fruit of long practice supplemented by a natural shrewdness, and to a quite extraordinary memory, which gave him almost total recall of anything he read even many years after the event.

Charles Taylor was, like his brother Isaac and like his forbears on his mother's side, a dissenter and a regular worshipper at the old meeting-house in Fetter Lane. He was, however, by temperament a deeply conservative man, as ordinary in his respect for social convention as he was extraordinary (and even eccentric) in his intellectual range and habits. He was, in apparent contrast to his father, who had supported Wilkes, a *'thorough-going Tory.'* His nephew speculates that his political opinions may have been formed by his experience in France and hardened by the events of the French Revolution. On his father's death in 1807, he inherited the bulk of his considerable fortune, though this does not appear to have altered his manner of living one jot. He died on 13 November 1823 and was buried with several of his forbears in the family vault in the Bunhill Fields burial ground. There is in the Taylor Collection in the Suffolk Record Office a photograph of a self-portrait of Charles Taylor as a young man. The original is in the possession of a descendant of Charles Taylor's father Isaac.

Isaac Taylor (1759–1829) and his wife Anne née Martin (1757–1830)

Isaac Taylor was born in London on 30 January 1759, but spent much of his childhood in Shenfield and probably attended what later became Brentwood Grammar School,[17] which *'he left not entirely ignorant of Latin and Greek'*. He was apprenticed to his father and learnt from him the techniques of the art of engraving. He became one of the finest of all English engravers – *'far surpass[ing] his father in every artistic quality'* – combining great skill with a flair for design, qualities which he also demonstrated as a painter of both portraits and landscapes.

In 1790, he exhibited at the Society of Arts[18] a large engraving (which had been commissioned by Boydell[19] for the then enormous sum of 250 guineas) of *The Assassination of Rizzio*, after a painting by John Opie. It won him ten guineas and the Society's Gold Palette, awarded annually for the best engraving of the year. It was considered to be significantly finer than the original painting, itself reckoned to be one of Opie's best. In 1802, at a time when the market for engraving was still much depressed, he received 500 guineas, also from Boydell, for an engraving after Thomas Stothard of Henry VIII's first sight of Anne Boleyn.[20] One of his finest works, published by himself and his brother Josiah in 1796, was *Specimens of Gothic Ornaments*, a series of engravings illustrating the architectural details of the parish church of St Peter & St Paul in Lavenham.

As an artist alone, he was a remarkable man, but this was very far from being the full extent of his achievements. He combined an unquenchable intellectual curiosity with the energy, perseverance, discipline and methodical approach to apply what he learnt to the best effect and with an infectious enthusiasm which enabled him to impart his own intellectual excitement to others. At Lavenham, where he was a deacon of the Independent congregation, he started a Sunday School. He excelled as a pioneer in educational techniques. Packed lectures which he regularly gave to the youth of Colchester on a range of subjects as diverse as geography and mechanics were enlivened by meticulously produced visual aids (as we should call them now), a few of which have survived. The same approach was taken to the education of his own children, which he undertook in close partnership with his wife. Later in life, when in Ongar, he published a very successful series of illustrated educational books for children.

On his arrival in Ongar in 1811, the influence of Isaac Taylor was felt almost immediately, and Ongar benefited from his experience at Lavenham and at Colchester. By the end of the year, the Sunday School[21] had been reopened after an interval of thirteen years, and a weekly lecture and a weekly prayer meeting had been instituted. A book society already existed in the town, having been started in 1808 with a quarterly subscription of half a crown for the purchase of books and a monthly meeting to discuss them. Isaac Taylor was soon an active member; he served as its treasurer and appears to have wielded considerable influence over the selection of books. (The society survived until at least 1843.)

In addition, Isaac Taylor was throughout his life a devout Christian and, for its last thirty-three years, a dedicated Independent minister, setting a high standard of moral conduct, rejuvenating the congregation at Ongar and earning the ungrudging respect even of the established church. In accepting the call to the pastorate at Ongar, he wrote a letter[22] to the members of his future congregation which well expresses the spirit in which he was to fulfil his charge and makes clear the deep spiritual commitment which underpinned his many achievements in the temporal sphere. Many of the ideas he put forward in the letter and many of the individual phrases which he employed to express them were the normal stock in trade of any minister of the time, but the whole has the ring of sincerity. Here is a man of both principle and compassion, who will not confuse compassion with the condoning of wrongdoing, or principle with the withholding of compassion.

THE TAYLOR FAMILY OF ONGAR AND THEIR HOUSES THERE

Figure 7   The Rev. Isaac Taylor from an engraving by James Andrews.

The position of an Independent minister at this time was not an easy one either professionally or socially, there being constant resentment and opposition from the clergy of the established church. For instance, many of the early recruits to the Sunday School were soon withdrawn after pressure from the incumbents of neighbouring parishes, who themselves almost certainly offered no alternative source of pastoral care to the children of Ongar. It is a mark of the respect which Isaac Taylor earned even in these circles that, in the survey of nonconformist meeting houses commissioned by the Home Office from Church of England incumbents in 1829, he is, almost uniquely, accorded the courtesy of the title of Reverend.

But, above all perhaps, in equal partnership with his wife Ann, he created a family. Several of its members themselves also achieved fame and distinction in their own fields; all remained devoted to each other throughout their lives. Marriage and friendships – of which there were many and of great warmth – in no way weakened these bond of loyalty and mutual affection and respect. On the contrary, wives, husbands, friends and their families were gladly drawn in to an ever-widening Taylor family circle, which was enriched by their accession to it. Strong echoes of this sense of family as the foundation upon which all other relationships and all worthwhile achievements were based reverberated among

ASPECTS OF THE HISTORY OF ONGAR

Isaac Taylor's descendants well into the twentieth century. And yet that foundation was itself founded upon a natural, unassuming and steady faith in God and his Providence.

If one were required to cite only one illustration to epitomize the character of Isaac Taylor and the spirit of mutual devotion which imbued his family, it would have to be the following. At around the time at which the older children began, for various reasons, to leave home, it was agreed that, on the night of every full moon, at nine o'clock, each member of the family would take a few minutes to look upon the moon alone and thus to meet in thought, confident that the others, scattered throughout the country, would be doing the same. And Isaac Taylor, who was also nothing if not a practical man, supplied each of his absent children with a calendar of full-moon nights for the coming year. Several references in surviving letters make it clear that this tryst was faithfully kept. For instance, Isaac Taylor wrote from Castle House:

> *'It is nine o'clock, the full moon shines delightfully into my study, and the duty (for so we have agreed, and therefore it is a duty) – the pleasing duty calls me to think of my absent children; not that there would be any danger of my forgetting them, but I love to look at the bright moon, and to recollect what dear eyes are looking at the same object, what precious bosoms are beating, at thought of their father, their mother, their home!'*

And Ann to her husband in June 1814:

> *'If, on Saturday evening, you should be walking to Sheffield* [23] *remember the full moon will have a message for you; and if you are in some northern mail contrive to sit next to her, that at nine o'clock she may drop the wonted whisper, and make sign of love in the name of one upon whom she will be gazing beyond many a blue hill'.*

Isaac Taylor's own upbringing appears to have been very different. According to his daughter, his father '*though a strictly moral man...exhibited towards his family an austere reserve which was little calculated to awaken the domestic affections to genial life,*' while his mother, though '*possessing no small share of practical good sense, and real concern for the interests of the children, was yet so more than occupied in the labours of rearing them, and withal of a temper so heedless of the graces of life, that it seemed scarcely possible for kind and tender dispositions to expand under her influence....Her will was law, and in many respects her family reaped the advantage of such a parent, but it is perhaps surprising that a heart so warm as his, should have been trained under her hand.*' What is more, he had to endure – which he did with cheerful equanimity – having his good nature put upon; he was '*made something like the "fag" of the family.*'

Nor was his father a religious man – or, as Ann Gilbert puts it, '*under the influence of Christian principle.*' The younger Isaac, however, became a practising Christian early, and never wavered. At sixteen, he joined the congregation under the Rev. Mr Webb at Fetter Lane, where his brother Charles was to worship throughout his life.

THE TAYLOR FAMILY OF ONGAR AND THEIR HOUSES THERE

The bent towards nonconformity – an appellation which Isaac Taylor himself disliked – probably came from his mother, a legacy of the Hackshaws. For most of his adult life, it was his practice to rise at a quarter to six and to spend the hour between six and seven at prayer in his closet. To prevent '*the vagrancy of thought,*' he prayed aloud. The hour between eight and nine in the evening was almost always spent in the same way. His late entry to the ministry, in 1796, was due to severe illness which had frustrated an earlier calling.

One of Isaac Taylor's first important achievements as apprentice to his father was to oversee the preparation of the plates for the engravings for Dr Rees's revised edition of the *Cyclopaedia* of Ephraim Chambers, which began to appear in 1778. These engravings included a wide variety of scientific subjects. This work and his many discussions with Rees were, by his own account, what first filled him with a thirst for knowledge. Rees was generous in his support of the young man and lent him many books from his extensive library.

On 18 April 1781 at St Andrew's Church, Holborn, Isaac Taylor married Ann Martin, whom he had known from childhood, the daughter of a long-deceased disciple of Whitfield, Thomas Martin, the son of an estate-agent of Kensington, and his wife Mary (née Plaxton).

Ann Martin's mother, who must have been born in the 1730s, was by all accounts a strikingly beautiful woman. She married again twice, her second husband also dying within a short time of their marriage. In 1781, she was Mrs Hewitt; there is a portrait of her, described as Mrs Martin, in the Taylor Room in the Guildhall at Lavenham. Her grandfather and great-grandfather had been clergymen in Yorkshire.[24] Her father, Henry Plaxton (born 1686), appears to have invested unwisely in a building development in York and was ruined. Mary, then only sixteen, '*was sent off alone on the top of the York coach for London*' and never saw her family again. She lived for a time with a family in Kensington Square and '*married early*' at St Botolph, Bishopsgate, on 28 June 1756. Ann, the elder of two children, was born on 20 June 1757.

Ann's childhood was not a happy one. Her father, whom she adored, appears to have been a fundamentalist whose beliefs bordered on the deranged. '*He once called her to see a new and favourite toy thrown on the fire, hoping in this way to induce a salutary self-control!*' On the night he died, aged only twenty-nine and when Ann was six, she dreamt she saw him disappearing up to heaven in a chariot and beckoning her to follow. She awoke to be told that he was dead and was prostrated with grief to the extent that her mother feared for her life. For a time, she was sent to live with her paternal grandfather in Kensington, who alternately spoiled her and subjected his intelligent grandchild to the tedium of unimaginative instruction by rote; the latter experience determined her never to inflict such methods upon her own children.

Her mother's third marriage was fruitful. According to her daughter's account, Ann's step-father was a selfish man, who gave her no love or attention, while her step-brothers and step-sisters rewarded her affection for them by treating her, like

ASPECTS OF THE HISTORY OF ONGAR

Cinderella, with contempt, as little more than an unpaid servant. School was her salvation. She was quickly marked out as possessing an enquiring mind and an aptitude both for learning and for writing; her *'poetic and often satirical effusions soon gained her a local celebrity.'*

Isaac Taylor, who was eighteen months younger than she was, was one of a group of friends who sometimes visited the Hewitt household. He appears to have been smitten with Ann before she had shown any interest in him and seized the opportunity afforded by his being entrusted with the engraving of a silver tea-pot belonging to her to return it with a poem inside. She responded indignantly in kind, and there ensued a *'paper war, which, for a time, made the gossip of the little circle,'* but which ended in their engagement.[25] They were singularly well matched – in intelligence, in outlook, in talents and in shared experience of overcoming in childhood the handicap of a less than happy home life – and it was their daughter's firm and entirely credible belief that they remained deeply in love for the rest of their lives.

The early years: Islington/Holborn/Lavenham/Colchester

At the time of his marriage, Isaac Taylor's immediate financial prospects, although his father was a fairly wealthy man, were hardly dazzling. He could rely upon half a guinea a week for three days' work for his elder brother Charles, to which would be added whatever he could earn on his own account in the other three days. His capital amounted to £30. Ann brought with her a dowry of £100 in stock, a legacy from her grandfather, and some furniture. With this, they set up house in a rented first-floor apartment with a view of the Highgate Hills immediately opposite the parish church in Islington – then a country village, where Isaac was already living, having moved there to recuperate after his serious illness some time earlier.

Isaac Taylor's first independent venture in business was to use the £100 of Ann's dowry to commission a rising painter, Robert Smirke, to produce four circular paintings representing morning, noon, evening and night, which he then engraved and published. In 1783, he painted and engraved a series of views of the River Thames near London; there are copies of some of these engravings in the Taylor Collection in the Suffolk Record Office. Between 1783 and 1787, he was engaged (at first with his brother Charles, but then on his own, and finally, in 1787, with his younger brother Josiah) in an enterprise to produce illustrations to Shakespeare's plays. The designs, by other artists, including Robert Smirke, were then engraved by Charles and Isaac, though Charles seems to have dropped out of the picture by 1785. Josiah was involved only in the publishing. It was the success of this work which won Isaac the commission from Boydell to engrave Opie's *The Assassination of Rizzio*.

While Isaac was establishing himself as an engraver and beginning to strike out on his own, Ann was getting to grips with running a household and with motherhood. On Isaac's twenty-third birthday, 30 January 1782, their first child was born and christened Ann. Eighteen months later, at midsummer 1783, the family moved, to facilitate Isaac's growing business, to 54 Red Lion Street, Holborn. Three months later, on 23 September 1783, Jane Taylor was born, '*a little before midnight.*' On 20 July 1785, a son was born and christened Isaac, but died when less than a year old on 22 April 1786. Jane too was a sickly child, catching cold '*from the negligence of the attendants*' '*at the moment of her birth*', and giving constant occasion for anxiety in the first two years of her life. Her mother was convinced that this was '*a remote cause of her premature death*' forty years later.

At first, Ann found her new role hard. She appears to have had no training from her mother in the practical aspects of housekeeping and had everything to learn. Money was short and her children's health a constant concern. She was a conscientious mother, but inclined throughout her life to be a worrier. After the birth of her third child, her own health began to suffer and she began to be so weighed down with her burdens and responsibilities that she thought of little else. A forthright friend (who had herself the luxury of two servants!) then told her bluntly that, unless she did something to render herself less of a drudge, her husband was soon likely to lose interest in her. The shaft hit home, and it occurred to her with a pang that Isaac's recently acquired habit of reading a book at meal-times might be the first symptom of such a decline in their relationship. Having no other time to spare, she hit upon the notion of offering herself to read to her husband aloud at meal-times. This, at a stroke, banished the daily grind for a brief period of each day, kept her own mind active and provided the material for conversation on topics of mutual interest. The practice continued for forty years and in due course made an important contribution to their children's education too.

This was the only period of Isaac's life when he broke his rule of early rising, and perhaps even that of regular prayer. His sleep, as a parent of young children, was interrupted, and he gave in to the temptation to try to compensate by getting up, if not late, at least less early. He was forced to return to his earlier habits by an act of charity. A minister, who had fallen on hard times, asked him if he would buy, for half a guinea, an elaborately bound leather prayer-book. Half a guinea was much more than he could afford, but he hadn't the heart to refuse. He then resolved to work an extra hour each day in order to make up the money he had spent and to get up an hour earlier in order to achieve it. However, he was both tired and a heavy sleeper and found it hard to keep to his resolve. Having begun to sleep through the ringing of an alarm clock, he first added to its effect by balancing a pair of tongs so that it would fall with a crash when the weight of the alarm began to move. When this too soon failed to wake him, he took the more desperate measure of placing his watch under the weight of the alarm so that only an immediate response to the bell would save his precious watch from destruction. This worked for long enough for him to reacquire the habit of early rising.

Holborn, though convenient for business, was expensive. The annual rent on the apartment in Red Lion Street was £20, a large sum when compared, for instance, with half a guinea for half a week's work, and there were now more mouths to feed. Nor was London a healthy place, and almost every member of the family was constitutionally vulnerable to the risks of illness. Isaac Taylor was a methodical man, and he reasoned that, although neither he nor Ann had ever yet been more than twenty miles from Charing Cross, the advantages of retiring to the country would outweigh the disadvantages. Their money would go further and buy them in many ways a better quality of life. Their health could be expected to improve. Now that he was established as an engraver, distance from his clientele was an obstacle which could be overcome, the work itself being no more easily carried out in one place than in another. The principal drawback was separation from family and friends, and Ann at least embarked upon the enterprise not as something she had any wish to do, but as a necessary evil which must be endured.

With typical thoroughness, Isaac obtained the name of every Independent minister within a hundred miles of London and wrote to them all to enquire about the cost of living in each locality. He received a reply from the Rev. W. Hickman informing him of a house for rent in Lavenham in Suffolk. It belonged to an Anglican clergyman, Mr Cooke, and was known in those days simply as "Cooke's House". It was described by a cottager, when Isaac asked for directions, as *'the first grand house in Shilling Street.'* And grand it was, in terms of size at least, when compared with what Isaac and Ann were used to. The ground floor boasted *'three parlours, two kitchens, and a dairy, together with three other rooms never inhabited'* and there were six bedrooms above. There was a large garden with a meadow beyond and even a disused pig-sty, which Ann and Jane later appropriated for their own use. The rent asked was £6 a year – a mark, no doubt, of the extreme remoteness of Lavenham from what most eighteenth century people would have regarded as civilisation. Isaac Taylor, having travelled sixty miles to view the property, decided to take it.

This house is now known as The Grange. It is the sort of timber-framed building which features prominently in publications of the English Tourist Board, the model of what, if only he could afford it, every Englishman's house should be. In the Taylors' day, it did not in fact look like that at all: such features as exposed external timbers and upper floors overhanging the lower were thought to be hopelessly plebeian and passé. Cooke's House had been "Georgianized". Its subsequent history was one of decline and neglect. By the 1920s, it was virtually a ruin and came within a whisker of being demolished. Just in time it was saved and restored to its late fifteenth century appearance. Now, after further sensitive renovation, it is one of the glories of Lavenham, though, externally, it would be all but unrecognisable to the Taylors. Picture postcards of it tend to feature the attic window at which, it is claimed, Jane Taylor sat when she composed *Twinkle, Twinkle, Little Star* – which is odd, since the window in question was first put in in the 1930s![26]

The Taylors moved to Lavenham on 30 June 1786. After a grim first winter – during which Isaac was much away on business and Mrs Taylor's forebodings of inevitable misery away from her own family and her friends seemed to her to be fully justified – began one of several golden periods in the life of the family. It was clouded only by the deaths in infancy of three more children: another Isaac born shortly after their arrival, who survived for only two months; Harriet, who died in

THE TAYLOR FAMILY OF ONGAR AND THEIR HOUSES THERE

October 1791 aged 18 months; and Eliza, who lived for only four months and died shortly before her sister Harriet. However, three other children were born in Lavenham and survived into adulthood. All were boys: Isaac, born 17 August 1787; Martin, born 9 October 1788; and Jefferys (named after his paternal grandmother) born 30 October 1792.

Isaac Taylor's reputation as an engraver was rising fast, and the number of his commissions, and his income, with it. By the end of the decade, he was taking apprentices and more rooms of the house were given up to the business. Ann and Jane thrived on the country air and upon the opportunities for creative play offered by a large house and garden. Their formal education they received at home; their mother taught reading, needlework and the catechism, and their father, from his engraving stool, everything else. Less formally they also benefited from the ambience of simple piety, diligence, learning and intellectual curiosity created by their parents. The two girls, thrown much upon their own resources in a busy household, became inseparable. They gave free rein to their imaginations, endlessly creating and acting out characters, always in pairs, who ranged from two poor, but industrious, women known as Moll and Bet to mythical daughters of George III. Isaac Taylor found time, however, to make ingenious toys for his children, such as '*a landscape painted on cardboard, cut out and placed at different distances, through the lanes of which, by means of a wire turning underneath, there slowly wound a loaded waggon and other carriages.*' This '*was contained in a box about seven inches by twelve, and two in depth, with a glass in front.*'

Jane, at this age, was a '*saucy, lively, entertaining little thing.*' '*At the baker's shop, she used to be placed on the kneading board in order to preach, recite, narrate – to the great entertainment of his many visitors.*' Ann soon began to write for pleasure. From the age of about eight or nine, she composed verse, imitating the style of Isaac Watts, the only one she then knew. Even before that (according to their brother Isaac) both she and Jane regularly composed short snatches of verse and declaimed them to each other. Jane was even more precocious, producing at an early age verses and short stories[27] which would not have disgraced one twice as old.

In 1792, the Taylors' landlord, Mr Cooke, decided that he wished to occupy the house himself and gave them notice to quit. No other suitable property was available for rent, and Isaac Taylor eventually purchased for £250 the house next door (now Arundel House), which was then in a ruinous condition. He embarked with enthusiasm upon the task of restoration and of creating a house and garden precisely to his own specification. But the work had hardly begun when, just before Christmas, he fell dangerously ill of typhoid fever. For three months, he was confined to bed, his life frequently despaired of, and during this time he earned nothing. Work on Arundel House was stopped and his own apprentices laid off. The children's education was disrupted, as their mother poured her remaining strength into nursing her husband. Gradually, as spring approached, Isaac Taylor's condition improved, but it was not until May that he was able to resume work and to start to pay off the debts accumulated during his illness. (The capital saved from his success as an engraver was already committed to the acquisition of his new house.) A little earlier, when it was apparent that he was not going to die, work on Arundel House had been resumed, and at midsummer 1793 the Taylors occupied it. The renovation had cost a further £250, but, thanks to Isaac Taylor's careful and imaginative planning, house and garden, which then abutted on a common, had been transformed from dereliction to delight. *'The common parlour was pretty and comfortable as it could be, with a door and a large bay-window into the garden, and a sliding panel for convenient communication with the kitchen. China closets and store closets were large and commodious....The garden too was a particularly nice one. Happily there were several well-grown trees already in the ground, and a trellis arbour covered with honeysuckle stood on a rising ground underneath a picturesque old pear tree. Then there was a long shrubbery walk, and an exit by a white gate and rails to the common. A poultry yard, containing sometimes seventy fowls of different sorts was on the premises behind, and an excavated and paved pond for ducks.'* The family moved there as to a new beginning.

Isaac Taylor set to with a will to recoup his losses, the apprentices[28] returned and increased in number, the children's education resumed, other local children joined them and the house was soon a hive of purposeful activity. Mrs Taylor, however, was far from well, and suffered constant pain, her health, never good, further worn down by the strain of her husband's illness.

As soon as he had arrived in Lavenham, Isaac Taylor had become an active member of the Independent congregation, whose pastor was Mr Hickman. He was particularly involved in establishing its Sunday School. Before long, he became a deacon, and, when Mr Hickman decided to leave Lavenham, he proposed Isaac Taylor as his successor. The members of the congregation, however, were unwilling to see one of their own number appointed. Isaac Taylor had been invited to preach to various neighbouring congregations and thus came to the notice of a former resident of Lavenham then living in Colchester. The latter quickly decided that Isaac Taylor was the man to rejuvenate his own congregation, which had degenerated into heresy and apathy. An invitation was issued and, despite Mrs Taylor's reservations founded in her aversion to change (the once dreaded Lavenham was now her treasured home), it was accepted. On 1 November 1795, Isaac Taylor preached his first sermon to his new congregation in the chapel in Bucklersbury Lane, and, on 20 January 1796, the family left Lavenham for Colchester. Arundel House was not sold and remained Isaac Taylor's property for more than ten years.

The house which, after a few days, the family occupied was in a street then known as Angel Lane, but now and previously, more prosaically, as West Stockwell Street. As Anne Gilbert wrote many years later:

'It was nearly in the centre of the town, in a street which, though narrow and disagreeable at one end, became wider, and owned several excellent houses at the other. Ours was among the excellent houses, but it was not

one of them. It was just respectable, and would just hold us; and the garden, not a small one, contained some well-grown trees. Speedily, under my father's hand, it showed grass plots, and winding walks of good Essex gravel, a white seat, a vine-covered arbour, and so forth, besides laburnums and lilacs that warm my heart to think of even now'.

Next door was St Martin's Church, with '*a giant poplar towering over the broken, ivied tower.*' built in Norman times largely using Roman bricks. Shortly after their arrival, their tenth child was born and baptised Decimus. He died when he was five, of scarlet fever.

On 21 April 1796, Isaac Taylor was ordained and began his ministry to a congregation consisting of '*men of habit more than men of piety*' in a garrison town in which religious feeling was moribund among dissenters and members of the established church alike. He did not, however, cease his work as an engraver. Even if he had wanted to abandon it, which is most unlikely, it provided the principal means of supporting his growing family. The move to Colchester coincided with a period of high inflation and the collapse of the art market in the wake of the war with France. Isaac Taylor suffered '*a grievous reverse of fortune.*' It was as much as he could do to earn enough to feed his family and to keep out of debt. The man who had so recently won the Gold Palette of the Society of Arts was even reduced to engraving dog-collars.

After a time, the older children, the two girls included, were pressed into service to help their father in his secular profession, though they received wages for doing so, and the long workroom at the back of the house became in a real sense the hub of family life.[29] At a later stage, the three boys, Isaac, Martin and Jefferys, were formally apprenticed to their father, thereby gaining exemption from the attentions of the press gang!

In the complex process of producing a line engraving, one of the young Ann's tasks was to carry out the "biting" of the etched copper plate, that is, deepening the shallowly etched lines by the application of a solution of aquafortis (i.e. nitric acid). This was a delicate and iterative process usually taking several days to complete. Mistakes, leading to the acid's marking the plate where it was not intended, sometimes required months of painstaking work to rectify. Although the work was exacting and sometimes tedious, Ann at least remembered these as very happy times. In the workroom, Isaac and later Jefferys learnt the skills which in due course enabled them to earn a living; it seems that their father, so often ahead of his time, intended in this way to provide the means of future self-sufficiency for his daughters too; it also ensured – a pressing motive indeed in his eyes and those of Mrs Taylor – that the whole family was able to remain under one roof for as long as possible. Assistance to Mrs Taylor and the girls' practical education in housekeeping were provided by the expedient of their spending alternate weeks in engraving and in helping their mother. Whoever was on duty in the workroom was known as "Supra", the other as "Infra". The hours were long. Breakfast was at 8am, at which, as at other meals, Mrs Taylor read aloud. After a brief interlude which Isaac Taylor devoted to sketching while his wife continued to read, the family worked until 8pm with an hour's break for lunch and half an hour for tea. However, when schooling was not in progress in the workroom, conversation was encouraged and the children were allowed visits from their friends, who watched the work in hand with fascination.

As at Arundel House, the workroom was simultaneously the setting for the children's continuing education – and, as at Arundel House, for that of the children of a number of acquaintances (who speedily recognised Isaac Taylor's gifts in that direction), thus providing a welcome source of additional income in difficult times. Isaac Taylor taught, from his high stool, as he worked – or rather he helped his pupils to teach themselves. For instance, before breakfast, when his prayers were complete, he would devote time to drawing maps and anatomical studies, marking and identifying the individual features. He then engraved "blanks" of these drawings without the identifications and printed multiple copies of them. These were bound into books, one for each child, and the children were required to colour the blanks and to fill in the identifications, learning in the process to place Colchester or London on a map, and to distinguish a tibia from a fibula. At other times, one of the children was asked to read aloud, thus allowing the engraving assistants too to acquire other knowledge as they worked.

The curriculum was extensive: history, geography, anatomy, the sciences, current affairs, even fortification. Isaac Taylor's object was *'to give them a taste for every branch of knowledge that [could] well be made the subject of early instruction'*. To illustrate historic voyages and even the campaigns of the Napoleonic wars then in progress, he constructed a revolving cylinder around which he *'strained a large Mercator's chart'* and plotted the voyages and the movements of armies upon it by means of *'pith-headed pins.'* He believed that *'a principal object of education [is] to prevent the formation of a narrow and exclusive taste for particular pursuits, by exciting very early a lively interest in subjects of all kinds;' 'he aimed less to impart those shreds of information, which serve for little except to deck out ignorance with the show of knowledge, than to expand the mind by a general acquaintance with all the more important objects of science.'*

In late 1798, Isaac Taylor began a series of monthly lectures for young people on "scientific subjects", delivered, free of charge, in the parlour of his own house. The subjects covered comprised astronomy, geography, geometry, mechanics, general history and anatomy. These lectures, which were extremely popular and continued for three or four years thereafter, were illustrated by numerous visual aids, in the preparation of which his own children assisted, themselves learning in the process. Jane showed a particular interest in astronomy, as befitted the author of her most famous poem.

Both Ann and Jane continued to write. In this, they received little encouragement from their parents, and particularly from Mrs Taylor, who, despite her own early predilection for versifying, long held female authorship to be a symptom of the neglect of more important pursuits.[30] Early in the Taylors' time in Colchester, Ann was even upbraided, presumably by her mother, for "literary vanity". Mortified, she consigned all her existing manuscripts to the flames, resolving to write no more. But her resolve did not last long. In 1797, for instance, when she was fifteen, she composed an election song in support of the Whig interest in a local election. Although intended only for private reading, it *'happened to be seen, and was speedily printed, a distinction that no doubt I felt as somewhat dazzling.'* In her old age, however, she concluded that it exhibited *'sadly little wit.'*

Once the workroom regime was instituted, the girls' only time for writing (or for any other pursuits, such as regular walks in the summer) was before breakfast or between 8pm and a late supper at nine. However, Ann found ways to make notes of any ideas which occurred to her as she worked, which she developed later as soon as she was free. Indeed, the drafts of some of their early poems were scribbled *'on the margins of engraved plans for fortified towns.'*

In 1798, Ann bought herself a copy of the *Minor's Pocket Book* for that year. This annual, published by Messrs Darton & Harvey, combined the function of a diary and of an annual. It contained, among other things, poems submitted by readers, and competitions to solve enigmas, charades and rebuses, together with the winning entries to the previous year's competitions. Ann decided to try her hand and submitted, under the *non de plume* of "Juvenilia", solutions, in verse as was the convention, to enigma, charade and rebus and six charades of her own. Many months later, when the edition for 1799 came out, she found that the first prize had been awarded to "Juvenilia" and that all her own charades had been printed. From then on, until shortly after her marriage in 1813, she was a regular contributor to the *Minor's Pocket Book*, eventually becoming its editor. But of greater importance to her future and to Jane's was the association formed with Darton & Harvey, who were to publish their early books and thus to help make their literary reputations. Jane's first appearance in print was in the *Minor's Pocket Book* for 1804, a poem entitled *The Beggar Boy*, which won second prize to Ann's first prize for *The Cripple Child's Complaint*, a poem inspired by the lameness of her brother Jefferys.

In the previous year, their brother Isaac, then only fifteen, had submitted a solution to the competition in the form of a poem entitled *Consumption*, which attracted admiring comments from the judges and was awarded a special prize *'in consideration of his uncommon genius.'* This achievement was the more remarkable in that, according to his sister Jemima, Isaac had been regarded as *'the dunce of the family.'* He was, she relates, his mother's only failure in her role as a teacher, and had not learned to read until sent, at the age of about ten, to a dame school in Colchester, where the wife of the church clerk *'hammered it into him'*.[31] It seems that the poor boy may have been dyslexic.

Darton & Harvey, having discovered Ann's identity and her relationship to a highly regarded engraver, were quick to commission from the family small plates to illustrate their books for children. In June 1803, having now[32] seen evidence of great literary promise from two more members of the family, they went further and wrote to the Rev. Isaac Taylor proposing the publication for a young readership of a collection of his children's poems. This bore fruit as *Original Poems for Infant Minds*, which was published early in 1804. It contained twenty poems by Ann, including *My Mother*, twenty by Jane and three the work of the two Isaacs, father and son, together with seventeen poems by Adelaide O'Keefe and one by Bernard Barton (neither of whom had any connection with the Taylors). The book was stated to be by '*Several Young Persons*,' some of the poems being "signed" with initials or Christian names. Initially, the payment to the Taylors was £5, but it sold extremely well, and they soon received a further £5 and, on 19 November 1804, a commission arrived for a second volume, for which £15 was paid. This was published on 22 August 1805 and contained 29 poems by Ann, including *Meddlesome Matty*, 23 by Jane, and a further three by the two Isaacs and sixteen by Adelaide O'Keefe. Although more than fifty editions followed in the next hundred years, it is very rare to find one, even of the later ones, in good condition, since they tended to be read and read until they fell apart. Within a short time of their first publication, the poems had been translated into French, German, Dutch and Russian. Few authors can have enjoyed such a runaway literary success so early in their lives.

Further commissions followed thick and fast, and over the next few years appeared *Rural Scenes* (1805), *City Scenes* (1806), *Rhymes for the Nursery* (1806), which included *The Star* (the proper title of *Twinkle, Twinkle, Little Star*), *The New Cries of London* (1808), *Limed Twigs to Catch Young Birds* (1808) and several other titles. "Ownership" of *The Star* has been claimed by Lavenham and even by Ongar, but there can be little doubt that it was written in Colchester. Had it been written earlier than mid-1805, it would surely have appeared in *Original Poems*, the second volume of which was published in August of that year. *Rhymes for the Nursery* was published on 28 May 1806, which thus suggests a date of composition for *The Star* in the last six months of 1805 or in the first few months of 1806, when Jane Taylor was living in the house in Angel Lane, Colchester. Indeed, it seems a fairly safe conjecture that it was the product of her fondness for studying the night sky from the attic which she had appropriated as her special sanctum. As her brother was to write in his *Memoir*, '*The window commanded a view of the country, and a 'tract of sky' as a field for that nightly soaring of the fancy of which she was so fond,*' and Jane herself told a friend at about this time that her poems were composed in her own study.

The speed at which Ann and Jane had met the original commission from Darton & Harvey in not much more than six months from June 1803 is remarkable in itself, and the more so when one remembers that they were effectively in full-time employment, working at least an 11-hour day including meal-breaks. However, this was but the half of it, for this period coincided with a serious invasion scare, mass panic in Colchester and the temporary break-up of the household in Angel Lane. On 11 October 1803, Jane, then twenty, her brothers Isaac and Jefferys and her young sister Jemima (who had been born on 27 December 1798) were evacuated, in the company of over twenty wives and children of soldiers garrisoned in the town, by heavily laden goods waggon to Lavenham. The journey took eleven and a half hours. Fortunately, Arundel House happened to be without a tenant. Here Jane and Isaac set up a second Taylor household, complete with its own workroom, and here Jane, in between her duties as a surrogate mother and as an engraver, composed many of the poems which appeared in the first volume of *Original Poems*. For the next four months, the family was divided between Colchester and Lavenham, though at the turn of the year Jane swapped places with Mrs Taylor and Ann. On 18 February 1804, the danger being judged to be past, they were all reunited in the house in Angel Lane. And it was not only commissioned verses that were written at this time. Their accustomed correspondence with friends was supplemented by a stream of letters between Colchester and Lavenham, many of which survive, at least in transcript – and they are among the liveliest and most vivid of the entire canon.

The next few years were busy and productive even by the standards of the Taylors, and the children's happiness was clouded only by the deaths in 1804 and 1806 of their four friends, the Stapleton sisters. In 1808, the younger Isaac Taylor fell dangerously ill and, although he recovered, it was the beginning of a long period of recurring ill health and the first of several such crises over the next five or more years. In 1809, Martin Taylor, who was clearly not cut out to be an engraver, left home for London, where he joined a firm of publishers, '*the first breach in our family circle.*' The following year, on 2 January 1810, the younger Isaac also left for London and embarked upon a career as an artist, specialising in designs for engraved book illustrations and portraits, principally miniatures.

On 21 June 1810, the Rev. Isaac Taylor, exasperated by the apparently ineradicable heretical tendencies of many in his congregation,[33] announced his resignation from his pastorate in Colchester. These doctrinal difficulties were of long standing, and he had as long struggled against them, suffering "persecution", his son Isaac tells us, even from his own deacons (a circumstance which was the first step in the younger Isaac's disillusionment with non conformity). However, since the death of his father in 1807 and the sale at last in 1808 of his house in Lavenham (though at a considerable loss), his financial situation had improved. By early 1810, his two elder sons had left home for London and become modestly independent, thus reducing the size of the family for which he had to provide. He may have felt that, financially at least, he and his family could now afford to take the risk of a break with the past even without immediate prospect of a new pastorate, though surviving letters from the younger Isaac show that this was a time of considerable anxiety. Furthermore, Ann's and Jane's literary works were beginning to provide healthy returns, despite the bankruptcy of Thomas Conder,[34] an old friend of the family and the publisher of *The Associate Minstrels* and of *Hymns for Infant Minds*, which both first appeared in 1810. *The Associate Minstrels* (which, like all their work to date, was published anonymously) was written for an adult readership rather than for children and contained poems not only by Ann and Jane, but also by a number of their friends including Josiah Conder, Thomas Conder's nephew. It elicted glowing letters of appreciation from Walter Scott and from Robert Southey. *The Maniac's Song*, one of Ann's contributions, was perhaps her finest poem.

For the time being the family remained in Colchester, and Isaac Taylor seems to

ASPECTS OF THE HISTORY OF ONGAR

have offered his services, or been invited to give them, as an occasional preacher to congregations elsewhere in Essex. On one such occasion in 1811, he had preached at Brentwood. The following day he walked to Ongar.

> 'On coming to an angle in the road, from which the pretty little town is visible within the distance of a field or two, he rested against a gate to look at it, and said to himself, 'Well, I could be content to live and die in that spot'. And so it was to be, he lived and died there; spending more than eighteen years as the assiduous and beloved pastor of its little church. On the 14th of July that year he received a call to the pastorate'.

The houses

The family of the Rev. Isaac Taylor lived in three houses in Ongar, or on its outskirts, all of which are still standing: Castle House, New House Farm and that which is now 10, Castle Street. Only the last of these was owned by Isaac Taylor, the other two being rented. The younger Isaac Taylor lived for forty years, from 1825 until his death in 1865, at Stanforf Rivers House on what is now the A113 just beyond Little End. Josiah Gilbert, the eldest child of the Rev. Isaac Taylor's eldest child Ann, lived in his granfather's household in Ongar from 1819 until his death in 1829. In 1843, he returned to Ongar and rented, and later bought, the large house in Marden Ash called Dyers.

The purpose of the pages that follow is to present some of the contemporary evidence, mostly from the pens of members of the family, for the appearance and character of those houses and of the Taylors' feelings for them. The passages quoted also offer insights into the characters of the Taylors themselves and particularly into their striking sense of place, which was an important aspect of their sense of family. It was of great importance to the members of the family, and especially to Ann Gilbert, to be able to visualize in great detail the physical surroundings of those they loved and from whom they were separated. Verbal descriptions were frequently complemented by detailed plans and even by scale models of rooms. As, for instance, Ann wrote to her parents on their move to Win Lane (Castle Street):

> 'I want exceedingly a catalogue raisonée of your rooms, closets, and conveniences, that I may be able to feel my way pretty well about your new habitation. I have solid satisfaction in thinking of you in it, and airy regrets when I think of the other, – of which, indeed, I do not much like to think'.

And earlier, in writing to Jane, who had, in 1816, visited Rotherham with her brother Isaac before returning to Ongar after their long absence in Ilfracombe and Marazion:

> 'I enjoyed more than I can describe your account of your arrival at Ongar. I only wished to have known the exact time. I always want those little points of circumstance which may enable me to realise with all possible precision. I so enjoy your enjoyment of the sweet spot of which I

have said so often – 'Oh, it is delightful!' for now I can believe in your entire sympathy when I say again – 'Isn't it?"

It is in the nature of the sources that there is more to be quoted, and of greater interest, about some of the houses than about others.

Figure 8 Castle House, a sketch by Jane Taylor in Ann Gilbert's Album.

Castle House

On Saturday, 31 August 1811, the work-room in the house in Angel Lane, Colchester, in which Ann and Jane had for many years assisted their father in his engraving business (and in which the younger Isaac and his brother Jefferys had learned their trade as engravers), was closed up for the last time. The next ten days, Sabbaths excluded, were spent in packing. On Tuesday, 10 September, the waggon carrying the bulk of the family's furniture and effects left for Ongar. Isaac Taylor had preceded it to make arrangements for its reception. The house he had rented was already well over two hundred years old in 1811: Castle House, now and for many years the home of the Buxtons. The following day, the rest of the family – Mrs Taylor, Ann, Jane, Jefferys and Jemima, the cat Nutty and her kitten, '*named 'Pack' by way of memorial'* – set out by laden chaise. Less than two weeks later, Ann gave the following account in a letter to her friend Luck Conder:[35]

> *'And now, follow us, dear Luck, till we turn into the Ongar Road at Chelmsford. It was a fine afternoon; quite new country opening upon us at every step, and expectation, which had begun to doze, was all alive again. Father had directed us how to descry the white steeple of Ongar, and the Castle house and trees, about three miles before we reached it, and this gave us most interesting employment, till, at length, we all*

ASPECTS OF THE HISTORY OF ONGAR

exclaimed, 'There it is!' The road then turned off, and we saw it no more till – O that pleasant moment! – after driving about half way through the town we turned up the lane and round a sharp corner, and the three peaks[36] *and the castle trees appeared in view....The house was built upon the site of the ancient castle, in the reign of Queen Elizabeth, who once honoured it with a visit. The hall-door, studded with clump-headed nails an inch in diameter, measures 6 feet by 4 feet 7. The front is covered by a vine; before it is a flower garden; on the right, as pretty a village church among the trees as you ever saw; and close on the left the castle trees rising upon a high mount, with a moat of deep water encircling it.*[37] *From every window in front we command a rich and beautiful valley, and behind see the town just peeping through a line of elms on a terrace beside an outer moat. Immediately adjacent is a farm-yard, and we have not only the usual live stock of such a scene, but a fine pair of swans, three cygnets, moorfowl, and solan geese upon the moat; rabbits running wild upon the mount; a rookery, wood doves, and, we are told, nightingales in the castle trees. Now, you may fancy, perhaps, that with all this appropriate scenery the house must be haunted, or, at least, hauntable; that there are nooks and vaults, and niches at every turn; and that, sitting as I do now, a broad moon shining in at my window, and the village clock striking eleven, the next thing must be a tall gliding figure patting down the stairs which wind from my room door, within the northern turret. But I assure you we are the picture of cheerfulness and comfort. The rooms are light and pleasant, not in the least ghostly, and fitted up with every modern convenience. We have a hall, two parlours, kitchen, store-room, &c, on the ground floor; three chambers above; and a good workroom, study, two bed-chambers, and a light closet on the attic floor. We had to saw the ivy from the back parlour window before we could see it, but some still remains to fringe the mullions; we have beautiful walks in every direction; and we have placed our garden seat at the end of a retired field, surrounded by the moats and the terrace elms immediately behind the house'.*

The northern turret containing the stairway now exists only at ground floor level, having been largely demolished at some point in the last century before 1874. It is clearly visible in the wash drawing of 1821 by Jane Taylor and in a print of Castle House dated 1832. Curiously, a matching southern turret, visible on the print, is not shown in Jane's picture, which merely shows a wider gable at the south end of the house. Today there is the vestigial stump of a southern turret at ground floor level symmetrical with that of the northern one. It would seem that Jane was simply in error, for Josiah Gilbert, writing in the 1870s as an almost life-long resident of Ongar, says: '*The old house has since been much altered; the two turrets, in one of which was her writing closet, have been pulled down, and the whole has been re-fronted.*'

Ann's room was, at her request, '*on the attic floor commanding a beautiful country view, and having the advantage of a closet where I could sit and write.'* However, although this was the room in which Ann began to write for *The Eclectic Review*[38] – including the first reviews of works of fiction to appear in that periodical – she spent relatively little time at Castle House, and Jane was there even less. The two sisters spent much of the winter of 1811–12 in London at the house of the Conders in Clapton, preparing themselves for an enterprise, urged upon them by friends, *'to take pupils,'* which ultimately proved abortive. On 18 February 1812, they returned to Ongar, as they thought to stay indefinitely.

However, it was not to be. Less than a year earlier, their brother Isaac had again suffered a serious breakdown in his health, brought on (it was thought) by long hours spent on a commission to produce a series of anatomical drawings in a London dissecting room. He had left London for Ongar, exhibiting symptoms which his anxious mother appears to have taken for consumption. According to his sister Jemima, he had in fact *'ruptured a bloodvessel on the lungs.'* Although he seems to have recovered enough to return briefly to London, on 1 July 1811, he had left once more to spend the winter convalescing in the milder air of the West Country and fulfilling some commissions for miniatures from friends who had moved there. In April, he had returned but, at the approach of the winter of 1812, he was advised by his doctors to return to the West Country. It was decided that Ann and Jane should accompany him.[39] On 28 September, they set out via London for Ilfracombe, not returning until 23 July the following year. Jane and Isaac stayed for less than three months before leaving again for Ilfracombe, and later Marazion, in Cornwall, where they remained until June 1816. Nor did Ann stay in Ongar for very much longer. On Christmas Eve 1813, she married the Rev. Joseph Gilbert at the parish church of St Martin in Ongar[40] and, on New Year's Day 1814, after a brief honeymoon in Cambridge, set out with her husband for her new home in Masborough near Rotherham.

Jane had written to Ann on the occasion of her wedding:

> *'I cannot suffer this interesting morning to pass without something of a salutation from Ilfracombe; and I dare say this letter will arrive in good company; but I am sure no one will address you who can feel on this occasion either so glad or so sorry as I do. So far as you only are concerned, I think I am entirely glad, and feel as perfectly satisfied and happy as one can do about untried circumstances. But I cannot forget that this morning, which forms one indissoluble partnership, dissolves another, which we had almost considered so. From the early days of 'Moll and Bett', down to these last times, we have been more inseparable companions than sisters usually are, and our pursuits and interests have been the same....I cannot – no, I cannot realize the busy scene at the Castle House, nor fancy you in your bridal appearance. I intend to place myself before the view of the house, about the time I imagine you will be walking down the gravel-walk, and stand there while you are at the church, and till I think you are coming back again. How strange – how sad that I cannot*

be with you! What a world is this, that its brightest pleasures are, almost invariably, attended with the keenest heart-rendings.'

Although Ann never again made her home in Ongar, she visited it many times during the remainder of her long life. It held a special place in her heart, both as the home of he beloved parents and later of her eldest child Josiah and as one of several places – Lavenham, Colchester, Ongar, Nottingham – in which she herself felt truly at home. The parting from it and from her family had been hard for her to bear – '*one of those bitter pains which we sometimes have to pay for pleasures of an earthly kind'* – and her mother, herself distraught, noted that '*When she was seated in the chaise, her eye roved from window to window of the house, and rested with unspeakable expression on that of her own room'.*

When, in June 1814, Ann visited her parents at the newly occupied Peaked Farm, despite her enthusiasm for the new house, Castle House was by no means forgotten: '*Yesterday Mother and I went over the Castle House, and I could not leave the scene of so many changes without tears. – It was a short but eventful period, and the last family meeting took place there, which is probably for a long time indeed.*[41] *– It is a pretty place.'*

In 1853, shortly after she was widowed, Ann Gilbert stayed for several months at her brother's home in Stanford Rivers and, during this lengthy visit, made a special pilgrimage to the scene of those events forty years ago:

> '*On the day before Christmas, her wedding day, she contrived, at seventy-two, to walk to Ongar alone [from Stanford Rivers], and to do a memorable thing: 'I made my way to the Castle House, then to the church, up one lane, and down the other, and finding the church-door open for Christmas decorations, I went in and stood at the Altar! Very, very strange! Sad, and yet merciful, at the end of forty years, to stand on the same spot, and see everything just as it looked then! To feel myself embosomed in the love of a new generation, near and distant, and to visit the many dear graves, at that time, little thought of...'*".

The move from Castle House to the Peaked Farm

Shortly after Isaac and Jane left for Ilfracombe, their parents received notice to quit Castle House, which was presumably required again by its owner. At the time, this seemed a severe blow, since it was a fine house, which had quickly become a much loved home. However, as so often with the Taylors, good fortune was born of apparent adversity. They had about six months in which to find somewhere else to live, and, in June 1814, they moved to the house which they came to love probably more than any other. New House Farm – almost invariably referred to by the Taylors as The Peaked Farm – is an Elizabethan farmhouse on the Stondon Massey road on the outskirts of Marden Ash. The house was more extensive in the Taylors' time, and they themselves pulled down a barn and removed a farmyard to enlarge the garden. The house survives today, lovingly restored to its full glory by the Padfield family who lived there for almost three quarters of a century.

THE TAYLOR FAMILY OF ONGAR AND THEIR HOUSES THERE

The move, eventful, exhausting and traumatic, was vividly described by Mrs Taylor (in her characteristic eighteenth century orthography, capitalisation and punctuation) in a letter to her absent children in the West Country written a few weeks after the event:

> '...Our moving though to so small a distance has been quite as fatiguing as ye last – I was packing for a week previously nor need I describe to you the confusion we were in – On ye Tuesday morng Mr Slaters waggon arrived at 7 o clock It was loaded at ye back door and a narrow escape of almost utter ruin we had – when <u>all</u> your Father's books and <u>all</u> his copper[42] were in ye shaft horse set off tore up part of the moat railing and had not your Father by the greatest exertion stoped him or had he backed one inch ye Waggon with all its contents & a horse worth 60£ would have plunged into ye moat! What a merciful escape!! The very thought of it filled us with horror – Your Father was at ye house to receive while we remained at ye Castle to send off at noon a second waggon went but your father willing to avail himself of such conveyance worth 3 guineas was disposed to retain it for a third load by bribing ye men – for this I was totally unprepared & the consequence was all our best furniture almost unpacked was torn down and thrown into ye waggon very carelefsly ye men were so anxious to earn extra money that they cared not what they did this with the mistaken notion that as it was such a little way lefs care was requisite did all ye mischief that might have been anticipated The mahogany beaureau[43] & bedstead fell from ye waggon as soon as it was out of ye gate & shatter almost to pieces, a hamper of wine shared ye same fate – 4 bottle of Elder, 1 of parsnip, 2 of raisin, 2 of <u>port</u> and 1 of sherry were broken – not a pair of drawers that was not impaired more or lefs a little packing case of china ware was so shattered that I have not been able to discover what ye fragments once were Add to this sundry [illegible word] aches bruises pinches and scratches on our persons with various tares and rends on our apparel As for me ye first I night which was Wednesday that I slept in ye new house I shall not soon forget A violent cholic seized me just before I went to bed & continued with excruciating agony ye whole night – nothing but ye worn out state of ye family prevented me from calling them all up I think I never was worse & the next day in ye midst of all ye confusion I could only sit over ye fire & look at them – however I am happy to say that we have got tollerably settled already which is surprising considering the time it took us at ye Castle house – We like our situation right well in all respects and so I am sure would you for convenience our situation is certainly much improved and though quite different we are equally pleasant – We have lost poor Pack [44] – We brough him up but he ran back again & must have found his way over ye footbridge though he was brought blinded – We brought him a second time but he again made his excape & after lingering about ye Castle house a few days has totally disappeared and poor fellow is quite lost – I am indeed <u>very</u> sorry – So much for moving – My little study over

the porch is more delightful to me than I can describe – in it I find ye pleasantest retreat from ye world I ever was favoured with – The first time I sat down to enjoy it I actually wept for pleasure...'.

The Peaked Farm

Ann Gilbert was an early visitor to the Peaked Farm, arriving on the evening of 20 June and staying six weeks while her husband was away '*upon an ordination tour in Cumberland and elsewhere.*' She has left not one, but two, detailed accounts of the new house, in letters respectively to her husband and to Isaac and Jane – though they are so similar that it would seem that, although there are unique details in both, she copied wholesale from the former in writing the latter! The letter to Isaac and Jane also describes her journey south from Rotherham by stage coach – she was five months pregnant with the future Josiah Gilbert at the time – and her stay in London which coincided with the state visits of the Tsar of Russia and the King of Prussia. In transcript, it fills five A4 sides of typescript. Yet, almost incredibly, the single demy sheet on which it is written also contains the letter from Ann Taylor quoted above and a meticulous floor plan of the Peaked Farm!

'*At the turning off of the Ingatestone road Jefferys was waiting, and I got out of the coach. – Father met me on the way, and Mother and Jemima were planted at their rural window to watch my approach; – it was very strange to see them in such a new situation; – I hope you clearly understand which is the house, – if not I will try and make you sensible. – It is really exceedingly pleasant and convenient; large, low, farmhouse rooms in abundance, innumerable closets and lumberrooms, and the inhabited part even more convenient, tho' not so well fitted up, as the Castle'. 'The house, newly whitewashed, looked exceedingly pretty among the trees, covered with vine, which clings round the porch, and surrounded by a large countrified garden, laid out, by father's unconquerable contrivance, in the prettiest rural style. There is an arched gateway of yew over the wicket entrance, a fine row of poplars on one side, and fruit and flowers in abundance*'. '*On the ground floor are, the parlour, 18 feet square. – The library, 14 by 15, a very comfortable room, where company can be asked without seeing a trace of the business, and which would on occasion answer the end of another parlour. – a commodious workroom, and what Father calls his <u>cabinet</u>, containing prints, pictures, and everything of that kind. Kitchen, dairy, very comfortable storeroom, and outplaces of all sorts. – Above, Mothers room, large and very pleasant opening into the little study over the porch, which is furnished with all the family pictures, and is her delight. – The spare-room, in which Jemima sleeps, with her closet adjoining, a nice, green, country room. – Jefferys's very rural, and the Servants. – Beside this several others could be fitted up if necessary. It is quite the farm house, but exceedingly pleasant and comfortable, which is a great mercy, considering especially what they have left*'.

One curious article which went with the Taylors from Castle House to the Peaked Farm was a curved altar rail. This had been found surplus to requirement in a local church and bought by Isaac Taylor for £1. It was first positioned by the moat at Castle House, but found a more practical use at the Peaked Farm – as a gate between the garden and the adjoining field. As Mrs Taylor put it in a letter now sadly lost *'the part which used to let the parson in lets us out into the field.'* However, the rail itself has achieved a sort of immortality. It appears in a picture of the Peaked Farm by the Rev. Isaac Taylor now in the Taylor collection at Bury St Edmunds and again in an engraved vignette used as the frontispiece of the eighth edition of Jane Taylor's *Contributions of QQ*.

In mid-August 1816, Jane and Isaac returned at last to Ongar, and Jane saw for the first time with her own eyes the Peaked Farm which she had learned to love through the letters of her parents and of her sister Ann. The homecoming was a fond one:

> *'It was, indeed, a joyful meeting; and when, that evening, we once more knelt around the family altar, I believe our hearts glowed with gratitude to Him who had permitted us thus to assemble in peace and comfort, and had disappointed all our fears. Here we are again in complete retirement; and a sweeter retreat I do not wish for. We are nearly a mile from the town, and surrounded with the green fields. The house is an old-fashioned place, with a pretty garden, which it is the delight of my father and mother to cultivate; at the door is a rural porch, covered with a vine. Here we are rarely interrupted by any one; and, although only twenty miles from the great world of London, we enjoy the most delightful seclusion. The rooms are large and pleasant, and the whole has that rural air which we all so much admire'.*

And looking back in December of the same year:

> *'Oh, what a pleasure it was to be welcomed by kind parents to a home! Nothing could exceed their kindness and indulgence all the time we were there; and after so long an interval, we knew how to value this affection. They thought me not looking well, and it has been my dear mother's constant business to nurse me up during my stay. Our house stands alone in a pretty country: it is an old farmhouse – more picturesque than splendid – and therefore it suits both our tastes and our fortunes. I enjoyed exceedingly the three quiet months we spent there; all my love of nature returned in a scene so well adapted to excite it, and it was delightful to see our dear father and mother enjoying, in their declining years, so peaceful a retreat, and wishing for no other pleasures than their house and garden and their mutual affection afford'.*

In July 1817, Joseph and Ann Gilbert moved from Rotherham to Hull, where Joseph Gilbert had accepted an invitation to be minister to the thriving congregation at the Fish Street Chapel. Almost immediately, Ann began to lay plans for a visit by her parents, using every argument she could find to convince them how cheaply – £2 16s from London to Barton on the south side of the Humber –

and safely it might be done. However, for the moment, her mother's fears of the ferry crossing of the Humber prevailed, and the Gilberts visited Ongar instead – no hardship for Ann indeed, to whom even to think of Ongar was a '*a constant rest to her spirit.*' For five happy weeks in May and June 1818, Ann revelled in the joy of being surrounded by her family again. For good measure, she and Jane took Joseph to see Colchester, the first time they had visited the home of their childhood since they left it in 1811. At the Peaked Farm, a constant stream of improvements was in hand: '*Dear little J[osiah] is much engaged in watching the gardener, and the carpenter, and the bricklayer who has been paving the Hermitage in the shrubbery; and 'Master Wood', who has been clearing out the pond; and the sheep-shearers, who have been busy in the farm-yard.*' Jane and Isaac having by this time returned from Marazion, a visit from their younger brother Martin made it possible that '*we shall once more assemble an entire family at our father's table, and with one pretty sample of a third generation.*'

Figure 9 The Peaked Farm, a water colour sketch by the Rev. Isaac Taylor in Ann Gilbert's Album.

Soon after the Gilberts had returned to Hull (taking Jemima with them for an extended stay), sickness struck the family at the Peaked Farm. In succession, Jane, her father and one of her brothers – it is unclear whether this was Isaac or Jefferys – fell dangerously ill. Even before this, Jane's health had begun to deteriorate. A year earlier she had been diagnosed as suffering from breast cancer, the first symptom of which, '*an induration of the breast,*' had appeared in April 1817. In these circumstances, she concluded, in the autumn of 1818, that she was unlikely to move from Ongar again and allowed herself the indulgence of setting up a study for herself at the Peaked Farm, a room which she came to love as much as any she had had.

THE TAYLOR FAMILY OF ONGAR AND THEIR HOUSES THERE

Jane's cancer and (until the autumn of 1820, the recurring serious illness of her father with rheumatic fever) gave constant cause for concern. But in other respects this period was a golden one for the Taylors, to be compared with the years in Colchester before the two elder sons, Isaac and Martin, left to work in London.

Jane and Isaac were now living at home again. Martin, though resident in London, could reach Ongar in a matter of hours and seems to have been a regular visitor. Even Ann, for whom the journey was a more formidable proposition, spent several weeks at a time in her parents' house as often as she could. Neither Jefferys nor Jemima had yet left home, and Josiah Gilbert, who had come to live with his grandparents in the autumn of 1819, represented the third generation. Josiah, writing many years later, vividly captures the character of the house, of each member of the family and of the relationship between them:

> '...the old house and its inhabitants offered a remarkable spectacle – a literary and artistic workshop. A large, low, wainscotted parlour was the common room for the very lively meals and winter-evening gatherings. At these the father sat in an arm-chair on one side of the fire, the mother on the other, leaning with her hand behind her ear to catch the sounds; Isaac, Jane, Jefferys, Jemima, completed the circle. Some one might then read the latest composition amidst a running fire of comments, – sarcastic from the mother, genial from the father, acute from Jane, sedate, though not without humour, from Isaac, droll from Jefferys; Jemima, the youngest of the circle, joining in with quiet little hits that left their mark. When Ann was of the party, pun and repartee abounded more than ever. The writer well remembers hearing his uncle Jefferys read the 'Tolling Bell' one winter night, the wind roaring in the chimney, and wailing among the tall poplars outside, so that it became quite impossible to go to bed up the black oak creaking staircase, except well accompanied, and with a candle left in the room till sleep should come.
>
> The father's study, furnished with the best English literature, opened from an adjoining passage, and on the other side of the same passage, what was called the "brown room" was entered. This was used for engraving, and was redolent of oil and asphaltum, of aquafortis and copper-plates, but always warm and cosy, and even picturesque, for it was oak pannelled, and the wide mantle-piece displayed elaborate carving. Beyond this, a small room was fitted up as a cabinet for pictures, collected during the long art-life of the father, all of them good, and some carrying well-known names. Upstairs were roomy bedrooms; that of the father and mother opened into a small chamber over the "vine-clad porch", occupied as a study by the latter. Here were collected several family treasures, in the shape of china, books, and miniatures, and here her writing-table stood. Jane's bedroom, smaller than the rest, looked out behind, over the green meadows of the Roding Valley...
>
> Isaac's study...was a strange remote place, approached by dark and

> narrow stairs across the kitchen and a dreary lumber-room. Its one window, high up, opened under the spreading branches of the elm tree, and had scarcely any other prospect. This room was not unpleasantly perfumed with Indian ink, his designs for books being always executed in that delicate pigment. Miniatures were also frequently in hand, and shelves were beginning to be laden with vellum-bound editions of the Fathers; but literary work was always carefully hidden away under lock and key. The "sanctum" of Jefferys was still more out of the way. A range of attics at the top of the house was unused; the floors of some were understood to be dangerous, and one of the huge stacks of chimneys was always regarded with anxiety by the inmates in windy weather. One of these attics, looking towards the west, between the waving poplars, and very rarely intruded upon by any but the owner, belonged to Jefferys, and contained, besides a few books, a turning lathe, and numerous odd bits of machinery; for, like his brother Isaac, he possessed a strong mechanical genius, and here invented a machine for ruling such portions of engraving work as required straight and close lines, which at one time was of much pecuniary advantage to him. Here too, "Harry's Holiday", and "Aesop in Rhyme", were written, with other popular works; fragments of MSS. lay carelessly enough.
>
> Such was the dear old "rabbit-warren", as somebody called it, never long absent from my mother's thoughts in her distant home'.

However, by the time that Josiah Gilbert was writing in the late 1860s, 'The "yew tree", the "vine-leaved porch", half of the gabled peaks, one of the massive chimney-stacks, the surrounding poplars, have all been improved away. The elm tree itself, last remnant of a rookery, has been lopped of its noble arms; and the garden has gone to ruin'.

The Peaked Farm, though in itself an ancient house in which the advantages of history and character had no doubt to be paid for in the coin of a certain amount of inconvenience and discomfort, was not entirely without amenities in the Taylors' time. In 1819, they acquired a "cooking machine", by which, apparently, was meant a kitchen range. In a letter to Ann Gilbert, Mrs Taylor devotes a lengthy and enthusiastic postscript to it:

> 'I wish you could see our cooking machine it is an unspeakable comfort and enables us to make a great improvement in our table by a variety of dishes (at a distance as we are from ye bakers)[45] which we could not [sc. otherwise] have. The top is completely enclosed and ye pots and kettles stand on ye iron plate and boil ye same as on a fire There is a copper with water always hot an excellent oven and ye fire can be wound up[46] to ye depth of only a few inches – Martin is so interested that when he is here he does not know how to leave ye kitchen. My brother who is used to see such things says it is ye most complete apparatus he ever say – We had it a bargain – only twelve guineas'.

THE TAYLOR FAMILY OF ONGAR AND THEIR HOUSES THERE

Win Lane (10, Castle Street)

At about this time, the Taylors' landlord, Capel Cure Esq. of Blake Hall, gave notice that he wished to repossess the Peaked Farm in order to let the farm again as a unit with its farm-house. The exact order of events is problematical. A letter from Ann Gilbert to her father in late January 1822 refers to the notice to quit in terms which seem to suggest that it was recent news. The letter also makes it clear that the Taylors' departure from the Peaked Farm had not by then taken place, which is corroborated by an annotation by Ann Gilbert to a watercolour of the house in her Album by her brother Isaac, which reads *'Entered June 1814, quitted May 1822.'* However, the accounts of the Blake Hall estate show that the farm was let at Michaelmas 1821 to a former tenant by the name of Hadsel(e)y at an annual rent of £185 10s. As part of the tenancy agreement, he was allowed £222, together with the use of materials to be salvaged from demolition of part of the farm-house, towards the cost of carrying out repairs to the rest of the house. There seems good reason to conclude that the Taylors' move from the Peaked Farm did not take place until May 1822. It is strange, if the tenancy passed to Hadseley at Michaelmas 1821, that Ann should not have been aware almost immediately that her parents' days in the house were numbered.

In the letter referred to above, nostalgic regret characteristically vying with optimism and practical good sense, Ann wrote:

> *'As to Ongar, and all that is dear to me in it, I do not know how to think, and, of course, not how to speak of it. It seems to me a sort of dream that you are going to leave the house, and how to think of you in the course of a few months I cannot tell. Yet Providence has always favoured your particular tastes, and allowed you something better than brick and mortar to look at, and I hope you may be equally favoured now. It will be in some respects no disadvantage to have both house and garden on a smaller scale, and if a little more air-tight within doors, so much the better also, – and then there are the chimnies! So that it may happen, as when you left the Castle, that you will not really regret the change, though the parting must be painful. Oh, that 'low white porch where the vine leaves cling'! I shall never forget it'.*

It proved difficult to find another house, but eventually Isaac Taylor purchased one in what was then apparently called Win Lane[47] *'on the outskirts of the town'*. The house is now 10, Castle Street. The younger Isaac Taylor described it as *'altogether more commodious,'* by which presumably he meant convenient rather than spacious. Though quite substantial by modern standards, it is, of course, very much smaller even than New House Farm as it stands today. It had *'some pleasant views from the upstairs windows'* – among which was one which included the Independent meeting house and its burial ground – but *'a sadly small plot of garden attached.' 'Mr Taylor built a study, and a cabinet for his pictures, adapted an outbuilding for his "brown room" and did wonders with the garden'*.

ASPECTS OF THE HISTORY OF ONGAR

He also contributed a wash drawing of the house to Ann Gilbert's Album, which clearly shows that the '*sadly small plot of garden*' was very much larger, in an easterly direction, than that which survives today. Several years later, Isaac Taylor was still making improvements. In 1826, his jobbing builder, Richard Noble, was employed to sink and brick a new cesspool for the privy and to improve and deepen the well; the following year he rebuilt a chimney and '*put a block to the statue*'. He was also regularly employed for miscellaneous tasks of maintenance, including clearing out the privy – £1 4s 4d for '*labour, candles, liquor, etc*' – and '*stink-traps*' and even taking down and rehanging curtains.

Figure 10   10 Castle Street, a water colour sketch by the Rev. Isaac Taylor in Ann Gilbert's Album.

Isaac Taylor's response to misfortune or disappointment was to busy himself with practical matters and to seek opportunities to turn his new circumstances to good effect. For Jane, however, ill as she was, the move from the Peaked Farm seems almost to have symbolised the extinction of earthly hopes, including that for her own survival. Her brother Isaac concluded that '*it evidently increased the depression of her spirits; and thus hastened the progress of her disorder.*' Her younger sister Jemima wrote many years later: '*From 1822 we lived in that more compact house in Ongar – far better suited to my parents in their declining years, but beside that the garden was small & the situation, comparatively, townified – a feeling of melancholy attaches to it, for Aunt Jane's health declined from the time we entered it...*'. By the end of 1823, the cancer had spread from her breast to her lungs, though she seems to have suffered surprisingly little pain. By the following spring, she was so weak that her brother Isaac had to carry her, morning and evening, from her bedroom to the parlour and back again. On 13 April 1824, at a little after half past five in the afternoon, in her bedroom overlooking Win Lane, Jane Taylor died.

Her body was interred on 20 April in the burial-ground of the chapel at Ongar. Ann, who, alerted by a letter from Isaac, had hurried south too late, described the occasion in a letter to her daughter Anne:

> 'Yesterday morning the coffin was brought down into uncle Isaac's study, and after breakfast we all went in to look at her for the last time....At twelve o'clock we began to move to the chapel, which is very near. First the coffin, then grandpapa and I, then uncle Isaac and aunt Jemima, then uncle Martin and uncle Jefferys, and then papa and J[osiah]. She lies close by a tall poplar near the vestry door, and poor grandmama was at one of the back windows here, and could see her let down into the grave. There is only one garden and one field between. Though we all grieve very much, yet we are all comforted and thankful to think of the goodness of God towards her. She was in her life kind, tender, active, generous, and always anxious to be useful to others. She was willing to deny herself of everything, and was never so happy as when she was doing a kindness to her brothers and sisters. Above all, she feared God from her youth, and did not leave that great work till she came to die'.

The spot by the poplar tree near the vestry door now lies under the vestry floor of the new building. The grave-stone may still be seen by lifting a trap-door. The inscription reads: *'Beneath this stone lie the mortal remains of Jane Taylor second daughter of the Rev. Isaac Taylor. She died April 13th 1824 in the fortieth year of her age. 'Let her works praise her'*.

Three years later, Ann, still in mourning for the death of her fourth child Edward, visited Ongar again:

> 'In July of this year, 1827, Mrs Gilbert, with two of her boys, paid what was destined to be the last visit to her mother and father at Ongar....At Ongar, this once more, stood her father's genial portly figure, now touching his 70th year, his cheek ruddy with apple tints; no Jane was at his side, but Ann had once remarked 'it is not my custom to bury living pleasures in the graves of dead ones', and so she wrote: 'I, just now, feel myself as happy as the scene that surrounds me is beautiful – the little house in trim order, the evening exceedingly fine, and the green slopes and trees, seen from my bedroom window, looking quite lovely'. From that chamber,[48] she could see the venerable chimneys of the old 'peaked farm', the 'chase-way' to the Castle-house of earlier memory, and the white glimmer among the trees of Jane Taylor's tombstone'.

Less than eighteen months later, the Rev. Isaac Taylor was dead. On the afternoon of Wednesday 9 December, he suddenly found it difficult to breathe. At about 9am on the Saturday morning, 12 December, in his bedroom looking eastwards over what was then the garden, he died. Again, Ann Gilbert describes the funeral in a letter to her children in Nottingham:

ASPECTS OF THE HISTORY OF ONGAR

> 'On the following Saturday, at twelve o'clock, the funeral took place; six ministers attended as pall-bearers. All the congregation who could leave their homes, all the young people, and the children of the Sunday schools, in black ribbons, followed....He lies in a new, deep grave, by the side of aunt Jane. Aunt Isaac [i.e. Elizabeth Taylor, wife of Ann's brother Isaac] stayed with grandmamma, who would see the funeral leave the house, and watched it from what was aunt Jane's window, as far as she could see. They then waited to see it in the Meeting-yard, from the other side of the house, but the sun shone so brightly on the mist, that after an hour's waiting, all they could see – and grandmamma did not even see that – was, for one moment, the white edge of the pall, as it was drawn from the coffin'.

The coffin and the grave are described in the account books of Richard Noble, who clearly also acted as the local undertaker and sexton (and whose arithmetic is hard to follow!):

> 'A stout elm shell with fine flannel lining and Ruffles fine quilted Bed flannel sheet pillow and depositing the body 3s 10d.
>
> A stout elm coffin covered with fine black cloth Embellished with treble row of black nails four pair of large Cherub handles chased plate of inscription gloria & so on £7
>
> Sinking and bricking the grave filling in and leavelling the ground over. £3.1s.0d
>
> Materials labour Beer & eating for men arching over grave pall-bearing & miscellaneous
>
> Total 24.8s.5d
>
> Settled by cash of Mr Isaac Taylor'.

A few months later, Mrs Ann Taylor too was dead. She died, in her bedroom on the south side of the house, on 27 May 1830, and was buried beside her husband and daughter. Her funeral, which took place on 4 June, was slightly less costly at £19 12s 4d.

> 'With that death the household at Ongar was finally broken up. All the memorials of a family life, artistic and literary, of more than fifty years, –furniture of the first home at Islington, relics from Lavenham and Colchester, family portraits, drawings and paintings of home scenes and people, inumerable educational contrivances of the busy, benevolent father, – all were mournfully divided...'

Stanford Rivers House

Shortly after the death of his sister Jane, the younger Isaac Taylor became engaged to Elizabeth Medland. On the death of her mother some years earlier, Elizabeth had, with her brothers and sisters, become a particular protégé of Jane's – and the recipient of long letters of earnest moral exhortation. (Elizabeth's father, James Medland of Newington, had proposed to Jane in 1821, but, although she at first accepted, she almost immediately, and to the great sadness of both parties, broke the engagement on account of her declining health. James Medland himself died in June 1823.) In preparation for his marriage, which took place on 17 August 1825, Isaac Taylor bought Stanford Rivers House.

In a letter of 21 July 1825 to his wife Ann, the Rev. Joseph Gilbert wrote:

> 'A most pleasant ride brought me to Stanford Rivers; there I was arrested in my journey by Isaac, Jemima, and J[osiah], and after looking round the delightful domain of your brother, came here by a pleasant footpath to sleep. Isaac is really situated just as I have always thought I should like to be: the house neat, commodious, comfortable, pleasantly surrounded with clean gravel walks, grass plots, roses, fruit – everything that is 'pleasant to the eye and good for food'. It is just what one would like to take a simple-hearted, tender, good-tempered, cheerful, kind, contented young bride to. They are to be happy in less than a month'.

The short memoir of Isaac Taylor included by his son Isaac in *The Family Pen* contains the following passage:

> 'In preparation for his marriage, Mr Taylor had established himself at Stanford Rivers, a secluded country village, distant some two miles from his father's residence at Ongar. This house at Stanford Rivers, which was to be the scene of his literary labours, and of his silent meditations for more than forty years, was not unfitted for the retreat of a literary recluse. It was a rambling, old-fashioned farmhouse, standing in a large garden. It commanded a somewhat extensive view of the numerous shaws, the well-timbered hedge-rows, and the undulating pasturages, which are characteristic of that part of Essex; while at a distance of some half-mile from the house the little river Roden [sic] meanders through the broad meadows. The house was speedily adapted to its new purposes; barns, and other farm outbuildings, were pulled down, the garden was replanted and laid out afresh, with a characteristic provision of spacious gravel-walks for meditative purposes'.

Isaac's sister Jemima, who became Mrs Thomas Herbert, recollected the newly married couple's arrival at Stanford Rivers in a letter written to her niece Jane in 1869:

> 'I well remember the bright summer evening in August on which I walked up and down the shrubbery watching for the first glimpse of the carriage which brought him & his young and happy bride to their home! From that time to the death of my dear Parents, visits to the bright Stanford Rivers home were a frequently recurring treat to all of us. It was a great solace to his parents to see him thus surrounded by so much that constitutes earthly happiness, & the love & companionship of your Mother – as well

> as your Father – was to me a great boon, while their continual visits to us at Ongar enlivened many a quiet hour...'

Josiah Gilbert thus described a visit by his mother to Ongar in 1827:

> 'This time it was not only at the last hill hiding the view of Ongar that my mother's heart began to beat with happy expectation; for now, two miles earlier on the road [from London], at Stanford Rivers, her brother Isaac and his charming young wife were at their garden gate to welcome her, and the coach, in the leisurely neighbourliness of those days, pulled up for a few minutes to accommodate them. He had been married nearly two years, and was settled in the simple old house with its large garden, and no other view than that of woods and fields, which has ever since been associated with his name. Here for forty years he accumulated his 'Patristic' folios, and wrote the works which gave him his high place in literature. Here, to seek 'the recluse of Stanford Rivers', came one and another of the band of thinkers he had gathered round him in England, Scotland, and America....For all the years that followed, Stanford Rivers was another heart-centre to that sister's thoughts'.

After the death of Mrs Ann Taylor and the breaking up of the household in Win Lane, Jemima Taylor at first went to live with her brother Isaac, as reported by Josiah Gilbert:

> 'A pretty attic at Stanford Rivers was fitted up as a temporary residence for this bereaved one, and her sister [i.e. Ann Gilbert] rejoiced that it was so exactly the counterpart of 'dear Jane's at Colchester'. A country attic, with sloping ceilings, small-paned dormer windows, near neighbourhood of birds and trees, and out-of-the-wayness from the bustle of the house, had always special charms for the members of this family; and each could look back to the particular attic that, at some period of life, had been a much loved refuge'.

Or as Jemima herself remembered it in her old age:

> 'Late one evening in August I left my Father's house, with a desolate and sorrowful heart. The full moon was just rising in the east as my brother drove me to his own home. There I had a tender, loving welcome from your dear Mother. A little attic had been fitted up for me, with a pretty view across the road & fields, & everything around looked cheerful & soothing. I lived there a year & during that to me sorrowful time, the loving affection & unselfish kindness of both your dear Parents were more precious to me than I can express...'[49]

We also have a description of the house and household at Stanford Rivers from someone who was not a family member. Mrs Staffen, the sister of Jean Ingelow, a minor poet and family friend of the Isaac Taylors, recalls in a memoir of her sister published in 1901 a visit of her own, apparently in the mid to late 1840s:

THE TAYLOR FAMILY OF ONGAR AND THEIR HOUSES THERE

'The Taylors' house at Stanford Rivers was a delightful one to visit. The keenly intellectual father, the beautiful mother, the large family of young people, full of variety, yet much alike, in that one and all they were enthusiastic [50] and romantic in their attachment to and admiration of their friends, formed a group at once unworldly and fascinating. In that house, Jean must have found much that was congenial in both generations. Mrs Taylor, without being, perhaps, more intelligent than many other cultivated women, had the art of throwing a halo over all her surroundings which I have never seen equalled – for I, too, 'have dwelt in Arcadia' when I was a visitor at Stanford Rivers.... One was made to feel, and that without an effort, that everything was touching and home-like and delightful; and yet the house was neither large nor handsome, the garden was not half so pretty as many one might see, the children were not all equally gifted or companionable, the amusements were few, and of gaieties there were none. Yet when you sat on the couch behind a tiny table in the small drawing-room at six o'clock tea, the family seated round the large table in the middle of the room – Jane, the eldest daughter, presiding at the urn, and you, the favoured guest, allowed to share the sofa with Mrs Taylor; perhaps the youngest child, the little Euphemia, tucked into a corner of the said sofa, with its somewhat faded chintz cover – you felt that you were privileged beyond the ordinary run of mortals. I can see Mrs Taylor now, in her pretty lilac-silk gown, and her dainty cap with its pink ribbons; the little table you shared with her, while some young member of the family handed you tea and muffins or bread and butter. All seemed to admire everything and everybody. But it was Mrs Taylor who did it; it was she who cast the glamour over ordinary surroundings. Then the lovely walks to Epping Forest, Navestock, and Ongar were all within easy reach of Stanford Rivers'.

Finally, in 1853, the recently widowed Ann Gilbert responded again to the charm of Stanford Rivers and of her beloved Ongar:

'How beautiful everything looks! It is hard to decide between winter and summer months under a bright sun; each has its loveliness. Stripped as the trees now are, there is so much variety of pencilling – so much evergreen, such sweeps, and fingers of gold and brown, and such brilliancy in the white frosts, that on the whole, we have beauty everywhere, even now. You cannot think how much I enjoy my temporary residence once more, near Ongar. The pretty little town is, almost to a brick, the same as it was forty years ago. Door-plates are altered, and there a few new buildings, but the general appearance is the same...'

Marden Ash

The house chosen by Josiah Gilbert when he returned to Ongar in 1843 was an old one. It dates from 1556, though it has been enlarged more than once since and a façade was added in the mid-eighteenth century. In the sixteenth century, as today, it was known as Dyers. Josiah Gilbert, however, seems not to have used the name: in family correspondence and in Susan Gilbert's diaries, it is referred to simply as "Marden Ash", which was also the address on Josiah Gilbert's own writing-paper.

Ann Gilbert, although she appears to have been in two minds, before the decision was made, about the wisdom of Josiah's becoming involved in the development of her brother Isaac's invention, had no doubts about the desirability of the move to Ongar which it involved. The house quickly won a place in her affections alongside the other family houses in Ongar. As Josiah himself recalled:

> *'But perhaps the removal of her eldest son from London to the country was even more interesting to her, for it was to Ongar that he came. Near the 'three wants-way', where visitors for the old Peaked Farm used to leave the coach, and which, marked by an ash tree in the middle, was named Marden Ash, stood a house well bowered in trees. There he made his home, and it became a favourite haunt of her's for many years. Nor was the cause of the removal less interesting to her, since it was the association of her son with her brother Isaac, in the artistic management of his remarkable invention, for applying mechanism to the delicate and complex processes of line-engraving'.*

Josiah appears to have made the decision to move before finally deciding to accept Isaac Taylor's invitation. At this point, Ann Gilbert wrote:

> *'My thoughts, when free from the anxiety of indecision, and dwelling only on your present, and, to me, pleasant location, feel to breathe a freer air, and to be tinted with brighter colours than when they hovered over you in London; and to you, whose early and happy home it was, I think it must be full of delightful interest. But, oh, the final yea or nay! I do dread it.*
>
> *Do not be afraid of death from suffocation from those beautiful trees. You will get to love them; and how sweet they are, with the winds and the birds, and the flowers, and the grass plots, and all the lovely items of a country garden – that one earthly good which I have coveted all my life, and do not possess! Think of turning out on to your own gravel walks before breakfast, and bringing in a fresh radish to help your appetite, if then needing help! But these radishes will make me poetical, and I must forbear. I cannot express my astonishment and admiration, knowing as I do what engraving is, at the effects you describe. Nothing in modern invention seems to me more marvellous'.*

Susan Gilbert, in her diaries for 1843, gives a laconic and more prosaic account of the move itself:

> *Sunday, 24 September. 'The last Sunday we spent in Berners Street, felt rather melancholy about it. Went to Craven*[51] *in the morning & staid at home in the evening packed a little & Josiah wrote to his Mama'.*

THE TAYLOR FAMILY OF ONGAR AND THEIR HOUSES THERE

Monday, 25 September. 'Rose early and packed all day till 3 o'clock when we all set off by coach for Stanford [Rivers] very heavy shower for the packing got in to tea found Mrs Hay [52] at the Taylors'.

Tuesday, 26 September. 'Josiah went directly after breakfast to Marden Ash I followed with Lucy [53] & joined the furniture vans with Martins, [54] went back to Mr Taylor's & dined early returned in the afternoon to see the furniture unpacked'.

Wednesday, 27 September. 'Very cold went with Josiah to Marden Ash & remained till dinner time 4 o'clock Mrs Cecil [55] called to see us at our new house unpacked and put away as much as we could very cold'.

Friday, 6 October. 'rather wet & showery Josiah went to the house I remained at home for a rest he returned to dinner & Mr Taylor drove us out by moonlight to take possession and sleep for the first time at our new residence'.

Saturday, 7 October. 'My dear husband's birthday spent in thorough hard work getting things straight hanging pictures etc Martins left in the afternoon. J Taylor [56] poorly with erysipelas'.

Sunday, 8 October. 'Showers All went to Chapel dined early & went again in the Afternoon no service in the evening Josiah read to me and wrote home'.

Monday, 9 October. 'Very wet morning Josiah began regular work [57] leaving at 9 in the morning returned to dinner at 4 began 'Evelina' [58] in the evening'.

Tuesday, 10 October. 'Showery. Lucy & I went in the chaise to the Chapel house and walked home with Josiah. Mrs Taylor & Rosa [59] called Josiah & Mr Taylor went to the book meeting'.[60]

Wednesday, 11 October. 'Very wet morning. Josiah stayed till 12 putting up pictures etc. Lucy broke my watch'.

Author's acknowledgements

The help and encouragement received by the author over the last nine years has been extraordinary, not only for its unfailing generosity, but also for the range of people who have given it. Amongst those who have welcomed me as a perfect stranger into their houses (associated with the Taylors) are Neil and Mary Clayton, Tim and Gilli Pitt, Cecil and Pat Halliday and Joy Donnelly; and in Ongar, Paul and Margaret Buxton, Andrew and Maureen Morrison, and Nicholas and Bronwen Raine. Warm thanks are due to family members, including John Taylor, David Taylor, Veronica O'Neal and Clare Wilson (whose Wilson forebears[61] are also closely associated with Ongar). Others who have given invaluable help include: staff of the record offices, archives, libraries, museums and art galleries mentioned in the sources below, and of the Worcester Record Office; Mr Alan Bell, Librarian of the London Library; Mr A. V. Griffiths of the Dept of Prints & Drawings, British Museum; the late Cliff Hardy; Bruce Neville; James Hodsdon; Claire Lamont; Dana Tenny; and, above all, Christina Duff Stewart. Last, but far from least, are my friends from the United Reformed Church in Ongar, Jean Easter, Rodney Kinzett and Marie Korf; and our editor, Michael Leach. To all these I am sincerely grateful.

Sources

The primary sources for the Taylor family are unusually rich and prolific. They were, amongst their many other accomplishments, a family of writers and a family which placed a high value on family relationships. As a result, as well as the usual sources such as wills and parish registers, there are several published accounts, written by members of the family, of their own lives and of the lives of family members whom they knew well, some of which include information about the early history of the family. These accounts, based in part upon contemporary notebooks, diaries and letters, include many precise details of events, and a considerable amount of circumstantial detail about places, people and family life.

What is more, the Taylors were great letter-writers, and hundreds of their letters survive, containing, as well as more high flown passages about literature and religion and occasional references to public events, a great deal of contemporary news, much of it extraordinarily detailed and precise. Ann Gilbert, the Rev. Isaac Taylor's eldest daughter, also kept an Album[62] (see also FAAG below) throughout most of her married life, in which family events were recorded and in which visitors to the Gilbert household were invited to contribute poems, drawings and other mementoes.

The Taylors (and the Rev. Isaac Taylor's grandson, Josiah Gilbert) were also artists. Many portraits survive of family members by family members (and a few by other artists) and several contemporary pictures of the houses in which they lived. We also have a detailed floor plan by Ann Gilbert née Taylor of New House Farm (the Peaked Farm) showing what each room was used for, and by whom. Inserted in the back of Ann Gilbert's Album (which also contains drawings of the exterior of several Taylor houses, and of the chapel in Ongar in which they worshipped) are two detailed three dimensional models. One is of the parlour of the house on the quay at Ilfracombe where Ann, Jane and Isaac lived for a time, and the other of the newly married Ann Gilbert's parlour in Masborough (always spelt Masboro' by the Taylors) near Rotherham.

The formal details of all these sources are given below.

THE TAYLOR FAMILY OF ONGAR AND THEIR HOUSES THERE

Published sources

1) *BMIT*: *A Biographical Memoir of the late Isaac Taylor, engraver, F.S.A. etc.*, a part of *RCAE*: *Recollections of the circumstances connected with the art of engraving etc.* by (anonymously) Charles Taylor in *TLP*: *The Literary Panorama*, vol 3 (London, March 1808) pp. 588–594 and vol 4 (London 1808) pp. 809–816. This is the principal source for the early history of the family, and provides important information on engraving in the eighteenth century.

2) *MCT*: *Memoir of the late Mr Charles Taylor* by Isaac Taylor (1787–1865), a preface to *CDB Calmet's Dictionary of the Bible* ed. Charles Taylor, 6th edition (1837). This complements and supplements information in *FP* below.

3) *MBLTF*: *The Family Pen, Memorials, Biographical and Literary, of the Taylor Family of Ongar* vol 1, (London, 1867) edited by Isaac Taylor (1829–1901). This contains

   a) *FP*: *The Family Pen* by Isaac Taylor (1787–1865) first printed in *Good Words* in 1864, a substantial essay on the literary achievements of various members of the family. Important for unique biographical details of Charles Taylor.

   b) *LIT*: *The Late Isaac Taylor* by Isaac Taylor (1829–1901), a short biographical sketch of Isaac Taylor of Stanford Rivers by his son.

   c) *MCJT*: *Memoirs and Correspondence of Jane Taylor* by Isaac Taylor (1787–1865) has a short history of Jane Taylor's ancestors (*MBLTF* pp. 80–84), but is mainly a revised and recast version of:

4) *MPRJT*: *Memoirs and Poetical remains of the late Jane Taylor with extracts from her Correspondence* (London,1825) by Isaac Taylor (1787–1865). Written to preserve the memory, particularly the pious memory, of the author's sister. Jane's letters and her mother's are extensively quoted but the latter (less numerous, but full of lively observation) are generally a richer source of historical and anecdotal detail.

5) *AOMMG*: *Autobiography and other Memorials of Mrs Gilbert (formerly Ann Taylor)*, edited by Josiah Gilbert (2 volumes, London, 1874). This work consists of an Introductory Note by Josiah Gilbert (giving a few brief details of the early history of the family, culled, he says, from notes compiled by the Rev. Isaac Taylor) and of two main parts:

   a) an autobiographical memoir by Ann Gilbert, written in old age, drawing on contemporary letters and her own "pocket books". It deals briefly with her parents' upbringing, and very fully with the family in her own lifetime up to just before her marriage in 1813. The preface suggests that it was edited by Josiah, but it is not clear to what extent. He added footnotes, some of which contain unique information. The whereabouts of the pocket books, if they have survived, is not known.

   b) an account by Josiah Gilbert of the remainder of his mother's life, which draws extensively upon family correspondence.

6) *FAAG*: *The Family Album of Mrs Ann Gilbert*, published as *ATGA*: *Ann Taylor Gilbert's Album*[62] edited by Christina Duff Stewart[64] (Garland Publishing, London & New York, 1978). The published version has black and white photographic reproductions of all the completed pages of the Album, with an introduction and extensive notes and indexes by Miss Stewart.

7) *PTO*: *Pedigree of the Taylors of Ongar,* compiled by Henry Taylor[65] (1837–1916), privately printed by him in 1895. A version of this, fallibly extended to include later descendants, is displayed in the Taylor Room at Lavenham.

8) *TTO*: *The Taylors of Ongar, Portrait of an English Family of the Eighteenth and Nineteenth Centuries drawn from Family Records by the Great-great niece of Ann & Jane Taylor* by Doris Mary Armitage[66] (Cambridge, 1939). The standard modern account and entertainingly written, but heavily dependent on previously published accounts. It rarely adequately identifies its sources.

9) *ABB*: *The Taylors of Ongar: An Analytical Bio-Bibliography,* 2 volumes, by Christina Duff Stewart[64] (Garland Publishing, London & New York, 1975). This monumental work of scholarship seeks to describe in detail every published work (including contributions to periodicals) by the immediate family of Rev. Isaac Taylor (excluding the scholarly works of Isaac Taylor of Stanford Rivers) and indicates where copies may be found. There is also information on published drawings and engravings and their whereabouts, on unpublished letters and other manuscripts, on books and articles about the Taylors, and on nineteenth century booksellers and printers associated with the Taylors' published works.

ASPECTS OF THE HISTORY OF ONGAR

10) *DNB*: *Dictionary of National Biography* on various members of the family. Heavily dependent on other published material, these articles are now being re-written for the new edition.

Unpublished sources

1) the extensive collection of letters, paintings, drawings, engravings and other Taylor memorabilia amassed by Henry Taylor[65] (1837–1916); inherited by his daughter Ursula Gertrude Taylor (1879–1969), who donated items to Colchester in 1929; those at Bury St Edmunds and Lavenham were donated by her nephew, David Harold Leigh Taylor (b. 1920). The collection is now divided between:
   a) the Taylor Collection: Suffolk Record Office at Bury St Edmunds: HD/588
   b) the Taylor Room in the Guildhall at Lavenham which also has other items donated or lent by other Taylor descendants
   c) the Museum Resource Centre at Colchester
   d) descendants of Henry Taylor.
2) a collection of letters, pictures and other Taylor memorabilia (including *FAAG*) presented, together with many early editions of books by the Taylors, to the Osborne Collection of Children's Literature in the Toronto Public Library by the Taylors' bibliographer, Christina Duff Stewart.[64]
3) diaries of Susan Gilbert née Green (1809–1871). The diaries, which are laconic in style and rather repetitive, cover 1841 to 1866, with gaps from 1847–1850 and 1853–1856: Essex Record Office: D/DU 1545/1–18
4) account book of Richard Noble, builder. Essex Record Office: D/DU 413/1
5) material relating to Ann Gilbert (née Taylor) & her husband Rev. Joseph Gilbert in Nottinghamshire Archives, Nottingham County Library, University of Nottingham Library and the Brian O'Malley Central Library at Rotherham.
6) Ann Gilbert's commonplace book, into which she transcribed verses written for each member of her family every Christmas between 1856 & 1862: Alexander Turnbull Library, Wellington, New Zealand.
7) minute books and other records of the Incorporated Society of Artists of Great Britain: Royal Academy archives: SA/ -
8) registers & meeting books: United Reformed Church, Ongar.
9) letters and other material owned by various descendants of the Taylor family, including the author of this chapter.

Portraits of the Taylors and Gilberts (accessible to the public, some by appointment only)

1) portrait in oils of Ann & Jane Taylor as girls in garden at Lavenham (rest of family in background) by the Rev. Isaac Taylor (1791 or 1793): Bath Preservation Trust, Bath (on loan from National Portrait Gallery)
2) sketchbooks of the Rev. Isaac Taylor with portraits of Mrs Ann Taylor, Ann & Jane Taylor (as young girls), Isaac Taylor of Stanford Rivers and Martin Taylor (as babies): Suffolk Record Office (SRO): HD 588/4/30
3) pastel portrait of Mrs Isaac Taylor of Stanford Rivers and pencil sketches of her & her husband by Josiah Gilbert: SRO: HD 588/12/27, 23 &24
4) pencil & ink sketch of his wife to be, Elizabeth Medland, by Isaac Taylor of Stanford Rivers: SRO: HD 588/12/25
5) silhouettes & outline sketches (probably by Isaac Taylor of Stanford Rivers) of Ann, Jane, Martin & Jefferys Taylor: SRO; HD 588/12/55, 60, 58, 57 & 62
6) numerous photos, & copies of portrait prints, of members of the family: SRO
7) portrait in oils of Isaac Taylor of Stanford Rivers (in early middle age) by Josiah Gilbert: Museum Resource Centre, Colchester
8) self portrait in oils, & portrait in oils of his wife Sarah by Isaac Taylor (1730–1807): Taylor Room, Lavenham Guildhall (TR)
9) portrait of Mary Hewitt (formerly Mrs Martin née Plaxton), mother of Mrs Ann Taylor: TR
10) portrait of Mrs Ann Taylor by the Rev. Isaac Taylor (c. 1790): TR
11) sketch of his daughter Ann by the Rev. Isaac Taylor: TR

THE TAYLOR FAMILY OF ONGAR AND THEIR HOUSES THERE

12) miniature of Jane Taylor by Isaac Taylor of Stanford Rivers: TR
13) miniatures of Mrs Ann Taylor (in old age), the Rev. Joseph Gilbert (in early middle age), Mrs Ann Gilbert (as a young woman) and Jemima Taylor: TR
14) portrait of Isaac Taylor of Stanford Rivers by Josiah Gilbert (1854): TR
15) portraits of Mrs Isaac Taylor of Stanford Rivers by Josiah Gilbert (1844 or 1845) & by her husband: TR
16) miniature of the Rev. Isaac Taylor, probably a self portrait: TR
17) charcoal portrait, alleged to be of Jane Taylor (but dated 1831 & identification very doubtful): National Portrait Gallery (NPG) Archives, London
18) Isaac Taylor of Stanford Rivers by Josiah Gilbert (copy made by JG in 1890 from his own crayon drawing of 1862): NPG
19) the Rev. Joseph Gilbert by W. Gauci: Nottingham Castle Museum & Art Gallery (NCM)
20) Mrs Ann Gilbert by Josiah Gilbert: NCM
21) portraits of Josiah Gilbert by Rev. Isaac Taylor and by Sylvanus Redgate (1827–1907): NCM
22) many Alpine landscapes by Josiah Gilbert: NCM
23) portrait of the Rev. Joseph Gilbert in old age, probably by Josiah Gilbert: Nottingham County Library (NCL)
24) portrait of Mrs Ann Gilbert in late middle age: NCL
25) photos of Isaac Taylor of Stanford Rivers, Josiah Gilbert, and a copy of a detail of (1) above: Ongar United Reformed Church
26) copy (?contemporary) in oils of (1) above: Osborne Collection, Toronto Public Library, Canada (OC)
27) pastel portrait of Mrs Ann Gilbert by Josiah Gilbert (1855): OC
28) Ann Gilbert's Album including
    (a) portraits of Mrs Ann Taylor in late middle age, copy by Josiah Gilbert of original by the Rev. Isaac Taylor, Mrs Ann Taylor in extreme old age, by Josiah Gilbert (1830), the Rev. Joseph Gilbert by Elizabeth Westoby (1823), silhouette of Jemima Taylor by Isaac Taylor of Stanford River, and Jemima Taylor by Ann Gilbert (?1831/32), and
    (b) drawings, paintings & photos of many of the houses occupied by the family, including Castle House by Jane Taylor; New House Farm (Peaked Farm) by Isaac Taylor of Stanford Rivers; 10 Castle Street by the Rev. Isaac Taylor; Stanford Rivers House by Edith Haddon Herbert; pre-war photos of Stanford Rivers House & Dyers; and various Ongar & Stanford Rivers scenes (including the meeting house & the burial ground) by Isaac Taylor of Stanford Rivers: OC

Endnotes

1 they were so called to distinguish them from another contemporary literary family known as the Taylors of Norwich.
2 two examples may illustrate their universality: a Sino-Portugese friend of the author learnt *My Mother* from his Chinese mother in Hong Kong in the 1940s; another friend found *Twinkle, Twinkle, Little Star* on the wall of a school in a remote part of Nepal in the 1980s.
3 no other literary project was pursued by Jane Taylor with such single minded excitement as *Essays in Rhyme on Morals and Manners* (1816) – *MCJT* in *MBLTF*, vol 1, pp. 312–313
4 Rev. Joseph Gilbert (1779–1852), Congregational minister & theologian, was at this time pastor of the Nether Chapel in Sheffield and tutor in Classics & Mathematics at the Independent College of Rotherham (the nearest equivalent to a university available to dissenters). He was later a minister in Hull and in Nottingham, where the Friar Lane Chapel was founded for him. His brother-in-law, Isaac Taylor, described him as *'a man of the warmest benevolence, of extraordinary intelligence, extensive acquirements, excellent judgement in common affairs, and withal of deep and elevated piety'.*
5 *TTO*, pp. 84–85
6 anon letter to Canon Isaac Taylor dated 15 October 1867 in Suffolk RO: HD 588/4/7 offering for sale MS poems exchanged between Isaac Taylor & Ann Martin. Present whereabouts of this MS unknown.
7 Isaac Charles Gilbert (1822–1885) at one time employed Fothergill Watson (1841–1928), later architect of the Budworth Hall. Gilbert's Sunday School building was almost entirely destroyed by

ASPECTS OF THE HISTORY OF ONGAR

fire in the early hours of 27 February 1919, an event clearly remembered by Miss Korf, who saw the flames from her bedroom window.

8   Mary Gilbert (1835–1925) née Steward, formerly Angas, daughter of a prominent dissenting minister, married Josiah Gilbert in August 1880. She is remembered by Miss Korf as a formidable, but generous, lady, quite small, grey haired and "slung shouldered".

9   Edith Haddon Herbert (186/–post-February 1939). Probably living in Ongar by 1900, when her poem *Golden Days – Essex* (which confusingly alluded to Ann & Jane Taylor as children) was published in the *Essex Review*, No. 9, pp.116–117. Apparently painted several copies of the Lavenham portrait of Ann & Jane Taylor, one of which (now lost) was presented to Colchester Town Hall (letter from Henry Taylor dated 4 April 1903 in Suffolk RO: HD 588/5/5)

10 John Wilkes (1727–1797) scapegrace, radical politician and scourge of the establishment. He also became a symbol of free speech, which perhaps explains support from ostensibly as unlikely a source as the father of the Rev. Isaac Taylor. At this time, £1000 was an enormous sum.

11 The Society of Artists of Great Britain, founded 1761, had auspicious beginnings – Reynolds, Gainsborough and Hogarth were all involved – and royal patronage, but quickly became driven by faction (out of which, by secession, the Royal Academy was born) and later plagued by debt. The Society's annual exhibitions continued for some years, but they were years of inexorable decline.

12 Bewick wrote sadly, but without rancour, of his estrangement in 1776 from Isaac Taylor, who took offence at his determination to throw up his bright prospects in London and to return to Northumberland. They never met again, but, shortly before Isaac Taylor died, Bewick wrote to him in the warmest terms, enclosing a copy of his *Birds*; the text of the letter was reproduced in Isaac Taylor's obituary in *The Literary Panorama*.

13 Thomas Jefferys (died 1771) see <u>DNB</u>. He married Elizabeth Raikes, sister of Robert Raikes, the promoter of Sunday Schools, a field in which the Rev. Isaac Taylor was to become active.

14 Henry Taylor & other contemporaries attempted to prove on the flimsiest evidence that the Jefferys brothers were of the same stock as John Milton's mother, Sara Jeffrey (1572–1637). See Suffolk RO: HD 588/1/25ff.

15 Bunhill Fields burial ground, much favoured by dissenters, in Finsbury. Henry Taylor's sister Rosa visited on 15 October 1893 to sketch the memorial and copy the inscriptions. See Suffolk RO: HD 588/1/40 and HD 588/1/49.

16 Isaac Taylor of Stanford Rivers (<u>FP</u> in <u>MBLTF</u>, vol 1, p. 2; <u>MCT</u>, p. ii) states that Charles Taylor, (and his brother Isaac) received *'a common education' 'at a grammar school near Brentwood'* (presumably Sir Anthony Browne's school, later Brentwood Grammar School) and left it *'not wholly ignorant of Latin, nor perhaps of Greek'* for a school in the City. Notes by the Rev Isaac Taylor (Suffolk RO: HD/4/14) state that Charles was taught only English at a day school run by a Mr Green in Wych Street (presumably in Brentwood or Shenfield) before spending a year *'at a higher school in Lothbury'* (in the City) where he learnt *'French, dancing, perhaps Latin, I believe not Greek'*.

17 see endnote 16 above

18 The Royal Society for the Encouragement of Arts, Manufactures and Commerce, founded in 1754 and still flourishing, is to be distinguished from the Society of Artists (see endnote 11 above), but the aims of the two bodies were similar.

19 John Boydell (1719–1804) sometime Sheriff, Alderman and Lord Mayor of London. An engraver by training, and a publisher who encouraged the art. His nephew, Josiah Boydell (1752–1817) succeeded to his engraving and publishing business, & commissioned the younger Isaac Taylor to design, and his father to engrave, the plates for *Illustrations of Holy Writ* (1814 to 1818)

20 published in Boydell's *The Dramatic Works of Shakespeare* (1802) which was illustrated by leading artists and engravers of the time. The book plates were also sold separately as engraved prints.

21 Ongar's Sunday School regularly celebrated its anniversary in the 1820s. *'The children arrived in tilted waggons and carts from outlying villages; an excellent dinner was provided for them and the visitors in a large barn, decorated with flowers and evergreens, and two of the most eminent preachers of the day preached the sermons'*. On one such occasion, Ann Gilbert wryly noted that Dr Ripon preached for an hour & twenty minutes *'from the gospel of St Parenthesis, a loose paraphrase of which he gave from the first to the fiftieth chapter inclusive!'*. On another occasion, the great Edward Irving, *'in the zenith of his fame, gave a magnificent oration, two hours long, upon*

THE TAYLOR FAMILY OF ONGAR AND THEIR HOUSES THERE

the somewhat unsuitable subject of the battle of Armageddon, the chapel windows being taken out to allow the crowd outside to participate in the service'.

22   printed in full in Pinchback, H., *Ongar Congregational Church – A Short History* (1937) Ongar
23   Joseph Gilbert was simultaneously minister in Sheffield & lecturer at Rotherham. He usually walked from Rotherham to Sheffield on Saturday evening or Sunday morning.
24   see the Rev. Isaac Taylor's notes in Suffolk RO: HD 588/1/147. Also *AOMMG*, vol 1 p. 12.
25   see endnote 6.
26   see Lingard's *Lavenham, A Photographic Tour of Lavenham Past* (1990) pp. 27–28. However the caption on page 27 perpetuates the error.
27   original MS of *The Adventures of Don Floris in Spain* is lost. Photocopy in Osborne Collection, Toronto and typed transcript in Suffolk RO: HD 588/1/181.
28   one apprentice was Nathan Branwhite (1775–1857) who became a distinguished miniaturist and portrait painter. He apparently followed Isaac Taylor to Colchester & subsequently made a proposal of marriage to Ann. She was flattered, but turned him down.
29   the workroom ran at right angles eastwards from the back wall of the house, from which it was originally separate (*AOMMG*, vol 1, p.101). E. J. Reedsdale, assistant at Colchester Museum wrote to Doris Armitage in March 1939 *'the famous workshop was pulled down a few years ago'*. (Copy of letter in Colchester Museum Resource Centre)
30   Ann Taylor was wont to declare that lady authors *'would have done better to employ themselves in mending the family stockings'*. It is ironical that later she was the first female member of the family to publish a book in her own name.
31   this is hard to reconcile with the fact that Isaac Taylor's lost diaries began in 1793 (*ABB*, F7, p.884), suggesting that he could write at the age of five or six.
32   the chronology may seem wrong, but *Minor's Pocket Book* for 1804 was published at the end of 1803; the material in it would have been contributed in response to the 1803 edition, published at the end of 1802.
33   *AOMMG*, vol 1, p. 188, with a footnote by Josiah Gilbert. The heresy was antinomianism, the belief that Christians are saved by faith and grace alone, & thus freed from any obligation to adhere to the moral law. Such excuses for moral laxity would have been unacceptable to Isaac Taylor. The Bucklersbury Lane congregation had a reputation for unorthodoxy, see Blaxill, E. A., *The Nonconformist Churches of Colchester* (1948) Colchester.
34   Thomas Conder (1747–1831) map engraver & bookseller of London. His brother, Samuel, was a very old friend of Rev. Isaac and Mrs Ann Taylor. Thomas's son, Josiah (1789–1855) was a close friend of Ann & Jane Taylor, & their brother Isaac, & influential in furthering their literary careers
35   Sarah Luck Conder (died 1837), daughter of Mr and Mrs Samuel Conder of Clapton, niece of Thomas Conder (see endnote 34 above) and later Mrs Whitty, became Jane Taylor's closest friend. She and her elder sister Susan (later Mrs Wenham) were lifelong correspondents of Ann and Jane. The letter, dated 23 September 1811 from Castle House, quoted at length in *AOMMG*, vol 1, pp. 192–200, is in the possession of the author.
36   the "three peaks" are presumably the three main gables of the house itself.
37   "left" and "right" are from the point of view of someone with his back to the house.
38   *The Eclectic Review*, edited at this time by Daniel Parken, a nonconformist periodical with more liberal political views & a more catholic range of literary reviews than its contemporary *The Evangelical Magazine*. Ann was brought to Parken's attention by Josiah Conder, later *The Review*'s editor. Isaac thought his sister's chief literary talent was as a reviewer (*AOMMG*, vol 1, p. 236.)
39   the evidence for the chronology of Isaac's illness and travels at this time is contradictory. Not even Isaac's son Henry was able to reconstruct the order of events with certainty.
40   at that time a marriage could not legally be solemnized in England by an Independent minister, with the result that dissenters were still married according to the rites of the Church of England.
41   Ann was correct. It was not until the summer of 1818 that the whole family was again assembled in one place.
42   i.e. the copper plates on which the engraving was done.
43   this word is difficult to read, but probably a misspelling of "bureau".
44   the cat which as a kitten came from Colchester with the Taylors.

ASPECTS OF THE HISTORY OF ONGAR

45 it was usual at this time for housewives to do their roasting & baking in the ovens of the local baker.
46 the significance of "winding up" the fire is unclear.
47 notes of Euphemia Taylor (transcribed by her brother Henry, now in Suffolk RO: HD 588/6/38) suggest that Henry had some reason to believe that what is now Castle Street was known in the Taylor's time as Win Lane. Euphemia, sent to investigate this in 1913, failed to find anyone in Ongar with any memory of this name.
48 during this stay, Ann appears to have occupied a first floor room at the south east corner of the house, with windows facing east & south. Her parents' rooms adjoined, with windows facing east & south respectively.
49 I am grateful to the Suffolk Record Office for permission to print this extract from HD 588/6/107.
50 Isaac Taylor would not have approved of the use of this word. In his view, enthusiasm was an undesirable quality, akin to fanaticism.
51 a nonconformist preacher, whose chapel the Gilberts attended when in London.
52 probably Lucy Jane, wife of the Rev. John Hay, elder daughter of the Rev. & Mrs Richard Cecil (see endnote 55).
53 Lucy was a child (not their daughter) living with the Gilberts. She may have been a relative, perhaps an orphaned younger sister of Susan Gilbert. In 1841–2 she was old enough to go for walks in the park, but young enough to have tantrums.
54 "Martins" may be shorthand for Mr & Mrs Martin Taylor, who may have come to assist with the move.
55 Mrs Cecil (c.1799–1844), born Salome Goodricke, wife of the Rev. Richard Cecil (1799–1863) the Independent minister at Ongar at this time. Richard Cecil, whose parents were old friends of the Taylors, had been a pupil of Rev. Joseph Gilbert at Rotherham. Salome had been Gilbert's ward, the orphaned niece of his first wife, Sarah (nee Chapman). In 1825, Gilbert became co-pastor with Cecil at St James Street Chapel, Nottingham, but the arrangement did not work out. Cecil's rather rigid religious conservatism did not mix well with Gilbert's more liberal & rational outlook. Their friendship, however, survived. Henry Taylor claimed that Cecil's preaching gradually emptied the Ongar chapel. (Suffolk RO: HD 588/6/104). In 1847, he returned to an earlier pastorate at Turvey, Bedfordshire.
56 three of Isaac & Elizabeth Taylor's children had the initial J; Jane (b. 1828), James Medland (b. 1834) & Jessie (b. 1841). At least in later life, James was usually known by his second name. Possibly Jane was the sufferer here.
57 presumably in connection with Isaac's invention, rather than portrait painting.
58 the handwriting is hard to read. If Susan Gilbert wrote "Evelina", it may be the book of that name by Fanny Burney.
59 Rosa (b. 1835) was the Taylors' sixth child.
60 the "book meeting" was presumably a meeting of the Ongar Book Society in which the Rev. Isaac Taylor had been closely involved.
61 Thomas Wilson (1764–1843), the son of a wealthy Derbyshire manufacturer, was a major benefactor of the Congregational Church, a director of the London Missionary Society and founder member of the Council of University College, London.. He appears to have owned land in the vicinity of Ongar. His son, Joshua Wilson ((1795–1874), a barrister, was a leading scholar of the history of dissent, and his grandson Thomas Wilson (1841–1915) married Jessie, one of the daughters of Isaac Taylor of Stanford Rivers, and lived for a time at Stanford Rivers Hall, which was owned by his family. Their son, Geoffrey Remington Wilson (1874–1943), became a GP and practised for many years in Ongar. His son, Peter Remington Wilson (1911–1997), born in Ongar and also a doctor, was the father of Clare Wilson.
62 The blank Album of about 500 pages was given to Ann by a friend probably in 1820 (*AOMMG*, vol 2, pp. 29–30, *ATGA* Preface, p. xi). The earliest entry dated is 24 July 1820, the last in Ann Gilbert's lifetime 12 June 1866. Other members of the family added occasional entries over the next 70 years, the final one being a charming water colour dated 1939 by Ann's grand daughter, Annie Laurie Gilbert (1851–1943) (see endnote 63), of the Gilberts' Nottingham home from 1830 to 1841. The Album seems to have passed from Ann Gilbert to her grand – daughter Jane Taylor Neville

THE TAYLOR FAMILY OF ONGAR AND THEIR HOUSES THERE

(née Gilbert), possibly via Ann's sister Jemima Herbert, then to Edith Haddon Herbert (see endnote 9), from her to Doris Armitage (see endnote 66) and then to Christina Duff Stewart (see endnote 64) who presented it to the Osborne Collection in Toronto.

63. Annie Laurie Gilbert Gilbert (1851–1941) the eldest child of Isaac Charles Gilbert (see endnote 7) and his wife Anne, née Gee, appears to have been baptised thus, though why the name Gilbert was repeated is not clear. She was named Laurie after Anna Laurie (née Forbes), a great friend of her grandmother, Ann Gilbert. Annie Gilbert became a talented artist, and her water colours of Nottingham and the surrounding area are invaluable to local historians. A view of Ongar High Street (reproduced on the cover of this book) and another of Stanford Rivers are in the possession of Clare Wilson (see endnote 61), a great-great-granddaughter of the Rev. Isaac Taylor.
64. Christina Duff Stewart, the foremost authority on the literary works of the Taylors, was born a Scot. She emigrated to Canada and became a librarian at the University of Toronto, and book selector for graduate research. In 1967 she was asked by the Director of the Osborne Collection to write an introduction to a facsimile edition of the Rev. Isaac Taylor's *Scenes in America*. Thus began a long fascination with the Taylors, which bore fruit in the *Analytical Bio-Bibliography* and the facsimile edition of Ann Gilbert's Album. Miss Stewart spent much time researching in England in the 1960s and 1970s, made contact with several Taylor descendants, and became acquainted with Doris Armitage, with whom she subsequently corresponded.
65. Henry Taylor practised as an architect in Manchester. In the early 1890s he retired on medical grounds and devoted the rest of his life to family history, with particular emphasis on the artistic achievements of his father, Isaac Taylor of Stanford Rivers.
66. Doris Mary Armitage (1887–1974), only child of Joseph Armitage (d. 1941), a furniture manufacturer, and his wife Gertrude, née Herbert, (1862–1958) who was the eldest child of the Rev. Thomas Martin Herbert (1835–1877), professor of Philosophy and Church History at the Lancashire Independent College, himself the eldest child of Thomas Herbert (1794–1878), a lace manufacturer and Alderman of Nottingham, and his wife Jemima, née Taylor (1798–1886), the youngest of the children of the Rev. Isaac Taylor.

Editor's note: A much fuller version of the author's endnotes has been deposited at the Ongar Library and at the Essex Record Office.

ASPECTS OF THE HISTORY OF ONGAR

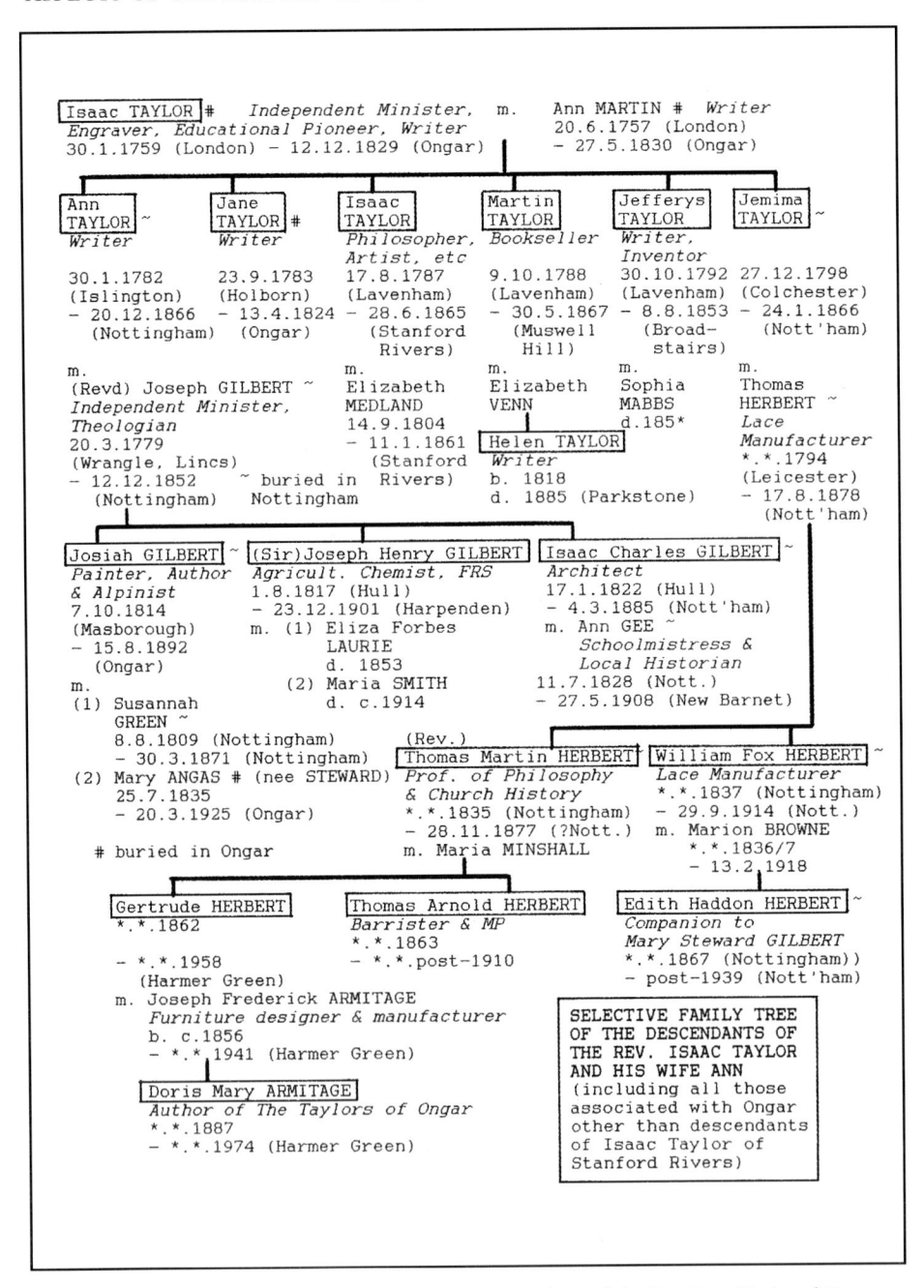

```
Isaac TAYLOR #    Independent Minister,    m.    Ann MARTIN #    Writer
Engraver, Educational Pioneer, Writer            20.6.1757 (London)
30.1.1759 (London) - 12.12.1829 (Ongar)          - 27.5.1830 (Ongar)
```

Ann TAYLOR ~	Jane TAYLOR #	Isaac TAYLOR	Martin TAYLOR	Jefferys TAYLOR	Jemima TAYLOR ~
Writer	Writer	Philosopher, Artist, etc	Bookseller	Writer, Inventor	
30.1.1782 (Islington)	23.9.1783 (Holborn)	17.8.1787 (Lavenham)	9.10.1788 (Lavenham)	30.10.1792 (Lavenham)	27.12.1798 (Colchester)
- 20.12.1866 (Nottingham)	- 13.4.1824 (Ongar)	- 28.6.1865 (Stanford Rivers)	- 30.5.1867 (Muswell Hill)	- 8.8.1853 (Broadstairs)	- 24.1.1866 (Nott'ham)
m. (Revd) Joseph GILBERT ~ Independent Minister, Theologian 20.3.1779 (Wrangle, Lincs) - 12.12.1852 (Nottingham)	~ buried in Nottingham	m. Elizabeth MEDLAND 14.9.1804 - 11.1.1861 (Stanford Rivers)	m. Elizabeth VENN Helen TAYLOR Writer b. 1818 d. 1885 (Parkstone)	m. Sophia MABBS d.185*	m. Thomas HERBERT ~ Lace Manufacturer *.*.1794 (Leicester) - 17.8.1878 (Nott'ham)

```
Josiah GILBERT ~      (Sir) Joseph Henry GILBERT    Isaac Charles GILBERT ~
Painter, Author       Agricult. Chemist, FRS        Architect
& Alpinist            1.8.1817 (Hull)               17.1.1822 (Hull)
7.10.1814             - 23.12.1901 (Harpenden)      - 4.3.1885 (Nott'ham)
(Masborough)          m. (1) Eliza Forbes           m. Ann GEE ~
- 15.8.1892               LAURIE                        Schoolmistress &
(Ongar)                   d. 1853                       Local Historian
m.                    (2) Maria SMITH               11.7.1828 (Nott.)
(1) Susannah              d. c.1914                 - 27.5.1908 (New Barnet)
    GREEN ~
    8.8.1809 (Nottingham)    (Rev.)
    - 30.3.1871 (Nottingham) Thomas Martin HERBERT    William Fox HERBERT ~
(2) Mary ANGAS # (nee STEWARD) Prof. of Philosophy    Lace Manufacturer
    25.7.1835                 & Church History        *.*.1837 (Nottingham)
    - 20.3.1925 (Ongar)       *.*.1835 (Nottingham)   - 29.9.1914 (Nott.)
                              - 28.11.1877 (?Nott.)   m. Marion BROWNE
    # buried in Ongar         m. Maria MINSHALL         *.*.1836/7
                                                        - 13.2.1918
```

```
    Gertrude HERBERT      Thomas Arnold HERBERT      Edith Haddon HERBERT ~
    *.*.1862              Barrister & MP             Companion to
                          *.*.1863                   Mary Steward GILBERT
    - *.*.1958            - *.*.post-1910            *.*.1867 (Nottingham))
    (Harmer Green)                                   - post-1939 (Nott'ham)
    m. Joseph Frederick ARMITAGE
       Furniture designer & manufacturer
       b. c.1856
       - *.*.1941 (Harmer Green)

       Doris Mary ARMITAGE
       Author of The Taylors of Ongar
       *.*.1887
       - *.*.1974 (Harmer Green)
```

SELECTIVE FAMILY TREE OF THE DESCENDANTS OF THE REV. ISAAC TAYLOR AND HIS WIFE ANN (including all those associated with Ongar other than descendants of Isaac Taylor of Stanford Rivers)

Figure 11   Descendants of the Rev. Isaac Taylor of Ongar

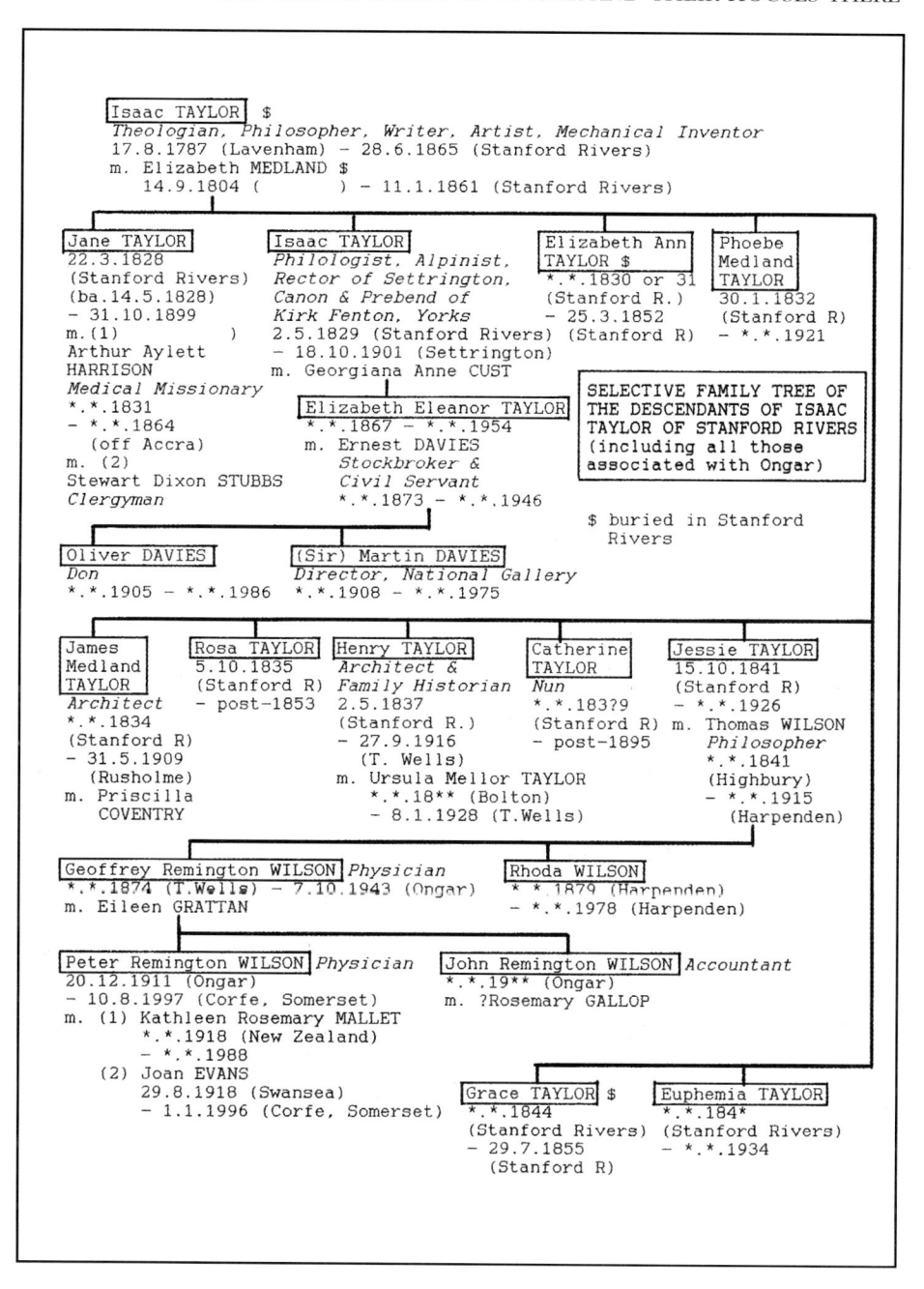

THE TAYLOR FAMILY OF ONGAR AND THEIR HOUSES THERE

```
Isaac TAYLOR  $
Theologian, Philosopher, Writer, Artist, Mechanical Inventor
17.8.1787 (Lavenham) - 28.6.1865 (Stanford Rivers)
m. Elizabeth MEDLAND $
     14.9.1804 (        ) - 11.1.1861 (Stanford Rivers)
```

Jane TAYLOR	Isaac TAYLOR	Elizabeth Ann	Phoebe
22.3.1828	Philologist, Alpinist,	TAYLOR $	Medland
(Stanford Rivers)	Rector of Settrington,	*.*.1830 or 31	TAYLOR
(ba.14.5.1828)	Canon & Prebend of	(Stanford R.)	30.1.1832
- 31.10.1899	Kirk Fenton, Yorks	- 25.3.1852	(Stanford R)
m.(1) ( )	2.5.1829 (Stanford Rivers)	(Stanford R)	- *.*.1921
Arthur Aylett	- 18.10.1901 (Settrington)		
HARRISON	m. Georgiana Anne CUST		
Medical Missionary			
..1831	Elizabeth Eleanor TAYLOR	SELECTIVE FAMILY TREE OF
- *.*.1864	*.*.1867 - *.*.1954	THE DESCENDANTS OF ISAAC
(off Accra)	m. Ernest DAVIES	TAYLOR OF STANFORD RIVERS
m. (2)	Stockbroker &	(including all those
Stewart Dixon STUBBS	Civil Servant	associated with Ongar)
Clergyman	*.*.1873 - *.*.1946	

$ buried in Stanford Rivers

Oliver DAVIES	(Sir) Martin DAVIES
Don	Director, National Gallery
..1905 - *.*.1986	*.*.1908 - *.*.1975

James	Rosa TAYLOR	Henry TAYLOR	Catherine	Jessie TAYLOR
Medland	5.10.1835	Architect &	TAYLOR	15.10.1841
TAYLOR	(Stanford R)	Family Historian	Nun	(Stanford R)
Architect	- post-1853	2.5.1837	*.*.183?9	- *.*.1926
..1834		(Stanford R.)	(Stanford R)	m. Thomas WILSON
(Stanford R)		- 27.9.1916	- post-1895	Philosopher
- 31.5.1909		(T. Wells)		*.*.1841
(Rusholme)		m. Ursula Mellor TAYLOR		(Highbury)
m. Priscilla		*.*.18** (Bolton)		- *.*.1915
COVENTRY		- 8.1.1928 (T.Wells)		(Harpenden)

Geoffrey Remington WILSON Physician	Rhoda WILSON
..1874 (T.Wells) - 7.10.1943 (Ongar)	*.*.1879 (Harpenden)
m. Eileen GRATTAN	- *.*.1978 (Harpenden)

Peter Remington WILSON Physician	John Remington WILSON Accountant
20.12.1911 (Ongar)	*.*.19** (Ongar)
- 10.8.1997 (Corfe, Somerset)	m. ?Rosemary GALLOP
m. (1) Kathleen Rosemary MALLET	
..1918 (New Zealand)	
- *.*.1988	
(2) Joan EVANS	Grace TAYLOR $	Euphemia TAYLOR
29.8.1918 (Swansea)	*.*.1844	*.*.184*
- 1.1.1996 (Corfe, Somerset)	(Stanford Rivers)	(Stanford Rivers)
	- 29.7.1855	- *.*.1934
	(Stanford R)	

Figure 12   Descendants of Isaac Taylor of Stanford Rivers

chapter 9

Local government in Ongar

by Jenny Main

Introduction

As local government is such a vast subject area, this chapter will aim to give a flavour of the issues and responsibilities undertaken by the various local bodies responsible for Ongar's local government through the ages. Availability of material has largely been responsible for the shape of this survey. This means that there is only a cursory look at local government generally prior to the sixteenth century. Ongar's local government is then looked at in some detail from 1743, when the Ongar vestry minute books begin, up until the beginning of the twentieth century, when the amount of material becomes too overwhelming. In addition, an attempt has been made to look at the changing roles and relationships between the different boards and committees, and how the various responsibilities have moved between them.

Early years

King Alfred (871–901) was initially responsible for handing over routine administrative matters for each shire to an official called an "ealdorman". Later in the tenth century as the "ealdorman" came to exercise control over more than one shire, the role of sheriff began to emerge. The sheriff would preside over the biennial shire moot as the King's representative whenever the "ealdorman" was absent. The shire moot was an assembly of freemen of the shire for administrative, judicial and financial purposes.

The shires were further divided into hundreds, whose main importance during the tenth and eleventh centuries derived from the regularly held court where customary law was administered, and as a unit for the collection of local taxes. At the shire moot each hundred was represented by "reeve" or bailiff, four "best men" and the priest, while at the hundred moot each village was represented. At the "tun-scipe" or township level there was the town moot where every freeman helped to settle local matters

William the Conqueror removed many local powers back to central government, although the parish retained its importance. The shire moot was replaced by the manor court, which was controlled by the lord's bailiff. If there was more than one bailiff, then the leading bailiff became known as the major bailiff or major (hence mayor). The manor court had two main forms, the court baron to deal with agricultural problems and issues of land, and the court leet for criminal offences. Each court appointed officers for one year's compulsory service with

LOCAL GOVERNMENT IN ONGAR

responsibility as haywards (looking after fences and animal stock), hedge surveyors, pinders (who were in charge of the pound for stray animals), and ale-tasters.

The creation of justices of the peace was also an important step towards local government. In 1361 Edward II enacted that every county should appoint one lord and three or four worthies to keep the peace. By 1388 they were assembling at Quarter Sessions to deal with criminal and administrative matters, and by Tudor times they were the main agents of royal power, with each county having 30 or 40 justices of the peace. Their civil powers, which included oversight of the poor law, markets, the regulation of wages and prices, and the upkeep of roads and bridges, were eventually transferred to local government in the late nineteenth century.[1] Interestingly, there is little mention of the local justices of the peace in the Ongar vestry minutes.[2]

The parish had always been an important unit ecclesiastically but, as the manor declined in the sixteenth century, so the parish vestry developed further as a unit of local secular government. In 1555 a Highways Act passed responsibility for the upkeep of local roads to the parish. Under the Tudors, one of the most important and arduous functions of the parish became its involvement with the relief of the poor. In 1563 each parish appointed two collectors of charitable alms. In 1572 the office of overseer of the poor was created and the vestry was responsible for their appointment. The principle of differing categories of poor relief for the able-bodied, the infirm and the aged was introduced in 1601, but the principle of a parish workhouse was not introduced until the General Workhouse Act of 1723.

Figure 13   The Old Town Hall in 1818, a pen and ink sketch by M. A. Newbey The vestry, the board of guardians, the burial board, the Ongar Friendly Society and many others met in the upper room until the demolition of the building in 1896.

ASPECTS OF THE HISTORY OF ONGAR
The vestry era

Matters discussed at the parish vestry meetings were those of "common concern." All principal and best-educated residents would take their turn on the vestry and various officers were elected to serve their community in an unpaid capacity for one year. These included:

- the churchwarden, who was custodian of the parish and trustee of its common property
- the constable, who was responsible for supervising beggars and the poor, as part of his law and order role
- the surveyor of highways, who was responsible for road maintenance
- the overseer of the poor, who administered poor relief.

The monthly meeting was open to all male ratepayers, who could just turn up and vote. Attendance was variable. The main Easter meeting may have attracted 15 to 20 people, but more normally the attendance would be around eight people. The vestry was presided over by the squire or the vicar. Income was from church collections and voluntary benevolence, but by the eighteenth century rate collection was the main source of income.

The vestry minutes for Chipping Ongar begin in 1743[2] with the Rector, Thomas Velley, in the chair. Throughout the vestry minutes available it would appear, that apart from a few periods, there was usually a church representative present at the meetings, sometimes in the person of the curate instead of the rector. The Chipping Ongar vestry was responsible for the appointment of the churchwardens, the overseers, surveyors and constables for the parish. The accounts of all of these officials had to be presented to the vestry at regular intervals for approval and payment.

Examples of early business include church repairs, such as:

> 'churchyard railed and paled in 1701 at the charge of Parish of Chipping Ongar Philip Trahearn and ffrances Sadler being then churchwardens.
>
> Witness John Campe Minister'[3]

and an order for new pews in 1749, and for four new windows in the church roof to give more light in the gallery in 1752. Also repairs to the parish almshouses seemed to have been a personal concern of the Rev. Thomas Velley in 1748:

> 'At a vestry held in this parish church of Chipping Ongar on Wednesday the 13th April 1748 it is proposed by the Revd Mr Tho Velley Rector of this said parish to tyle that end of the Almshouses next towards the Dwelling House of the said Mr Velley so far as the first chimney or as much farther as he thinks fitt at his own expense. This therefore agreed at the said Vestry that the parishioners of the said parish of Chipping Ongar will allow the price of thatching to the said Mr Velley towards the doing

LOCAL GOVERNMENT IN ONGAR

> *thereof and also hold the same in repair with tyling at all times hereafter within our hands.'*

Various statements on local matters are made from time to time, which can only hint at an underlying problem. For example, the vestry minutes of 27 March 1749 announce that:

> *'We the underwritten inhabitants of this parish of Chipping Ongar in the County of Essex do hereby certifie that a foot path leading from Ongar Church through the lands of Richard Bull Esq commonly called Barnfield into a field called Bushey Leas is only on sufferance and not an old accustomed and usual path.*
>
> *Thomas Velley, Rector*
> *John Till, Churchwarden.'*

One can only guess at what caused this pronouncement to be made.

The office of parish clerk was an important one, dating back to King Ethelbert.[4] Although the specific duties of the clerk were modified over the years, the role was to serve the parish and the church in whatever way was required. In Ongar, in 1770, the parish clerk was given a salary of 40 shillings per year:

> *'whereas he is to find mopps and brooms to keep church and church yard clean and decent and do all duties belonging to the office of Parish Clerk.'*

Initially the duties included keeping the church bells in order, to ring them as necessary, to clean the church, to accompany the priest, to sing and read the epistle and lesson, but over the years some of the liturgical and musical functions were lost. However, maintaining the parish register was a major and ongoing task, as well as keeping the vestry minutes.

As the years pass the vestry minutes become increasingly dominated by the problem of the relief of the poor of the parish. The role of the overseer of the parish seemed a particularly arduous one, and for little reward. Besides being responsible for the collection of the poor rate, and chasing up defaulters, they held responsibility for the administration of outdoor relief in money and kind to those of the poor who were not resident in the workhouse. In addition they were also responsible for the provision of doctors and nurses, housing, care of the aged, sick and insane, managing smallpox outbreaks, the boarding out and apprenticing of orphans and children of the poor, and bargaining with tradesmen for goods!

Obviously the expense of maintaining the poor of the parish fell on those with the means to pay, which included those who attended the parish vestry. Thus there is a lot of discussion on the cost of doctors' fees, and keeping sick people out of Ongar. In order to control expenses, the vestry kept a close watch on provision of health care to the poor of the town, and on 20 April 1748 they ordered:

> *'that for the future no surgeon or appothecary shall be paid or allowed*

> *any Bill or sum of money from the parishioners of this said parish for anything done to any of the poor of the said parish unless the same shall be done by order in writing under the hand of one of the Churchwardens or Overseers of the poor of the said parish for the time being.*
>
> *At the same time it is agreed that Mr John Boodle and Mr James Beasing shall take care of the poor of this said parish alternately each year and that Mr James Beasing shall take care of them this present year and that nothing extraordinary shall be ordered for the poor without consent of Vestry.'*

By 1770, the amount available to pay surgeons and apothecaries for taking care of the poor had been limited to £4 per year. Smallpox was a particular concern, confirmed by the minutes of 9 June 1767, which report that:

> *'it is agreed by the Rector, Churchwardens, overseers and the principle Inhabitants of the Town to Prosecute any person or persons that shall take in, bring or cause to be brought into the said parish any Person or persons with the small pox, either in the Natural way or by inoculation at the Expense of the Parish.'*

The poor rate and the accounts of the overseers become the main focus of the vestry's interest as we move into the nineteenth century, together with incidences of extravagance at the local workhouse!

A poorhouse had been established in Ongar by 1748, adjacent to the rectory. This was replaced by a new larger building on glebe land near the church in 1797 at a cost of £153.[5] The amount of poor rate collected from the inhabitants of Ongar rose steadily from £119 in 1744 to £350 in 1798 (extra to pay for the new workhouse perhaps), and £674 in 1806. By 1821 members of the vestry were showing a level of concern over the finances of poor relief in Ongar:

> *'it appears to this Vestry, proper attention has not been given for some years back by the Overseer of the Poor of this Parish to inforce from divers of the Inhabitants punctual money payments for their proportion of the rates granted That there is a want of a proper system for keeping the Overseers accounts That the Poor Rates have increased to an alarming amount That the Parish has been continued in Debt from year to year for Articles furnished to the Poor – and that the accounts such as they be are in a very erratic factor [sic] state.'*[6]

The meeting resolved, on presentation of this sorry state of affairs, to appoint a permanent committee of audit to check future accounts and ordered the overseer to report annually to the vestry at Easter. The overseers were also instructed to keep a cash book for receipts and payments, a ledger to record the assessed payments of poor rate by individuals and an order book for the purchase of "shop goodes." Receipts were to be obtained from every person who received a payment, with the exception of paupers, and these receipts were to be affixed in an alphabetical index. All these various books were to be balanced monthly and laid before the vestry for inspection, and a record made in the vestry minutes.

These records can be seen in the following years' vestry minute books and appear to be the main subject of business until after the establishment of the Ongar Union in 1835, which took over control of local poor relief.

The quality of the overseers obviously varied from year to year. We read of congratulations being handed out to some overseers for their clear accounts, whilst others are admonished for *'being personally in advance of money for the Parish amounting to £50'* and being summoned to appear before the local magistrate to explain the situation. Further control was established over the cost of poor relief by the appointment of a governor, or master, of the workhouse. The job description was established at the vestry meeting of 2 March 1828. The master was to keep a register of all names and ages of residents in the workhouse, and he was to establish rules and regulations to ensure cleanliness, sobriety, peace, piety and no gambling. An inventory of the contents of the workhouse was to be started and maintained. The master was to be responsible for keeping the inmates inside the workhouse and for holding morning prayers at 8am and evening prayers at 7pm (or 9pm in the summer). He was also to ensure that all inmates attended church at least once each Sabbath.

The Poor Law Amendment Act of 1834 was an attempt to deal with the national problem of the relief of the poor in a more organised way. The act had three main aims. These were to establish central control through the Poor Law Commission, to join parishes together as "unions" for the provision of poor relief, and to provide for a locally elected board of guardians (who were responsible for the workhouse and poor relief). In Ongar a meeting was held on 7 May 1835 for all inhabitants paying more than £5 per annum in rates to consider the implications of the 1834 Act. The meeting passed a resolution to establish a union with neighbouring parishes and a board of guardians to manage the affairs locally. However, the vestry kept the powers of the overseers, as well as the levying and collection of the rates.

The board of guardians and the union were examples of the early ad hoc authorities established to deal with a specific issue. The boundaries of the union did not follow historic boundaries but related solely to the individual issue that was to be tackled. This was the beginning of the principle of different boundaries for different services that was to proliferate later, rather than a standard geographic area and one authority being applicable for all services.

The first minute book of the Ongar Union records the initial meeting of the board of guardians, which took place on 12 April 1836 at the workhouse in Stanford Rivers. Capel Cure Esq. was chairman and the two guardians from Chipping Ongar parish were James Haslam and William Coe, who was also chairman of the vestry at the time. The board meetings were held each Tuesday morning in Chipping Ongar town hall, at a cost of 5s 0d a week for the hire of the room. Most of the

ASPECTS OF THE HISTORY OF ONGAR

business was to establish contracts for the supply of essential goods for the workhouse, thus advertisements were placed in the *Chelmsford Chronicle* for the supply of flour, bread, meat and other provisions for the use of the union.[7] Initial tenders were received from around the local area:

> '*Mr Edward Cousins of Willingale Doe, baker – flour and bread*
> *Mr James Webster, High Ongar, baker – bread, flour and salt*
> *Mr John Smitherman, Stanford Rivers, miller – flour*
> *Mr Francis Boyce – soap, butter and candles*
> *Mr John Cooper – meat.*'

It was also stated that the parish guardians should communicate with the churchwardens and overseers concerning the contracts for medical men, implying a joint responsibility for their employment and costs. The later minute books show evidence of the union summoning doctors to explain their failure to make house visits, which resulted in the deaths of the patients in question.[8]

Looking at the later minutes of the Ongar Union, it appears that they felt that their responsibilities, on occasions, stretched further than just the workhouse. The union made itself into a sanitary authority, employed an architect to draw up a sewerage scheme for Ongar and appointed an inspector. However they were unable to persuade the Ongar vestry to take up the sewerage scheme. On one occasion the union identified a 'nuisance' at the Two Brewers public house, built a brick drain at their own expense and then tried to recover their costs from the publican. The union was also anxious to make claims on other parishes for the care of their residents, just like the modern National Health Service. One young man on his way from Thaxted to London fell off a wagon as it passed through Stanford Rivers, resulting in a broken thigh, 76 days in the Ongar Union workhouse infirmary plus the accompanying surgeon's fees. The union consequently made a claim for the costs to Dunmow Union.

Meanwhile, the Ongar vestry having lost most of its powers over poor relief turned its attention to other local considerations. No doubt urgent matters had not been neglected in the past, but as some of the more routine matters seemed to take care of themselves, they did not require much discussion or comment at meetings, unlike the subject of the poor. This of course means that there is less detail available in the minutes concerning these other local issues. However we can find several references to drainage, church repairs and issues concerning the housing of the fire engine, together with the annual appointment of the constables, surveyors of the roads, and lighting and gas inspectors.

The church repairs were fairly standard. In 1826, it was a question of white washing and painting as required, putting swing casements in the gallery windows, repairing the fence and gravelling the paths, while in 1844 it was agreed by the vestry to pay £4 per annum to have the church clock kept in better time.

Commercial directories for the nineteenth century show that Ongar was well served by fire insurance agents from early on. The 1826–27 *Pigot's Directory* lists

LOCAL GOVERNMENT IN ONGAR

both the County and Royal Exchange Insurance companies as being represented in the town, while the 1859 *Post Office Directory* lists a whole host of insurance agencies, at least five of which included fire cover for residents who could afford to pay. From the vestry minutes we also know that by this time the Royal Exchange Fire Assurance Company maintained a fire engine at Chipping Ongar. In 1853 the vestry had written to the company:

> 'with notice forthwith to remove the Royal Exchange Engine from the Building attached to the Old Cage situate at the South Entrance of this Town both being the property of this Parish and being in such a dilapidated and dangerous state that we as Parish Officers deem it incumbent upon us to remove these, as a great portion of the said Building having fell in.'

The minute book of the Ongar Voluntary Fire Brigade reports that at a public meeting of inhabitants on 25 September 1840, it was resolved to have a fire engine and raise a subscription to pay for it.[9] It is not until the 1886 *Kelly's Directory* that mention of a fire brigade is found.

The constables were elected by the vestry each year with a salary, reported in 1826, to be 7 guineas per annum. Other than their election and salary they do not feature in the minutes of the vestry in terms of their duties and activities. However, in about 1830, the possibility of appointing a night watch in Ongar was being considered.

By 1842, after the arrival of the County Police Act of 1839 and the establishment of an Essex police force, the vestry minuted that it:

> 'Resolved unanimously that it does not appear to this meeting to be necessary to have one or more police constables for this Parish.'

This resolution was passed annually for the next few years, and in 1848 there is mention of a county rate to pay towards the cost of the police.

The Lighting and Watching Act of 1833 allowed towns with a population of 5000 or more to appoint paid watchmen. Ongar adopted the provisions of the Act in 1836, and the vestry meeting on 25 February 1836 appointed six inspectors who were to report back to the vestry at regular intervals and granted £60 for the implementation of the Act. Earlier in the 1830s, it had been considered necessary to set up a night watch for Ongar:

> 'In consequence of depredations recently committed in the Town of Ongar and the Numerous Vagrants and suspicious Characters which are seen about at night

> It is suggested as a measure conducive to check the progress and return of such proceedings That the Inhabitants of Ongar Appoint a young and respectable Man as Night Watchman, who will otherwise be appointed Special Constable

ASPECTS OF THE HISTORY OF ONGAR

> *The expence probably would not exceed a guinea weekly which if 60 Householders in Ongar would contribute four pence each weekly would meet the demand.*[10]

The lighting and watching inspectors collected a rate twice a year from the inhabitants of Ongar, presumably to cover the costs of checking the street lights and maintaining the night watch. From the inspector's rate books, it seems that in the 1840s and 1850s the rate on each household was about 5d in the pound. The gas inspector's rate books have also survived, showing a rate over the same period of between 3d and 4d in the pound.[11] Presumably this was used to pay for the gas used in lighting the town. Kelly's *Directory* of 1891 reports that the town was lighted by gas, although gas lights did not appear in Marden Ash until 1906.

The burial boards were established by the Burials Act of 1853. At the first meeting of the Ongar burial board in 1863, the search begins for a suitable burial site, as required by the Act. Various options are put forward and rejected, a part of Admiral Swinburne's land at Great Stony Field known as Mill Field at the back of Miss Shadrack's, an area of Stony field at the back of the Glebe known as Springpond (but this was considered too near to the town), an area of Bushy Lees at the back of Mrs Gibson's house, a piece of Wantz Farm, and many others. The first mention of Love Lane comes with an enquiry from the committee clerk to Miss Shadrack about the sale of the field known as Silvercroft, adjoining Love Lane for £300, which was refused. Negotiations were in hand to purchase an area at Little Bansons when it would appear that Miss Shadrack died, as an offer of £450 for Silvercroft was submitted to the executors of her estate in June 1864. All decisions and costs had to be sanctioned by the vestry. The total expenses were estimated at £1030, which included the purchase of Silvercroft for £450, conveyancing expenses at £120, the building of a chapel (designed by I.C. Gilbert, architect of Nottingham) estimated at £380 and enhancement of gates, fencing and grounds being £80.[12] The tenders received for the chapel building surprised the committee when they came in between £600 and £955. This resulted in a smaller chapel being built. Time was pressing as the churchyard was due to close in April 1866, so penalty clauses were put in to the builder's contract. The cemetery opened in 1866, and the burial board minutes continue to deal with expenses of maintenance and reserving burial plots for the inhabitants of Ongar.

As the twentieth century approaches, there is already a marked change from the system of the parish being the single local self-governing unit towards a system of centralised bureaucracy.[13] The days of the parish vestry managing numerous issues through one meeting is being rapidly superceded by a situation where many of the different responsibilities have been devolved to separate bodies through the implementation of central government legislation. The Poor Law Amendment Act of 1834 had started the trend with the arrival of the parish union and the board of guardians. This had been continued by the Highways Act 1835, which allowed the parish to appoint a highways board to look after the maintenance of the roads, the County Police Act, various public health acts which established sanitary authorities and burial boards, and finally the Local Government Acts of 1888 and 1894, which in turn established the county councils, urban and rural district councils, together with the parish council.

The parish council begins

The parish as a governing unit was revived with the introduction of the parish council by the Local Government Act of 1894 for rural areas with more than 300 inhabitants. Chipping Ongar with a population of 813 in 1891[14] was entitled to elect a parish council, rather than continue with the parish meeting or vestry. The vestry, of course, still had a role and continued to meet, but with all their civil responsibilities being transferred to the new parish council, the issues they were left with were largely related to the church itself. At the last vestry meeting, prior to the election of the parish council, it was recorded that:

> *'a vote of thanks of parishioners be given to Mr Charles Rose for his services as clerk to the Vestry with an expression of regret that they are deprived of his services by the operation of the Local Government Act 1894.'* [15]

However, where Mr Charles Rose went to, there is no record, and he does not appear to have been involved with the new Ongar parish council. Perhaps he had gone to the rural district council or the county council?

The parish council was the third tier of local government, after the county councils established in 1888, and the rural district councils, also created by the 1894 Act, which were based largely on consolidated sanitary districts. The Ongar Rural District Council comprised of the 26 parishes that made up the Ongar Union and their main function was to look after public health and highways. Unfortunately the early minutes of the Ongar RDC are missing, so we are unable to discover exactly how the council established itself and exercised its new powers. The physical area that the rural district council covered was an area of 47,230 acres and the population in 1891 was 10,557. The twenty-six parishes of the union and the Ongar RDC were Beauchamp Roothing, Berners Roothing, Blackmore, Bobbingworth, Chipping Ongar, Doddinghurst, Fyfield, Greensted, High Laver, High Ongar, Kelvedon Hatch, Lambourne, Little Laver, Moreton, Navestock, Norton Mandeville, Shelley, Shellow Bowells, Stanford Rivers, Stapleford Abbots, Stapleford Tawney, Stondon Massey, Theydon Mount, Willingale Doe and Willingale Spain.[14] The parish council, it is often said, took on a largely consultative role in the post-1894 system of local government, yet they inherited all the non-ecclesiastical powers, duties and liabilities of the vestry. There is no complete listing of the transferred powers because the role of the vestry had never been laid down by statute, but had evolved by custom and practice, and in each parish vestry it was different. However, certain elements were undoubtedly handed over, including the following:

- the return of names of persons to serve in the office of constable
  (even though county police forces had been established 40 years earlier)
- the power to rate owners rather than occupiers

ASPECTS OF THE HISTORY OF ONGAR

- the power to appeal against the valuation list
- the duty to appoint overseers and assistant overseers of the poor
- the control of village greens and allotments
- the provision of parish books, a vestry room or parochial office, a parish chest, and a fire engine and fire escape.

In addition, the parish councils were also given some new powers, some of which were shared with the rural district councils. These included:

- to deal with nuisances prejudicial to health
- to use wells and streams for water supply
- other public health powers as delegated by the rural district council
- to maintain footpaths and provide land for public walks and recreation-grounds.[16]

Nationally there was a mixture of enthusiasm and scepticism for the new parish councils. W. T. Stead of *The Times* had written to Henry Fowler, president of the Local Government Board, who had presented the 1894 Bill to Parliament:

> *'Your parish councils will be the old vestries over again – the squire and the parson will find that instead of being disestablished their power has only received consecration at the hands of Democracy.'* [17]

Lack of money and the absence of any general powers to promote the welfare of the parish may have squashed any enthusiasm or progressive ideas. In addition, the parish council had no obligatory functions, apart from having to hold meetings. On the positive side the 1894 Act brought some order to the chaos of local administration and spread local democracy to all rate-paying inhabitants.

The Local Government Act of 1894 laid down the procedure for the election of the first parish councils at parish meetings to be held on Tuesday, 4 December 1894, and Chipping Ongar was no exception. Ongar's meeting was held at the King's Trust school room, with Mr Leonard Pelly, a magistrate, of Bowes, Ongar elected as chairman for the duration of the election. Fifteen valid nominations were put forward and read to the meeting in alphabetical order by the chairman. Fifteen minutes after having taken the chair, the chairman then read the names to the meeting again, with the number of votes for each cast by a show of hands. Each elector had as many votes as there were vacancies, so in this case it was seven. If demanded by one or more electors, a poll could be taken by ballot. The names of the seven persons with the most votes were read out again, and after allowing a short time as stipulated, and no poll being demanded, the following were duly elected as parish councillors:

Name and number of votes

Clark W. C. 76	Christie C. H. F. 72	Cowee T. 70	Tanner J. 70
Rose T. E. 61	Gibson H. W. 52	Hayward R. 50	

Certificates of election were then drawn up for publication, and one sent to the returning officer, and a certificate sent to each of the elected members.[18] By totalling the votes for the 15 nominated candidates, a total of 673 votes is arrived at, and allowing each elector 7 votes, implies there must have been at least 76 people present at the meeting who were entitled to vote. Nationally, the *Contemporary Review* calculated that between a third and a half of the parish council seats were won by farmers, about a quarter by craftsmen, and most of the rest by labourers, with a sprinkling of parsons, gentry, professional men, non-conformist ministers and women.[19] This was not the case in Ongar! By checking the 1895 *Kelly's Directory* it is possible to trace most of the candidates and elected members. Of those elected to serve on the parish council, Dr William Clark was headmaster of Ongar Grammar School and the Rev. James Tanner was the rector of St Martin's church. Charles Christie, a magistrate, lived at the Wilderness and Henry Gibson, who lived at the White House, was clerk of the peace for the county. The traders of Ongar were represented by Thomas Rose, a tailor and hatter, Robert Hayward, a grocer, and Thomas Cowee, a butcher. The unsuccessful candidates included the superintendent of the fire brigade, a seedsman and florist, a builder, an insurance agent, a farmer, the secretary of Ongar Cricket Club, plus two unlisted names. The first meeting of the newly elected Chipping Ongar parish council was held at the Trust school room on Thursday 13 December 1894. The Rev. James Tanner was elected to be chairman until the annual meeting, required by the Act to take place in April of each year, and Dr William Clark was elected as vice chairman, but it was decided to sign all declarations of acceptance of office at the next meeting. The first few meetings of the new parish council are understandably dominated by the appointment of officers, establishment of duties and routines, and wary steps towards the business of local government. This certainly appears to have been the case between the council's election and its first annual meeting held on 19 April 1895.

The appointment of parish clerk was an important early responsibility of the council, which at their first meeting on 13 December 1894 they agreed to defer, with councillor H. W. Gibson as acting clerk for the time being. The acting clerk was instructed to obtain a minute book and a book of declaration for the next meeting. At the meeting of 14 January 1895, applications for the post of parish clerk were invited to be received by 28 January 1895. For a salary of £10 per annum, the clerk would be expected to perform all duties connected with Ongar parish council and the Ongar parish meeting, other than those under the Burial and Lighting Acts. At the meeting of 30 January 1895 the new clerk was appointed from the two applications received. The successful candidate was Mr F. W. B. Stocker, who had beautiful handwriting, but unfortunately is not listed in the 1895 *Kelly's Directory* so we do not know his trade. The terms of his appointment were three months notice, no pension or compensation for loss of office, and it was carefully stated that, '*his duties shall not extend to advising the Council.*' Later in August 1896, a letter from the Local Government Board clarified the position of the assistant overseers. In effect, the appointment of an assistant overseer terminated

ASPECTS OF THE HISTORY OF ONGAR

the appointment of a paid clerk, in that the assistant overseer acted "ex officio" as clerk to the parish council. From this time on Ongar appointed two assistant overseers, one to maintain the duties of the clerk and the duty of overseer of the by-laws of the Ongar RDC, and the other to carry out all the rate collecting and other official duties.

Equally important was the appointment of a treasurer for the parish council. The council agreed to a security of a sum equivalent to 9d in the pound on the rateable value of the parish, and approached the firm of Messrs Sparrow, Tufnell and Co, bankers of Chelmsford to ask one of their members to act as treasurer. A reply was received from the bank in early January reporting that they were unable to permit any partner or principal clerk to be nominated treasurer to any parish, unless they were resident there, and on the council. However they agreed to take on the account providing a small balance was kept and it was never overdrawn. The parish council therefore appointed one of its own members, Mr C. H. F. Christie, as treasurer. A year later it appears that the Chelmsford bank had changed its mind, saying that they were agreeable to accept the treasurership of the council if required, and that the council should have received a circular to this effect in January 1895. The council, had however, decided to refuse this offer as they already had a treasurer in whom they have perfect confidence. In 1897 Mr Christie no longer felt able to continue as treasurer, and this led to the appointment of Mr Robert Woodhead of Chelmsford, from the firm of Messrs Barclay and Co. as treasurer to the council.

As to the role and responsibilities of the new council, they moved very gingerly with constant deferments, and communications with and from the Local Government Board as to what they should and should not do. The parish council was keen to leave the management of gas and the cemetery to the gas inspectors and burial board until after the first annual meeting in March 1895. At the meeting of 14 January 1895 it was happy to let the existing burial board (Mr F. Noble, W. Hancock, T. Cowee, Charles Rose, F. Silcock and Dr Clark, and the gas inspectors, Mr P. B. Brown, T. H. Kirby, A. Smith, H. Barlow, F. Silcock and F. Gibbs) carry on. In fact, the council was very unclear as to its powers under the Lighting and Watching Act and the Burial Act. The clerk was instructed to write to the Local Government Board to enquire whether the council should themselves act as gas inspectors and burial board or whether they should appoint such officials from their own body or outside. At the meeting of 19 April 1895, a reply was received from the secretary to the Local Government Board which stated that the powers of the burial boards and gas inspectors were transferred to the parish council by section 7(5) of the Local Government Act 1894.

Other communications from the Local Government Board were received which laid down the rules for polls consequent on a parish meeting, set out forms and notices for the appointment of overseers and forms of precept to the overseers, as well as giving details of the powers and duties with respect to roadside wastes and commons.

LOCAL GOVERNMENT IN ONGAR

The routine matter of room hire was dealt with by the clerk. The early meetings were held in the Trust school room at a cost of 2s 0d or 2s 6d per meeting. In January 1895, the acting clerk was instructed to negotiate with the Budworth Hall letting committee on the council's use of a room, with cost not to exceed 3s 0d per meeting. The reply from Mr Fenn, secretary of the Budworth Institute, was reported to the annual meeting of Ongar parish council in April 1895, offering the council use of the committee room for meetings at a cost of 2s 6d, which would include fire and gas as required. These terms were accepted and by this time, the first parish council meeting at the Budworth Hall had already been held on 11 March 1895.

Actual practical matters of local government appear to have been few and far between in these early months. The roads were an apparent priority at the meeting of 13 December 1894, as the surveyors of the highways were requested to repair the roads in the parish, apart from the main roads. Greensted Road and Castle Street required gravelling and shaping. The lack of works was due mainly to the council's reluctance to set a rate, as Mr Herbert B. Brown, surveyor, reported to the meeting of 14 January 1895:

> *'I have to inform the Council that the balance in the hands of the Surveyors on 25th March last was only £3-6-4 and that during the past nine months Mr Camp has spent something beyond this amount in cleaning these roads from time to time. I have therefore no funds with which to carry out the suggestions of the Council and do not think that under the present arrangements I am called upon to personally incur the expense and trouble of making and gathering a rate. If however the Council through their collector would arrange to collect the rate I have no doubt that Mr Camp would be happy to undertake spending the money.'*

However the council resolved to take no further action.

A more forward thinking move was also taken early on, in the form of a circular to every householder in Ongar to find out the state of water supply in the town. The questions asked were:

> *'Have you a supply of drinking water on your premises – if not where do you obtain it from?*
> *Are you satisfied with your present water supply?*
> *Have you a water closet for your house alone?*
> *Are you in favour of a parish Assistant Overseer being appointed for Ongar?*
> *Is there any matter which you wish to bring before the council, if so please give particulars?'*

To cover themselves there was a disclaimer as a footnote:

> *'NB You must not consider that the Council are neglecting their duty if the above matters do not receive attention as they may not fall entirely within their province.'*

ASPECTS OF THE HISTORY OF ONGAR

This sentence had been amended from the original draft, which might have implicated Ongar RDC! By April 1895, 121 replies had been received from a total of the 173 circulars that had been sent out. An impressive response! Of these, 61 had answered each question in the affirmative, and of the remaining 60, six had a supply of drinking water on the premises, while 54 did not. Twenty-seven householders were satisfied with their present supply, while nineteen had no privies for their house alone. No answers to the last question are reported although there is mention of verbal reports of defective drainage.

The first annual meeting of Chipping Ongar parish council was held at the Budworth Hall on 19 April 1895. The chairman of the council, the Rev. James Tanner, and the vice-chairman, Dr W. C. Clark, were both re-elected to their posts, and overseers of the poor were appointed. Elections for the Ongar parish council itself had not been held at the annual parish meeting on 26 March 1895, coming so soon after the establishment of the council the previous December. However, in following years the full council would be elected at the annual parish meeting in March, prior to the parish council's annual meeting in April. This practice was to continue annually until the Parish Councillor Terms of Office Act 1899 came into force in 1900, and this allowed for elections every three years. The annual meeting also resolved that quarterly meetings of the parish council be held in April, July, October and January, if possible, and that meetings should not be open to the public. Representatives of the press should not be present either but they should be given copies of resolutions and decisions taken after each meeting. So the regular business of local government began.

Certainly in the early years of the parish council, the minute books show that business tended to follow on from the vestry era, with a continuation of concern about sanitary conditions, lighting, roads, and the cemetery, together with new issues of the railway and fire hydrants.

The sanitary condition of the town was a concern of both the parish council and Ongar RDC, and resulted in a joint committee being established in 1898, which we shall come onto later. At the annual parish meeting in 1895 an extract from the annual report of the medical officer of health, Dr Quennell, was read out. He referred to *'the insanitary condition of the Town of Ongar and the necessity of a system of drainage.'* The council resolved to write to Dr Quennell and ask him, *'to state what was required in the way of drainage, and what particular portions of the Town were in need thereof.'* The people of Ongar were obviously concerned by the state of Cripsey Brook, and held a public meeting of the inhabitants of the parish on 25 September 1895 where they established a committee to deal with the cleaning of the river. The parish council was happy to let the cleaning of the river proceed, and at the meeting on 4 November 1895, the council did agree to pay £15 for the labour costs of cleaning out the Cripsey Brook. However this process led to a slight disagreement between the council and Mr Camp, a former surveyor of the parish. In order to allow for the cleaning of the Cripsey Brook, Mr Camp had removed a dam from the river without permission, and kept for himself the

LOCAL GOVERNMENT IN ONGAR

materials which in theory belonged to the parish. On enquiry by the parish clerk, Mr Camp reminded the council that they had refused to pay the original account, as being outside the remit of the surveyor, so in fact the dam and materials were nothing to do with the council at all!

Water supply was a major concern of the parish council. They approached various landowners including those of Castle Farm and Bowes to utilise the springs on their land, or bore for water for use by the town. By 7 October 1895, they decided to take the step of writing to the Herts and Essex Waterworks Company to see if they had plans to extend their mains water to Ongar. The company replied that they were willing to come to Ongar if there were enough people to warrant it, meaning assured revenue of £250 per annum. As a result a public meeting was called for residents of Ongar and surrounding parishes for 28 January 1896 to consider the proposals of the Herts and Essex Waterworks Company. What happened at this public meeting is not recorded in the minute book, even as a report to the next parish council meeting. The next references to water supply however refer to the statement by Herts and Essex Waterworks Company that no other company can be called on to supply water in the Ongar area. This then leads on to discussions about the formation of a private water company to provide a mains water supply for Ongar.

Maintenance of some roads had always been a responsibility of the parish, but a nation-wide campaign to transfer control over parish highways to the parish councils and parish meetings was proposed by the Local Government Highways Bill of 1896. This campaign was organised by the *Councils Gazette*. Although the Bill was drafted, and petitions were received from all over the country, including Ongar, no opportunity ever came for the Bill to be introduced to Parliament. The parish council was left to make complaints to the county council or rural district council about the state of the roads. However it seems to have been the footpaths that were a particular grievance in the town. On 18 August 1896, the clerk reported that he had received complaints about the dangerous condition of the footpath between Ongar Bridge and the Two Brewers Inn. The council resolved to write to Essex County Council thanking them for the great improvement in the footpath from Ongar station to the Wantz, but also asking for the kerbing of the footpath at the other end of the town. Later Castle Street is also held up as in need of footpath improvement and kerbing.

A new problem was also beginning to appear – the motor car. Following receipt of a letter from the clerk to Grays Thurrock Urban District Council about lights on vehicles, it is minuted that the following resolution was passed:

> *'That Essex County Council be asked to make a bye-law enforcing the carrying of one light on all vehicles passing along the public roads between the hours of one hour after sunset and one hour before sunrise, such lamp to be carried on the off side of such vehicles and to show a light in the direction in which the same are proceeding which shall be visible to any person meeting such vehicles.'*

ASPECTS OF THE HISTORY OF ONGAR

By 1902 traffic through the town was becoming a problem, and the clerk was instructed to write to Essex County Council:

> 'drawing their attention to the danger caused to pedestrians and vehicular traffic in the High Street, Ongar through the high rate of speed at which Motor cars and Bicycles pass through the Town and suggesting that a Notice Board be affixed in some conspicuous place warning such persons to moderate their speed on passing through Ongar Town.'

A swift response from Essex County Council stated that the police had powers to prevent nuisances of this kind, so the clerk wrote to the local inspectors about the matter, but no further reports are given.

Lighting of the town seemed to have been a delicate business especially where the siting of the lamps were concerned. There are many reports in the parish minute books of individuals objecting to lamps being on or near their property. Also the payment for some lights appears to have been down to individuals too. After establishing that the powers of the gas inspectors had been transferred to the parish council, the Ongar annual parish meeting in March 1895 set a rate of 4d in the pound to cover the expenses of lighting the town. Mr Alfred Hall, clerk to the burial board and gas inspectors was kept on as an officer of the council, to cover all the business under the Burial and Lighting and Watching Acts. Thus having established its position, the council resolved to take over the responsibility for:

> 'the present lamp in the churchyard, place new lamps at the corner of Mr H Childs Gateway in the High Street, and at the Corner of the Chase in the Borough, and that the lamp near Mr Coe's House in the Borough be removed to the corner of Mr Smart's garden on the opposite side of the road, permission being obtained from the High Ongar Parish Council to place it there this part of the road being in that Parish.'

This land later turned out to be the private property of a Mr Venables who gave permission for the lamp to be placed on his land. At the same meeting it was decided to ask Ongar Gas Company to tender for the lighting of the lamps in the town. The reply was available for the next meeting on 23 August 1895 when the price quoted to light the public lamps from 1 September to 30 April was for 42s 0d per lamp, lighting the lamps within one hour of sunset and extinguishing them at midnight:

> 'excepting the night of full moon and two preceding nights when they shall remain unlit and that on the two following evenings they shall be lit at the usual hour and extinguished at 9 o'clock.'

The tender offer was accepted together with that for installing the new lamps and keeping them all in good repair. The parish council agreed to set up a committee to transact any business under the Lighting and Watching Act at the October meeting. The initial committee was made up of all those councillors who were not on the burial committee, the Rev. J Tanner, Dr W. C. Clark, Mr C. H. F. Christie, and

Mr T. Cowee. This committee, and the burial committee, both met for a quarter of an hour before each meeting of the council. Further reports from the lighting and watching committee are concerned with the repair and maintenance of the existing lamps and the extension of lighting in the town, especially to the areas around the station, the Rectory and the Wantz, without increasing the rate being levied to pay for it.

As already mentioned the council also had a burial committee to deal with all the issues and responsibilities under the Burial Acts, carrying on from the burial boards. This committee was made up of the other half of the parish council, Mr H. W. Gibson, R. Hayward and T. E. Rose. They were authorised to co-opt another member and obtain estimates for the erection of a tool shed at the cemetery. The contract for the new tool shed was given to Mr F. Noble for a sum of £9 5s 0d, and Mr S. Hadsley was taken on to attend the cemetery for two days a week at 2s 6d per day. In addition, an offer was received from Mr Walter Lacey to cut the grass in the cemetery providing he was able to keep the cuttings. The committee had to wait a while for the tool shed. Mr Noble was given 14 days to complete the job in October 1895, and the council was informed at the November meeting that the tool shed had been completed. However by the same token, it was not until March 1896 that a cheque was drawn to pay Mr Noble for the tool shed and clearance of rubbish. Once this issue was settled there was little business to be reported back to the full council, other than the annual accounts and rate to be levied for the year and the occasional instance of flowers being stolen from graves. The Burial Act of 1900 made certain changes, including the need for a fixed table of fees to be paid to ministers and sextons for their services.

The railway had arrived in Ongar in 1865, and the parish council was keen to remind the railway company of its responsibilities as a landowner. In October 1895, the clerk was instructed to write to the Great Eastern Railway to call their attention to the bad state of repair of the approach to Ongar railway station stating:

> *'that it would increase the comfort of passengers if the road is placed in good order and the footpaths paved and kerbed in the same way as the footpaths of the Town and a crossing is provided.'*

The council was also quick to see the possible benefits to Ongar of an extension to the railway when the proposals for the Ongar Dunmow and Yeldham light railway came to its attention in 1898. They passed a resolution in favour of the line's construction:

> *'being of the opinion that the District traversed by the line is urgently in need of increased railway facilities and that the railway as proposed will be a material benefit to all classes of the community and give a great impetus to the trade of the district.'*

Unfortunately the proposed line never came to fruition. Interestingly, a petition was submitted and signed by several members of the council in March 1899

ASPECTS OF THE HISTORY OF ONGAR

asking the Great Eastern Railway Company to provide a faster service of trains between Ongar and London. Signatures were also sought from residents of Ongar and neighbourhood.

A fire brigade was established in Ongar some time between 1878 and 1886, according to entries in the *Kelly's Directory* for these years. The Ongar Waterworks Company was in operation by 1898, and was offering free supply of water for the extinguishing of fires if the parish council would install and maintain the necessary number of hydrants, costing around 75s each. The council decided to approach the several fire insurance companies operating in the area to see if they would be willing to subscribe to the costs of the works. However, the fire insurance companies all declined the offer, leaving the parish council, with the permission of the annual parish meeting, to provide a sufficient number of hydrants for the town. An estimate for eight hydrants was received from Messrs J Tyler and Sons of Newgate Street, London for a sum of £42 16s 0d, and in March 1899 Mr Childs, secretary of Ongar Waterworks Company suggested suitable locations for the hydrants:

No 1 *Between the Railway Station and Rectory*
No 2 *Between the grammar school and Mr Noble's [builders]*
No 3 *Opposite Mr Ashdown's [drapers]*
No 4 *Opposite Mr Cowee's for Church etc .[butcher]*
No 5 *Council House for Castle Street*
No 6 *Congregational Chapel*
No 7 *Entrance to Mr Cowee's field opposite Mr Gadsdon's shop [coach builder]*
No 8 *The Borough.*

The council accepted these recommendations subject to an inspection of the relevant sites. The next mention of hydrants in the minutes is in December 1901, when Mr Cowee was appointed:

> *'to ascertain if the Fire Brigade Hose fitted the hydrants of the Town and that if necessary he be empowered to purchase a sufficient length of hose to fit the same.'*

Estimates are later received for two lengths of hose amounting to £20, and the railway fare and expenses of Mr Ely, captain of the Ongar Fire Brigade, are paid to enable him to visit Messrs Shand and Mason, London, to choose suitable hoses. An agreement was then drawn up with Mr Wightman, draper of High Street, Ongar to store the hose on his premises, padlocked for security, for the sum of 1s per annum.

As the end of the century approaches consideration is given to the Diamond Jubilee celebrations for Queen Victoria in 1897. Various suggestions were put forward at a special parish meeting in May 1897:

LOCAL GOVERNMENT IN ONGAR

The erection of an ornamental lamp and bust of the Queen on the site of the Old Town Hall
The lighting of the Town with Incandescent Light in place of that at present used
That additional lamps be provided between the Railway Station and Shelley
That the Main Street be widened at its narrowest part
That a recreation ground be provided for the children of Ongar.

All suggestions were rejected apart from that of the recreation ground. A special committee of local residents was established to raise funds and arrange the celebrations for the Diamond Jubilee, but there is no further information given in the minute book as to what actually happened.

Relationship with Ongar Rural District Council

Throughout these early years of the parish council there was a continual dialogue with the Ongar RDC, largely brought about by the restricted power of the parish itself. The earliest mentioned communication in the parish minute book is the request from the Ongar RDC to buy a portion of the waste ground at the front of the cemetery in order to build a council house for themselves to meet in. This request was quickly rejected by the parish council. Ongar RDC went on to build the council house on the corner of Castle Street in 1896, now Essex House. Once this venue was operational, Ongar parish council was advised by the Local Government Board that it had the right to use the council house for meetings too, as the building had been paid for by local rates. So from 18 March 1897 onwards the parish council meetings were held there.

Representation of the parish on Ongar RDC became an issue in 1896, with a county council proposal to alter the representation of certain parishes in the county. For Ongar the proposal was that the parishes of Chipping Ongar and Greensted should be combined to allow only two representatives for the combined parishes instead of three. The parish council's reply was to reject such an idea, being:

> '*very much surprised at any alteration being suggested in the way of diminishing representation of certain Parishes in the County, especially with regard to Ongar which is the Metropolis of the Union.*'

They even went on to suggest that the representation for Chipping Ongar itself should be increased to three seats.

Other than road repairs, the majority of communication between the two councils seems to have been over the matter of the sanitary condition of the town. Ongar RDC was the local sanitary authority so had the powers to deal with some of the concerns. The condition of the Cripsey Brook at Ongar Bridge was the catalyst for a joint committee to meet to consider the option of a dam to improve the river, and to consider a report on the general sanitary condition of the town.

ASPECTS OF THE HISTORY OF ONGAR

The report from the county medical officer of health in August 1896 recommended that Ongar RDC be called upon:

> 'To provide a proper water supply for the Parish of Chipping Ongar
> To provide a proper system of sewerage for the same Parish
> To cease to pollute the Cripsey Brook by discharging crude sewage therein.'

The RDC surveyor had drawn up plans for the sewerage of Ongar by April 1897 and a joint committee was again established to inspect these plans. The final decision was then postponed due to a visit to Exeter to see an automatic system. However, at the parish council meeting of 11 May 1898 it was decided that:

> 'the field marked No 83 on Ordnance map is recommended as a suitable site for the proposed Drainage Works of Chipping Ongar and Marden Ash' and 'that the scheme of drainage be on the septic tank system.'

Cripsey Brook was still being described as dangerous and a health hazard in August 1899, but progress was being made on the new sewerage works with claims for compensation being paid to landowners of the chosen site in September 1902.

Meantime the district council had decided to delegate its powers under the Public Health Act in regard to the removal of household refuse to the parish council, who were then responsible for tendering for a contractor to collect the town's rubbish.

It is unfortunate that the corresponding minute book for Ongar RDC after its establishment is missing, so it is not possible to see the same issues from the opposite perspective. It appears that parish councils from the outset were as much lobbyists for the parish cause as authorities in their own right. They made demands on rural district and county councils for improvements to sanitation or highways that went beyond their own powers or pockets, as well as complaining to railway authorities, water suppliers and poor law guardians. Most parish councils around this time would have had about 20 items on the agenda for each meeting, of which a quarter would often be about the activities of bodies other than themselves.[20]

Into the twentieth century

Parish council business carried on in a similar vein for a number of years. Looking ten years on in the minute books, the business was still dominated by public lamps, the cemetery, the provision of a fire engine and the speed of motor vehicles. The Small Holdings and Allotments Act of 1907 brought a new issue on to the agenda. Ongar Parish Council received plenty of requests from residents wanting to have an allotment, but the council had terrible trouble trying to find some suitable land, despite newspaper advertisements. Other added powers during the early years of the century included the Open Spaces Act 1906, allowing parish councils to acquire and maintain open spaces.

LOCAL GOVERNMENT IN ONGAR

As the years passed, there appeared to be a general slipping away of local power. In 1902 local school boards were abolished and local education authorities were established. In 1919 the new Ministry of Health took over all public health issues, and the 1925 Rating and Valuation Act ended the reign of the overseers of the poor and made Ongar RDC the local rating authority. This trend was continued by the Local Government Act 1929, which introduced a consolidated general rate and abolished the boards of guardians. Further losses of responsibility came with the nationalisation of gas and electricity, regional water and sewerage authorities and regional hospital boards, and later health authorities. The idea of the single self-governing local unit has by now long since disappeared.[21]

With the advent of Harlow new town in the late 1940s, there was the need for a small reorganisation of authorities at district level, which lead to the establishment of the Epping and Ongar Rural District Council in 1955. The new council met at the offices in Castle Street once a month. Meanwhile the Parish Councils Act of 1957 gave some of the responsibilities of the old Lighting and Watching Acts back to the parish. These included the provision of clocks, seats and bus shelters. Litter bins were added by the Public Health Act of 1961. In 1965, the Civil Parish of Ongar was formed by the amalgamation of Chipping Ongar, Shelley, and Greensted parish councils together with Marden Ash.

In the big reorganisation of local government in 1972, the parish council was the only tier to come through relatively unscathed. Parish councils increased their areas of responsibility to include the arts, tourism and public conveniences, as well as the important principle of consultation on local planning issues. As Ongar became part of the larger Epping Forest District Council in 1974, with its large urban areas, Ongar parish council again took on an important role as the voice of its own local community.

References

1. For full details of early local government, see Jackson, P.W. *Local Government*, (1986) Macmillan.
2. Vestry minutes 1743–1775. ERO: D/P 124/8/1A. Most of the local information in this section is derived from these minute books.
3. Chipping Ongar parish register transcript. ERO: T/R 76
4. Vaughan, E. *The Essex Village in Days Gone By* (1930) Bentham, 2nd edition.
5. VCH Essex volume 4 (1956) p.168
6. Vestry minutes 1821–1863. ERO: D/P 124/8/3
7. Ongar Union minutes 1836. ERO: G/On M1
8. Ongar Union minutes 1865–1872. ERO: G/On M5
9. Ongar Voluntary Fire Brigade minute book. ERO D/Z 49
10. Vestry minutes 1743–1775. ERO: D/P 124/8/1A. The night watch subscription list is on a loose sheet in the back of this minute book but the names of the signatories date it to the 1830s.
11. Lighting and Gas Rate books. ERO: D/P 124/23/1
12. Ongar Burial Board minute book 1863–1885.
13. Vaughan, E., op. cit p.62
14. *Kelly's Directory* (1895)
15. Vestry minutes 1869–1921. ERO: D/P 124/8/5
16. Poole, K.P. *Parish Government 1894–1994*, (1994) National Association of Local Councils
17. ibid p.60

ASPECTS OF THE HISTORY OF ONGAR

18 Ongar Parish Council minute book 1894–1903. This minute book is the source for all meeting details
19 Poole K.P. op cit p.43
20 ibid p.56
21 Byrne, T. *Local Government in England,* (1994) Penguin, rev.ed.

chapter 10

Poor relief in Chipping Ongar

by Martyn Lockwood

The system of poor relief was started during the reign of Elizabeth I and was consolidated by the Poor Law Acts of 1597 and 1601 – a system that was to last until 1834 and which is generally considered the foundation of modern poor law. During this period the parish was the unit of administration and the Acts of 1597 and 1601 ordered the annual election of overseers of the poor, answerable to the parish vestry. In common with all parishes, they were elected at the Easter meeting of the vestry.

The Chipping Ongar vestry was responsible for poor relief prior to 1834 and membership consisted of the minister, churchwardens and leading parishioners. They elected the overseers, and constables who would serve for a period of 12 months. From 1759 monthly meetings were held of the vestry to discuss matters relating to poor relief, especially the costs of providing such relief.

There were two overseers for Chipping Ongar, who were unpaid, and were empowered, in conjunction with the churchwardens, to levy a poor rate for the purpose of providing such sums as might be necessary to meet the expense of relieving the poor. At the Easter meeting of the vestry the overseers had to present their annual accounts of expenditure on the poor.

1803	Thomas Nichols	John Patmore
1806	James Haslam	William Cooper
1808	William Wright	John Dodd
1810	Thomas Shadrack	John Cowee
1811	Henry Starkey	George Archer
1813	William Darby	Daniel Rawlings
1818	Thomas Adams	John Cooper
1823	Francis Bayer	Elias Carter
1829	Edward Moss	William Meeres
1832	Thomas Edwards	William Parker

Table 1: some of the overseers appointed for Ongar

The poor were classified into one of three groups: the "able-bodied" poor who could not find employment and who were to have work provided for them; rogues and vagabonds, and sturdy beggars who were to be whipped, or otherwise punished, for their desire not to work; and the "impotent" poor – the old, sick or handicapped, who were to be relieved in almshouses.

The Poor Relief Act 1601 allowed the overseers to bind out as apprentices orphaned or abandoned children in their care who were under 14 (16 after 1696), although they had to obtain the consent of two justices of the peace. It was not easy to find masters for such apprentices for they were usually bound out at the age of seven and, in some parishes, no premium was paid. Consequently a further Act in 1696 compelled appropriate parishioners, chosen by rotation or ballot, to take on apprentices. Thus in May 1707 the vestry minutes reported, *'It appears by the preceding lists of parish apprentices placed out to the inhabitants, that it comes by rotation to Mr Henly's turn to take a child. Resolved that a girl be placed with W. Henley for a year.'* [1]

In 1662 the Settlement Act set out the ways in which a poor person could claim to be legally settled in a particular parish and gave the overseers power to remove anybody likely to become a burden on the parish and who did not possess a settlement guaranteeing them the right of relief in the parish. Every person had a place of legal settlement, often the parish where they were born, and if they later became too poor to support themselves they could be moved back to their place of settlement. After 1697 anyone moving to find work was required to bring with them a settlement certificate stating they were legally settled in a particular parish and could legally be returned there by a magistrates "removal order" if they needed maintenance. In 1757 the vestry had been served with a settlement order from the overseers of a parish in Wiltshire but at their meeting in January it was decided *'that the Churchwardens and Overseers of the said parish (Chipping Ongar) shall appeal to the order at the City of New Sarum in the County of Wilts, against the settlement of Finch and her three children.'* [2]

In 1772 a pauper by the name of Samuel Offord, who had been hired at the annual statute fair in Chipping Ongar in 1763 by a man from Navestock, was removed together with his wife to Stondon Massey. On appeal to the Quarter Sessions it was decided that the man, who had resided and worked in Navestock for 12 months, had gained a settlement in the parish.[3]

In 1804 the vestry, concerned at the costs imposed on them, reported *'Mr Patmore the Overseer having visited Wm Travell in Warburton Mad-House Bethnall Green reports that the man in his opinion seems to have his proper intellect. It is therefore the opinion of the Vestry that he should return to the workhouse.'*[1]

In 1723 Knatchbull's General Workhouse Act was passed which allowed a parish to erect a workhouse. There are records that suggest a poor-house existed in Chipping Ongar in 1748 and was situated adjacent to the Rectory.[4] In 1795 it was resolved to pull down the poorhouses and that one large building should be erected instead. In the same year it was decided *'that the site of the old building being inconvenient to the Rector, the parishioners do agree to exchange the present site for a portion of the glebe of equal extent now offered by the rector.'*

It is possible that the site of the new workhouse was built on the glebe to the north of St Martin's church. It was estimated that the cost of the new poorhouse would be £153 and the vestry agreed that £100 of this should be borrowed on a ten-year term. The building was carried out in 1797. John Crabb of Shelley Hall lent the £100 but in the same year required repayment. The vestry decided to meet half the debt immediately out of the rates and to borrow £50 from someone else.[4]

POOR RELIEF IN CHIPPING ONGAR

The cost of providing relief was a constant problem. In 1744 the poor rates were £119 but had risen to about £350 in 1798 and in 1800 they amounted to £454. At a vestry meeting in April 1748 *'it is ordered and agreed that for the future no surgeon or apothecary shall be allowed an Bill or sum of money from the parishioners of the said parish for anything done to any of the poor of the said parish, unless the same shall be done by order, first in writing under the hand of any of the churchwardens or Overseers of the poor of the said parish.'*[2] In 1761 a parish doctor was appointed at an annual salary of 5 guineas, but this was reduced in 1770 to £4. Before 1761 it would appear that medical treatment was paid for as each case arose.

In 1782 Gilbert's Act allowed parishes to combine into unions where the unemployed able-bodied were provided first with outdoor relief and then with work, while indoor relief was restricted to caring for the old, sick and dependant children. Examples of such outdoor relief include, in 1823, the overseers allowing the sum of seven shillings for *'William Parker, a pauper towards buying a bed,'* and in 1835 the following: *'Daniel Foster applied for relief being ill – Granted. John Whitbread's wife for relief – Granted. Will Sourby's family applied for assistance for shoes – Granted. Widow Wood for relief – To be allowed one shilling.'*[5]

In May 1800 it was resolved that every householder of sufficient ability should in turn either take an apprentice or yearly a servant, a boy or girl from the parish or should provide a suitable master for such child and in the following June it was decided to hold a ballot to decide the first allotment of pauper apprentices. In July 1800 the vestry decided to enlarge the workhouse although it is not clear whether this work was carried out. However in 1802 there was a fire which necessitated rebuilding work to be carried out, the cost coming from the poor rates. In 1807 the cost of finishing the back chamber of the workhouse amounted to £4 15s 0d. The poor rates continued to rise; in 1806 they were £674. In May 1815 a committee chaired by the Rev H. J. Parker was formed to investigate *'causes of the late great expense of the Poor House.'* To assist them in their enquiry the committee called the late overseers Messrs Darbey and Starkey to assist in their investigation. The expenditure for the years 1813 and 1814 were reported as follows:

Beer	£40 17s	*Bread*	£101 4s 3d
Meat	£90 4s ½d	*Vegetables*	£6
Firing	£38 10s 4d	*Grocery*	£101 15s 5 ½d
Milk	£12 11s 2d	*Mrs Cracknell's salary*	£21'

Its report revealed that in 1813 and 1814 the average number of persons in the poor house was eleven and the cost of maintaining each person was 7s 2d per week. In all £407 2s 3d had been spent, of which £63 was reckoned as the cost of maintaining the "governor" and her two children. The committee suggested that a plan be adopted for *'the diminution of such unnecessary expense.'* The method suggested to achieve this was to advertise in the county newspapers for a governor who *'will undertake to provide suitable and sufficient maintenance for*

ASPECTS OF THE HISTORY OF ONGAR

the paupers at such sum per head weekly as the vestry may think proper to stipulate for.'[1] In June 1815, a Mr Jessup from Epping was given the job. At the vestry meeting in April 1819 it was resolved to appoint a full time overseer who would also fill the role of vestry clerk at an annual salary of £15.

In 1820 problems over the expenses of the workhouse continued to trouble the vestry and John Heard replaced Jessup as governor. Heard was paid 4s 3d per person per week. In 1821 the vestry adopted a long and detailed code of regulations for the relief of the poor, with special reference to the keeping of the overseer's accounts. These are shown in Table 2. An audit of the accounts revealed a debt of £196. The state of the overseers' accounts was also called into question and a permanent committee of audit was formed to check the accounts. In 1822 John Osborne, a former schoolmaster, was appointed perpetual overseer at an annual salary of £15.

1. Master to enter in a book, names, ages of persons admitted and of those discharged or on death.
2. All inmates to be acquainted with the rules and regulations and same to be hung up.
3. Master to carefully promote cleanliness, industry, sobriety, peace and piety in the work house and to prevent contrary vices of sloth, idleness, wastefulness, intemperance, discord and immoral language and on no account suffer cards, dice, or any gambling in the said house.
4. All beds, linen, rooms and other parts of the house to be kept clean and decent and no damage done.
5. An inventory of all furniture, goods, linen, clothing, working implements be kept.
6. All linen and things capable of being marked be marked.
7. Prayers be read to inmates at 8 o' clock in the morning throughout the year and 7 o' clock in the evening during the winter half year and at 9 o' clock during the summer half year and all who are well and able be required to attend.
8. All who are well and able to attend parish Church or some other place of worship at least once on every Sabbath day.
9. Inmates required to be in the Poor House before the hour of nine in the evening during the summer half-year and before the hour of seven during the winter half year. Not to leave without permission of the Master and such permission be not granted except on urgent occasions.
10. Master to keep a strict charge and care of all the children in the Poor House who do not go out to work and that he be required to attend to their moral conduct, cleanliness and general good behaviour.

Table 2: Rules for the workhouse adopted in 1821[5]

In 1828 William Wood was appointed Master of the Poor House at an annual salary of £10 for his own and his wife's services. In addition he was allowed *'5d per head per week for the washing of those whom the parish officers may direct them to wash'*, and *'4s 4d per week for firing for the use of the Poor House.'* Improvements were also made to the work-house at this time. At their meeting in February 1829 the vestry considered a scheme to join a voluntary union with other parishes in the area, but it appears that they decided against the idea. However Stanford Rivers did join with nine other parishes to form a voluntary union which led to the building of the work-house at Stanford Rivers, later to be adopted as the workhouse for the Ongar Union. At a meeting held in June 1832 the Chipping Ongar vestry adopted a further set of rules, orders and regulations for the management of the workhouse.

1. No person whatever be admitted into the house as an inmate without a written order from churchwarden and overseer, or either of them.

2. That the earnings of the inmate be accounted for to the parish by such inmates respectively to the churchwardens and overseers.

3. That no goods or furniture or linen be brought into the house, or be removed from it without a special order from the overseer.

4. That the names and ages of all the persons, who shall be from time to time be admitted into the parish house or be discharged or die, be entered into a book kept for that purpose.

5. That the master be careful to promote cleanliness, industry, frugality, sobriety, peace and piety and to prevent sloth, idleness, waste, intemperance, discord and immoral language and no account to suffer tippling, or any kind of gambling whatever in the said house.

6. The Master be responsible to the parish officers for the safekeeping of the property of the poor house and that he mark every article with the parish mark COP.

7. That prayers be read to the inmates morning and evening throughout the year and that all who are able are required to attend the same.

8. That the inmates required to be in the House before the hour of nine in the evening during the summer half year and before the hour of seven during the winter half year, at which hour the doors be closed for the night.

9. That the Master do keep strict charge and care of all the children in the parish house.

10. That the Master with the sanction of the overseer be empowered to remove any pauper or paupers from room to room, as occasion requires.

11. That the Master do report any breach of the foregoing regulations to the parish officers without delay, in order that the offender may be taken before a Magistrate to answer for his or her misconduct.

12. That the poor be allowed to leave the house at any reasonable hour to lay their complaint before the parish officers.

13. That a copy of the Rules, Bylaws and Regulations be affixed to the wall of every room in the poor house.

Table 3: Rules for the Ongar workhouse adopted in 1832

ASPECTS OF THE HISTORY OF ONGAR

The Ongar Union:

Expenditure on the poor throughout England and Wales rose considerably during the late eighteenth and early nineteenth centuries and, as a result of increasing economic and social pressure, change was inevitable. A social policy designed for a largely rural population of some 4 million people could not cope with the rapid urbanisation that took place. An increase in population from 6 to 9 million in the second half of the eighteenth century and from 9 to 14 million by 1834 [6] was bound to lead to change. In 1832 a Royal Commission was established to consider the position of the poor within society, which until that time had been the responsibility of each parish. One of the commissioners, Edwin Chadwick, formulated a plan to take poor relief out of the hands of the parish and entrust its administration to salaried national government officers. However his suggestion was not adopted, a compromise being reached, and a locally controlled system of poor relief, supervised by central government was implemented on 14 August 1834.

The Poor Law Amendment Act, 1834 created a body called the Poor Law Commission who were responsible for forming unions of parishes for the purpose of poor relief. The unions were administered by a board of guardians, whose members were elected by open ballot from the ratepayers and local gentry in each parish. Thus power effectively was taken away from parishes and put into the hands of the board of guardians. To ensure uniform levels of poor relief, the Poor Law Commission appointed inspectors to inspect each union regularly, a fact bitterly resented.

At the Chipping Ongar vestry meeting held in May 1835 the following motion was under discussion:

> *'Notice is hereby given that a public vestry of the owners or occupiers of lands, tenements, or hereditaments assessed after their sale at five pounds per annum will be held at the poor house of this parish on Thursday May 7th 1835 at six o' clock in the evening, for the purpose of considering the propriety of adopting such of the provisions of an Act passed in the 22 year of his Majesty King George the Third, entitled 'An Act for the better relief and employment of the Poor' as are now in force, and of incorporating this Parish with the several parishes of Abbotts Roothing, Bobbingworth, Great Warley, Greensted, Little Laver, Stanford Rivers, Stapleford Abbotts, Stapleford Tawney, Stondon Massey and Shelley, already incorporated by virtue of the said Act, either alone or together with any other parishes.'* [5]

Those present at the meeting and voting agreed to this proposal and so Chipping Ongar voted to become part of the Ongar Union. The union consisted of the 26 parishes shown in Table 4. It was established in 1836; and the first meeting of the board of guardians was held at the Town Hall in Ongar on 26 April.

POOR RELIEF IN CHIPPING ONGAR

Abbess Roding	High Ongar	Shellow Bowells
Beauchamp Roding	Kelvedon Hatch	Stanford Rivers
Berners Roding.	Lambourne	Stapleford Abbots
Blackmore	High Laver	Stapleford Tawney
Bobbingworth	Little Laver	Stondon Massey
Chipping Ongar	Moreton	Theydon Mount
Doddinghurst	Navestock	Willingale Doe
Fyfield	Norton Mandeville	Willingale Spain
Greensted	Shelley	

Table 4: The 26 parishes forming the Ongar Union.

The total population of the union at this time was just under 11,000 people.[7] At their first meeting, the guardians were appointed. Each parish was allowed one guardian with the exception of Chipping Ongar, High Ongar and Stanford Rivers who were allowed two each. Capel Cure was appointed chairman, Thomas Horner vice-chairman and William Baker, a solicitor from Chipping Ongar, clerk to the guardians. William Coe (109 votes) and James Haslam (88 votes) were elected by the ratepayers as guardians for Chipping Ongar.

For the purpose of providing relief the union was divided into two districts and a relieving officer appointed for each. Robert Eve from Fyfield was appointed for the Fyfield district and John Palmer from Stanford Rivers for that district. Each was to receive a salary of £80 per year and because of the nature of the job each man was required to enter into a bond of £200 with two sureties each of £100 to ensure the proper discharge of their duties.

The board of guardians agreed to meet on the Tuesday of each week at the Town Hall in Chipping Ongar to carry out their business and Mr Baker was allowed the sum of 5s per week towards the cost of hiring the room for the meetings. George Keys the appointed constable for Chipping Ongar was appointed doorkeeper at a salary of 2s 6d per day *'for his attendance upon the Board during sittings.'*

A committee of guardians was formed to inspect each parish workhouse within the union and following their inspection it was agreed that use would be made of the work houses at Chipping Ongar and High Ongar for the next 12 months, in addition to that at Stanford Rivers which was to remain the union workhouse until its sale to a private company in 1923. The remaining parish workhouses would be sold off.

The workhouse at Stanford Rivers had been built in 1830–31, when Stanford Rivers, using Gilbert's Act of 1782, had formed a voluntary poor law union with nine other parishes. £300 had been raised on £50 bonds at four per cent in order to contribute to the cost of the building. A conveyance dated 23 March 1830 indicated that the land at London Road, Little End, was leased by the Capel Cure family to the *'Visitors and Guardians of Sundry Parishes.'*

Each of the three workhouses to be retained by the union was to be used for a different purpose: Chipping Ongar for the children of paupers, High Ongar for the aged and infirm and Stanford Rivers for the able bodied male and female paupers. However at their meeting held on the 10 May 1836, this was changed, with Stanford Rivers being divided into two parts, one for able-bodied males and the other for able-bodied females and children. It was decided to keep Chipping Ongar workhouse but that its use would be at the discretion of the guardians.

James Thomson and his wife Sarah were appointed master and matron of Stanford Rivers workhouse at a joint salary of £70 per annum; John Hurd and his wife Ann to the positions at High Ongar at a joint salary of £40, whilst George Keys and his wife were appointed to Chipping Ongar at a salary of £10. The board of guardians were empowered to appoint a number of paid officials, and these included a clerk to the guardians, treasurer, master and matron of the workhouse, schoolmaster and schoolmistress, porter and nurse as well as the relieving officers.

The workhouse at Stanford Rivers still belonged to the previous administration but a decision was made to enlarge it for the reception of an additional 140 paupers. The workhouse building was valued at £2335 whilst the land, furniture, fixtures and *'things therein'* were valued at £578 7s 9d. The board of guardians agreed to purchase the workhouse. It was also agreed that a schoolhouse should be built *'where the privies now stand of sufficient size to receive the whole of the inmates of the workhouse as a chapel.'* The population of the workhouses at this time was 210.

In 1837 the overseers for Chipping Ongar were ordered by the Board to adopt proceedings to compel George Bright, a pauper belonging to Chipping Ongar, to support his child who was chargeable to the parish. This was not unusual, for in every case where relief was given the guardians sought to ensure that those who were liable for the upkeep paid. Such was their enthusiasm to pursue those who were liable for maintenance that in 1894 the guardians offered a reward of £1 for the apprehension of Herbert Martin from Blackmore for deserting his wife and family who were being maintained at the expense of the union. The reward was increased the following year to £2 and in 1898 to £5, but there is no record of Martin having been apprehended.

Money was always an overriding consideration of the board. In 1849 the rate payers of Chipping Ongar recommended that the board should pay £7 towards the cost of apprenticing a boy, Joseph Whitbread, to the sea service, but this was turned down; but in 1879 they apprenticed an 18 year old orphan to Jane Carman, a milliner of Chipping Ongar, the cost of the indenture of apprenticeship costing £10. In 1884 Emily Weal *'a poor girl, lately an inmate of the workhouse and incapacitated for domestic service'* was apprenticed to Mrs Reynolds, widow and dressmaker of Chipping Ongar for three years. In 1890 Alfred Reed, described as a *'cripple boy'* was provided with clothing at a cost of £1 16s upon leaving the workhouse and a sum of 4s 3d per week paid to Mrs Smith, the wife of the wheelwright at Ongar, for agreeing to take the child.

In March 1837 the board of guardians agreed to stop using and to sell the workhouse at Chipping Ongar. The vestry unanimously agreed to the sale of their poor house, which was described in the sale notice as *'a timber built messuage used as a workhouse with the outhouses, yard, brickwall and appendages belonging thereto situate in the town of Chipping Ongar.'* The sale fetched £200, the monies being passed on to the board.[8]

Medical relief was provided for the poor and the union was divided into six districts with a medical officer appointed for each. An infirmary was provided at the workhouse and a school building built for the education of the children. A chaplain was also appointed for the moral welfare of the inmates. The diet of the inmates was strictly controlled, but extra rations were usually provided at Christmas and hot cross buns at Easter. In 1852 it was proposed that the *'the adult paupers should have half a pound of meat, half a pound of plum pudding and a pint of beer, and the children half such quantities for dinner on Christmas day.'*[9] In 1897 the guardians agreed to provide *'a meat tea of beef and ham with beer and tobacco for the men and tea and sugar for the women to commemorate the Queen's Jubilee.'* On Christmas day 1906, it was reported that dinner consisted of roast beef, roast pork and stuffing, greens, parsnips, plum pudding and mince pies, ale and milk.[10]

Local residents did their best to brighten up the lives of the inhabitants. In 1891 the chaplain, the Rev. Cochrane requested that entertainments be provided during the winter months and each year the Stanford Rivers "Cottage Garden Show" sent invitations for the children to attend. On New Year's day 1906 the chaplain the Rev. J. Thomas and a number of friends gave an entertainment for the inmates which was much enjoyed. A delightful feature was a violin trio by the Misses Raby, and the Rector's song "The Maid of the Mill" *'gave intense pleasure.'*[11]

The conditions in the workhouse came in for criticism on several occasions by the Inspectors. In 1865 it was agreed to spend £500 to *'remedy those evils in the workhouse.'* In 1883 Mr Lockwood, the inspector from the Local Government Board, described the schoolmistress's sleeping apartments as *'injurious to health';*[12] and in 1886 the sanitary conditions were considered unsatisfactory with respect to the water supply. The death rate amongst inmates at this time was considered excessive with outbreaks of typhoid fever being reported. In 1895 the receiving ward was described as a *'damp and unwholesome bedroom.'* Several outbreaks of smallpox were also reported and in 1882 the nurse at the workhouse, Nurse Bowman, contracted the disease. In 1904 12 cases were reported in the infirmary, the patients being isolated in the smallpox tents at Toot Hill.

Tramps and vagrants visited the workhouse where they received a night's lodging. They first had to obtain an order from the police inspector at Ongar police station (who held the position of assistant relieving officer for vagrants) and then present it at the workhouse before being admitted. In 1894 a committee of

ASPECTS OF THE HISTORY OF ONGAR

guardians were concerned at the increased number of "casuals" visiting the workhouse, which they put down to the inspector indiscriminately granting orders. In 1895 there was accommodation for nine vagrants, but it was reported that in the pea picking season it was made to serve twenty-five. It was recommended to the guardians that a new receiving ward should be built, but this was rejected in favour of three stone-breaking cages, in which vagrants would be locked to ensure they carried out their work, and a disinfecting room.

In return for their keep the tramps were required to break 4cwt of stones before being released. In December of the same year three tramps received 10 days hard labour each for insubordination at the workhouse.[13] In March 1902 a tramp, George Simpkins, refused to carry out the allotted task and was taken before the magistrates. He was sentenced to 14 days hard labour. In June 1904 a man was charged with refusing to break stone. He had broken 1cwt instead of the amount required. He stated in his defence that he had had no food for three days prior to entering the workhouse, but he was sent back by the magistrates to complete his task. On 1 June 1912, 50 tramps visited the workhouse and the supply of bread ran out.

In 1905 the Conservative government of A. J. Balfour appointed a Royal Commission to investigate the working of the poor law. It sat from 1905 until 1908 before finally producing two reports, a majority and a minority report. Children were finally removed from workhouses in 1908 and in the same year the importance of the poor law was much reduced by the introduction of old age pensions. In 1911 the first state sickness and unemployment insurance schemes were introduced. These gradually led to an alternative approach to social welfare. In 1920 the guardians recommended that the workhouse should be closed down and that the resident inmates should be transferred to the workhouse at Epping. The board of guardians continued in being until 1930.

In October 1923 the building was sold to the Island Manufacturing Company, but this concern seems to have had a short existence as it was liquidated in 1926.[11] The workhouse buildings remain to this day, mainly unaltered, a sad testimony to a chapter in the history of social welfare and reform. It is claimed that the building is haunted and employees still refuse to work in certain parts. The building is currently owned by Piggott Brothers.

References

1. ERO: D/P 124/8/2
2. ERO: D/P 124/8/1A
3. ERO: QSBb 268
4. VCH Essex vol 4 (1956) p.168
5. ERO: D/P 124/8/3
6. Digby, A. *The Poor Law in Nineteenth Century England* (1982) The Historical Association
7. Second Annual Report of the Poor Law Commissioners (1836), ERO. The population in 1851 was 11,855, but by 1891 had fallen to 10,557. In 1931, just after the closure of the workhouse, the population in the 26 parishes was 11,520.
8. Fourth Annual Report of the Poor Law Commissioners (1838), ERO.

9   ERO: G/OnM4
10 ERO: G/OnM13
11 Scott, H. *Stanford Rivers* (1973). Published privately
12 ERO: G/OnM8
13 ERO: G/OnM16

chapter 11

Law and order in Chipping Ongar

by Martyn Lockwood

The parish constable

The office of constable is manorial in origin and provided the link between the lord of the manor and his tenants and the keeper of law and order. He was appointed by the court leet, but by the eighteenth century the parish vestry meeting made the appointment. The vestry books for Chipping Ongar survive for the periods 1743 to 1775 and 1780 to 1863[1] and at the Easter meetings the constable was appointed for the following year. The parish constable received no salary for his year in office and therefore took fees for such tasks as executing warrants, searching for witnesses, or even attending court. He was part-time, often a shopkeeper or artisan, ignorant of the substantive law, but responsible for maintaining law and order in the parish. In 1562 at the Ongar Hundred petty sessions, William Tynge of Stanford Rivers was ordered *'that he shall not further frequent the society of Joan Palmer, widow of Chipping Ongar, because they are suspected persons and of dishonest conversation, under a penalty to forfeit as often as they are found associating, to wit William 13s 4d and Joan 6s 8d.'*[2]

At other times the role of constable could prove difficult. In 1678, William Holbrook of Chipping Ongar was charged at the Essex Quarter Sessions with assaulting Samuel Binckes and his men with a "naked sword" at the Greyhound Inn, Ongar. Holbrook, it would appear, was attempting to release a man who had been taken into custody by Binckes who was constable of the Ongar Hundred.

It would appear from the vestry books that Chipping Ongar appointed two constables each year. Table 1 shows the names of some of those appointed to the position:

1749	John Wright	John Mitchell
1765	Richard Carey	Richard Guy
1803	John Crossingham	William Ainsworth
1808	William Slaughter	Henry Starkey
1812	Abraham Hodsoll	George Keys

Table 1: names of parish constables for Chipping Ongar

In 1812 George Keys was appointed the parish constable for Chipping Ongar. He apparently liked the job for he held the position until 1836, when his name disappears from the records. In 1842 a meeting of the vestry was held *'to nominate six persons qualified and liable to serve as constables within the parish...and to consider the propriety of appointing one or more paid constables for this parish.'*[3] The following were appointed: William Penson, carpenter, Jeremiah

Bridge,shoemaker, William Pavitt, tailor, John Keys, whitesmith, Charley Gidley, schoolmaster, and Richard Oliver, farrier. However it was resolved unanimously by the meeting that it was not necessary to have one or more paid constables.

In one of the Ongar vestry books is a loose, undated sheet of paper, dating from the nineteenth century. It is entitled *'Proposed Night Watch at the Town of Ongar.'* It states:

> *'In consequence of the depredations recently committed in the Town of Ongar and the numerous vagrants and suspicious characters which are seen about it at night, it is suggested as a measure conducive to check the progress and return of such proceedings that the inhabitants of Ongar appoint a young and respectable Man as Night Watchman, who will otherwise be appointed Special Constable. The expense would probably not exceed a guinea weekly which if 60 householders in Ongar would contribute four pence each weekly would meet the demand'.*

Under this are the names of 69 inhabitants supporting the proposal. There is no evidence that such a person was appointed.

The birth of modern policing

Essex was one of the first counties to avail itself of the County Police Act 1839 and to form a professional police force. In April 1840, 100 constables and 15 superintendents[4] were appointed under the command of a chief constable, Captain (later Admiral) John Bunch Bonnemaison McHardy, a retired Naval officer. From the outset, Ongar became one of the fourteen divisions that was to make up the force, under the direction of Superintendent John McInnes, a former sergeant in the 2nd Battalion Scots Fusiliers, born in Ayr; and three constables. A further two constables were stationed at Blackmore. McInnes, who was over 40 years of age when he joined, was replaced in 1848 by Superintendent Henry Flood, who before joining had been employed as a glassblower.

Records held by the Essex Police Museum provide us with the details of some of the early constables stationed at Ongar. One of the first was a Joseph Darlington, a 23-year-old plumber, born in Glasgow, who had only joined the force on 23 March 1841. He was living in the High Street with his wife Sophie and 10 month old son Robert, but the rigours of being a constable did not suit him as he resigned on 17 March 1842. Another was William Finch, a native of Ingatestone who joined the police on 22 June 1848 when he was 23, having previously been a groom. He became Constable 22 and in the census of 1851 was living in Two Brewers Row at Two Brewers End with his 30-year-old wife Mary and three year old son John. He resigned due to ill health in 1854.

The 1871 census showed that living at Cherry Garden Cottage, Ongar, was a Jeremiah Raison, described as an "assistant Superintendent of Police". This may be a mistake for "retired". He lived with his wife Phoebe, who, like her husband had been born at Dedham. He was 50 and she 49, which seems quite young for

ASPECTS OF THE HISTORY OF ONGAR

a senior officer to retire. Living with them were three daughters, Clara (aged 20), Emily (aged 13) and Lydia (aged 11). Raison joined the force on 1 November 1845, having previously been a soldier. Another register gave his date of birth as 1819 and said that retirement on 31 December 1870 was due to *'infirmity of mind.'*

In 1843 an application to build a lock-up was made, the application being supported by a letter from the Under Secretary of State, who declared that a lock-up should be built at Ongar. The argument failed to convince the justices, who decided in favour of a police station at Epping.[5] However in 1847, Mr Budworth offered land for a police station and this, together with a magistrates court was built in 1855, by Mr Henry Hayward, who was also responsible for building the police stations at Dunmow and Latchingdon. The cost was £1500, on land purchased for £205 in the High Street, on a site now occupied by the present station. The original building was to remain until 1964 when it was demolished and the present building erected at a cost of £30,000.[6]

1840	Superintendent John McInnes
1848	Superintendent Henry Flood
1855	Superintendent Joseph Catchpole
1867	Inspector Charles Fox
1871–1893	Inspector Charles Foster Robinson
1893–1899	Inspector Patrick Gallagher
1902–1904	Inspector James William Burrell
1908	Inspector Arthur Brown
1912–1913	Inspector Richard Giggins
1913–1915	Inspector Charles Fordham
1915–1921	Inspector Arthur Edward Brown
1921–1922	Inspector Thomas Browning
1923–1928	Inspector Percy Poulton
1928–1933	Inspector Charles Weeden
1933–1946	Inspector Alfred E. Butcher
1946–1946	Inspector John Silwood
1946–1950	Inspector Alex Woolner
1950–1960	Inspector Rupert Green
1960–1965	Inspector Ronald Payne
1965–1967	Inspector Doug Badcock
1967–1979	Inspector/Chief Inspector Alan Cartwright.

Table 2: officers in charge of Ongar Police Sub-division 1840–1979

By 1855 Superintendent Joseph Catchpole was in charge, but in that year Ongar ceased to be a Division in its own right and became a sub-division of the Epping Division, under the command of Superintendent William Pattinson. From 1855 the officer in charge at Ongar held the rank of inspector.[7] Table 2 lists the names of those in charge at Ongar, from 1840 until 1979. In 1866 gas lighting was installed in the police station, the gas being supplied by the Ongar Gas Company.

In addition to maintaining law and order police officers were also responsible for enforcing the law in respect of other matters. These included Relieving Officers (Poor Law), Inspectors of Petroleum, Explosives, Horse Slaughtering Yards, Hackney Carriages, Contagious Diseases (Animals) Acts, Pleasure Grounds and Forecourts, Common Lodging Houses, Food and Drugs and Employment of Children.[8] Superintendent McInnes was one of the first officers to be appointed an Inspector of Weights and Measures in 1843.[9] In 1849 the Chief Constable agreed that Superintendent Henry Flood could undertake the role of Assistant Relieving Officer *'so far as concerns the wandering poor'* for the Ongar Union.[10]

In November 1855 a George Joslin of Moreton was robbed near Ongar by two men, one of whom held him in a ditch whilst the other stole £1 3s 6d. The two men were later caught and sentenced to 12 months and eight months hard labour respectively.[11]

In the 1870s there was growing concern in Essex over the number of criminals who were moving out from London to commit crime. The railway had been extended to Ongar in 1865, allowing for easier travel, and crime, including burglaries and horse stealing, was prevalent in the area. In 1885, following the murder of Inspector Thomas Simmons at Rainham, police officers patrolling rural areas bordering on the Metropolis were given the option of carrying firearms and two revolvers were held by the Inspector at Ongar to be issued to men *'who desire to have them when employed on night duty.'*

Horse-stealing had always been a serious problem in rural areas. In 1825 James Mallett had been hanged for stealing a horse at Stanford Rivers. In 1885, the Chief Constable, William Poyntz, published the following account of an incident that had occurred in Ongar in General Orders as an example for the rest of the force.

> *'A case having occurred at Ongar in which a considerable want of ordinary sharpness and intelligence shown by an Inspector and constable resulting in the escape of a horse stealer, the Chief Constable hereby publishes the facts as a warning to members of the force to be more careful under similar circumstances. On the night of 30th ultimo, at a quarter to eleven, a man rode into Ongar on a horse with only a common halter and without a saddle and bridle. He was stopped by the Inspector and challenged as to where he had had the animal and where he was going. His answers being satisfactory the inspector allowed him to pass. He was then met by the constable who, in a similar manner stopped, questioned and permitted him to go on his way. Next morning it was reported that the horse, one of considerable value, had been stolen. Though it was entirely an error of judgement on the part of both officers still considering (1) the time of night, (2) that horse stealing is prevalent around Ongar, (3) there was only a common halter on the horse and it*

ASPECTS OF THE HISTORY OF ONGAR

> *was being ridden, (4) that the place the thief stated he had bought the horse was only a short distance from Ongar, and (5) that the county cart and horse were available at the station and might at once have been used to ascertain whether the man's statement was true or otherwise.*
>
> *The Chief Constable is of the opinion that both officers acted very unwisely by their mistaken confidence, and as the expense to the county endeavouring unsuccessfully to trace the thief amounts to £1 17s 9d he directs that two-thirds of this sum be defrayed by the Inspector and one-third by the constable.'* [12]

The annual fair held at Ongar on the 12 and 13 October was also said to provide problems, and in April 1872 a petition was sent to the Home Office for its abolition. This suggestion led to a very vocal opposition in the town, the press and in correspondence with the Home Office. It had been asserted that the fair led to drunkenness, riot and immorality, but an opposition letter signed by, among others, the rector's churchwarden pointed out '....*that statements relating to drunkenness etc are not easily made out, but, if true, easily proved. For the drunkenness and riot we beg to call your attention to the provable fact that on the mornings after the fair, the police cells are unusually empty. For immorality a reference to the return of illegitimate births will prove at all events that seduction finds no place in our little town.*'

An opposition meeting had to adjourn from the Town Hall to the schoolroom because of the numbers attending the meeting and even this was not large enough to hold all those who wished to attend. Because of the opposition, the Home Office sought the opinion of the police. Superintendent Simpson reported on the 6 September, that he had been in the Division for four years and eight months and '*I have attended the Ongar fair annually and I never saw it attended with any disorder or immorality. I find...that there has not been any conviction at Ongar arising from the Fair for the last 10 years and I think the reasonable enjoyment of the agricultural labourers would be interfered with by its abolition.*' The Home Office refused the application and the fair continued until 1892 when a further appeal for its abolition was granted.[13]

In September 1927, PC George Gutteridge, the village policeman at Stapleford Abbotts, was brutally murdered whilst on night patrol by two men who had stolen a car from Billericay. Scotland Yard investigated the crime, which shocked the nation, and eventually the two men were arrested.[14]

During the First World War, many police officers were called to the colours and this left a shortage to police Essex. As a consequence some 6000 special constables were utilised and a number of local men rallied to the cause in Ongar and made a valuable contribution to the war effort. Table 3 shows the names of some of the special constables who served at Chipping Ongar and Shelley during the period 1914–18.

In 1979 following reorganisation, Ongar and Epping were amalgamated into one sub-division, under the command of a chief inspector and inspector based at

LAW AND ORDER IN CHIPPING ONGAR

Epping. Further changes have seen the number of police officers based at Ongar reduced, and the closure of the village police stations, and the reduction in the hours of opening at the police station in Ongar. As we move into the next millennium, what further changes in policing await us?

Chipping Ongar		Shelley	
Ashdown	John Alfred	Broom	Alfred Edward
Chandler	George	Blundell	John
Comerford	Hugh	Boram	Charles
Cornell	Herbert	Boram	James
Dicker	Frederick Herbert	Brett	Percy Edward
Fenn	John Patrick	Cook	Henry John
Hammond	Charles William	Gould	Frank E
Hall	Alfred	Monk	Alfred
Kent	Henry William	Spells	Ernest George
Lacey	William Edward	Schweir	Ernest Frederick
Mead	Albert Frederick	Wilmot	Albert
Mead	Harry		
Mott	Frank		
Merchant	Harold Edgar		
Noble	Frederick Harold		
Pay	Benjamin Joseph		
Simmons	Sidney Mainwaring		
Surridge	John		
Taylor	George Albert		
Traveller	Jesse		
Wildman	Albert Charles Ansley		
Westlake	Herbert		

Table 3: names of special constables during the First World War

References

1. ERO: D/P 124/8/1–4.
2. Emmison, F. G. *Elizabethan Life and Disorder* (1970) ERO
3. ERO: D/P 124/8/1–4
4. The additional ranks of inspector (November 1840) and sergeant (1854) were introduced later.
5. Woodgate, J. *The Essex Police* (1985) Dalton
6. ibid
7. In 1969 inspectors in charge of sub-division were promoted to the rank of chief inspector.
8. Tabrum, B. *A Short History of the Essex Constabulary* (1911) Essex Chronicle
9. In 1843 all Weights and Measures Inspectors were dismissed so that police superintendents could take on the role.
10. Minutes of the Ongar Guardians dated 12 June ERO: G/On M3. This role was eventually undertaken by the police inspector at Ongar
11. Gray, A. *Crime and Criminals in Victorian Essex* (1988) Countryside Books
12. General Orders, number 330, dated 19 October 1885.
13. Boyes, J. "Essex and the 1871 Fairs Act" in Neale, K. (ed) *An Essex Tribute* (1987) Leopards Head Press
14. The men, William Kennedy and Frederick Browne, were both hanged for the crime in 1929.

chapter 12

The Joseph King Trust

by Gillian Sheldrick

Joseph King died in 1679, and in his will he left money to provide an education for six poor boys and four poor girls,[1] or as King himself described it, *'the education of poor children in true reformed Protestant Religion and good learning that they may be capable of some good calling, trade and employment that they may come to live comfortably and to love and bless God for that education by which they were fitted for such a way of living.'* His motives for leaving his money in this way were, he stated *'to testifie to my humble thankfullness to* [God's] *divine Goodness from which I confess myself to have received all I have.'* Although at his death, King was described *as 'Citizen and Ironmonger of London,'*[2] his roots were in Ongar, where he and his parents are buried.[3]

His bequest had far-reaching effects in Ongar, for this was the origin both of what is now the Ongar Primary School, at one time known as the Kings' Trust School, and of the Joseph King Educational Trust.

In the seventeenth century it was not unusual for rich men to make good use of their fortunes by founding educational charities. Many other schools in Essex and elsewhere were founded in a similar way around the same time. A local example is in Fyfield. Dr Anthony Walker, the rector who died in 1692, left two houses in his will to found a school which is now, like that founded by Joseph King, the local primary school.[4]

To ensure a regular and sufficient income for the Trust, King left five cottages in trust and it was essentially the rents from these which gave the Trust its income. These cottages are the five seventeenth century[5] shops next to the Budworth Hall, which still belong to the Trust today. In addition to educating poor children, the Trust was charged with providing bibles for the poor. Provision was also made for the sexton to clean the tablet in St Martin's church recording the bequest, as well as for 10s 0d a year to provide an annual dinner for the trustees.[1] Although payments for bibles and for cleaning the tablet were still made in the twentieth century,[6] the educational work of the charity was the most significant aspect of King's bequest, and this is the area which will be explored below.

It is unlikely that the Trust would have founded a new school in order to carry out the provisions of King's will. It is perhaps more likely that they paid the money as fees for the selected children to teachers who were already established in Ongar, and who almost certainly taught other (fee-paying) children as well as the children paid for by the Trust. There are hints in the early minutes which seem to

THE JOSEPH KING TRUST

confirm this. In 1681, for example, the trustees ordered *'that if any of the Boys whose teaching is paid for by this charity, or of the Girls, shall neglect to attend the Schools to which they are assigned'* another child would be paid for in their place. Again, in 1692 it was reported *'that George Allen has been absent from the School 36 days since Easter last'* so Richard Francis was educated in his place.[2] However, by guaranteeing a regular income to the teachers, the establishment of the Trust ensured continuity of educational provision in the town.

The first schoolmaster to benefit from the Trust was Benjamin Stebbing (sometimes spelt Stepping) who received ten pounds a year for teaching the six boys. He was a clergyman, and left his post as schoolmaster when he became rector of Stondon in 1690.[7] The first six boys to benefit were Nymphas Mayor, Robert Cliffe, George Francis, George Stane, John Waylett and William Francis. The girls were taught by two women: Widow Mayor (could she have been the mother of Nymphas?) taught Katherine Stane and Mary Fippes and Widow White taught Katherine Angier and Sarah White. The ages of the children varied: the oldest boy, Nymphas Mayor, was nearly fifteen, while the youngest, George Francis, was seven; Katherine Angier was not yet five years old, while the oldest girl, Katherine Stane, was almost ten.[8] Unfortunately, no details are recorded in the trustees' minutes about how the children were chosen. Was it for their aptitude for learning, or was coming from a respectable family more important? The school mistresses, unlike their male counterpart, only received a pound a year each for their work.[2] This discrepancy between the fees for the girls and the boys almost certainly reflected the difference in the standard of education considered appropriate at this time. The education of the boys would have included reading, writing and probably accounting. The girls would probably have learnt to read, and perhaps to write, but their main teaching would probably have been in domestic work.

In the early days of the Trust, the children would probably have been taught in the homes of their teachers, though in the case of the boys at least there may have been a school room within the house. There are hints that the girls' teachers lived in the Trust cottages, and this may have been true of the schoolmasters as well. In 1681, the tenants of the cottages included "widow Mayer" and "Henry White", which suggests at least a connection with the then schoolmistresses. And in 1702, Widow Seel was informed that if she *'make good the repairs wanting in her tenement'* before midsummer day, she would be allowed to continue as schoolmistress to the four girls, *'otherwise they* [i.e. the girls] *are to be taken from her.'*[2]

During the eighteenth century, the Trust flourished and in 1790 agreed to pay for the education of two extra boys in addition to the original six, though the fees (33s 0d per boy per year) remained unchanged. The trustees were also purchasing books for the children for whose education they were responsible: for example, in 1790 they spent a total of three shillings on'[4] *Writing Books for Westwood boy'* and *'2 Cyphering* [i.e. number] *books for ditto.'*[2] By the early nineteenth century the Trust was paying for sixteen extra children. By this time there was certainly a proper school, or at least a dedicated room, for in 1806 the minutes of the Trustees record a payment of £70 '*For repairs of School House*' and in 1814 a payment of 14s 0d for '*repairing the school room.*'[9]

In the mid-nineteenth century, education was becoming a matter of great national concern. The National Society for Promoting the Education of the Poor in the Principles of the Established Church, and its rival, the mainly nonconformist British and Foreign Schools Society were actively building schools, assisted by government grants.[10] It was no doubt this change in the national climate, as well as local circumstances, which led the trustees in 1846 to build a new school which could accommodate 63 children (both boys and girls).[1] This school was behind the Trust cottages, and though much enlarged later, was occupied until it was replaced by the new primary school building in 1968.[11] The Trust continued to distinguish in its accounts the payments for the education of the original six boys and four girls, but its role was now little different from the managers of a school, and from 1873 its income was supplemented by government grants for education.[9] By 1894 there was accommodation for 172 children[1] and there were five teachers: Mr and Mrs Rose, Miss Fewell, Miss Barlow and Miss Parker. As Mr Rose received £50 per year, Mrs Rose just £5 and the others £12 or £13, it is to be presumed that the headmaster took the lion's share of the work, probably concentrating on the older boys, while the others were almost certainly part-time teachers.[9] It is extremely unlikely that at this date classes would have been as small as the 35 children which a ratio of 172 children to five teachers might otherwise suggest. It is interesting to note that Mr and Mrs Rose occupied one of the Trust cottages.

From the beginning of the twentieth century, the history of the Trust and of what became the Ongar County Primary School began to diverge. In 1905, the Charity Commissioners approved the division of the Trust into two charities, the "King's Educational Foundation" for the portion of the charity dealing with the education of the ten children, and the "King's Charity for Bibles and Sexton" to cover the rest.[12] The school accommodation had become inadequate but the trustees were reluctant to spend the very large sum necessary to bring the school up to the necessary standard.[12&13] It must have been with some horror that they received – and refused – the request of Hackney Union in 1903 that the 300 children from the new home (i.e. Great Stony) attend the school, pleading lack of room.[12] Finally it was agreed that the school be handed over to the County Council, which had under the 1902 Education Act become the education authority for the county and as such had taken over the management of the school, though not the ownership or management of its premises.[12&13]

The school continued to flourish, and, although from this point it was no longer the direct concern of the Joseph King Trust, it is perhaps worth looking briefly at its history to the present day. At the time of the handover in 1913, the school was, as was usual at that date, for all ages – i.e. it took children right up to the school leaving age, which was then fourteen (though in some circumstances children could leave school earlier). An official visitor to the school described it in

THE JOSEPH KING TRUST

about 1905: *'The school...consists of two rooms, divided from one another by a glass partition...and there would be room to put up another class-room. At the time of my visit, I saw two elder boys in Standard VII* [who would be aged about 14] *doing more advanced work with the headmaster...nature lessons are given in the school, but there is at present no school garden. It is desirable that one should be provided. There should also be instruction in cookery and domestic science for the elder girls.'* [14]

The premises were enlarged in 1913, on additional land. The "temporary" green corrugated iron building erected in 1913 remained in use until the junior school moved to its new premises in Greensted Road. By the 1960s (if not before), it was used as kitchens, eating areas and two classrooms and had been supplemented by further "temporary" buildings.[15] In 1936, pressure on numbers, and the difficulties of teaching such a wide age range together, were relieved by the opening of the Ongar Secondary School in the Fyfield Road.[12] (This became the Ongar Comprehensive School, which closed in 1989, although the buildings are still – in 1999 – standing).[16] The Primary School, which so many must remember with gratitude, still flourishes as the successor to the work begun by Joseph King, though in new buildings in the Greensted Road. The nineteenth century buildings behind the Budworth Hall were demolished in 1992.[17] The site was sold to a developer in April 1998 and is now occupied by Sainsbury's supermarket.[18]

After surrendering control of the school, the King's Educational Foundation channelled its energies into new areas. A further reorganisation of the Trust was approved by the charity commissioners in 1983. The trustees are now the rector and two churchwardens, two members nominated by the Chelmsford Diocesan Education Committee, and a further four members co-opted by the trustees themselves. The co-opted members are individuals who by residence, occupation, employment, or otherwise, have a special knowledge of the parish of Ongar.[18] Grants were – and still are – made to children from Chipping Ongar for a wide variety of educational purposes. In 1928, for example, George Wyatt received £7 10s a year to attend the Leyton Engineering School; other children received money to cover their travel to grammar schools in Brentwood and elsewhere. In the 1950s, a number of children were given grants to purchase uniforms, while in the 1970s at least one child had the cost of her music lessons paid for.[19] In recent years, between 70 and 80 students a year receive grants to attend schools, colleges and universities, covering a very wide range of subjects.[18]

The work of the Trust today is very different from that envisaged by the founder, Joseph King, when he made his will in 1678, and it benefits more people each year than he would have thought possible. Even today, with educational opportunities available to all, many have reason to be grateful to Joseph King for his generosity.

References

1 VCH Essex vol 4 (1956) p.169
2 Minutes and accounts of the Joseph King Trust, 1679–1800. ERO: D/P 124/25/7
3 Monumental inscription in St Martin's Church, Ongar, recorded by William Holman in 1718

ASPECTS OF THE HISTORY OF ONGAR

4. VCH Essex vol 2, where many further examples can be found; see also 'The Endowed Schools of Essex' in the *Essex Review* vol VI (1897) p.108
5. Department of the Environment: List of Buildings of Special Architectural or Historical Interest
6. Accounts submitted to the Charity Commissioners, 1911–1913. ERO accession: A 6930 (part)
7. Various papers of the trust, including extracts from the Ongar Ruri-Decanal Magazine (1915–1916) concerning the history of the Trust. ERO: D/P 124/25/10
8. Ages based on dates of baptisms from the Ongar parish registers; I am grateful to Michael Leach for the information.
9. Joseph King Trust Minutes and Accounts 1799–1913. ERO: D/P 124/25/8
10. Sutherland, G. *Elementary Education in the Nineteenth Century* (1971) London Historical Assoc.
11. The Junior School moved to the Greensted Road site in December 1968 (ERO: E/ML268/6), though the infants school continued to occupy the old buildings for several years (personal knowledge)
12. Minutes of the Joseph King Trust 1893–1959. ERO: D/P 124/25/9
13. VCH Essex vol 4 (1956) p.170
14. Richard Sadler, Report (to ECC Education Committee) on Secondary and Higher Education in Essex, 1906; Sadler went on to recommend that a "higher department" should be developed at the school, with an additional teacher appointed to assist the headmaster
15. VCH Essex vol 4 (1956) p 170 and personal knowledge; the corrugated iron building was demolished in 1972 to provide room for a temporary library (*West Essex Gazette* 1972)
16. ERO: Schools Catalogue and personal knowledge
17. inf from M. Leach, 1998
18. inf. from T Blyth, secretary to Joseph King's Trust
19. ERO: D/P124/25/9 and personal knowledge

chapter 13

The history of Ongar Grammar School
Part one: 1811-1859

by I. L. Williams

Chipping Ongar, as its name implies, has always been noted for its market, even though this never belonged to the town, and was in the hands of the Lord of the Manor until 1841. It served particularly to supply the London market with dairy produce and hay. The market trade brought prosperity to the town, and by the end of the eighteenth century Ongar was already supporting a full range of shops, as well as a surgeon and an attorney. The needs of the farming community were fulfilled by those such as the blacksmith, the miller, the auctioneer and the land-surveyor, and the town was connected to London by two waggons and three coaches each week.[1] The Essex farming community was able to benefit from the rise in prices caused by the wars of 1793 to 1807, and even the labourers were able to demand higher wages, because so many of their number had enlisted that there was a shortage of hands. The prosperity of the town continued after peace returned, and by the middle of the nineteenth century Ongar was described as being *'partially paved, lighted with gas and amply supplied with water.'* [2]

Education has also been part of the life of the town for several centuries. Early schoolmasters include Thomas Glascock in 1637 (*'afterwards of Felsted'*) [3] and Benjamin Stebbing, the first master of the Joseph King Trust (see Chapter 12) who was in the town by 1670.[4] Godfrey Jones (rector from 1720 to 1733) is described as a schoolmaster at the time of his wife's death in 1718.[5] A copyhold deed of 1740 refers to a *'tenement in the occupation of John Green and used as a boarding school,'* [6] and Miss Buckle's "Boarding School for Ladies" was offering *'the strictest Attention…to every Branch of the Education of Young Ladies'* in 1787.[7] Many small schools were established over the next 150 years, but most of them were short lived.

Richard Stokes, the founder of Ongar Academy (later known as the Grammar School) was born in High Ongar in 1788. His father, Jonathan, and all his ancestors were farmers, as were three of his brothers. Only the youngest, Edward, moved away from the agricultural community, becoming a hatter in the City of London. Jonathan died in 1810 at the age of 59, the *Chelmsford Chronicle* of 9 March reporting: *'On Saturday last died Mr Stokes, a respectable farmer of High Ongar, leaving a numerous family to lament his loss.'* Richard was bequeathed £200 by his father, together with a share of the residue of the estate after his mother's death. Less than a year later Richard had set up his school, sending out handbills to the local gentry and tradespeople, and placing an advertisement in the *Chelmsford Chronicle* of 11 January 1811:

ASPECTS OF THE HISTORY OF ONGAR

> *'EDUCATION: CHIPPING ONGAR, ESSEX. R STOKES Respectfully acquaints his Friends and the Public, that his Academy for the Board and Education of twenty young Gentlemen, will open on Monday, 21st instant. Terms, Twenty Guineas per Annum.'*

Richard was probably counting on the increased prosperity of the local farmers and tradesmen to supply him with pupils, as well as the tendency of the time for boys to be educated in boarding rather than day schools. He seems originally to have envisaged teaching girls as well: an early handbill stated that a *'separate Apartment'* was available for the *'Instruction of Young Ladies,'* but no more is heard of this idea. His only rival in Ongar was the master of the charity school, who also took in fee-paying pupils.

When Richard advertised the opening of the school in a handbill, he stated that he had already had *'several Years' Practice in the Art of Teaching.'* Since he was only 23 years old at the time, he implies that he had started at a young age. This was not at all unusual in the early nineteenth century. Many teachers started their careers as students in the schools where they had been pupils, often beginning their training as young as the age of fourteen. It is not known where Richard was educated, but it was probably in the same type of proprietorial school which he founded in Ongar. These were flourishing by the end of the eighteenth century. Demand for secondary education was increasing at the time, partly due to the increase in the scope of national and local government. This administration was often supervised, in rural areas such as west Essex, by local farmers and tradespeople, just at a time when they were realising the need for better record keeping in their own businesses. The private schools usually offered a more practical and commercial education than the old endowed Grammar Schools, which were in any case going through a bad time in the late eighteenth and early nineteenth centuries. In the 1830s, for example, Colchester Royal Grammar School was referred to as *'nothing but an educational sham.'*[8] Many of the early proprietorial schools were founded by dissenters, who were often denied admission to the old grammar schools and other charitable foundations. This was not the case with Richard Stokes, however, since he was a staunch supporter of the established church.

Boys usually began their education at home or in dame schools, and were only sent to boarding school at the age of seven or eight. They remained until they were about 15 or 16, when they left to take up apprenticeships or enter their parents' businesses. The census of 1841 shows that there were only six boys less than 10 years old at Ongar Academy at that time, and the oldest pupil was 13: in 1851 the number under 10 had declined to three, but there were seven aged 14 and over. Many of the boys were the sons of farmers or tradesmen. Richard Stokes issued a handbill in the 1850s which gave the names of 65 men who had been his pupils, or had their sons educated by him. Of the 56 whose occupations have been traced, 17 were farmers, 21 were shopkeepers and small businessmen and only seven were of private means. Twelve were professional men. Most of them came

THE HISTORY OF ONGAR GRAMMAR SCHOOL/ PART ONE 1811-1859

from Essex or the London area, but the 1851 census also lists boys as having been born in Buckinghamshire, Worcestershire, Cornwall and even Newfoundland.[9] The numbers of boys at the school varied considerably over the years. Richard had envisaged 20 in his opening announcement, but a government enquiry into education in 1833 reported that there were only 13 pupils at the school.[10] By 1841 there were 47, the largest number under Richard's ownership, and in 1851 there were 30. In 1861, two years after Richard retired, there were 29. Three of the boys who were attending the school in 1851 were Richard's nephews: Edward Stokes was the son of his brother Edward, the London hatter, Richard Stokes was the younger son of his brother Thomas, who had taken over the tenancy at Chivers Hall Farm in High Ongar after their father Jonathan's death, while Henry West was the son of his sister Mary Ann, whose husband was a tallow-chandler in Stratford Broadway. Parents often preferred to send their children to schools run by relatives, expecting to obtain a reduction in fees, and hoping that the boys would be better looked after than by strangers.

When the Academy opened in 1811, Richard's fees were 20 guineas per annum. A later handbill, undated but probably from the late 1820s, states that the fees are 24 guineas per annum, with a charge of one guinea entrance fee. Washing cost 2 guineas per annum, while parents were required to pay one quarter's fees if they withdrew a boy without the customary one quarter's notice. By the 1850s Richard was charging £30 per annum for the younger boys and £35 per annum for those over twelve years of age. Many bills for school fees have survived in family papers of the era, and Richard's charges seem to be about average. Charles Spedding of Great Maplestead in north Essex was paying 30 guineas per annum for the older boy and 25 guineas for the younger when he sent his sons to Ashford Grammar School in the 1840s.[11] Setting a fee, and actually managing to collect it were, however, two different things, as many nineteenth century school proprietors found to their cost. They often had to visit the parents personally to collect their dues. A Somerset man, remembering his childhood, wrote, '*When I left this school, Mr Cooper, the master, came round during the holidays, as was customary, to collect his bills.*' [9] At least Richard did not have to find the money to buy his own premises when he opened the Academy. The building in Ongar High Street, now known as Central House, was bought by his brother Jonathan, a substantial farmer of Stapleford Abbotts, and was at first rented from him by Richard. Jonathan later sold part of the freehold to Richard, but it was not until Jonathan died in 1853 that Richard became sole owner of the building. The cost of equipping the school would have taken up most of the legacy which Richard received from his father. A Dorset schoolmaster paid £2 8s for four boys bedsteads in 1827, and in addition each of them cost £1 6s 5d for a mattress, bolster, sheets and bedspread,[13] while in 1831 Richard Stokes paid £1 3s 4d to a local builder, Richard Noble, to provide bookshelves in the dining room.[14]

Until Richard married in 1823 he must have employed a housekeeper to look after the boys, and even after that date there were female relatives of his living at the school to assist in the running of the house. The census of 1841 shows that his niece Emma Young, daughter of his deceased sister Jane, was resident at the school, and in 1851 another niece, Jane West, was listed in the census as "assistant". She was the daughter of Richard's sister Sarah and John West, the Chipping Ongar coach proprietor. Richard's bride was Elizabeth Shadrack, the daughter of Thomas Shadrack, a leading local citizen. Elizabeth was only 18 years old at the time of her marriage, while Richard was 35. She brought with her a dowry of £800, and received a considerable amount of property from the estate of her father when he died in 1828. Thomas Shadrack must also have lent money to Richard, since his will states that he forgave Richard '*all the debt or debts now owing by him to me.*' Although Richard was always a good schoolmaster, he does not seem to have been a very good businessman. When he retired in 1859 his brother James, the tenant of Cozens Farm in High Ongar, wrote to their brother Edward '*...I had a letter from Brother Richard of the same import as yours Stating he would sell his Freeholds in Ongar and relieve Himself from all debts...If his Estate is all Mortgaged as I fear it is, when all Expences and all debts are paid he wont have much left.*'

Richard and Elizabeth's marriage was childless, so they would have needed only a small part of the building for their private use, while the boys would have required a dormitory, a schoolroom and a dining room. The layout of the building at that time is not clear, and many alterations were carried out on it during the nineteenth century. In particular, the present top floor, which is known to have been the dormitory in the early twentieth century, was not added until a much later date. Boys normally had to share beds at boarding school. In a handbill issued by Richard in the 1850s, one of the extras which he charged was one guinea per annum for a separate bed for junior pupils. The 1828–32 ledger books of Richard Noble, the builder whose premises lay just to the south of the school, have survived in Essex Record Office.[15] Noble carried out all the maintenance needed on the building and its furnishings, and was also employed in a similar capacity by James Lane at Fyfield Academy. Boys swinging on the schoolroom door may well have caused its hinges to need repair in September 1829. Did the boys have a good hunt before Noble's men stopped up the rat-holes in the cellar? Was it a storm which caused one of the chimney pots to need replacing in April 1832? Spring cleaning at the school seems to have taken place during the Christmas vacation, since it was at that time of year that Noble provided men to take down the bedsteads, and put them back up again. The men were equally adept at repairing Venetian blinds, making a new roller for a towel or a new seat for the privy. We know something of the school diet from the work which Noble was paid for, the accounts mentioning a cattle crib, a dairy house, cucumber frames, chicken coops and a malt mill. The malt mill was needed for beer brewing, since the boys would each have received their pot of ale at lunchtime. Noble was not just a repair man, however, and in 1830 a separate set of accounts in his ledger book is headed '*To the alteration of Building to connect the House and Schoolroom.*' This seems to imply that the Schoolroom had been added as a separate structure at the back of the main building.

THE HISTORY OF ONGAR GRAMMAR SCHOOL/ PART ONE 1811-1859

The principal advantages that parents saw in private schools were their small size and their wide curriculum. By the 1850s Richard's handbill reads:

> *'The Course of Instruction embraces the Greek, Latin, French and German Languages, Penmanship, Arithmetic in all its branches, with Merchants' Accounts, Land-Surveying, and Algebra, the Mathematics, Geography, Astronomy, and History: thus including every subject that may be considered necessary for a sound Classical, Mathematical, or Commercial Education.'*

Although there was little science on the curriculum, this area was not neglected. In 1847 Walter Barlow, one of the sons of Dr Barlow of Blackmore, wrote home to tell his family that *'Tomorrow and the following day we are going to have two lectures on Electricity and Galvanism by Mr Thornthwaite, a lecturer from London.'* Clear handwriting was an essential requirement in commerce and administration in the days before the typewriter was invented, and Richard paid particular attention to good penmanship. A copybook of one of his pupils, John Shipman, has survived among the papers of Thomas Shadrack, and is a fine example of the kind of writing which was required of the boys.[16] It may have been John's holiday task, since the first page reads *'Specimens of penmanship written by John Shipman at Ongar Academy Christmas 1818'*, while on the last page he wrote *'The Vacation will terminate Monday the 18th of January 1819.'* The field at the back of the school building, which Richard rented from his mother-in-law, would have made a useful area for practical lessons in surveying, as well as being a home for the school cows. The field may well have been used for sports and games too, Richard having informed parents in 1811 that he provided an *'appropriate Play-ground.'* Religious instruction does not appear on the curriculum, but in a handbill produced in the 1850s Richard states that his course of instruction was based on Christian principles, and the boys attended church every Sunday. In 1830 Richard Noble had installed *'Boards for Childrens Hats under Seats at Church'*, and in the following year he had to put what he called "fences" round their pews to stop the boys tipping books over the top (perhaps their response to too long a sermon).

Something of the flavour of life at the school can be gained from a letter written to the school magazine in his 91st year by a former pupil, John Pertwee.[17]

> *'I believe that it was between the years 1836 and 1838 that I entered Ongar Grammar School as a boarder, and had to go through all those inquisitive questions which greet a new boy. In those days, the school was considered one of the principal private schools in the County of Essex. Mr Richard Stokes was the headmaster, and was a capital scholar. Everything was done for the comfort of the boys, and provision made for physical exercise as well as mental, for a good field was at the boys' disposal for sports, and many a happy game of cricket have I played in those irresponsible days of boyhood; I was considered a fair bowler, and dearly loved an afternoon with the willow and the leather. Three of my brothers entered the school after I had left; of their school life, I remember nothing, only it*

shows in what high esteem my parents held the school to have sent four sons there. I forget how many boys there were at Ongar in my day, but I do remember that I was the first boy in the school for Latin, Arithmetic and Writing. I still possess a few volumes of the Life of Napoleon bound in half calf which I received as a prize, for which subject I cannot be sure, but I fancy for Latin. The distance from my home at Woodham Ferris to Ongar is about sixteen miles, and I think my father used to drive me to school, but many of the boys used to come by coach.' Pertwee was almost certainly wrong in thinking that he had entered the school in the late 1830s. From his own account he would have been born in 1823, and would probably have gone to the school at the age of ten in 1833. He had certainly left by the date of the 1841 census which records other Pertwees, namely Henry aged 16, Alfred aged 12, and George, Joseph and Edward all aged 10. The 1851 census shows Arthur Pertwee aged 13, born at Woodham Ferris, so it seems that the school was favoured by other members of the family too.[18] We know of another prize winner, George Walter Elliot, who was presented in 1831 with a copy of *"The British Nepos: consisting of the Lives of Industrious Britons"* as a reward for merit.

Figure 14   Ongar Grammar School, from a prospectus of 1875, showing the building before the alteration to the south wing, and before the addition of the second storey of the central block. Engraved by Alfred Adlard from a drawing by T. M. Baynes (possibly the architect of the classical façade built in the 1840s).

In the following year, he received the same award and on this occasion the book was *"The History of Charles the Twelfth and Peter the Great"*. Both volumes are embellished with handsome printed book plates.[19]

Like many other schoolmasters, Richard Stokes often employed other teachers to help him. In the 1830s his assistant was John Parker, who later moved to Brighton to found his own school. In 1841 the assistant was William Casford, and in 1851 it was Augustus Noble, the youngest son of Richard Noble the builder, and a

THE HISTORY OF ONGAR GRAMMAR SCHOOL/ PART ONE 1811-1859

previous pupil at the Academy. Augustus died only two years later, at the tragically young age of 27, and is buried in St Martin's churchyard in Ongar. His father outlived him by only three months. It was John Parker who introduced Richard Stokes to the group of young schoolmasters who were instrumental in forming the College of Preceptors, the first organisation for school teachers, in 1846. At its inaugural meeting the principal motion was seconded by Richard:

> 'That, in the opinion of this meeting, it is desirable for the protection of the interests both of the Scholastic profession and the public, that some proof of qualification both as to the amount of knowledge, and the art of conveying it to others should be required,...of all persons who may by desirous of entering the profession....'

The College, which is still an active body, never achieved its initial aim of becoming the sole professional organisation for teachers in private schools, but its examinations for teachers have always been well subscribed to, and its examinations of scholars were the foundation on which the later School Certificate examinations were based. Richard remained a member of the College for the rest of his professional life, was often a member of its Council, and was elected a Fellow of the College in 1852. Reports of meetings of the College and its Council were regularly reported in the monthly *Educational Times* whose reports of the General Meetings of the College are their only surviving record. This is now the only place where we can read Richard's opinions on educational matters at first hand. During the discussion on the report of the Council at the half-yearly meeting held on 27 June 1850:

> 'Mr Stokes expressed his opinion, that the College should impress upon Parents the necessity of interesting themselves more particularly in the Education of their children; to enquire diligently and minutely into the fitness of the Educators to whom they committed so important a trust; and to assist their authority, influence, and active cooperation, in the moral, religious and literary training of their offspring.'

Three years later, when the half-yearly meeting was discussing the examination of teachers, Richard pointed out:

> 'the disadvantages, pecuniary and moral, which resulted to the properly qualified teacher, from the existence of pretenders to the art of teaching – men who made it their boast that the less they knew of any subject, the better they taught it, – and hoped to see examinations made compulsory.'

Present day teachers would be at one with Richard Stokes on both these issues.

Richard did not confine his public activities to the College of Preceptors, for he was also active in the life of the town of Chipping Ongar. During the first half of the nineteenth century Ongar was governed by a public vestry, and the minute books of its meetings show that Richard was a regular attender. The main business of the monthly meetings was to approve the accounts of the overseer of the poor. One of the former overseers was Richard's father-in-law, Thomas Shadrack, but by 1819 the town was employing a permanent overseer at a salary of £15 per annum. Since Elizabethan times each parish had been responsible for maintaining its own poor, and the cost of this was an ever increasing burden on the town and its rate-payers. By 1821 the Chipping Ongar vestry was alarmed to find that the overseer's accounts had not been properly kept for years, that the rates were unnecessarily high because so many people omitted to pay, and that the parish was quite heavily in debt. A committee, of which Richard was a member, was appointed to sort out the finances of the vestry. This committee directed the overseer that in future he was to use properly printed account books, and proposed that an extra rate of 2s in the pound per month should be levied until the parish debt of about £200 had been paid off. At the vestry meeting of 17 April 1823 it was unanimously resolved that *'the thanks of this Meeting be given to Mr Stokes for his able and impartial conduct in the Chair and for the Business of the Day as on all former Occasions in the affairs of the Parish.'*

The vestry also had charge of the parish poorhouse. In February 1828 Richard proposed that the building should be enlarged, but the motion was not carried. At the following meeting various suggestions for the better management of the poorhouse were put forward, and Richard proposed that its master was to promote '*Cleanliness, Industry, Frugality, Sobriety, Peace and Piety*' among the inmates, and to prevent the contrary vices of '*Sloth, Idleness, Wastefulness, Intemperance, Discord and Immoral language.*' Cards, dice and gambling were forbidden, the master was to read prayers twice a day, and the inmates were required to attend church or chapel every Sunday. Richard was elected churchwarden in March 1828, and continued in office until March 1836. In those days the church-wardens had rather more duties than they have today. They were particularly concerned to ensure that Sunday was properly observed in the parish, that no manual labour was carried out and no-one was visiting ale-houses during the hours of divine service. When Richard became churchwarden the parish rate stood at 6d in the pound, but in September 1831 it was increased to 9d. Perhaps this caused a protest among the ratepayers, since on 18 April 1832 the vestry decided that the rate assessment was unfair, and every rate-paying property was reassessed by a committee including the overseer and the churchwardens. Richard's new assessment was for £38, of which £20 was for the schoolhouse, £8 for the cottages which he owned at the north end of the town, and £10 for his rented fields. The poundage was, however, reduced to 3d.

Richard had celebrated his 60th birthday in 1848, and seems to have looked for a slower pace of life in his last years as proprietor of Ongar Academy. He took the chair at a vestry meeting for the last time in 1854, and did not attend at all after June 1856. He was also rarely seen at meetings of the College of Preceptors by that time. His old friend John Parker resigned as secretary of the College in 1859 after several years of conflict with the Council. Richard must have felt that he too should make way for a younger man, and some time in 1859 he sold the school and moved to Brighton, where several members of the family were already living. The boys presented him with a handmade chess set to mark his retirement.[20] From the scant evidence which remains he seems to have been a good and progressive teacher, and his boys held him in enough affection to have composed a bantering ditty at his expense:

> 'This time tomorrow where shall I be
> Not in this Academy
> And if I am I'll play my pranks
> And kick old Stokes's bandied shanks.'

Richard and Elizabeth lived in Brighton for the rest of their lives, although they seem to have made frequent visits to family and friends in Essex and Hertfordshire. After Elizabeth died in 1868, Richard wrote to one of his nieces that they had '*lived for upwards of 43 years together in unbroken harmony and affection.*' Richard himself died in July 1875, and was buried in Elizabeth's grave in Brighton Cemetery.

References

1. Universal British Directory, Volume 4, (1798), p.176
2. Lewis, S. *A Topographical Dictionary of England*, (1849), p.478
3. Smith, H. *The Sequence of the Parochial Clergy in the County of Essex 1640–1664*, undated typescript in ERO
4. Chipping Ongar parish register. ERO: T/R 76
5. Monumental inscription in St Martin's church, Chipping Ongar
6. ERO: T/B 203
7. *Chelmsford Chronicle* 6 July 1787
8. Davidoff, L. and Hall, C. *Family Fortunes: men and women of the English middle class 1780–1850* (1992) Routledge p.236
9. PRO: HO 107/336/15, 3–5; HO 107/1771, 267–8
10. Parliamentary Papers 1835, (62), XLI
11. ERO: D/DSe 33
12. Hunt, H. *The Memoirs of Henry Hunt Esquire, Written by himself, in his Majesty's Jail at Ilchester*, (1820), p.46
13. Hearl, T.W. *William Barnes, 1801–1886, The Schoolmaster*, (1966), Dorchester, p.43
14. ERO: D/DU 413/1
15. ERO: D/DU 413/1–3
16. ERO: D/DU 276/8
17. *The Ongarian* No. 2, March 1914, p10.
18. PRO: HO 107/336/15, 3–5; HO 107/1771, 267–8
19. These books are now in the possession of a descendant of G.W. Elliot, who kindly provided these details.
20. Karr, M. and Humphrey, M. *Out on a Limb* (1976) ms in ERO: Box 136, p.39

Editor's note: I am very grateful to the editor of the Transactions of the Essex Society for Archaeology and History for permission to print this article, a fuller version of which was published in Volume 29 of the Society's Transactions.

chapter 14
The history of Ongar Grammar School Part two: 1860-1940

by John Whaler

Introduction

In 1811 Richard Stokes had sent out to the gentry and tradesmen in the locality his respectful notification that he intended to open an academy for young gentlemen. It was then usual for the increasingly prosperous farmers and tradespeople to consider sending their sons to private boarding schools. Nineteenth century England was growing in wealth and power. There was a perceived need for competence and leadership and a keenness to pay for the appropriate education of the young men of the day. Consequently, any self-styled "good" private grammar school in the nineteenth century set out to equip pupils for their future positions in life, and to inculcate self-sufficiency, responsibility, joy in the refinements of life and loyalty to comrades. These were values seen as vital for the wider civilising process and – often more importantly – for success in life and society.

The general picture of English education until well into the twentieth century shows Ongar Grammar School to have been one of many select and privileged establishments. Its decline in its later years coincided with the growth of locally acceptable and attractive state secondary schools.

Up to the 1867 Reform Act, which led to the 1870 Education Act, progress towards a national system in England was minimal. There was an abundance of schools, but no pattern or compulsion. The 1870 Act set up School Boards, elected directly, empowered to make attendance compulsory to age 13 in their areas and to pay the fees of those unable to afford them. It had little early success. According to an article in the *Manchester Guardian* of 26 November 1898:

> 'Out of every hundred children attending English day schools, sixty five leave before they are eleven years old, and never return.'[1]

Private schools in Ongar flourished throughout the nineteenth century. A survey in 1833 recorded six day schools with 82 pupils, a boarding school ("Ongar Academy") with 13 boys and a dissenting school with seven girls; in 1845 there were reported to be 11 schools in the town, including the "Academy", as the Grammar School was then known.[2] In the Sadler Report in 1906 on secondary and higher education in Essex, three private schools in Ongar had provided information: Windsor House School, proprietors Mr and Mrs Dawson, coeducational; Roden House School, run since 1890 by Amy and Edith Bishop, '*a girls' school, admitting little boys to the younger classes*'[3]; Ongar Grammar School, principal O. W. Clark M.A., boys only, all boarders. The total number of pupils in

THE HISTORY OF ONGAR GRAMMAR SCHOOL/ PART TWO: 1860 –1940

these schools was 227 (164 boys, 63 girls), of whom 158 were boarders. Significantly, only 26 of them lived in Essex.[3]

The opening of the rail service between Ongar and London in 1865 brought both change and additional prosperity to the town and the development of Ongar Grammar School brought it considerable success.

Education of the individual, to suit the times

The names of the successive proprietors of the Ongar Academy (called from about 1900 "Ongar Grammar School" and finally, from about 1926, "Ongar School") were listed in the Post Office Directories under "Traders" or "Commercial", still in the latter category as late as 1917.[4] Economic realities had to control both philanthropy and educational zeal. Money talked. Nevertheless the school's prospectuses showed an impressive balance of moral and religious training, together with studies advertised as both practical and adapted to the age. There was proud reference to the spacious buildings and grounds, the attractiveness of the surrounding countryside and the salubriousness of the area. A prospectus from the 1920s is specific in this matter: *'Ongar is mentioned in one of the Census returns as being one of the twelve most healthy towns in England.'*

Popular educational needs were catered for in the lists of subjects, but enterprise and adaptability were always there. The course of instruction offered in the mid nineteenth century attempted to include every subject thought to be needed for a sound education in the classics, languages, mathematics or commerce, Greek, Latin, French, German, arithmetic, geography and history. Instruction in astronomy and penmanship reflected the particular requirements of the times. The special and recommended mathematical skills of the day appear also: algebra, merchants' accounts and land-surveying.

At this time annual charges, which changed little in the following 25 years, were £30 (for *'young gentlemen'* under 12) and £35 (for those over 12). French and German incurred an extra two guineas per annum, as did drawing in pencil. For an extra four guineas boys could enjoy drawing in colours, dancing or music. Use of the school library was also possible at a small annual charge. By 1875 the choice of subjects had been expanded to include elocution, grammar, composition, book-keeping (by single or double entry), geometry, trigonometry and chemistry.

Fifty years later a prospectus from the 1920s showed further refinements with the addition of English language and literature, religious knowledge, and natural history (all in the lower school). For those in the upper school following the commercial course, shorthand, commercial correspondence, economics, commercial law and secretarial practice reflected the new demands of business and trade between the World Wars.

During the First World War there were strong calls for more general improvements to commercial education. Allied to new approaches to science teaching, this was part of the drive to meet the country's expected post-war needs. There were cries for commercial education to take over from, say, Latin and Greek. Schools should ensure that boys could write a decent hand, add up figures accurately, write a letter, balance a ledger. Ongar Grammar School saw itself as a pioneer in this field. In an advertisement for the school published at the turn of the century the only reference to the curriculum was '*Pupils receive a thorough Mercantile Education*'.[5] In an article in *The Ongarian* (December 1916), James Travers states: '*We (ie O.G.S.) have been practically first in the field, and we venture to affirm that we give our boys a better commercial education than other more pretentious schools and colleges.*' In the same issue of *The Ongarian*, the science master, Mr G. J. Dawkins, is less content with current practice. He felt that science (then evidently a "senior" subject) should be introduced long before the end of a boy's scholastic career. In 1916 a knowledge of science was indispensable for improving ways of destroying the enemy, and after the war for keeping the country ahead in commerce. Other subjects without practical uses should give way. He wrote: '*The country will demand new mechanical devices, new methods of manufacture, new contrivances which will revolutionise the trade of the nation.*'

By the 1920s fees at Ongar Grammar School had increased to between £66 and £78 per annum (according to age), with reductions for sons of clergymen and brothers of current pupils. These fees included board, tuition and materials. There were separate "compulsory extras"; church subscriptions, school medicines and nursing, mending materials and porterage (all for 10s 6d per term); gymnastics and drilling (10s 6d); sports subscription (10s 6d). The optional extras were piano and violin instruction at £1 10s each per term. Science (including wireless), languages other than French and Latin, typewriting and machine drawing (at one guinea per term each) showed that new times called for new, although non-obligatory, skills. Boxing (fortunately '*including the use of gloves*') cost 10s 6d per term.

From the mid nineteenth century numbers at Ongar Grammar School appear not to have varied greatly. There were 130 boarders under the direction of Dr William Chignall Clark (headmaster since 1859) in 1878,[6] 164 in 1914[7] and 155 in 1916[8] with Mrs L. A. Brucesmith (principal) and Mr Albert Charles Anstey Wildman (headmaster). There were 140 boarders in 1926 (principal: Mr Percival Hubert Bingley, director of studies: William Attlee M.A.[9]) This provision for 140 boarders continued into the 1930s,[10] at which time there were also day boys. Mr Bingley had Mr Basil J. Ward as headmaster in 1929, Thomas Arthur Owen as joint principal in 1937. Mr Bingley died in 1939.

The population of Ongar increased over this period from 867 in 1862 to 967 in 1901 ('*inclusive of 120 paupers and officials at the Union Workhouse*')[11] and 1142 in the 1920s.[9]

The school, then, was never a large one, which made it both practicable and distinctive to offer a feature thought to set it above other schools of a similar kind; that of adapting the studies of each pupil '*…with a special regard to the position he is expected to occupy in after life.*'[12]

THE HISTORY OF ONGAR GRAMMAR SCHOOL/ PART TWO: 1860 –1940

This approach in the last quarter of the nineteenth century meant that, unusually, there were many courses of study in operation at the same time. Dr Clark promised that he was able to employ enough qualified and trained teachers to allow every pupil a good deal of individual tuition. Academically, all attention seems to have been directed at subjects relevant to the student's chosen career – usually in business or commerce. They would not, said the principal, have to study subjects they would not require. Parents' wishes were decisive in this matter and career advice appears to have been either deferential or completely absent. Dr Clark continued to run the school into the early years of the twentieth century.

The school's task, of course, was to ensure that what was really useful was also really learnt. Its additional task was, through the "hidden curriculum", to instil values of serious industry, self-sufficiency and honour, so vital for sending good and worthy young men out into society.

Teaching method and moral training

Dr Clark and his colleagues attached great importance to purposeful and carefully selected reading – good poetry and respectable newspapers are mentioned – and particularly reading aloud, which was expected to show understanding and be pleasant to listen to. Arithmetical skills were acquired not by repetition, a method still favoured well into the twentieth century, but by careful explanation of the rules and reasons of mathematics. Mental arithmetic and book-keeping, said to be so essential in "the counting house", were thought to be just as important as working out problems. Everything was tailored to the practical needs of life and business. The school offered practical ends and practical means, fortified by a codified and persuasive disciplinary system.

Moral and religious training was given the importance expected in such establishments in Victorian England. Boys in 1875 went out to church twice on Sundays, and had morning and evening prayers at school every day. The day must never, it was thought, be dull. As to the rules of discipline, they were declared to be not harsh, but firm. Common sense should persuade pupils that obedience was beneficial to them and protected them from harm: '*All are thus taught to govern themselves, and cultivate a spirit of justice, order and self-reliance, which must do very much towards fitting them for positions of trust and usefulness.*'[12]

The prospectus considered that the happiness and the high moral tone of the school were proof that its methods worked.

Military exercises, later to be such a distinctive and distinguished aspect of the school, were already in use in the 1870s to promote good health, seemly deportment and proper habit. The regime in the 1920s and 1930s had similar aims; to maintain a high code of honour and "esprit de corps," whilst refusing to accept or retain morally unsuitable pupils. Mr Bingley did not allow his staff to administer corporal punishment of any kind and investigated personally all breaches of discipline.

ASPECTS OF THE HISTORY OF ONGAR

'The house and premises are spacious and commodious'

This description of the spacious, purpose-built premises and extensive grounds is repeatedly mentioned in advertisements and prospectuses through the nineteenth century, together with its healthy locality. This was described as dry, 200 feet above sea level, on gravel soil and close to "famed" Epping Forest – an ideal situation, it was claimed, for an attractive and successful school. Ongar was recommended as a delightful and charming country town, neat, picturesque, relaxed, neighbourly and within easy reach of London. The size and extent of the building and the grounds can still be appreciated today.

In 1932, eight years before closure, the buildings included nine classrooms, library, music room, chemical laboratory, gymnasium, large covered swimming bath (built in 1885), carpentry shop and rifle range. There were said to be playing fields and grounds of well over 100 acres.[10] The school, certainly from the beginning of the twentieth century, had its own dairy farm and vegetable garden. The advert for the school dating from the turn of the century mentioned above refers to pure milk from its own dairy farm, as well as the attractions of a *'grand tepid swimming pool.'* A prospectus from the 1920s refers to the plentiful supply of milk from the School herd of British Friesian Milk Recorded Cows. (The fire brigade put out a fire in one of the cattle sheds at the rear of the swimming bath, the property of the late Mr Bingley, on 20 June 1940.[13])

An *Ongar Guide* issued around 1930 refers to the addition of classrooms in 1921. In 1924 the adjoining estate, comprising mansion (now called Bowes House) and 80 acres of grounds, was acquired; and in 1926 *'the Budworth Estate, including the famous Long Walk and parts of Ongar Woods, were purchased for the further development of the school.'*[14] Playing fields and grounds were stated in this document to cover 200 acres.

Photographs of the school and grounds show other aspects of these facilities. Fresh air and exercise were common features. The dormitories were visibly clean, spacious and light The swimming pool was 60ft by 20ft, housed in a separate building in the school grounds and made tepid when necessary. There were ample playing fields for football. The football club was formed in 1869 by N. D. Caton and hockey was introduced in 1918. Cricket and tennis were played and the sole-purpose gymnasium was bright and well-equipped. The uniformed cadet corps trained in the playground.

'Proper and healthful recreation'

This phrase from the 1875 prospectus indicates what care was taken to cater for the physical development of the pupils. This objective was usual in schools like Ongar Grammar School in the late nineteenth and early twentieth centuries. Rambles in the surrounding countryside were a regular feature, with the principal and his teachers joining in, as they did in most activities, indoor and outdoor.

THE HISTORY OF ONGAR GRAMMAR SCHOOL/ PART TWO: 1860–1940

Figure 15 Ongar Grammar School photographed in 1905.

Throughout the 1860–1940 period the cadet corps was clearly the organised expression of the school's declared ideals of discipline, development and corporate spirit. In 1875, participation in the cadet corps was optional but '...*advised as being producive* [sic] *of great benefits.*' At that time the uniform could be worn for everyday purposes, perhaps because of the school's conviction that all pupils should be involved. The cadet corps was at its peak of fame and efficiency in the 1920s and 30s. It was part of the curriculum, with a resident sergeant instructor both for the cadets and for physical training. Informally it had obvious links with the school rifle club, another proudly advertised activity which achieved the highest standards.

Former pupils of Ongar Grammar School to whom I have spoken all mentioned the local and even national supremacy of the corps. It was reported to be the oldest in Britain, and the official annual inspections often placed it first for efficiency. Copies of *The Ongarian* school magazine issued before and during the First World War illustrate the great importance of the corps. In July 1916, out of 155 boys in the school, the corps had well over 100 members. *The Ongarian* published a number of moving letters from old boys of the school fighting in France, thanking the school for the crucial benefits to them of their corps training. As the war continued, these letters often stressed the need to keep up the good work at school to ensure that after the war England's lead in commerce was not lost.

The corps provided a good advertisement for the school. The prospectus for the 1920s quotes from a recent annual official inspection report:

> '*The Essex Territorial Association congratulates you on this very good report. It proves that the spirit and administrative arrangements in your*

ASPECTS OF THE HISTORY OF ONGAR

> school are of a high order of excellence. The Association has circulated the report to all other cadet corps in the County as an example for their emulation. The drill throughout was excellent and the turnout was beyond praise. A really smart, clean, well-set-up body, of excellent physique and intelligence.'

The school rifle club had great success in the early twentieth century. Both juniors and seniors participated. They would have been encouraged during the war by the letters from the front, urging the increasing numbers of boys in the rifle club to improve their standard of shooting in the national interest and to *'keep your rifle clean.'*

Unquestioning acceptance of a link between healthy minds and healthy bodies can be seen in the importance attached to school sport and organised games. A *School Gazette* first appeared on Saturday 4 September 1869 and showed the determination of Dr Clark and his *'large staff of qualified masters'* in this regard:

> 'A senior and junior Athletic Club has been established...a running match of 100 yards will take place on Tuesday next between Mr Pollard and Mr Griffin (4 September 1869)....C. Godfree and W. Jones will be willing to instruct those wishing to learn the art of swimming. Terms moderate...a fencing club has been established (11 September 1869). An athletic club has been formed by A. C. Hall....Already the bathers have left the river, the cricketers are thinking about drawing their stumps...in short, most outdoor games must be discontinued and recreation sought in the schoolroom...in the winter nights we hope to see such indoor games as chess and draughts cultivated (18 September 1869).' [15]

Dr Clark, Mr Pollard and Mr Griffin seem to have been very prominent in school recreational pursuits at this time. Godfree and Jones proposed to teach the art of swimming, presumably in the nearby river.

Competitive events had to be as inclusive as possible in a school of this size. Sports day in July 1914 offered, as well as the normal measured athletic contests, throwing the cricket ball, obstacle race, sack race, three-legged race, and so on. There was even a *'young ladies' race.'* Staff and boys, not unusually in this type of establishment, played team games together. In the 1914 cricket side, bowling honours went to Mr Laurence (also editor of *The Ongarian*), whose many outstanding performances included 7 for 12 against Brentwood Gas Works. A record was made in December 1916, when the school fielded four football teams in one day; the senior side was captained by the headmaster, Mr Wildman, also captain and commanding officer in the cadet corps. It was stated, not surprisingly, that *'lack of practice has hampered much of his play.'* [16] Boxing was "scientifically" taught to those wishing to learn – for an extra charge (as mentioned above).

'No better guarantee of kind and proper treatment can be offered'

Ongar Grammar School under the direction of Dr W. Clark had four divisions:

THE HISTORY OF ONGAR GRAMMAR SCHOOL/ PART TWO: 1860 –1940

preparatory, junior, intermediate and senior, an arrangement still adopted well into the twentieth century. By the 1930s the boarders were in four houses: Budworth, Cripsey, St Martin's and School. The link with St Martin's church was well-established, and it was usual for the rector of St Martin's to be school chaplain.

Parents sending their boys to Ongar expected care, kindness and personal attention to be given. The 1875 Prospectus gives reassurance on each of these: the principal's personal supervision of work and welfare, the guarantee of individual attention and – importantly – a monthly report to parents or guardians on progress, conduct and health. Mrs Sanders (Dr Clark's daughter) supervised the domestic arrangements, careful to make boys feel at home with well-aired clothing and bed linen, a bed for each pupil and an *'unlimited supply of the best provisions.'* Even then the school kept its own cows. Fifty years later the comfort of the boarders was entirely in the hands of the principal's wife, Mrs Percival Bingley, assisted by an experienced matron (who was also a fully-trained nurse) and an assistant matron. The school's own laundry ensured proper, hygienic and sanitary service.

At the end of each term throughout this period (Dr Clark to Mr Bingley) the principal accompanied pupils to London, and arranged for them to be met ('...*at any of the London Railway Stations*') at the start of each term. Mr Bingley took the boys to Liverpool Street Station and met them there at the start of each term. One ex-pupil spoke of a special train being available for this purpose in the 1920s. Pupils came to Ongar from far and wide. *The Ongarian* for April 1915 referred to the smallest dormitory, where there were two Arabians, two Egyptians, three Anglo-Indians and five English boys. A former pupil recalls that he sat next to a boy from New Zealand.

Homely comforts included acceptable pastimes. Small advertisements in the *School Gazette* of 1869 illustrate this well. Apart from the setting up of a number of private circulating libraries (*'of all kinds of literature'*), there was the exchange of stamps and the creation of beneficial societies to improve elocution and mathematics. Boys were able (for one farthing a line) to express their various needs. A. Mootham wanted a long light chain for his sparrowhawk; a boy offered for sale a fine Himalaya doe, with nine young ones, complete with hutch and padlocks; another wished to sell his pair of mice, with cage. There were letters, notes and queries, puzzles (*'none but very ingenious puzzles'*), lists of masters on duty.[15]

Dr Clark was to run the mathematical society. Mr Pollard was chairman of the elocution society, which about 30 "gentlemen" wanted to join. The editor hoped that this halfpenny bulletin would '...*tend considerably to strengthen those bonds of friendship and fraternal love which should exist between gentlemen who, while they remain at school, may be considered brothers.'*

For humanitarian and commercial reasons it was of course essential from around 1860 to disown the nightmare of Dickensian schools – an abhorrent picture of the misery of oppressed, victimised and ill-fed children. Proper treatment had to include proper nourishment.

ASPECTS OF THE HISTORY OF ONGAR

Reference to the availability in 1875 of '*an unlimited supply of the best provisions,*' with about 10 school cows providing the milk, has been made above. At eight o'clock there was breakfast, consisting mainly of bread and butter with milk or coffee. At midday, lunch was usually biscuits and again bread and butter with milk. Dinner (taken at three o'clock) was more copious – beef or pork and a pudding. Finally, at seven o'clock boys were yet again given bread and butter with their tea.[17] The brief advertisement for Ongar Grammar School dating from the turn of the century announced '*Diet unlimited,*' along with the thorough commercial education, the sport and the fishing. In the 1920s the diet was stated to be plain, wholesome and plentiful rather than unlimited. Variety had by now replaced the tedium of the regime 50 years before: boys had porridge, sausage or bacon for breakfast; midday dinner offered different menus, with a range of meats, rabbit pies, steak and kidney puddings, fresh fish and fresh vegetables. Puddings were equally varied and jam came with the bread and butter at teatime. The diet of more delicate boarders was given special attention.

Throughout this period parents were encouraged to correspond confidentially with the principal on matters concerning the treatment of their sons. Later they could visit the school at any time outside school hours (preferably Wednesday and Saturday afternoons, which were free of lessons). The Kings Head Hotel in Ongar ('*an old-fashioned Coaching House*') was recommended for parents needing accommodation. Apart from pupils from overseas, it seems that a good number came from distant parts of the country. The school's attractions of smallish numbers (with the assurance of close personal attention), the oldest cadet corps in Great Britain and healthy surroundings were probably enhanced in the 1930s by the two University leaving scholarships of £30 a year, tenable for two years.

From the fairly rigid list in the 1870s, school clothing requirements seem to have become less prescriptive, no doubt as fashions changed. As will be seen, however, departure from generally identifiable school uniform probably added smartness and dignity. Dr Clark in 1875, having said that parents could send whatever clothing they thought proper, then asked them to include all the items on his long list. He required three suits of clothes (best, second best and "school"). The pupil could join the cadet corps if the second best suit (costing 44s 0d) consisted of tunic, trousers, shako and belt. These were available from Mr Rose of Ongar. Two caps, "best" and "playground", were needed. The college cap (for best), black and with tassel, was obtainable at school for 6s 6d – wholesale price, from the supply sent by Mr Houghton of Oxford. Pupils' boxes (height 14 inches maximum) should also contain three pairs of boots, six handkerchieves, a pair of slippers, six white or three coloured shirts (and pieces for mending), eight collars, six pairs of socks, bathing drawers, three nightshirts, four towels and four table napkins. A rug for the grass in summer was an interesting additional item.

Fifty years after this, overcoat and mackintosh were required. Three suits were again listed, but now grey tweeds for winter, flannels for summer and compulsory dark Westminster lounge suit for Sundays. One pair of the boots had

THE HISTORY OF ONGAR GRAMMAR SCHOOL/ PART TWO: 1860 –1940

to be black for Sundays and soft collars were allowed on weekdays. The listing of vests and pants, dressing gown, gloves, hairbrushes, clothes brush, toothbrush and nail scissors pointed to a more refined and self-conscious turnout in the 1920s and 1930s.

'Good men and worthy citizens'

This title comes from an article in *The Ongarian* of July 1914 by Alfred Goodall, a superintendent for the College of Preceptors examinations, for which Ongar Grammar School pupils were then being prepared. He refers to the very high standard of work and conduct achieved at the school, going so far as to say that failure was almost unknown. He had not once, he said, had to rebuke a candidate. The school had an excellent record in the College of Preceptors' exams. The subjects taken, some with distinction, were algebra, arithmetic, English, scripture history, drawing, book-keeping, French, music and geography. In 1914 the school had a record number of successes. In 1915 it became a centre for National Shorthand Association exams. There were good results too in the exams of the Associated Board of the Royal Academy of Music and the Royal College of Music. In 1914 three of these candidates also entered successfully for the College of Violinists' exams. Examination choices widened rapidly in the first half of the twentieth century and by the mid 1920s Ongar Grammar School was preparing candidates for the Oxford and Cambridge Local exams, London matriculation, London Chamber of Commerce and the Trinity College of Music.

In December 1913 the Ongar Grammar School Old Boys' Club (president: Oswald W. Clark, M.A.) was founded. It grew slowly – to only 43 (including members of the school staff) after six months. *The Ongarian* thought this a poor record. Inevitably the war took many likely Old Ongarians away from the reach and relevance of such an association, and it was only after the Armistice that the O.B.s were able to regroup. News of former pupils serving in France in World War I did, as has been seen, get back to the school. Letters from the front were published in *The Ongarian*, the correspondents at first jubilantly impatient for action but later numb with disbelief at the horror and pity of war. War torn Old Boys visited the school.

One French Old Ongarian, L. Camus, joined the French army; 2nd Lt Edward Sanger was awarded the M.C. for exemplary bravery in the trenches. The Roll of Honour grew inexorably.

The successes of some school societies, in particular those of the cadet corps and the rifle club, have already been described in this study. The rising popularity of affordable photography in the first quarter of the twentieth century produced a very active photographic club at the school. Much of the club's work took members on cycling or walking excursions in the area: Maldon, Epping Forest, Chingford (July 1915: '...*to view the aeroplanes*'). The library grew, thanks to the benevolence of such as the principal, Mrs Brucesmith, who was, in 1914, the main donor of over 50 '*entirely new*' books.[18] The optional extra of science

ASPECTS OF THE HISTORY OF ONGAR

(including wireless) costing one guinea per term has been mentioned already. Old Ongarian O. B. Morgan wrote to the editor of *The Ongarian* from the trenches in December 1915, referring to the *'old wireless station'*: *'...when I get out of this, I will go to Ongar and send a few messages.'*

Ongar Grammar School continued its work to closure in 1940. Popular and varied speculation about its decline includes the damaging effect of what the *Ongar and District Chamber of Commerce Guide, 1961–62* describes as *'an unfortunate court case'* (reported in 1921), as well as competition from other schools, both private and county-provided. Essex County Council opened a secondary school in Fyfield Road in 1936, and Buckhurst Hill County High School (a selective grammar school attended by many Ongar boys) in 1938. Some former pupils said that fewer parents seemed to want to send their sons to Ongar Grammar School. Day boys were admitted through the 1930s, but the end came in the early months of the Second World War.

Sixty years later a surprising number of the town's citizens are unaware that in the neat but austere symmetry of Central House on the west side of today's High Street was once the Ongar Grammar School. Central House now contains shops and offices; the school grounds remain largely undeveloped and overgrown. Near the foot of their sloping wilderness the crumbling and entangled hollow of the swimming pool can still be seen – a touching reminder of healthy cavortings sixty or more years ago.

References

1. Ayerst, D. (Ed), *The Guardian Omnibus 1821 – 1971*, (1973), Collins, p.242: extract from an article by C.E. Ratcliffe, giving an account of school conditions in Middlesex, Bucks, Kent, Lincoln and Cornwall
2. VCH Essex vol 4, (1956)
3. The Sadler Report on Secondary and Higher Education in Essex, (1906), County Offices in Chelmsford.
4. (1) Post Office Directory of Essex, Herts, Kent, Middlesex, Surrey and Sussex, (1855), London, Kelly & Co (2) ERO: Kelly's Directory, (1917)
5. Pewsey, S. *Epping and Ongar – A Pictorial History*, (1997) Phillimore
6. Kelly's *Post Office Directory of the Six Home Counties*, (1878)
7. Kelly's *Directory of Essex*, (1914)
8. *The Ongarian* – the Organ of Ongar Grammar School, (July 1916)
9. Kelly's *Directory*, (1926)
10. Kelly's *Directory*, (1932)
11. Kelly's *Directory*, (1902)
12. Prospectus of the Ongar Grammar School, 1875
13. *Essex Weekly News* (28 June 1940), County Library, Chelmsford.
14. *Ongar Guide*, undated
15. *The School Gazette*, (1869)
16. *The Ongarian*, (December 1916)
17. Wingham, R.A. *Ongar in Old Picture Postcards*, (1987), European Library, Zaltbommel, Netherlands.
18. *The Ongarian*, (March 1914)

chapter 15

Secondary education in Ongar 1936-1989

by John Harrop (& John Swallow on the closure saga)

The early years

Before the opening of the secondary school at Fyfield Road, Shelley, children over the age of 11 were educated either at one of the grammar schools in neighbouring towns, or remained at Ongar School (the former King's Trust school) situated behind the Budworth Hall. Chipping Ongar Senior School opened in 1936. The first entries in the official log book reveal that certain things were little different sixty years or so ago. Written in the headmaster's own copper plate handwriting they read

> *11th May 1936*: *I, Gustavus George Cater, commenced duty as Headmaster. No scholars are attending as the building is unfinished.*
> *18th May 1936*: *Mr E. G. Balls and Miss G. A. Storey appointed to the staff commenced today. The school should have been open to scholars today, but as the building is not yet finished, the opening has been postponed until the 8th June.*
> *4th June 1936*: *The school was officially opened today by Councillor J. W. Carlow. A large number of guests and parents attended on the invitation of the education Committee and Miss Tabor, Chairman of the Committee, presided.*
> *8th June 1936*: *The school was opened for the scholars to attend today. The total number of children attending was 348. The day was spent in organising the school and rehearsing the various details of the daily routine. In the afternoon, an intelligence test was set for the whole school to enable classification to be carried out.'*

Other things, however, were very different when the school opened. There were separate entrances for boys and girls – at the time of writing the legends can still be seen over the doorways of the 1936 building. There were separate staff rooms for male and female members of staff. Each day began with the whole school joining in together in morning prayers and a hymn. For this, the boys and girls were mixed, as indeed they were for lessons. At break time, however, the two sexes were segregated into separate playgrounds. Lunch was taken in the hall, with all the teachers present at a separate table on a raised stage. No-one began to eat until the headmaster arrived. The headmaster made regular rounds of the school to check on progress and discipline. He was not alone, however, as he was normally accompanied by a small dark terrier, who perhaps pointed out anything that he had missed! Progress was needed if punishment was to be avoided. The most common reason for receiving the cane at this time was "slacking in class."

ASPECTS OF THE HISTORY OF ONGAR

Though there were some striking omissions, the subjects studied will be familiar to many. They comprised:

Arithmetic	English	History	Geography
Art	Religious instruction	Physical education	Woodwork
Metalwork	Cookery	Music	Rural science
Handicraft	Country dancing		

Cookery was studied by both sexes, though separately, as were metalwork and woodwork. In case anyone should suppose that country dancing was a soft option, it should be noted that it was taken very seriously at Ongar. A thriving competitive team existed which performed with distinction around the county.

The outbreak of war in 1939 brought changes to the school, as elsewhere. Large numbers of evacuees sought refuge in the area. Air raid shelters were constructed, gas masks worn, and regular air raid drills held. One can see from the punishment book that not all pupils took these drills as seriously as the headmaster thought they should. Up to this point, the most serious punishment handed out to any pupil had been two strokes of the cane. Mr Cater recorded having administered six strokes to some miscreant who acted in a manner '*which, in a real emergency, would have been likely to endanger life.*'

On the evening of 10 December 1945, Mr Cater died suddenly at home. Miss Mabel Hadler took charge of the school until a replacement headmaster was appointed. This proved to be Mr George Fleet, who assumed the role on 1 September 1946. He was obviously not such an assiduous diarist as Mr Cater, since his entries in the school log book during the six years of his tenure occupy only 86 pages, and consist almost entirely of staff absences and meetings attended. No clues as to curriculum development are to be found. A general inspection was carried out in October 1951 and a governors' meeting was held in November to hear the results – the log book, however, makes no comment.

The middle period

Mr Fleet left at Christmas 1951 to take up a position as assistant inspector of schools with the East Sussex Education Committee, and Mr John William Butler succeeded him on 1 January 1952. It would seem that he had many problems to contend with. In his first month of office the school log book mentions:

- the theft of a staff watch from the staff room by a boy who was to eventually end up in a remand school.
- the refusal of 30 boys out of 40 to play football, even though clothing was provided
- the refusal of classes 4B and 4C to change for physical education
- complaints by six members of staff about the unruly behaviour of children
- problems with children going to Shelley shops at break time and lunch time
- pupils in the third year possessing and reading obscene literature
- smoking in the playground
- trouble on the 339 bus

SECONDARY EDUCATION IN ONGAR IN 1936-1989

- staff wanting to leave early to catch their bus home.

None of these matters were referred to again, so one can assume that the "new broom" dealt with them effectively. The log books of Mr Cater's and Mr Butler's times would be worth publishing in their own rights (with suitable editing, of course!). Mr Butler, in particular, had a neat turn of phrase and a wry sense of humour. For example:

> **3 March**: *An interesting experience. Mr A again lost control of his class – sent out D and J. J openly defiant to myself! I think he will apologise tomorrow.*
>
> **4 March**: *J apologised? No he did not! He was even more insolent. His mother arrived in the afternoon and explained that J was an adopted child (when a fortnight old!)'*

Eight years later:

> '**15 January**: *Father of Robert L visited the school and made violent threats to HM for caning his son for misbehaving on the bus, throwing rice into the hair of the conductress and in the general direction of Mrs M (member of staff). Father only departed on threat of Police – for whom he cared more than he cared for HM. Father considered that all boys could and should fool around on the bus and even should not be punished. Asked if he would have complained if his son had been hit in the eye, he said it had nothing to do with it. Father very violent indeed – dreadful threats!'*

It was not always the pupils that caused problems:

> '**5 December**: *Miss Z insubordinate. Has been absent from Junior Assembly since return from absence on 15 November. When asked for reasons, in the presence of a witness refused to give a written explanation (actually making tea for a colleague!). Miss Z suspended from duty and DEO informed by letter.*
>
> **6 December**: *Miss Z to see DEO in Chelmsford at 4pm – given afternoon off to make her way there.*
>
> **13 December**: *Letter received from DEO stating Miss Z had sincerely expressed her regrets to him (but not to me!). HM replied that he hoped that Miss Z would not be in a position to say that she had won a victory, and so could continue on the insubordinate way.*
>
> **17 January**: *HM and Miss Z seen separately by DEO. Miss Z was to write a letter of apology.*
>
> **19 January**: *Letter received form Miss Z by registered post – carefully phrased – ignored her open insubordination, quoted permission she had never obtained, nor was in a position to obtain, and glossed over her*

ASPECTS OF THE HISTORY OF ONGAR

insubordination. <u>BUT</u> the School must go on, so I suppose once again her insubordination must be tolerated!'

The early years of Mr Butler's tenure as headmaster saw the school complete its transition from an area senior school to a secondary modern school, in accordance with the provisions of the 1944 Education Act. With the brighter pupils creamed off to grammar schools elsewhere by the 11+ exam, the school's curriculum inevitably catered for the less academic children. Thus, while providing the main core subjects – English, maths, history, geography, religious and physical education etc. – other subjects leaned towards the practical rather than the academic. Thus, woodwork and metalwork were thriving subjects for boys, and domestic science and needlework for the girls. The sciences were catered for by rural science (including gardening) and by general science (instead of biology, physics and chemistry). For this reason, the school was not looked upon with much favour by the newer more affluent parents in the post war housing estates which, in hindsight, may have sown the seeds of the disaster described in the final paragraphs of this history. Had the school become the Ongar Grammar School, the outcome could have been so different.

Nevertheless, when the school was subjected to a full inspection in May 1960, the report said that the tone of the school was excellent. The staff also received praise for the good manners and self-control of the children. It seems that Mr Butler was steering his ship on the right course. As the years passed by, the curriculum broadened, and increasing numbers of pupils obtained GCE certificates in academic subjects as well as in practical ones. As pupil numbers increased, and accommodation became more cramped, a building programme was planned. However, in Mr Butler's time, only the first stage was implemented, resulting in a new science laboratory built in isolation between the workshops and the main school block.

At a governors' meeting on 6 February 1969, Mr Butler informed the Divisional Education Officer that he intended to retire in July of that year, on reaching the age of 60. It was probably a very wise decision on his part, as he was obviously aware that sweeping changes lay ahead. On the evening of 19 March 1969, an important meeting of the governors was held with the West Essex Division to discuss comprehensive plans for Ongar. The executive proposal seemed to be that Ongar school should be comprehensive for children up to 16 years of age and that sixth formers would attend Chigwell schools as an interim measure, to free grammar school places there. After a long discussion, the governors decided to press for Ongar to be a full comprehensive with a sixth form, and that 11+ candidates should have Ongar as one of their choices. This recommendation was to be sent by the DEO to the county council and, in readiness for it, a new building programme was prepared and implemented. When finished, it provided a new hall, administration offices, a second gymnasium, a new kitchen for school meals, and some specialist classrooms (used at various times as science rooms, art rooms and workshops).

SECONDARY EDUCATION IN ONGAR 1936-1989

On 29 April 1969 interviews were held for the appointment of a new headmaster. Six candidates were short listed, but only four were interviewed as two had withdrawn. Mr J. P. Swallow, from North Romford Comprehensive School, was appointed from 1 September 1969. He had a year to prepare for the change to comprehensive education, during which time the new buildings were completed, extra staff were appointed and the pastoral structure of the school finalised.

The comprehensive era

In September 1970, Ongar Secondary School became Ongar Comprehensive School. The roll at the time stood at 820, but was soon to rise to over 1500. To ensure that every pupil in such a large school was individually cared for on the pastoral side, the house system (which had existed in rudimentary form before for sports and competitive events) was developed to cater for this. The school was divided into four houses (later five) named, by the original heads of houses, after the rivers Frome, Lea, Roding and Trent (and, later, Cam). Each head of house had a deputy of the opposite sex, so that both boys and girls had someone that they could turn to if necessary. The mixed ability classes were house based. To begin with, the small sixth form also belonged to the houses, but later, as it grew, it became a separate unit with its own director and deputy.

The curriculum was expanded to cover all the requirements of 11 to 18 year olds of all abilities, and was eventually crystallised into four distinct areas:

- creative arts, embracing art, music, drama, technical subjects and physical education
- language development, embracing English and modern languages
- community education embracing history, geography, economics, religious education
- mathematical & scientific development, embracing maths, computer studies, the sciences and food & nutrition.

In the upper school, the course choices for examination and other purposes required pupils to select (apart from English and maths, which were compulsory) at least one subject from each curriculum area, thus ensuring a balanced education as a basis for whatever career he or she should choose.

Over the years, Ongar Comprehensive School acquired a considerable reputation for the quality of its public performances. At its height, the school concert band contained over 70 wind and brass players, and was able to divide itself into a brass band, a Glenn Miller style show band and a jazz band. End of term concerts were a sell out. Similarly, the drama productions were ambitious and well attended.

The increasing size of the school meant that accommodation was again getting cramped, and another building programme was necessary to overcome this. This

ASPECTS OF THE HISTORY OF ONGAR

provided seven new science laboratories, a large maths department, new art rooms and a fully equipped drama studio. The movement of these subjects to the new building enabled others to expand into the areas that they had vacated. Although the school roll was falling, due largely to the realignment of catchment area described in the following section, the school was riding high in 1986. It had obtained one of the first Curriculum Awards in 1984 and was looking to even greater things, unaware of the blow that was shortly to fall.

The closure saga

At the end of the booklet published to commemorate the fiftieth anniversary of the school in 1986, the then headteacher, John Swallow, wrote these words:

> *'What next? Human beings are still, thank goodness, unable to predict the future. However, we can endeavour to plan to the best of our ability to enable all our young people and their parents to realise their aspirations. Educationally we are living in turbulent but dynamic times. I believe that our overriding task is to end the isolation of the educational process from the rest of society's activities – and that perhaps is a greater national task than it is a local one. Here we are, hopefully, in the words of the Curriculum Award, already "at the heart of the community." We have the strongest links with industry and commerce, further education and all sections of local society. This is how we want the school to continue and to develop so that school-in-community is a living reality. We want the educational aspirations of all age groups, adults as well as young people, to be centred upon it.'*

Of course, that was not to be. Instead we have a tale of swift metamorphosis so that a school, not unknown in its heyday both for innovative curriculum development and serious attempts to foster capability in all, rapidly proceeded to its extinction. "Ongar Comp", to employ the local colloquialism, was granted one of the first Curriculum Awards in 1984 and seemed set fair to celebrate the first fifty years of its life in 1986, and to embark on its second half century in full confidence of its ability to extend and define community education at the secondary stage. But this school, that started life in 1936 as an area senior school, that experienced short lived secondary modern status and that was transformed in 1970 into a community comprehensive (with brand new buildings and facilities, and a roll of over 1500), fell victim to reorganisation.

Ongar set out on the rural community comprehensive road immediately after the decision to reorganise it had been taken in 1969 – an ideal central location vis-à-vis "daschund and daimler" country to the east and south, pre-war local authority housing estates to the west, and traditional thatch-bedecked villages to the north – a splendid mix. The area school was welcomed. The expansion of opportunities here, instead of in relatively distant towns, was seen as a great asset, and people moved into the district in order to take advantage of the new educational facilities. The roll expanded rapidly until 1975 when the local education authority proposed a smaller catchment area by excluding "the five parishes" (i.e. Blackmore, Doddinghurst, Kelvedon Hatch, Navestock and Stondon Massey). At that time, catchment areas governed intakes. Tragically and ironically, the head and staff supported this move and even persuaded vociferous meetings of parents (who were all strongly opposed to the change) to accept the plan. Who could then have forecast events 12 years ahead? So the school never became over-full, and there followed a period of steady pupil numbers and a time of lively, organic curriculum development conducted by lively committed teachers. Spice was injected into the calm when a High Court action by a parent challenged an upper school course structure which was designed to eliminate options and to establish for all a broad balanced curriculum to 16+ – the hallmark of any half decent school today.

Roll decline set in endemically in the early 1980s but this process, if anything, provided a spur to new curricular moves, notably in the field of pre-vocational education, as the pressure of a larger pupil population diminished. And now the local education authority (LEA) stepped in with a consultation exercise – but with no proposals at this stage – designed to make people aware of falling school roll problems throughout West Essex. But why was Ongar included in the West Essex area of which it was not part? Ongar is solidly East Saxon; West Essex is leafy London. Few considered that destructive forces were at work; almost everyone dismissed the exercise as an interesting academic affair conducted by a paternal county authority. And indeed nothing whatsoever followed the consultation (is this currently the most abused word in the language?) other than county council elections that resulted in a "hung" political situation. So the calm continued. Was it significant that the two opposition parties could agree on nothing procedurally (let alone philosophically), save the reinvestment of the former Conservative party with all its traditional power and influence, exercised through the officerships of the council, and the committee positions, to which the opposition parties gave their consent?

In August 1985, when vigilance was diminished, the authority's intention to seek the closure of the school was announced – so everyone was flung into a heady headlong campaign, school and community led, to defeat the unthinkable, the unspeakable. The *Ongar Gazette* immediately started its own "Save Our School" campaign, and public meetings were held in all the primary schools in the district – both in the traditional catchment area and "the five parishes". All county councillors on the education committee were invited to visit the school and those who came (19 out of 58) were given a tour by sixth formers. The first phase of the campaign culminated in a meeting in the Budworth Hall – nothing less than a full community rally that ended with the unanimous resolution that ECC do all in its power to support and preserve Ongar Comprehensive School and to recognise the overwhelming wish of the community that the school should continue to act as the focus for local life, and as an example of excellent practice. But the schools sub-committee, at its meeting on 15 January 1986, recommended closure in August

ASPECTS OF THE HISTORY OF ONGAR

1989 – a recommendation that was not adopted by the full education committee, such was the fine balance on the issue between the main political parties.

Immediately all members of the education committee were furnished with fresh statements about the quality of the school, flooded with letters from parents, and lobbied intensively – notably at their home addresses by sixth formers. On 4 March 1986 the full council met in the council chamber, faced with a public gallery packed to the rafters with Ongar partisans. The occasion in no way maintained the staid, calm atmosphere which that chamber was accustomed to. At the end of a long, very fraught and continually interrupted debate (during which the education committee chairman, Paul White, attacked the headmaster personally for leading the campaign to save his school) the vote for closure was passed by the narrow majority of three. That majority must be ascribed to two members of the minority Labour group, who defied their party's whip because they feared closure of a school, or schools, in their own areas if Ongar survived.

And so the county council approved the impossible, with not only the community in general but also the two minor local authorities (Ongar parish council and Epping Forest District Council) ranged implacably against it. And what of the powerless, toothless political opposition that displayed its contemptible impotence for all to see? At no point was there any semblance of the unity that could so easily have defeated and condemned the iniquity now recommended to the government.

Had the community any remedy open to it which might restore the faith in the true meaning of consultation, in the right of people to be heard, in the paramount social and educational needs of young people? There was a final phase of the campaign. A detailed paper was produced indicating serious flaws in the official consultation process. A solicitor versed in education law, Peter Liell, was consulted about the feasibility of taking legal action against Essex County Council on the grounds of flawed consultation. The School Association Action Group, chaired by Dr Michael Leach, was formed to continue the campaign under the banner "Save Ongar School – Save Ongar Town", and the parish council agreed to fund all costs of the legal action investigations taking place. This courageous stance of the parish council enabled a judicial review to be heard in the High Court in October 1986 on the grounds that consultation had been unsatisfactory. Naturally, Essex County Council's decision per se could not be challenged in the court. On legal grounds – but not on moral – this action failed on the third day, and thus the Secretary of State for Education was to be the last port of call. A community delegation was arranged to see him. This consisted of the MP, Robert McCrindle, Peter Nightingale (chair of governors), Tony Sutherland (chair of parish council), Michael Leach (chair of action group), Jill Coward (past chair of school association) and John Swallow (headmaster). The delegation departed on 25 March 1987 with a send off from the town – bands, balloons, banners and billboards – worthy of royalty. Once again, everyone felt better, and there was renewed enthusiasm for some splendid fiftieth anniversary events. There followed a long summer of silence.

SECONDARY EDUCATION IN ONGAR 1936-1989

Then, in mid autumn, with Ongar enjoying the status of a national test case, rumours started flying; radio, television, newspapers, all had something and all were convinced (even the local MP) that decision time was imminent. And half way through the half term break, they were right. On 27 October 1987, with television cameras present, the call came through that the Secretary of State was to support the County Council's closure plan. Campaigning, with all its exhilaration, was over, and the sad negativity of retrenchment, and curriculum standstill, and moving pupils and colleagues out, and all the activities that are the very reverse of what the school had stood for over the different phases of its fifty years were to begin and end 18 months later.

In June 1989 in a school now bereft of its pupils, the governors held their final meeting. At the end of his report to that governing body, John Swallow said:

> *'It is, of course, beyond measure regrettable that other things remain to be said. Perhaps it was naïve of us to assume in 1969 that everyone in the local community would support what we were trying to do; perhaps in a democracy no school will ever receive the unanimous support of those who come within its sphere. What would have transpired had the school responded to the considerable pressure during the 1970s to drop the word "Comprehensive" in its title? In the case of this school, the word has never been universally accepted in this district, although we have always felt it to be a significant word, signifying as it does full provision for all. Nevertheless, there have always been parents who, because of their opposition to the principle of comprehensive secondary education, have sent their children to schools other than the neighbourhood institution. That has been sad and though it has in no way diminished the quality of the work and of the achievements, it did give the local authority a specious reason, which they utilised to the full in the campaign to preserve the school, for presenting a case for complete closure. Although we know that the substance is very different, that specious reason, together with the acutely falling roll situation afflicting both West and Central Essex, was enough to tip the balance against preservation. There has never been a case for closure on moral, on educational, on community grounds; indeed on all of these grounds I have cited, the case for preservation is undeniable. Sadly, we here, and the whole district with us, now have to accept that the decision has been made by people who never tried to understand the damage that was being done to a discrete community that had already lost services which it had every right to expect should be provided. I earnestly hope that the closure of our s chool will not herald the demise of the community in which we have worked for 53 years; rather I hope most fervently, that the site will continue in educational use – as will be the case in the immediate future – until such time as wiser counsels prevail, and the need for neighbourhood secondary education is recognised'.*

ASPECTS OF THE HISTORY OF ONGAR

Postscript

It is now ten years since the ill-considered West Essex reorganisation deprived Ongar of its only secondary school, as well as being responsible for the demise of other long established schools further south. It is perhaps inevitable, and certainly ironic, that at the end of the century the education authorities are faced with a shortage of secondary school places. This crisis can only be exacerbated by the sale of the Comprehensive School site for housing purposes as well as similar developments at the defunct Great Stony School, itself the subject of a similar short sighted act by a different education authority.

Sources

1   Ongar School log books 1936–1969
2   *Towards a better School* (1987) Ongar Comprehensive School
3   *Valedictory Celebrations* (1989) Ongar Comprehensive School
4   early school records
5   press cuttings 1969–1989
6   J. P. Swallow private papers
7   personal knowledge (both authors)

chapter 16

A home for the homeless: from Ongar Cottage Homes to Great Stony School

by Ron Barnes

Introduction

During the Elizabethan period, each parish assumed responsibility for their own poor by provision of outdoor relief. The increasing demands of poor relief necessitated the 1834 Poor Law Amendment Act which led to the building of many workhouses, in which all ages were confined. The children in these institutions were vulnerable to sexual abuse and were subjected to other forms of immorality by the adult paupers. Many workhouses became "dens of iniquity" and were overfilled with the illiterate poor.

Subsequent reforms led to the removal of children from workhouses and their placement in large "industrial schools" later in the nineteenth century. It had became clear that these children were likely to end up in the adult workhouses unless some provision was made for their training. The size of these industrial schools (often 100 or more, with only two officers to look after them) meant that they had little in the way of home comforts. Boards of guardians made attempts to find foster homes and other smaller homes in their areas. In the metropolis this proved difficult, and guardians often looked for placements outside the urban area. One such was the Hackney board of guardians which is the subject of this study.

The size of the problem

In 1899 a meeting of the Hackney board of guardians expressed concern about the size of families, especially amongst the poorer sections of the community. Families with a dozen or fifteen (or sometimes more) children were often unable to feed or clothe them all, and it was not unusual for the older children to be turned out of the home to fend for themselves. These children had to be picked up off the streets and taken to a "pound", before being returned to the board of guardians responsible for the area that they had come from. Hackney was dealing with two or three hundred children at any time, herded into industrial schools.

We will have to build, but where?

The school committee report of the guardians on 16 March 1900 showed that it was urgently considering the need for additional accommodation for children who were the responsibility of the guardians, as well for their maintenance and education. Three months earlier, the committee had agreed to engage Mr W. Bramham as surveyor to assist in the search for a suitable site for a new children's home.

ASPECTS OF THE HISTORY OF ONGAR

Into the new century

The Hackney board of guardians (covering the vestries of Hackney and Stoke Newington, with South Hornsey parish as a later addition) already had a school for pauper children in Brentwood, a workhouse like building known as the "Barrack." This was inadequate by 1899, and in 1901, due to overcrowding, its quota was reduced to 446 children. The problem was aggravated by legislation in 1889 and 1899 which obliged guardians to take into care children of "dissolute parents", as well as younger children about to be turned out by their families. All this was in addition to the normal responsibilities towards pauper children in the workhouse, orphans and foundlings. The guardians tried in vain to find foster homes for the increasing number of children in their care.

By 1901 the total number of children in Hackney's care had risen to 826. A number of empty houses in Sidney Street, Hackney Wick, were taken over, and organised as cottage homes, mainly for younger children. Two years' search had failed to find a suitable site for a new home in London, or to find suitable foster parents willing to work long hours on their own bringing up children. The "Sheffield scheme" had been considered. This involved placing children in scattered foster homes around a fairly large neighbourhood. The children would have attended normal schools, and there would have been a small purpose built centre containing an infirmary and temporary hostel. Hackney favoured this scheme but was unable to implement it due to the shortage of foster parents, and the lack of a suitable site in Hackney on which to build the centre.

As a result of these difficulties, Hackney sought places in Brentwood and the surrounding villages. It appears to have been particularly successful in Ongar. Foster parents were paid and, initially, inspected by board officials at regular intervals. Unfortunately, "out of sight, out of mind," the latter duty fell into abeyance. An inspection of foster homes in the summer of 1900 showed that all was not well. A motion to stop such visits, on the grounds that they infringed the foster parents' privacy, was rejected by the chairman, and the guardians nominated four members to follow the matter up. Their report showed that the foster homes left a lot to be desired, with children poorly clothed and infested with head lice. This made members more determined to build their own home.

Where to build?

Mr Bramham and his team examined 21 sites, eventually reducing this to ten possible ones to be considered by the guardians. Three were at Pilgrim's Hatch, two in Ongar and one each at Warley, Beacon Hill, Kelvedon Common, Theydon Bois, and Westwood Park in Brentwood. Members of the board visited all these sites, though the ones at Theydon and Westwood Park were viewed while passing in the train! A short list of three was produced – Pilgrim's Hatch, Warley and one of the Ongar sites. After consideration, it was unanimously agreed that the Ongar site was by far the most suitable on the following grounds.

Position: the site was considered to be in an excellent position, with good views

A HOME FOR THE HOMELESS:
FROM ONGAR COTTAGE HOMES TO GREAT STONY SCHOOL

and suitable for building, in a healthy neighbourhood near to a Great Eastern railway station, and eight miles from the board's other home in Brentwood.

Frontage: 1,150 ft frontage to the London Road, and 1500 ft frontage to the Chelmsford Road.

Facilities: gas was available at 3s 3d per 1000 cubic ft, water at 1s 6d per 1000 gallons and the local authority was willing to seek approval from the Local Government Board to install a sewerage system.

Local community: over the years the board had successfully found foster homes for many of the children in their care in the local area.

Altitude and contour: a clay soil, freely intermixed with pebbles. The highest point was 212 ft, the lowest 180 feet. The approximate site area was 40 acres, with an asking price of £200 per acre.

Concerns: the vendors mentioned that there had been a plan in 1898 to build a light railway through part of the site. Inspection of the plans, however, showed that it would only touch the site at one corner, and would not interfere with the guardians' intentions. The vendors were not happy with the board's wish to fence the whole site, particularly with an unclimbable fence, and it was agreed to strike out the word "unclimbable." In spite of this, the final fence was topped with two strands of barbed wire.

The purchase was agreed and finalised, with the tenant farmer, Mr Pratt, being permitted to crop the land until the end of his tenancy. He would be compensated for any crop damage. In November 1902, the guardians received the estimated costs of building the homes: 994,000 cubic feet of building at ninepence half penny a foot – £39,345 16s 8d; cost of work and drainage – £1200; engineering works to laundry – £300; building walls and fences – £700; digging, carting, levelling and road making – £1,300. This totalled £42,845 16s 8d. There were additional costs of: furnishing – £2,600; architect's fee – £2,142; quantity surveyor's fee – £550; clerk of works – £200; cost of raising loan – £50; contingencies – £612 3s 4d, making a grand total of £49,000. In the New Year of 1903, it was agreed that the guardians could borrow the whole sum, of which £4,400 was to be paid back in 15 years and the remainder in 30 years.

Schooling and church attendance

The original intention was for the children to go to school in the town. In February 1903, the board met the Rev. Tanner and three other members of the Joseph King Trust to discuss a plan to allow the guardians to extend the King's Trust school in order to accommodate the large number of extra children from the home. In due course, this offer was declined because of the difficulties that it would have caused the Trust. The guardians were therefore obliged to plan and build school buildings on its own site, but these could not be completed before the homes were ready. Children would have to receive their instruction in their cottages until the new

ASPECTS OF THE HISTORY OF ONGAR

Administrative block and SuperIntendents house

Receiving house

Administrative block

Infirmary

Figure 16 Cottage Homes at Ongar for the Hackney Union from the *Builders' Journal and Architectural Record* of 29 March 1905.

school was finished. Agreement was also reached at this time for children to attend whichever local church corresponded with their parents' religious denomination. In June 1903 the guardians, as the new landowner, received a request for £188 4s 7d in respect of the Ongar tithe rent.

The building of the Ongar Cottage Homes

Having received revised drawings for the administration block, specifications were sent out to 32 different firms for estimates. These tenders were opened on 29 July 1903 and ranged from £59,835 to £47,987. The lowest was from McCormick & Sons, of Northampton Street, Essex Road, London. The guardians were delighted that the lowest tender was within their estimated costs. However, one member proposed an amendment that consideration of the tenders should be delayed for six months, and this amendment was seconded and carried. Upset by this delay, another member sent the chairman a notice of a motion to rescind this decision. An extraordinary meeting of the board was duly held in August 1903, the previously amended motion was put to the meeting and defeated, and Messrs McCormick were asked to go ahead.

The original plan provided a communal kitchen and dining room. As the number of children were to be in the region of 300, it was decided that it would be better to provide each cottage with its own kitchen and dining area by means of a rear extension. This involved the architect, W. A. Finch, in considerable alterations to the drawings, and there were other changes too, including glazed pipes for drainage, and blue bricks on the cottage fronts. Then the weather stepped in. Just before Christmas 1903, the contractor asked for more time to complete, as bad weather and flooding had caused some delay. In February 1904, it was impossible to get on the site as the conditions were so bad.

The weather improved in the spring, but there were new problems. The tenant farmer, Mr Pratt, who had permission to crop the land while building proceeded, complained about poaching on the site. A search revealed six wire snares, and the finger of suspicion was pointed at the workmen. The poaching stopped. Another boiler was found to be necessary as the original could not get hot water to the second floor. In October 1904 the board decided that the buildings should be lit by electricity at an annual estimated cost of £604 8s 0d. A generating plant was to be installed together with a ten ton weighbridge at the porter's lodge. The contractor pointed out that this would save the cost of cutting out the walls to take the gas pipes for lighting. Autumn also saw problems with the toilets and the bathroom flooring.

Messrs McCormick must have been glad to have seen the end of 1904. However, things did not improve. In the New Year the infirmary was struck by lightning and had to be partly rebuilt. Then one of the board members, who was not in favour of electricity, put an amendment to the committee in favour of gas lighting. After considerable debate, this was approved, though McCormick pointed out that this would increase the cost as the walls would have to be hacked out to put the pipes in. The board then instructed the builder to fix the gas pipes on the surface of the walls! It also decided to provide a laundry capable of dealing with 4,000 to 5,000 articles of clothing a week, and approved the additional cost of £1,500.

Completion, at last!

Messrs McCormick handed the buildings over on 6 November 1905. It had been decided that the houses should be named after members of the Hackney board of guardians. Starting from the administration house (to be called the Fenton Jones house) they were to be named Howlett, Weston, Russell Morely, Carlise, Warick, Shaftsbury, May and the Hospital. A month before the handover, the guardians had accepted the lowest tender for the school building, being £6987 from F. E. Davey Ltd of Southend. Contrary to their previous decision to educate the children in the cottages, it was decided to leave the buildings empty until the school buildings were completed. As there was no central heating, a caretaker was employed to light and maintain fires in the houses in order to keep the buildings dry. After some time, he complained that he could not keep up with this task, as by the time he had dealt with the last fire, the first one had gone out! He was given an assistant who was paid £1 per week. Nevertheless, the buildings deteriorated in the three years that they were empty, and all the ceilings in the large rooms had to be hacked out and replastered. During this time, objections had been raised about the naming of the houses and, on 28 September 1908, it was decided that they should be renamed after the tree planted in front of each building.

Preparing for the intake

Before the completion of the school, it had been agreed to appoint Mr Spencer from the Brentwood school as superintendent/head schoolmaster at a salary of £150 per annum, with a biannual rise of £10 to a maximum of £180. His wife was appointed as the matron and would receive £40 per annum, rising in £5 increments to a maximum of £60. With their two children, they were also to have full board and laundry. Recruitment of other staff followed, and naturally teachers from the Brentwood school were anxious to transfer to this lovely new environment. Five were successful, followed by the clerk and storekeeper. Other appointments included a specialist teacher in drill, drawing and music (at £90 per annum), assistant matron, porters, engineers, stokers, night watchmen, two needlewomen, three laundrymaids, an ironer and helper, bandmaster, carpenter, plumber, gardeners, tailor, shoemender and 21 foster parents. Many Ongar families found jobs in the new home, one such notable being Flo Ethel Bolden. As senior laundry woman, she turned the laundry into a small business, taking in washing from several other Hackney establishments. By October 1908, all 114 staff had been appointed and the first children were admitted from Brentwood on 12 November 1908.

Inevitably questions were asked about the £8,550 overspend. After numerous visits by the guardians and government officials, it was agreed that the costs were justified. The result was a well designed home in open country, with plenty of

A HOME FOR THE HOMELESS:
FROM ONGAR COTTAGE HOMES TO GREAT STONY SCHOOL

open space for its 300 children, with 126 of them being educated in its own school. All the members of the Hackney board of guardians were pleased with the result of their eight years work. The unsuitable Brentwood school could now be closed and consideration given to building a more suitable replacement. The guardians' original intention was for the home to provide accommodation and education only, but it was reported that in the first two years 90% of leavers ended up in the workhouse. The guardians did not want the home to become a workhouse feeder. Therefore the various tradesmen who had already been employed were upgraded to become instructors, and by 1910 the leavers were trained for a trade and all found work. Ironically, as education was not considered important for girls, it had always been the intention for them to be trained for service. The superintendent's wife kept a watchful eye on several in her own home.

The children who were transferred must have been overjoyed to be removed from such crowded and outdated conditions. The new Hackney Homes (as they came to be called) must have seemed heavenly. Ongar itself benefited too, both from the new jobs and from the new houses that McCormick had put up for their employees. Some of these in the Fyfield Road were sold to the guardians and were used to accommodate non-residential staff.

Has the pendulum swung too far?

Not everyone was happy with the result. A descriptive article appeared in *The Builders' Journal and Architectural Record* of 29 March 1905, some eight months before completion. It stated *'the children's colony of the Hackney Guardians in the quiet little town of Chipping Ongar in Essex, shows that so far as creature comforts are concerned, the lot of the workhouse child is not devoid of its advantages. It is indeed a question whether in the revulsion from the former severity with which Boards of Guardians were wont to regard their hapless charges, they have not allowed solicitude for their welfare to urge the pendulum unduly in the other direction.'* It then went on to criticise the size of the cottages, designed to house 40 children each, *'as being prejudicial to the cottage character of these buildings'* and expressed the view that they should have been limited to two storeys in height. The writer seems to have been rather out of touch with the enormous problems facing the guardians, who had 800 children in care, many in very overcrowded and prison-like accommodation, with 100 children under the care of one officer. Those who returned later, to show their own children where they had grown up, never spoke about being overcrowded. Later in the century, with changing requirements, the numbers were reduced. By 1964 the cottages accommodated 30, and in the 1970s fire regulations reduced the number to 20.

It was the only home I knew

For 22 years these buildings were home to the pauper and foundling children of Hackney. The author instituted an annual reunion in the 1970s, and the elderly attenders spoke well of their time at Ongar where they were well fed, well clothed and well looked after. For many it was the only home that they could remember, as their early years were so traumatic. During their stay, they had been reminded how lucky they were, and how grateful they should be to the wonderful board of guardians. Girls were instructed to curtsy to visitors looking around, while the boys had to doff their hats. They all learnt a trade before they left so that they would not follow their parents into the workhouse. Fruit and vegetables were grown in the garden to reduce costs, any surplus being sold to other Hackney establishments. Much of the children's clothing was made or altered in the sewing room. The sewing ladies, assisted by the girls in training, saw to all the curtains, bedding and so forth. Both boys and girls were trained as tailors, and many lads learned how to make shoes. It is ironical that by taking these children away from their impoverished families, mothers were often able to go out to work to supplement the family income. There is nothing new about counter-productive social policies!

The end of the Poor Law

The Act of 1929 ceased the funding of the Poor Law system, and a survey of all children's homes was undertaken. Concern was expressed about the poor fire escape facilities at Ongar, that the roads and pavements were cracking and in need of repair, and that the school needed more room. Times were changing and the Ongar Homes had seen their best years. The buildings, and the responsibility for the children, passed to the London County Council on 1 April 1930. The Ongar Cottage Homes were now called the Ongar Residential (Public Assistance) School. Nine years later the school closed, and was re-opened by the London County Education Committee as a residential school for mentally defective boys under part 5 of the 1921 Education Act. The new head was Mr W. Uden, transferred from a similar school in Acres Lane, Brixton, on a salary of £546 per annum. Mrs Uden was appointed matron. During the war years many of the boys were evacuees. After the war, Bowes Farm, on the other side of the road, was purchased for £5,650 for the housing and training of the more difficult boys.

Mr and Mrs Uden retired in 1956, and were replaced as head and matron by Mr and Mrs Stanard from a London school for deaf children. By this time, the name "residential school" was not felt to be correct and there was a staff competition to suggest alternatives. After some deliberation, the name Great Stony School was adopted. The Stanards retired after eight years and Mr R. Barnes was appointed headmaster in 1963, taking up the post on 1 April 1964. The matron was Miss Deacon, Mrs Barnes not wishing to be appointed as she was more interested in teaching. Mr and Mrs Barnes were rather surprised on their arrival to find three maids at their disposal, as well as the fact that the main gates were locked at 10pm! The maids were quickly re-deployed, and the gates removed.

Soon after, the Education Department was separated from the London County Council (LCC) and became the Inner London Education Authority (ILEA). In the early 1990s, with the abolition of the Greater London Council (which was the successor of the LCC), Great Stony School was returned to the borough of Hackney and the circle was complete.

A HOME FOR THE HOMELESS: FROM ONGAR COTTAGE HOMES TO GREAT STONY SCHOOL

The end of the school and a new beginning

Mr Barnes retired in August 1988. With the threat of closure hanging over the school, Mr Clive Tombs was appointed in his place. The intention was to close the school as soon as the ILEA was wound up, but the government would not allow this and insisted that it should be returned to the Borough of Hackney. Initially Hackney refused, but changed its mind on being reassured that they would be allowed to sell the property. The campaign to keep the school open was doomed from this point, and there was a steady drop in pupil intake until the school was not an economic proposition. Closure inevitably followed and the buildings remained empty for several years apart from their use in filming "The Clockwork Mice" in the summer of 1995. Hackney sold the site to Taywood Homes in September 1997 and at the time of writing, the builders are struggling with a particularly wet winter (shades of 1904!) to convert the cottages into luxury homes for sale.

Sources

1. Ancient Monuments Society vol. 42 (1998) p. 81–102
2. Gautrey, T. *Lux mihi laus – School Board Memories* (1937) Link House Publications
3. Philpott, H. B. *London at School* (1904) Unwin
4. Maclure, S. *A History of Education in London 1870–1990* (1990) Allen Lane
5. English Heritage report, *Great Stony* (1989)
6. *The Builders' Record and Architectural Journal* 29 March 1905 p.163
7. Weiner, D. E. B. *The Institution of Popular Education: Architectural Form & Social Policy in the London Board Schools* (1985) Ann Arbor
8. Hackney Board of Guardians, minutes: Ha BG 1 – 100 (1899–1909)
9. ibid, visiting committee: Ongar Children's Home Ha BG 148–150
10. ibid, admissions: Ha BG 246
11. ibid, registers: Ha BG 248
12. ibid, register of apprentices: Ha BG 250
13. ibid, superintendent's record book: Ha BG 252
14. ibid, financial records: Ha BG 276
15. ibid, register of officers at Ongar: Ha BG 297
16. London Education Committee minutes 1947–1965

chapter 17

A history of trade and commerce in Chipping Ongar

by Elisabeth Barrett

Introduction

Trade and commerce has been the mainstay of many inhabitants of Ongar for centuries and, of course, continues today. Documentary evidence of this is difficult to obtain before the beginning of the nineteenth century. There are references to people's trades in parish registers and wills prior to this time, but the trade directories and census returns of the nineteenth century enable a much fuller picture to emerge. Trade directories continue to be useful source of information for the first half of the twentieth century (although information from census returns is not available) while the last fifty years is within the memory of many local people. The High Street was not numbered until the 1950s and house names have changed over the years, so this chapter will use present day numbers and names.

Markets and fairs

Although there has not been a thriving market for more than a century, Chipping Ongar was for '*many years a market town.*'[1] It is likely that a market was held as early as the twelfth century[2] although no market charter has survived. This would have been at the time when the castle was important and the town itself was the administrative centre of the Ongar Hundred. The first explicit reference occurs in 1287 '– *in the market of Angre –*.' In 1372 the market belonged to the manor and was being held on Tuesdays.[3] By the 1770s the market was described as '*a poor affair*', overshadowed by Romford, Epping and Chelmsford.[2] It was being held on Saturdays although it is not known when the day changed. It remained in the possession of the lord of the manor until 1841, when the market tolls were sold by Sir John Swinburne to P. Chaplin of Harlow.

There is a market house in Ongar dating from the seventeenth century (sometimes referred to as the Butter Market.) It adjoins the south side of the King's Inn and is a two storey timber framed building with attics and basement. The lower part was formerly open with three arches on the east side and the upper floor, which projects a little, rests on massive oak posts. It was converted into shops during the nineteenth century, possibly before 1835.[4] During the nineteenth century the market was held in a building (later called the Town Hall) which stood detached in the High Street close to the lane leading to St Martin's Church. In 1798 it was described as '*a noble building of brick built by R. Bennet Esq who is lord of the manor.*'[5] Later part of the building was used as a jail. It fell into disrepair and the deeds were bought for £250 in December 1896 by Thomas Cowee, who undertook to pull the building down by 25 March 1897, making the High Street more accessible to traffic.[6]

A HISTORY OF TRADE AND COMMERCE IN CHIPPING ONGAR

As well as an ancient market, Ongar also had an annual fair, held in the autumn. Fairs were originally established for trading goods and livestock and for hiring labourers, but became more of an occasion for entertainment and merry-making during the eighteenth century. For farm labourers and their families it was an eagerly anticipated occasion, but for the gentry it came to be regarded as an excuse for drunkenness and debauchery. The Fairs Act of 1871 allowed for abolition where fairs caused grievous immorality, nuisance to residents etc. In 1872 Henry Gibson, Clerk of the Peace for Essex, who lived at the White House in Ongar, applied for the abolition of Ongar's October fair. The move was rigorously opposed by the town and they found a champion for the cause in Captain Budworth of Greensted Hall who was chairman of the fair committee. An opposition meeting attracted so many people that the venue had to be changed from the town hall to the schoolroom. The application was refused by the Home Office, after receiving the views of the local police superintendent, but a further application in 1892 was successful.[7]

At about this time the weekly market ceased. There was a brief, unsuccessful attempt to revive the market between 1927 and 1930 when a poultry market for chickens, ducks, rabbits and goats was held behind the Lion Hotel once a week.[8] The sale of poultry was later transferred to the King's Head Inn, but in 1952 the poultry boxes were dismantled. For a brief period at the end of the nineteenth century, a weekly cattle market was held close to the goods shed at Ongar station, at the time when Scottish farmers had brought cattle farming to the area.[9] A general market was revived in 1995, and now takes place in the Pleasance car park on Wednesdays.

Figure 17 An early Victorian view of the High Street, already paved and probably lit by gas (rather than oil), from a woodcut by R. Hind. The Market House is open at ground floor level.

ASPECTS OF THE HISTORY OF ONGAR
Butchers

There have been butchers in Chipping Ongar wherever there are records of occupations. The names of Abraham Offin (1626), Nathaniel Rachell (1696), William Playle (1786), William Carter (1812), William Carter (1835) are found in Essex wills, and Thomas Anzer (1602), John Archer (1627), Thomas Anger jnr (1685), Thomas Cooper (1709) and George Tabour (1712) in the parish registers. Between 1770 and 1775 Chipping Ongar had a population of four hundred and there were two butchers.[3] Between 1798 and 1867 there were four butchers trading at any one time, but this fell to two by the end of that century, at the time of the great agricultural depression of the 1880s. Butchers' names at this time include Carter, Cooper, Cowee, Perry and Camp. Throughout most of this century there have been three butchers' shops. At 167 High Street there has been Frank Paul and P. J. Carter, at 121 High Street, Warr, George Carter, and Hocking, and at 103, Lavender, Church and Padmore. All three butchers slaughtered their own meat at the rear of their premises. Carter's bought their animals at Epping and Chelmsford markets and they were walked to Ongar. They were kept in Church Fields (now Shakletons) and driven along the High Street to the rear of their premises at 7 o'clock on Sunday mornings. They were stabled in an old barn and slaughtered on Monday morning.[10] While the other two butchers ceased selling home-killed meat several decades ago, Carter's continued until 1987, when they were the last slaughter house in the Epping Forest area. Butchers were well-to-do amongst the traders in the town. Thomas Cowee bought Greylands (155 High Street) in 1885[11] and Frank Paul lived at Holmlea, (116 High Street), both substantial properties.

The butchery business tends to stay in a family and Carter's is an example of this. The premises at 167 High Street, built in 1702 in front of the "George" pub[12] has probably been a butcher's shop since 1750. The name Carter as a butcher appears first in 1798.[6] William Carter, who died quite young in 1835[13] was probably related, and his business was at 167 High Street. His widow Mary remarried, to Thomas Cowee, and they carried on the butcher's business in the shop.[14] One of Mary's sons by her first marriage, William Worters Carter, born in 1834, appears in the 1871 census as a butcher, married and living in the Borough (Greensted Road) with several children, one of whom was Patrick then aged four. The Carters had not inherited the shop from their step-father, Thomas Cowee; he had passed it to his son, Thomas junior. The business was sold to Frank Paul in 1902.[10] Meanwhile in 1891, Patrick Carter, then aged 23, was living above Cowee's shop and was a butcher's assistant.[15] He married Elizabeth Bretton, whose family owned the Two Brewers pub in Ongar and Queen's Head pub in Fyfield.[10] Patrick and Elizabeth moved to Bethnal Green in London and, in 1912, had a butcher's shop in Chadwell Heath.[16] They kept in touch with Ongar through visits to the Bretton family and when Frank Paul's shop was sold in about 1929 it was Patrick's son, William, who bought it. The business had returned to the Carter family after three generations. This business thrived once the 1930s depression ended and William's son, Peter, subsequently joined the business. The shop had been open-fronted with shutters but this was replaced by a shop-front in 1958. The next door premises, number 169, was acquired in 1962 and the butcher's occupied the whole building with its own slaughter house at the rear. It continued as a butcher's until 1993.[10] With the closure of Carter's, two butchers remain in the town at the millennium, Hocking's and Padmore's, trading in competition with supermarkets as well as each other.

Grocers

The grocery trade in Ongar probably started, as did so many businesses, from small beginnings a few centuries ago to reach their zenith in the first half of the twentieth century and then to change radically by the end of this century.

There is evidence of the trade in the town in the seventeenth century. Joshua Beard and Simon Rous were described as grocers in their wills. In 1750 there were seven '*general shops*' in the town,[3] some of which would probably have supplied provisions. In 1798 there were two grocers, Richard Davey, and Joseph Brockes[5] who was also a tea dealer. By the nineteenth century there were as many as five grocers at any one time and the trade directories record frequent name changes. This may indicate that it was difficult to get established or that the rewards were not very great. However three names dominate, those of Boyer, Brown and Hayward.

Francis Boyer was a grocer in 1823.[17] In 1841, when he was forty-eight and unmarried, his shop was at 183 High Street next to the old Post Office and he employed his nephew, Charles Brown, as his shopman.[14] Five years later the shop was Boyer and Brown, Mr Boyer having become a wine and spirit merchant and an agent for Sparrow & Co's bank.[18] The grocer's was listed as Brown's from 1850 onwards, changing to Brown & Son in 1878.[19] Percy Boyer Brown, Charles' son by his second marriage, had the grocer's shop in 1891, when he is described as a retired tea merchant.[15] Possibly he had been away learning the trade before returning to run the family business. Another son, Herbert Boyer Brown, had a wine merchant's at 190 High Street for many years and lived by Manor Square in the house that has since become a wine shop.[9] From 1867, Robert Hayward had his grocery business on the east side of the street at number 204, next to Ongar House. According to the 1891 census, Robert Hayward's son had a grocer's shop at the other end of town, at 51 High Street, a shop previously run by Mr Horide. The grocery businesses at these three premises dominated the trade well into the twentieth century, when grocers were important tradesmen employing staff to serve and deliver to their customers.

The twentieth century saw a gradual change from "family grocers" to grocery chains and then to supermarkets. The grocery chain, International Stores, had a small shop next to Barclays Bank around 1900[9] and they had bought the business of Brown & Son by about 1910, and moved into those premises. The grocer's cellar at that time extended beneath the old Post Office. Cheese was stored there and the smell was apparent to those queuing to buy stamps and postal orders, especially after a weekend![20] International Stores expanded their business, firstly into the Post Office premises when the new Post Office was built further down the

ASPECTS OF THE HISTORY OF ONGAR

street in the 1960s, and then by building behind to create a large self-service store. Hayward's grocers became Star Tea Company and then Star Supplies. These premises, number 204, are now divided into two shops, but had an archway on the north side leading to store rooms. This was where the delivery cart was kept.[8] Star Supplies closed in the 1960s. The grocer at the south end of the town, which had been in the ownership of Hayward in 1891, became H. W. Mihill's "Ongar Stores". A photograph exists showing it to be a fine store, employing several assistants and with a cart for delivering both in the town and to the surrounding villages and country houses.[20] In the 1920s it became a branch of T. Liddle & Sons of South Woodford, and closed as a grocer's sometime in the 1960s.

150 High Street, now March's jewellers, has seen use as a baker's and grocer's. For a time at about the turn of this century it was No.3 Branch of the Epping & District Co-operative Society.[21] The Co-operative Society grocery moved to larger premises at number 156, which had been Chanell's printing works. Their original premises continued as Eastaugh & Wright, and then Blakeley's grocers until the 1950s. Number 156, partly occupied by Moseley's music shop, was replaced in 1935 by the London Co-operative Society to provide a detached purpose built shop. This building was demolished in the 1970s to make way for the larger premises needed for a modern food hall. During the rebuilding, the Co-op temporarily moved in to 53 High Street, the former Liddle's grocery.

By the 1970s, grocers in Ongar had been replaced by supermarkets, the Co-op and International Stores. The International Stores group was disappearing by the end of that decade, and changed to a discount store called Shoppers Paradise for a few years before closing. Ongar then had the Coop supermarket in the town centre and four convenience stores, at 19 High Street, in Marden Ash (Shepherd's Dairy), on the Fyfield Road and on the Shelley estate. The 1990s have seen the arrival in Ongar of two national supermarket chains, Tesco and Sainsbury. Tesco opened a new concept "Express Store", incorporating, a petrol station with a small supermarket on the site of a former garage, Whites of Ongar. Sainsbury have built a "Country Town Store" on the site of the former primary school, the land sold to them by the Joseph King Trust. Prior to the opening of these stores, much of the residents' food shopping was done outside Ongar, requiring travel by car and bus to surrounding towns. This can be contrasted with the beginning of the century when most people's needs were catered for within the town.

Bakers

Bakery is an ancient trade and an integral part of both town and village life. Several bakers are mentioned in the records of occupations of the seventeenth and eighteenth centuries. In 1798 there were two bakers, Thomas Adams, and Francis Sadler who was also a miller and cornfactor.[5] Most people would have bought flour ground at the windmills and watermills in the villages around Ongar and made their own bread. But there was enough demand for the produce of local bakers to sustain at least two bakers, perhaps supplying more luxury items. One baker, Henry Smith from Kings Lynn, who had a shop in the 1890s at 150 High Street, (the timber-framed corner building dated 1642), advertised as a *'fancy bread and biscuit baker, pastrycook and confectioner.'* [22]

During the nineteenth century, several bakers' names appear in the trade directories, and like the grocers there seem to be frequent changes. However the family names Cowee, Giblin, Parsons and Mead were established for considerable periods. There was a baker's shop at 121 High Street throughout the nineteenth century, first run by the Cowees,[14] and then by the Parsons. Sarah Parson carried on the business after her husband's death,[15] as often seemed to be the case at that time; there were families to support and no state help. Sometime between 1900 and 1920 the business closed and the shop became a butcher's. The ovens were bricked up and were only exposed recently as a result of building work carried out by the present owners.[23] For most of the twentieth century there was a baker's on the opposite side of the street at number 134. Maryon's baked their bread in a small building behind the shop, separated by an alleyway.[8] This business changed hands in the 1920s to Nickelson's, baker, pastrycook and general provisions merchant who also had a shop in Chelmsford.[20] There was a further change of ownership in the thirties to the bakery chain, Barton's.

Mead's was a baker's of longstanding. Thomas Mead was born in High Ongar in 1838 and the 1871 census describes him as a baker with his own business living at 109 High Street with his wife and children. These premises were the right side of a pair of shops built out in front of an old timber-framed house on the west side of the street to the south of the "narrows." The business has been described thus: *'Bread was baked daily in ovens at the rear and was carried to customers throughout the town in the handcart.'* [20] The business continued under this name until the 1930s when the name changed to Curtis and then to Pullens. It closed as a bakery in the 1960s. Ongar Bakery opened in 1982 in the adjoining premises, which had been an ironmongers and furniture shop, and with Pearce's further up the High Street there are still two bakers in the town.

Greengrocers

Fruit and vegetables have traditionally been traded on market stalls. In a small market town, serving a mainly agriculture-based community, there would have been limited need for a shop trading in these goods. People had access to pockets of land to grow their own produce and the large estates would have been mainly self sufficient with their extensive kitchen gardens. Going back several centuries, the consumption of vegetables by all classes was very limited, bread, meat and cheese dominating the diet.

However, there have been a number of greengrocers in Ongar, at least since 1832 when J. Playl is described as a fruiterer.[17] In 1859 there were four greengrocers but this declined to one, Fred Holt, by 1886.[25] The local economy must have been affected by the agricultural depression at this time. In the 1891 census there is no-one trading as a greengrocer and the weekly market was coming to an end. Fred Holt, whose shop was at 161 High Street, next to Greylands, gave his occupation as labourer at this time.[15]

For almost a century, there was a market garden close to the town centre. It was run from the 1850s by George Searle, who came to Ongar as a nursery foreman with his wife Sarah and two small children.[36] The market garden occupied the land between Bansons Lane and the Police Station, running down from the High Street to the Cripsey Brook, (now car park, telephone exchange and doctors' surgery). George, nurseryman and seedsman, continued the business with his son Samuel until the beginning of the twentieth century, when it was taken over by his grandsons, Robert and George.[42] The two brothers had been sent to Bishops Stortford for training and one brother specialised in greenhouse work and the other in pruning. Some of the produce was sent up to London by train, but most was sold in the greengrocer's shop run by Samuel's widow, Mary, in the building on the north side of the Bell Inn.[42] (Theses premises was demolished in the 1960s to make way for the new Post Office.) The shop had closed by the 1930s but the market garden continued until after the Second World War.

Another greengrocer was John Root who opened his shop in 1914 at 153 High Street, which had been Giffen's bootmakers. *'He had a costermonger's barrow which he loaded with fruit and veg from the goods train at Ongar Station.'* [8] This business continued until 1951 when it changed hands to King's the greengrocer for a few more years before closing. During the second half of this century there has been Freeston and Matthew Reeve in the town centre, and a greengrocer's in the parade of shops near Ongar Bridge. In the last two decades of this century the trade has steadily declined and no business has been able to hold its own against the competition of the supermarkets. However, in the 1990s the market has been revived and there is a fruit and vegetable stall, so the trade has perhaps gone full circle over two centuries

Drapers and bootmakers

Until the end of this century, most clothes and shoes required by the local population could be obtained in our market town. Types of trade and crafts varied according to the fashions prevailing at the time. In the seventeenth century John Wels was a whale bone body maker, Giles Miller, a weaver, and there were several glovers, tailors and shoemakers.[24] These trades required working in leather or tough materials and so were men's occupations. There must have been dressmakers and milliners, but there are no records of such traders who would have been mostly women. Women were usually described in contemporary records by their marital status and their occupation is rarely given. The first list of trades, the Universal Directory of 1798, lists makers of stays, breeches and shoes, as well as linen and wool drapers and tailors. Again women's names do not appear but it is reasonable to suppose that widows and spinsters were earning their livings in the town at this time. However, the trade directories of the nineteenth century give fuller information and women traders as well as men are listed. Ladies described as milliners and dressmakers include Martha Taylor (1839), Fanny Gidley (1850–1878), Elizabeth Playl (1870) and Ellen Reynolds (1874–1890).[25]

The nineteenth century saw the establishment of some longstanding businesses. In the 1870s Edward Rose had a tailor's shop at 169 High Street,[26] adjoining Cowee's

A HISTORY OF TRADE AND COMMERCE IN CHIPPING ONGAR

butchers. This was a bespoke tailor and breeches maker and they also made uniforms for members of the Essex hunt. In 1891 the business was run by his son Thomas.[15] The workshop was behind their premises, over the butcher's slaughter house[8] and employed several men. One of these employees was Hermann Korf, originally from Germany, who had come to Ongar from London's West End. He married one of the daughters of Peter Lacey, a cordwainer in the High Street and set up his own business at 1, Livingstone Cottages. He was a ladies tailor and, by arrangement with Roses, he made the ladies riding habits while they tailored for the gentlemen. Mr Korf was interned at the beginning of the First World War and his business closed.[27] Rose's, however, lasted for nearly a century, closing in the 1950s.

Giffen's was a boot and shoemaker in 1798[5] and this business continued until the 1900s. This shop was at 153 High Street, the three-gabled timber-framed building the other half of which was subsequently occupied by Baugh's Chemists. The workshop was probably in a room above the shop, as scraps of leather have been found under the floorboards during recent restoration of the building. The name of Lacey also became established as bootmakers and repairers. In 1859, Peter Lacey, who was born in Thaxted, had a bootmaker's shop at 149 High Street. He and his wife lived over the shop and had eight children.[27] The shop passed to one of his sons, William, and continued as a bootmaker's until William's son, Ernest, changed the business to Lacey's drug store and then, in 1931, Lacey's Chemist.[28] Further south down the High Street, at No 129 next to the Ongar Bell public house another of Peter's sons, Albert, set up as a shoemaker and shoe repairer.[27] His shop window advertised "Nugget Polishes." He repaired the shoes of the McCorquodales of Forest Hall. He was helped by his son William who lived next door.[21] This business was closed by the 1940s.

During the Victorian era drapers supplied most clothing needs, stocking haberdashery and materials and employed dressmakers and milliners to make ladies' and girls' clothes in the latest styles. They sold men's and boys' clothes of every description. They might also have sold carpets and upholstery, sewing machines and even furnished funerals.[22] There were two drapers at the end of the nineteenth century, Childs' and Ashdown's, close together on the east side of the street at numbers 192 and 196 respectively.[15] The first mention of Henry Childs was in 1867. The business was later run by his son William Henry Childs and changed hands in 1906 to Wightman's and later still Craigen's, who had had a small draper's shop further down the street. The first mention of Ashdown's, linen draper, was in 1878. The shop at 196 High Street had enlarged by the 1900s, having two entrances and full length plate-glass windows to display their extensive stock.[21] The business expanded over the next sixty years to other premises in the town. In about 1917, they took over Price & Co., clothiers of 146/148 High Street and this became their men's clothes and shoe shop. On the opposite side of the road at number 145, during the 1930s, they had a furnishing shop with a store room at the back, now occupied by the postal sorting office. Further up the High Street, in the Joseph King cottages, they kept carpets.[29] At the end of the 1930s, the business was taken over by London Co-operative Society (LCS) which retained the drapers and the men's shop, but closed the furnisher's.

As well as these larger shops there have been small shops selling drapery goods in the High Street throughout the twentieth century. Mrs Wilson sold second-hand clothes, as did Mrs Donavon, who described her business as a "wardrobe dealer." There was Traveller's clothes at number 123, which changed to Buther's drapers. There was a wool shop for many years at 101 High Street, firstly run by Mary O'Sullivan and then by Mrs Hocking. The only shop in the High Street selling haberdashery and wool at the end of the century is Blinds, Bobbins and Spools at number 178.

As this century has progressed there has been a change to shops selling factory made shoes and clothes and Ongar has had several shoe shops, including Johnson Bros, Pateman's and Everyday Shoes. Men's clothing could be purchased at Ashdown's and then LCS Men's shop, or at Coles, gentlemen's outfitters, who opened a branch in the Trust cottages in the 1950s and continue today as Peter Gold's. In the 1960s fashion boutiques, selling ladies' clothing, became popular and Ongar's small shop premises were ideal for this type of retailing. Examples of such shops have been Audrey Ruth, Domino, Tudor Rose and Francesca. Clothes retailing is now dominated by the vast selection available in large town shopping centres and out-of-town precincts, and there is little trade to be done in small towns like Ongar.

Newsagents and stationers

These shops first make their appearance in Chipping Ongar during the Victorian age. There is no record of shops selling newspapers or stationery before 1823, though other shops probably sold this type of merchandise as a side line. Ongar is recorded as having a postal service since 1717,[30] but it was not until 1845, when Miss Maria (Anna) Scruby was postmistress, that there is a reference to a *'post office issuing money orders.'* [31] Soon after this the postmaster, William Scruby, is listed as a stationer in trade directories[31] and continues as such, as well as postmaster, until 1886.

The first documented stationer was William Wright. In 1823, he was trading as a watchmaker.[17] Later he was selling books and then stationery.[14] He no longer appears in the trade directory of 1839, but in his place is the name Mott as a bookseller and stationer.[31] Mott's premises were at 185 High Street, a detached building between the King's Trust cottages and Brown's grocers. The business had changed to a china and glass dealer by 1867, run by Charles Mott and then by his widow, Ann, before becoming a paper shop by the turn of the century run by Fred ("Smasher") Mott.[8&9] Mott's described themselves as a newsagent and stationer at this time, and published postcards. Postcards were an important means of communication early this century. There were several posts each day; a postcard sent in the morning could be delivered in the afternoon and used for messages in the same way that telegrams, and then the telephone, were later used. They also became very collectable and were used as a means of advertising by those who published them.[20] So stationers were well established in the town during the nineteenth century, and specialising as newsagents or printers as the century turned and trade became larger.

In 1891, there was a printer's and stationer's at 156 High Street belonging to Sarah Burgess. She had been born in Gravesend and was at this time a widow aged 47, living there with her children.[15] About 1910 this business had changed to Chanell's Printing Works who, despite their trading name, also offered a bookbinding service and had a shop selling stationery and art jewellery.[20] These shop premises were taken over by the Co-op grocers in about 1920, but there was another printer, William Ward Jenkins, at 138 High Street until 1933. After this there appears to have been no printer in the High Street until J. Lewis opened his print and stationery shop at 101 High Street in 1985.

The newsagents during this century include Dement, Walkley, Senner, Mott and Sawkin. Dement's newsagent occupied the small premises next to Carter's butchers at 165 High Street for a short time at the beginning of this century.[20] J C Walkley took over Dement's business and then moved his shop premises in 1912 to 180 High Street, which had been for many years Chapman's chemist and druggist, and then Kirby's. As well as newspapers they published postcards and sold cigarettes.[20] In 1936 this business changed to Senner's, newsagent, stationer and tobacconist. It has traded under this name (with a change of ownership in 1963 to D. Hubbard Ltd.) until the present time, and now sells confectionery and toys as well as newspapers, magazines and stationery. The shop has been considerably enlarged, to include Mr Senner's downstairs living accommodation.[33] Mott's became Sawkins and traded as a newsagent and stationer until 1970, when the premises were demolished to make way for Midland Bank.

Cigarettes could be bought at the newsagents, but Ongar also had a tobacconist for many years occupying premises in the old Market House at number 171. In 1882 the proprietor was Mary Parker, described in 1891 as a forty-two year old widow with her mother, two children and a boarder living with her.[15] Pipe-smoking, often with clay pipes, would have been common at this time among men. The business changed hands and in 1910 was run by Mr Herbert. By 1922 the shop traded as Ongar Tobacco Stores Co. This tobacconist business had ceased trading in the High Street by the middle of the century although loose tobacco continued to be sold at Senner's.[33]

Sweets and toys

The location of sweet shops and toy shops are readily remembered by people reminiscing about the High Street of their childhood. The sweet shop seems to be another Victorian introduction. The first mention in Ongar is in 1850, a shop run by Webster[31] although it appeared to be short-lived. In 1878 there were two confectioners, J. Lawrence and A. Fewell.[25] Mr Lawrence's shop was at 147 High Street[15] and sweets were sold from these premises right through this century until the 1990s. The name changed at frequent intervals; Taff, Lavender, Kerridge, Atkinson and finally the Chocolate Box were all fondly remembered by different generations. There was a sweet shop for many years in the Trust cottages, Fewell's from 1874 to the 1890s and then Charles Lacey (another son of Peter Lacey the cordwainer) followed by Mrs Wilmott and Cordell until the 1950s. In the 1900s children had very little money and what they had they often earned, perhaps by running errands. As a twelve year old in 1900, D.W. White considered himself rich because he earned money selling rabbits he netted in Greensted Wood, using ferrets and a dog, for a shilling each. But sweets were cheap – twelve aniseed balls or four caramels for a penny.[9] Sweets were sold from large jars lined up on the shelves behind the counter or in the window and weighed or counted out. The Chocolate Box still sold sweets this way until it closed. There was another sweet shop for many years next to Greylands, run by Mrs Holt and then Mrs Butt. Fred Powell recalls Mrs Holt's shop in the 1920s where sweets were in jars and got stuck together. He says *'We would watch the window to see when the contents got low in the jar, then go in and ask for those sweets. She would let us have all she could dig out for a penny.'*[8] For the children on the south side of town, Mrs Mabon had a sweet shop next to her tea shop.[27] The newsagents also sold sweets and these shops, together with supermarkets and convenience stores, are the places where confectionery is now bought, wrapped and displayed for self-selection.

A toy shop was opened in Ongar for the first time after the Second World War. It was run by two former WRNS (Women's Royal Naval Service), Miss Tustin and Miss Smith, in the small house, now called Wren House, at the entrance to St Martin's churchyard. This house had been used by many different traders and craftsmen over the centuries, including a glazier and saddler and (in this century) Tucker's Taxis office. Between 1870 and 1936 it was owned by the 6th Essex Yeomanry and used as the Sergeant-at-Arms' residence, as well as a recruiting office. The building behind was the drill hall for the regiment.[33] When the Misses Tustin and Smith bought the house in 1946, Ongar was a candidate for London overspill development. Although this did not happen, new estates were built to the north and south of the town where young families settled to bring up their children. Tustin and Smith is remembered as a lovely shop with a Hornby train set laid out in the back room.[34] They also sold antiques in the drill house behind. For a short time in the 1960s there was a toy shop near Ongar Bridge run by Peter Trundle and then by D Hubbard. In 1966, Hubbard's bought the toy shop in Wren House, changed the name to Timothy Toys and closed their original shop. This toy shop closed in the 1980s and returned to being a private residence.[33] Another toy shop opened in the parade of shops near Ongar Bridge, Toys Galore. This shop sold art materials as well as toys, but in the 1990s fell victim to rising rents for shop premises. Also at this time the warehouse-style retailing chain "Toys R Us" swept in from the United States, resulting in the closure of small toy shops across the country.

Ironmongers

Until very recently, Ongar has had at least one ironmonger or hardware dealer in the High Street over the last two hundred years. As with many High Street traders, the first, John Wright, appears in the early nineteenth century.[17] Another John Wright was trading as an ironmonger at 151 High Street in 1851.[36] In the garden behind this shop were several outbuildings including a blacksmith's shop and a nail house.[37] They perhaps made some of their own ironware. In the about 1865, John Wright junior left Ongar and moved to Birmingham where he set up a factory, called the Ongar Works, to manufacture a gas burner he invented.[38] When the Wright's left the High Street, John Kerr opened an ironmongers[39] at number 145,[15] a few doors away, and this business passed from father to son until the 1930s. *'John was always "going to London tomorrow" if he hadn't got what you required'*![9] In 1886, George Snelling took over the ironmonger's which had been run by J. Penson since the 1850s and this was another business of longstanding. The shop adjoined Mead's bakers south of the "narrows" at number 107.[15] They were furnishing ironmongers, and agents for agricultural implements. They also had premises further down the High Street, "Snelling's bottom shop", where they kept garden equipment. Yet another ironmonger's opened in the 1900s, F. Cornell at 126 High Street [9] where the White Horse pub had been. These three shops traded up to the time of the Second World War.

After the war, Cornell's were still trading but Snelling's became a furnishing store. The former grocer's shops of Star Supply and Mihill's, at opposite ends of town, both became hardware and DIY shops (as ironmongers were then more commonly known) for a time. Newcombe's opened a business at number 43, in the new parade of shops, but one by one these shops had closed by the end of the 1980s. Ongar now no longer has any of these versatile shops.

John Wright had started with a small trading business in Ongar and had moved on to greater things. Another Ongar resident did likewise in this century. Bob Myson took over the Matthew's blacksmith's in the 1950s and changed the business to a do-it-yourself and hardware shop. In the workshop at the back of these premises, small engineering work was done and a sailing boat, the "Silhouette", was designed and made. This was the beginning of Myson Marine, one of the Myson Group of companies. In about 1959, the business moved to a small factory unit at Hallsford Bridge, next to Thurston Engineering, and engineered parts for production machinery for the Ford Motor Company. Within five years the company had changed to producing commercial heaters called "multivectors" and then fan-convectors. By the end of the 1960s Myson's was a small group of companies based in Ongar but with manufacturing units elsewhere. The company was floated on the stock exchange as Myson Heat Exchangers and, in 1970s, took over a radiator manufacturer in Hull and a boiler maker in Liverpool. Through the 1980s the company continued to grow into a multi-national firm, one of the biggest and most successful within the heating industry in the United Kingdom at that time, employing about two thousand five hundred people and having a turnover in the order of £120million.[40] Bob Myson lost control of the company when it was taken over by a consortium, but the group continued to have its Head Office in Ongar until 1989 when it was taken over by Blue Circle.[41] This company closed down operations in Ongar but a Myson Company managing director, Gary Webster, took many of the employees from the Ongar site and started a new company, Smith's Environmental Products Ltd, in South Woodhams Ferrers, *'continuing the Myson spirit'*[40] and manufacturing fan convectors.

ASPECTS OF THE HISTORY OF ONGAR

Horses, bicycles and motor cars

Before the internal combustion engine took over, trades allied to the use of horses were very important. Most villages had a blacksmith and wheelwright but collar and harness-makers, saddlers and coach builders were more likely to trade in local towns. Ongar had all these craftsmen to meet local demand and also to service the wagons passing between rural Essex and London and the coach routes to Aldgate.[2] Names that appear in seventeenth and eighteenth century records include wheelwrights John Dickinson (1618), Samual Whitehead (1719)[32] and John Witham (1796),[13] collar-makers and saddlers George Burrel and George Nicholls (1798)[5] and blacksmiths Jasper Smyth (1621),[24] Henry Lacey (1682) [55] and Jeames Cornell (1688).[24]

During the nineteenth and early twentieth centuries there were two blacksmith's, one in the centre of town next to the Crown Inn and the other near Ongar Bridge at the south end of town. Typically, they were family concerns, the Sucklings and the Barltrops. Wheelwrights became incorporated into the blacksmith's trade; Ammon Barltrop and Thomas Suckling were both so described in the trade directory.[25] Other traders at this time were saddlers: Silcock and later Stokes at 205 High Street, harness-makers Wild and later Ted Wilson next to the Royal Oak pub, coach builder Nathan Cook and later the firm of Matthews and Barker. Around 1900 the saddlers and harness-maker were kept busy making and repairing the tackle used by local farmers, Stoke's employing four men and Wild's three.[9]

Matthews and Barker was a coach works on the west side of the High Street close to the bridge over the Cripsey Brook:

> *The firm built coaches, carriages and traps from scratch, making the wheels and shafts in the woodwork shop and then to the paint and varnish shops where they would be decorated with the name and trade if built for local businesses. Other sources of work were traps and carts for the big houses in the district and in its heyday the firm employed between ten and fifteen tradesmen. Small ironwork items could be dealt with by the firm but larger items went up the road to Matthews, the blacksmith's at 142 High Street.'* [21]

By the 1920s signwriting was an important part of the business, but the firm closed in the 1930s as the change to motor transport was in full swing. The blacksmiths adapted to changing times by diversifying into bicycle sales and repairs[21] and of course horses continued to be used on farms and for local deliveries until after the Second World War. But it was about this time that the blacksmiths and saddlers left Ongar. Barltrop's smithy changed hands during this century to J Smith's and Ransome's, eventually becoming Wingar's cycle shop, Matthews diversified into wrought iron work and oxyacetylene welding before becoming Myson's hardware and timber merchants in the 1950s. Silcock's saddlery became a leather goods shop, Godfrey's. There have been two saddleries in the town in recent years serving pony and horse owners but they have only traded for a short time.

A HISTORY OF TRADE AND COMMERCE IN CHIPPING ONGAR

As these trades faded, the motor trade took over, Surridge's being a name synonymous with transport in the town. In 1908 John Surridge had Mikado Motor Cycle Works at 101 High Street, next to the Royal Oak pub. The sign on the side of the premises said *'Ford Cars, Motors and Cycles'* and they also sold gramophones and phonographs and were the first to stock gramophone records. In the 1920s, they sold petrol and had a garage behind their house at 45 High Street, called Brooklands after the racing circuit (since demolished and replaced by modern shop units). The petrol pumps had arms which came out over the footpath[35] and had to be cranked up and down to deliver one gallon, a slow process.[8] Victor Surridge raced motor cycles and was tragically killed, at the age of nineteen, at an early TT race on the Isle of Man.[21] Surridge junior continued the cycle and motor cycle business at number 101. Bikes could be hired for half-a-crown a week. Later there was a Surridge's shop at 145 High Street, having taken over premises vacated by Ashdown's furniture shop, which sold cycles and radios and charged accumulators. This closed when the building was demolished to make way for the new post office. A. V. Surridge cycles continued at number 85 but had closed by the 1970s, and the motor trade had long since moved to larger sites, such as Bridge Motors and White's Garage.

Banks

Banking came to Ongar in the middle of the nineteenth century when the Chelmsford Bank of Sparrow, Tufnell & Co appointed an agent in the town. The exact date is not known but F. Boyer, who had a grocer's shop in the High Street, was their agent for probably ten years before his death in 1851. He was succeeded by Charles Brown, his nephew, who had taken over his grocery business. In 1859 a regular bank office was fitted up, partly paid for by Sparrow, Tufnell & Co and partly by Mr Brown, in an upper floor room in the building at 181/183 High Street which also housed the grocer's business and the Post Office.[43] In 1883 the bank moved into its present premises at 186 High Street[21] when the bank agent was Walter Fenn.[25] In 1896, at a time when private bankers were disappearing, Sparrow, Tufnell & Co joined Barclay & Co Ltd and the Ongar bank became a branch of Barclays, with Walter Fenn as manager until he died in 1903.[44] The premises at this time was divided between the bankroom and office, and accommodation for the bank manager which was quite substantial, having five bedrooms, outbuildings including a stable and garden reaching to the castle moat at the rear. It was valued at the time of transfer at £1265.[45] The building has been updated over the subsequent century, the living accommodation has gone and the building has been plastered externally. The access arch at the north end of the building has been walled in and the entrance moved. Banking hours have changed also. In 1909 the bank was open from 10am to 4pm daily except Wednesday, half day, and on Saturday, market day, from 10am to 5pm.[21]

Until about 1926, two pollarded trees grew close together outside the bank. These trees were a noted feature of the High Street and appear in many photos taken at the beginning of this century, offering a shady resting place. They were probably elms[46] (although they were often referred to as *'the last oaks of Epping Forest'*) and gradually died, necessitating their removal.[47]

ASPECTS OF THE HISTORY OF ONGAR

On 2 March 1970, the Midland Bank opened a branch in the High Street at number 185. The site was redeveloped, the original building having been a newsagent and stationer, Mott's and then Sawkin's.[20]

Builders

Occupations of townsfolk recorded in Ongar parish registers and wills from the seventeenth century onwards include various building trades – carpenters, bricklayers, plumbers and glaziers. It is not known whether any of these men operated a building business as we would know it today. The first such business in the town, which is documented, was that of Noble's.

Richard Noble was born in Woodford in 1790 and is thought to have had a building business since 1829,[48] although a bill head from 1920 states *'founded 1805.'* He appears in a trade directory of 1839 under the heading of carpenter and builder.[49] In the 1837 tithe assessment, Richard Noble occupied the house, shop, yard and garden at Manor House, owned by William Baker.[50] In 1839, the Greensted tithe lists Richard Noble occupying road, shed and yard on a site which is now the south end of Fairfield Road.[51] This was possibly a depot for building materials near his brickyard which was on the site of the present Kilnfield housing development. Richard and his wife Maria had eight children and the business was continued by the family. A grandson of Richard, Frederick Miller Noble (1863 – 1944), of Manor House, was in partnership with his son F. H. N. Noble when the business was converted to a limited liability company in 1924.[48] The business premises were next to the Police Station, the office at the front, workshops behind, one of which was a timber store. As late as the 1960s there was an old deep saw pit for sawing trees into timber. They were undertakers, as were most builders before the Second World War, and the top hats and horses plumes were kept in boxes in the office.[35] They owned a brickyard firstly to the south of Ongar Bridge, then at the end of Mill Lane, High Ongar, and were proprietors of the Ongar gas works for a time.[21] The business was sold in 1948 to Charles Foster & Sons of Loughton. The firm continued in the same premises, trading as Nobles of Ongar until they incorporated the business of Eric Taylor and changed to Noble and Taylor (Ongar) Ltd.[48] Examples of significant work undertaken by Nobles in Ongar include the rebuilding of the front of Ongar Grammar School and the White House,[9] building the Budworth Hall and, during this century, Ongar War Memorial Hospital.

Eric Taylor's building firm, called E. M. Taylor, was set up in 1947. He was born in Ongar in 1920, the only child of Albert Taylor, a woodwork teacher at Great Stony School, and his second wife Alice. As a local magistrate she did a lot of work for Ongar War Memorial Hospital, where a brass plaque acknowledges her work. Eric was apprenticed with Noble's when he left school. He served in the Second World War and was a Japanese prisoner-of-war. He set up on his own on returning home and the business grew from small beginnings, doing mainly war damage repair work. He married Emily and they bought Brooklands, the Surridge's house and garage in the High Street, where they occupied half the house (the other half was home to evacuees) and had a small office at the back. The firm purchased The Gables, a nurses' and gentlewomen's retirement home on the Stondon Road on the edge of Ongar and demolished some of the building to build several detached houses. The remaining wing of the Gables became Knowleton Hall. They replaced Brooklands with a row of shops and ran the firm from the yard and offices behind. The business eventually employed forty men and built mainly private housing in Ongar, while, outside the town, they carried out commercial building work such as a factory in Harold Hill and work for Charringtons and Grays breweries.[52] In 1970 Eric Taylor retired on medical advice and sold his business to Nobles, who took responsibility for his staff, incorporated his name into the company, Noble and Taylor, and leased his premises in the High Street.[52] Eric continued a property company and built on a smaller scale from a yard behind the cottages at 79 to 85 High Street. He died in 1994.

Another builder's of note in the town was Barlow's. Henry Barlow was a master builder in Ongar by 1867[53] and he ran his business from a yard next to his house, Barncroft, at 60 High Street.[8] His son, Harry had taken over the business by 1891.[15] The yard beside the house had barns on the road and sheds on the land behind. As well as building work, coffins were made in the carpentry sheds. Harry had one son who was killed in the First World War and so when he died in 1920 the business was sold to Shawe's Builders. Harry Barlow's widow moved into Roden House, 50/52 High Street,[27] which had been a school for young ladies, founded in 1872. The school had moved to Holmlea further up the High Street in about 1910.[27] The brick facade of Roden House had probably been added by Barlow's onto an older timber framed building.[9] The London Co-operative Society eventually took over the builder's yard and allowed the grounds to be used for activities organised by the Congregational Church (United Reformed). The barn abutting the road was renovated in the 1940s and became Sally Lunn's café.[27] This is why the 1980s housing development on Barlow's yard was known locally as the Sally Lunn estate.

References

1. Morant, P. *History & Antiquities of the County of Essex vol 1* (1763–1768) London. Rep. 1978 by E. P. Publishing in collaboration with ECC Library
2. VCH Essex vol 4
3. Brown, A. F. *Essex at Work 1700–1815* (1969) ECC
4. Wright, T. *The History & Topography of the County of Essex* (1835) Geo. Virtue
5. *Universal British Directory of Trade, Commerce & Manufacturing* vol IV (1798)
6. *Essex Almanack* (1906)
7. *Essex Countryside Magazine* (January 1998)
8. Powell, F. *Tales of Old Ongar* (1992) Ongar Wine Circle
9. White, D. W., undated typescript
10. inf from Peter Carter
11. deeds of 155 High Street
12. ERO: D/DQ 55/71
13. Chelmsford Wills 1721–1857
14. 1841 census PRO: HO 107/336/15
15. 1891 census PRO: RG 12/1366
16. Kelly's *Trade Directory* (1912)

ASPECTS OF THE HISTORY OF ONGAR

17 Pigot's *Directory* (1823/4) and (1832) Kelly & Co. London
18 White's *Directory* (1848) ERO
19 *Post Office Directory* (1878) ERO
20 Wingham, R., Daniell, A. *Ongar in Old Postcards vol II* (1995) European Library
21 Wingham, R. *Ongar in Old Postcards* (1994) European Library
22 Pewsey, S. *Epping & Ongar – A Pictorial History* (1997) Phillimore
23 inf from Harold Wieland
24 Chipping Ongar parish registers ERO: T/R 76
25 Kelly's *Trade Directories* (1839 to 1890) ERO
26 1871 census PRO: RG 10/1643
27 inf from Marie Korf
28 *Annual Register of Premises* (1931) Pharmaceutical Society of Great Britain
29 inf from Mrs Pateman
30 *GPO General accounts vol III* (1711–1720)
31 *Kelly's Directory* (1845/1850)
32 Chelmsford Wills 1620–1720
33 inf from Brian Hubbard
34 inf from Dorothy Arnold
35 inf from Ray French
36 1851 census PRO: HO 107/1771
37 Deeds for 151 High Street (1866)
38 *Ongar W.E.A. Survey* directed by P. R. Banham, (1951) ERO: T/P 96
39 *Post Office Directory* (1867)
40 inf from Gary Webster
41 inf from Chris Funnell
42 inf from Phyllis Searle
43 Matthews, P., & Tuke, A. *History of Barclays Bank Limited* (1926) Blades, East & Blades (London)
44 Barclays Records Services: *Short History of Sparrow Tufnell & Co.*
45 Barclays Records Services: document acc 38/640 (1896)
46 Barclays Records Services: document acc 3/4426 undated
47 *The Spread Eagle* (Barclays Staff Magazine) March 1961
48 Foster, K. *History of Noble & Taylor (Ongar) Ltd,* (1997) typescript
49 Pigot's *Directory* (1839) ERO
50 Chipping Ongar tithe apportionment (1837) ERO: D/CT 262A
51 Greensted tithe apportionment (1839) ERO: D/CT 153A
52 inf from Emily Taylor
53 *Post Office Directory* (1867) ERO

chapter 18

Ongar's pubs and inns

by Ron Walker and Elisabeth Barrett

Gone but not forgotten

'In 1686 Ongar was evidently a fairly important place for travellers; according to a survey that year there was accommodation in the town for 71 lodgers and 104 horses. These figures were larger in both cases than those for Braintree, Harwich, Maldon, Witham and Coggeshall; for lodgers Ongar had more accommodation that Billericay, Dunmow, Kelvedon and Saffron Waldon and for horses there was more stabling than at Rayleigh.'[1] Indeed, like other villages and towns, Ongar's inns provided many services and were the focal point of social life. *'Before the 18th century the social life of Ongar was probably limited to the parish church, the court house and the inn.'*[1] Many inns are now no longer part of the Ongar scene, having made way for other developments, and, whilst local pubs provide a social life for many, they are obviously no longer the centre of activity that they were in the seventeenth to nineteenth centuries.

They performed more than one role

Writing in the *'Tales of Old Ongar,'* Fred Powell, a local resident, said of one local hostelry:

> *'A poultry market was held there once a week which sold chickens, ducks, rabbits and goats. There were stables on the left hand side, with coach houses at the back. During the First World War the stables were turned into our rest room and cook house and we drilled in the yard. I used to sneak out and have Guinness in the Lion nearly every dinner time Adjoining the Lion at the back was a fish and chip shop where I bought a penn'orth of chips and a ha'penny candle'.*[2]

The Red Lion

The Lion (or the Red Lion, as it was later known) was on the site of the present fire station in Ongar High Street. The Red Lion was a timber framed and plastered building. There is mention of Robert Stane, innkeeper, in 1697, and of the fact that Susannah Stane of the Lion was buried on 24 September 1750.[3] In 1798 the Lion was described as a *'Principle Inn'*[4] in the town. Thomas Nicholls was then the innkeeper and coach and wagon master – coaches left for the Three Nuns at Whitechapel each Monday, Wednesday and Friday at 9.00am. A wagon also left on Mondays and Thursdays, also for Whitechapel. The first reference to the Red Lion, as opposed to the Lion, was in 1823. It continued to dominate as a "coaching post"

ASPECTS OF THE HISTORY OF ONGAR

– from 1832 John West's coaches left for London,[5] and from 1850 it became the stopping point for coaches from Dunmow to London. Indeed, it was in 1870 that Charles Smith described the Red Lion as a *'Commercial Inn and Posting House'* – and later it was described as an *'hotel, a noted house for cyclists and tourists.'*[6] Alas, it was pulled down in 1953.

The Crown

If proof is needed that public houses, as they are now known, performed more than one role, the Crown is it. On 6 September 1650, the Crown was the meeting place for the Parochial Inquisition whose remit was *'to secure a preaching ministry and the better maintenance of the clergy.'* This was attended by six commissioners and 31 jurors, as well as witnesses called from most of the parishes in the Ongar and Waltham hundreds. On the face of it, the choice of venue is surprising, considering the puritans' aversion to alehouses! However this was probably the only place in town capable of providing a large enough room, as well as supplying food for those attending, and stabling for their horses.[8]

In the will of Francis Sadler in 1781 the inn represented one fourth of his estate which consisted of the inn on the site of the present 142–144 High Street and three acres of land.[7] In 1798 the owner of the pub was George Williams and he is described as a farmer and inn-keeper.[4] Like the Red Lion it was a coaching house and was thus described in 1832.[5] Coaches were introduced in 1826 to travel every weekday to and from the Bull at Aldgate, in London. The round trip was made in the day.[1] Interestingly, White's Directory of 1848 shows that the Ongar and Epping Building Society met at the Crown, every first Saturday of the month.

At the end of the nineteenth century the landlord was a gentleman named Spells and *'he used to harness up a pair of horses for the Fire Brigade and by the time he got to the bottom of the town where the fire engine house was and to the fire, it was usually burnt out....The engine was simply a large pump on four wheels operated by 8 men, four on each side who pushed the bar up and down working the pumps. It was about as effective as a stirrup pump and bucket.'*[9]

The Bull Inn

In August 1960 a local newspaper wrote: *'The long building (60ft frontage) is well over 200 years old, the brick facade being added about 1890. When it was the Bull Inn, many years ago, it was probably used by coaching services and carriers' wagons. The extensive stabling at the back was later used as a furniture warehouse.'*[10]

The Bull Inn was demolished in 1960 and stood on the site of the present Post Office in Ongar High Street. The reference to stabling is interesting because, in 1856, the sale particulars noted that *'the outbuildings, most of which are brick and have been lately built, comprise very superior stabling for twenty horses, including twelve loose boxes, chaise and harness houses and shed.'* It seems the stables were used to house the horses used in fox hunting because the sale document also stated *'The property being situated only two miles from the Kennel of Mr. Greaves's Fox Hounds, derives considerable emolument from the rent of stables, and other advantages*'[11] and in 1832 it appears as a *'Commercial inn and livery and hunting stables.*'[5] In 1960 the building was certainly well over two hundred years old. The first mention of the Bull was in 1692 when, on 4 November, they *'buried a souldier that died at the Bull'* and in 1693 *'December ye 10 Susanna King, wiffe of William King, at ye Bull'* and again, in 1694, *'William King, of ye Bull was buried September 25.'*[8]

In about 1850 the Bull built its own brewery – indeed, many inns and alehouses brewed their own beer. However, this brewery was particularly significant because of its size and because the landlord saw opportunities to extend the trade *'more particularly in the event of the anticipated Branch Line to the Eastern Counties Railway being constructed.'*[11] Such vision and enterprise was never rewarded and, despite the promotion in the sale catalogue, the Bull closed. By 1871 the premises were occupied by a corn merchant and his large household.[12] Later still it became two small shops and private accommodation.

The White Horse

Opposite the Bull stood the White Horse at 126 High Street. Little has been written or recorded about this alehouse and the first mention is the alehouse recognizances of 1769.[13] In 1798, Thomas Hendey was the victualler and the post office keeper.[4] By 1837 the White Horse was a tied house owned by Hawkes, Bird and Co, brewers of Chelmsford.[14] The licensee from 1848 to 1867 was Thomas Holt and his wife Susan continued as licensee until 1878. The White Horse is not mentioned in the trade directories after 1902 but we know at about this time the premises became Cornell's ironmonger shop – so by then this alehouse was no more.

The Bell

The building is still there but the pub is not. Originally known as the Blue Anchor (1769) and then the Anchor (1794),[13] the alehouse changed its name in 1862 to the Bell.[15] It occupies a precarious position in the narrowest part of town and the building has often been struck by passing high sided vehicles. From 1867 the Bretton family were landlords for 23 years and were also described as *'carriers to London.'*[16] In the 1871 census, George Bretton was described as publican and carrier, having a wife, four children, one general servant, three carmen, two lodgers, a hawker and a blacksmith. Quite a household! In 1895, though, William Henry Boyd became *'publican and cattle dealer'* and ceased to be a *'carrier.'*[17] The Bell ceased trading over 10 years ago and is now a residential property.

The George Inn

Another business which has long ceased trading is the George Inn which was situated behind Carter's shop at 167 High Street, on the west side of town. The area is still known to older residents as the George Yard. The first reference to the George Inn was in 1702[18] in the deeds of the present shop premises which were erected on the front of the site – whereas the George pub was set back from the High Street. The George is listed in alehouse recognizances between 1769 and 1785, but there is no mention of it after this date. What we do know is that the George, like many other inns in later years, performed more than one task. In 1761 the George is mentioned in relation to the *'sale – and use thereof – of the stallion for purposes of breeding. The George was chosen alongside the Crown in Brentwood, the Fox and Hounds, Romford and the Saracen's Head Chelmsford, to be the point of sale for the stallion's services.'*[19]

The Greyhound

And what of the Greyhound or Grayhown? We know that such an alehouse existed in 1677/78 because William Holbrook was charged with assaulting Samuel Bincks and his men, *'doing his utmost to rescue a prisoner at the 'Greyhown' in Ongar, with a naked sword.'*[20] We also know that the Greyhound was located towards the southern end of town, west of the High Street, but no other information is to hand.

The Red Cow

The last of the local public houses to disappear is the Red Cow on the Fyfield Road. Not a particularly old pub, for its first mention was in the census of 1871 which listed the Red Cow Inn, with licensed victualler James Ramball, aged 28, from Stapleford Tawney, with his wife, baby, servant and a boarder. The previous survey in 1861 did not list a beerseller in the parish of Shelley, although there was a certain William Oakes, a brewer living in the vicinity of Shelley House in 1851. In the censuses for 1881 and 1891, John Spells, from Southminster, is listed as licensed victualler of the Red Cow Inn. Was this the same Spells who, in 1887, provided the fire service with horses and was located at the Crown Inn? In Edwardian times the pub sold "London and Burton Fine Ales and Stout" and welcomed cyclists.[21] During the 1960s the public house was rebuilt, only to be converted into a restaurant, Smith's Brasserie, in about 1990.

They're still here

Though Ongar has lost many inns, some have survived and will continue to provide their traditional trade into the next millennium.

The Cock Tavern

This lays claim to be the oldest alehouse or public house now in town, but it is difficult to find evidence to support that statement. Although a framed history written by James Thirkell, at one stage hanging in the Cock, claimed that *'it has been an Ongar landmark since 1580,'* the first documented reference to the Cock Tavern is in 1765 when the returns of Surveyors of weights and measures declared his measures to be "good". It is also mentioned in 1766 under the *'Deeds of Sale from Richard Bennett to John Lenham, apothecary & surgeon, of dwelling house with yard, shop, stables, brewhouse, outhouses and garden – and the Cock*

ONGAR'S PUBS AND INNS

Alehouse yard and garden.'[22] Here again is the mention of a brewery or "brewhouse". It seems likely, though, that brewing had ceased in 1865 when, although continuing to own the alehouse, Mr. F. Starkey stopped running the place.[23] Various people ran the alehouse, but Francis Starkey continued to own it.

In 1872, though, that all changed when C. S. Gray and Son, brewers of Maldon, took over the lease at £20 per half year, for 21 years. Later, within five years, they had arranged to buy the Cock Inn in a rather unusual manner. They had to wait for the '*sellers to die before they could become the owners.*'[22] Gray's agreed to spend a considerable sum of money enlarging and improving the inn and aimed to purchase the property for £600 after the death of Francis Starkey and his wife, Charlotte. In the event Francis died in 1884 and his wife in 1897 – and then Gray's owned the public house.[22] Since then there have been a succession of landlords, but to this day it remains a "tied house" to Gray's Brewery.

The King's Head Inn

It was to the Cock Tavern that many who visited Ongar first went. Many from London and its eastern environs came by steam train to Ongar and the Cock was their first port of call. But the King's Head also attracted visitors from far and wide because of its central position in town. It is now called the King's Inn but it was formerly known as the King's Head Inn. It was a significant establishment and has been described as the largest inn in town with the highest coach entrance.[24] It is a seventeenth century coaching inn, brick fronted with a central arch. There was stabling on the north side with accommodation on the south. A terracotta plaque above the archway, dated 1697, could indicate the date it was built. The surname initial 'T', and the first names 'R' and 'S' around a heart, are thought to indicate a marriage. But there is evidence to suggest that before this date the King's Head was located elsewhere in Ongar. In the deeds (1613) to the property of 102 High Street (opposite what is now the Royal Oak) it mentions that the '*property adjoining on the north was the King's Head.*' [25] And in 1691 '*William Vdid, stranger of the parish, died at the King's Head.*'[8] With the date 1697 identified on the King's Head Inn it is possible to speculate that the inn was moved to its present location at that time.

Although the Universal Trade Directory of 1798 mentions the victualler at the King's Head it does not identify it as one of the three principles inns (those being the Bull, the Crown and the Lion).[4] Nevertheless, its rateable value of £16 in 1736 ranked it as eleventh (out of 77 properties) in Ongar – more than the rectory and glebe at £13, making it a significant establishment at that time.[26] Various landlords have occupied the King's Head Inn but one of the longest (1859 until 1878) was James Barlow who was also a builder.[27] In 1890 the King's Head was described as a family and commercial hotel.[28] In the early 1900s, it was a terminus for general omnibus vehicles. '*It was to the King's Head Hotel that the General Omnibus Company carried passengers from London (mostly Leyton) on open topped double-deckers. They would go sightseeing in Ongar, picnic in the fields and lay about like sheep. Then at about 6 o'clock they would all queue for the bus home, and the queue would go back as far as the Police Station. There were crowds of them.*' [2]

ASPECTS OF THE HISTORY OF ONGAR

The Royal Oak

Although the building probably dates back about 400 years, the origins of the public house, known as the Royal Oak, are vague. It is not listed in the trade directories, and its first mention is in the census of 1861, which described the occupant, James Auger, as a *'fishmonger and publican.'* Indeed, James Auger seems to have occupied the premises for a long time because both the 1871 and 1881 censuses still list him as a fishmonger.

In September 1875 the Royal Oak was put up for sale by auction. Ironically, the auction was held at the King's Head. It was handled by W. Sworder, estate agent. In its conditions and particulars of sale the Royal Oak was described as *'a substantially built house situated in the High Street...with a desirable freehold close of rich pasture land in the parish of Stondon Massey.'* William Willet of Abridge purchased the premises with a deposit of £73, leaving £657 to pay on completion of sale.[29] In the 1891 census Richard Giblin (aged 29) was listed as publican and fishmonger, with a wife, barmaid, servant, fishmonger's assistant and a boarder and visitor. Was it also, therefore, an inn? The fish shop remained for many years and at one time, during the early 1900s, three businesses operated from the building – a public house, a tea room and the fish shop.[21] Today, though, whilst you can get a cup of tea and a piece of fish for lunch, the entire building is known as the Royal Oak public house!

The Two Brewers

Just over the parish boundary in Marden Ash, this was probably built in the eighteenth century, and is mentioned in the alehouse recognizances of 1769 although an alehouse might have existed earlier on the site.[30] It is listed in the Universal Directory of 1798 with Joseph Osborne as victualler and it is also appears in trade directories from 1832. The census returns throughout the period 1841 to 1891 merely lists the publican, victualler or innkeeper. In 1841 John Sammes was shown as publican, and yet in 1851 George Frost Joy was a plumber and inn keeper. So was the Two Brewers an inn in the strictest sense? Certainly it would seem so because for thirty years the word innkeeper is shown in the census. In 1881 Walter Shaw became the licensed victualler, and 1891 Joseph Lee likewise. Joseph Lee is commemorated at the public house by two bricks in the wall of the outhouse – the inscription says, simply: *'J. H. Lee, 1895.'* At one stage in its recent history, the small bar of the Two Brewers was – wait for it! – a fish shop. What was the connection between fish and inns, alehouses or public houses?

The Stag

Just before leaving Ongar, on the Brentwood Road, is the Stag. It was built in the eighteenth century and was run as a "beerhouse" in 1851 by Edwin Derham from Devizes. He is described as a *'Master Cordwainer, with wife, four children and employing one man.'*[31] The significance of Mr Derham is that he ran the Stag (or the Stag Beerhouse as it was known) for over thirty years. But, as with other inns and alehouse keepers, Edwin Derham combined it with another trade – shoe and boot making. It wasn't until 1881 when Edwin was 67 that he became known merely as a beerseller. By 1891 the alehouse had reverted to its original name, the Stag, when Charles Rowden from Stapleford, Wiltshire was shown as the licensed victualler.[31] It seems that the Ongar Brewery owned the premises and in 1908 McMullens, a Hertford brewer, purchased the public house – and later, in 1921 and again in 1942, purchased adjoining land. In 1953 the Stag was granted a full license – prior to this date it did not sell spirits and was thus termed an ale house.

Ongar breweries and maltings

Throughout the history of Ongar's alehouses and public houses there is evidence that several brewed their own beer and there are references to corn dealers and maltsters – or just to maltsters. In 1713 Francis Sadler is described in his will as a maltster,[33] as is Andrew Brockes in 1798.[4]

Early in the nineteenth century, and possibly before, there was a maltings in Chipping Ongar High Street. Malting is the process by which the grain used to make beer, barley, is prepared for brewing. The grain is spread out on the floor of a barn-like building and water applied to begin germination, a process which takes about a week. The germinated grain is then heated in a kiln, usually in a taller "oasthouse-like" structure, to produce malt, which is fermented in a brewery to make beer. Such a set of premises is shown on the 1837 tithe map of Chipping Ongar[14] where there is now a row of cottages numbered 73–81 High Street, on the north side of the present fire station. A print of the kiln in Chipping Ongar dated 1832, shows a *'truncated cone surmounted by a cowl which was turned according to the direction of the wind by a fantail.'*[34] In an older print of Chipping Ongar, looking north from the bridge over the Cripsey Brook, a building of this description can be seen with smoke coming from the top. At the time of the tithe, the malting and adjacent grain store was in the ownership of the executors of the will of Elias Carter and occupied by John Porter Fordham.[14] It is possible that they were not at this time in use, because there is a tradition that the building was used by the Congregational church during the rebuilding of their chapel in 1833, John Fordham being a deacon at the church.[1]

In the accounts of the builder Richard Noble for 1828 to 1832, there are details of work carried out as a result of a fire at the maltings of Henry Alexander Johnston, maltster and corn dealer, who lived in Marden Ash. The location of these premises is not known but the account details the use of an engine, the employment of men to use an engine, watch the fire and move the grain under cover after the fire, and the cost of repairs. The total charge was £8 4s 6d.[35]

The tithe map of Marden Ash, 1848, indicates that there was a building used for malting or brewing on the road to Stanford Rivers, between the houses now known as Gate Cottage and Dyers.[36] In the 1851 Census this was occupied by Henry Johnston, his wife and children, and employed six persons.[31] Later this was the site of the Ongar Brewery, called "The Malting" in the Census Returns, and was run by Jonathan and James Palmer.[12] D.W. White, who was born in 1887 wrote in later years of his childhood memories, '*Not many people remember the Ongar Brewery. It was owned by James "Jimmie" Palmer – he lived at Bridge Farm* [in Stanford Rivers]. *The brewery was at the top of Marden Ash on the Stanford Rivers Road on the left.*' [9] The date when brewing started on this site is not known, nor is its closing although this was at the beginning of the twentieth century, maybe 1906. Henry Johnston is listed in trade directories as a maltster from 1848 to 1863. The first mention of Jonathan and James Palmer, brewers, is in 1870.[37] In 1886 the brewer was James Coleclough and the brewery is later called Coleclough & Palmer.[38] Colloquial reference is made to the Brewery Cottages (since demolished) on the Brentwood Road between the Stag public house and the junction of the road to Stanford Rivers. In the census returns these cottages are called Darby's Row and the occupations of the occupants do not indicate they all worked in the Brewery. There is however mention of Samuel Childs, maltmaker in 1871.[12]

Brewing also took place at the alehouses in Ongar. The Cock Tavern brewed its own beer until 1865. The Bull built its brewery in about 1850 and it was known as the Capital Brewery. It had a '*six-horse power steam boiler with apparatus for steamings, fourteen barrel round and underback, two coolers, two working squares, four stillions and force pump…with all other appendages fixed thereto. Also four twenty five barrel and two twelve barrel store vats and malt mill. The premises are in substantial repair and abundantly supplied with water.*' [11] For all this impressive equipment brewing at this inn did not last for long. The inn and brewery was for sale in 1856 and closed permanently in the 1860s.

References

1. *VCH Essex vol 4* (1956) OUP
2. Powell, F. *Tales of Old Ongar* (1992) Ongar Wine Circle
3. Chipping Ongar Parish Register ERO: T/P 76
4. Universal British Directory of Trade, Commerce & Manufacturing vol 4 (1798)
5. Piggot's *Directory* (1832/39)
6. Kelly's *Directory* (1902)
7. ERO: D/DU 418/63
8. Smith, H. *The Ecclesiastical History of Essex under the Long Parliament & Commonwealth* (1933) Colchester
9. White, D. W. *Memory Test – 1887 onwards* (undated typescript)
10. GPO Newsletter 12 Aug 1960
11. Sale Catalogue ERO: B2147 (29 Nov 1856)
12. Census (1871) PRO: RG 10/1643
13. Alehouse Recognizances (1769 – 1828) ERO: QRL v 24–80
14. Tithe apportionment for Chipping Ongar (1837) ERO: D/CT 262A
15. Kelly's *Directory* (1862)
16. Post Office Directory (1870)
17. Kelly's *Directory* (1895)
18. ERO: D/DQ 55/71
19. ERO: D/DU 497/18
20. Session Roll ERO: Q/SR/438/27
21. Wingham, R., & Daniell, A. *Ongar in Old Postcards vol 2* (1995) European Library
22. Jarvis, S. *The Cock, Chipping Ongar* (undated typescript)
23. Post Office Directory (1863)

ONGAR'S PUBS AND INNS

24 Morgan, G. *Romance of Essex Inns* (1974) Spurbooks
25 inf from R Harrap
26 Overseer's Poor Rate (1736) ERO: DP124/11/19
27 Census Return (1861) PRO: RG10/1643
28 Kelly's *Directory* (1890)
29 Sworder's Certificate of Sale (1865)
30 Gazette (1966)
31 Census Return (1851) PRO: HO 107/1771
32 Census Return (1891) PRO: RG 12/1366
33 Emmison F. G. *Wills at Chelmsford 1620 to 1720*
34 Booker, J. *Essex and the Industrial Revolution* (1974) ECC
35 Richard Noble's Account Book (1828–1832) ERO: D/DU 413/1
36 Tithe apportionment for the parish of High Ongar (1848) ERO: D/CT 314A
37 Post Office Directory (1870)
38 Kelly's *Directory* (1886/90)

chapter 19

Pharmacy in Ongar

by Elisabeth Barrett

Pharmacy as we know it today has evolved over the centuries, from self-medication with herbal remedies, collected from the countryside and brewed up to family recipes, through trading of chemical and plant medicines to the present highly regulated profession. Such evolution would have taken place in Ongar, although documentary evidence of this is almost non-existent before the nineteenth century.

Chemists and druggists, the forerunners of modern pharmacies, emerged during the eighteenth century as part of the commercialisation of Georgian society, at a time of growing affluence when the population had money to spend in excess of life's necessities.[1] Before this, the sale of medicinal remedies and advice on illnesses was given by apothecaries. They emerged as long ago as the fourteenth century as spicers and providers of drugs and medicines, and were distinct from physicians.[2] Only the very wealthy in society could afford the fees of physicians, who tended to practise in large towns and cities. A small town like Ongar would be unlikely to have had a physician, but probably had the services of an apothecary. The parish registers of Chipping Ongar mention, '*Sarah, the Wiffe of William Searl, appotecarie, buried at High Ongar March 16,1694/5.*'[3] Also, in 1626, Robert King an apothecary was (with Edward Peacock, a tallow chandler) in trouble for using and maintaining a house for melting tallow near the market place.[4] An apothecary's premises in the seventeenth and early eighteenth century did not correspond to our idea of a shop: a better description would be a combination of work-shop, storeroom, surgery and living room.[1] In the eighteenth century there was Mr Lenham, the Chipping Ongar apothecary who offered inoculations against smallpox. He had '*a Very Convenient House at a proper Distance*' from the town.[5] By the nineteenth century, apothecaries were coming to be seen as doctors, practising in premises with dispensaries and surgeries. A reference in another publication to Mr Lenham describes him as a doctor.[6] The 1851 census for Chipping Ongar lists '*Charles Balgarius, surgeon, apothecary & general practitioner.*' The transition to what we now know as general practitioners had begun.

Medicines derived from plants, materia medica, had been the basis of the apothecary's remedies. The sixteenth and seventeenth centuries saw the advent of chemical medicines, such as mercury compounds and various salts. Wholesale druggists who were importing medicinal plants into London from all over the world, including new plants from the Americas, were turning their attention to the manufacture of chemicals as well as galenicals (herbal medicines). This gave rise to an increase in self-treatment, the circulation of books on domestic medicine and

PHARMACY IN ONGAR

greater public awareness of what remedies were available. Anyone selling medicines could make a profit, so "chemists" and "druggists" were setting up shops and flourishing. By 1750 there were 150 such shops in London.[2] Where London led other towns and cities followed and small market towns like Ongar would in time have had such a shop. The Universal British Directory of 1798 listed no chemist or druggist in Ongar, but by 1823 there were two such shops.[7]

This new trade was posing a great threat to the livelihoods of the apothecaries who tried to stop the supply of drugs and dispensing of medicines by anyone who was not an apothecary. However, an Act of Parliament of 1815 contained a clause which said that *'nothing in the act was to affect the trade or business of chemists and druggists in buying, preparing, compounding, dispensing and vending of drugs, medicines and medicinal compounds, wholesale or retail.'* Chemists and druggists were established as suppliers of medicines and gave prominence to the retail side of their activities, making the premises attractive to the customer. Their shop windows were distinctive with a display of carboys and specie jars and the interiors were stocked with shelves of bottles and rows of drawers bearing labels only the shopkeeper could read. There were two such shops in Ongar when the Pigot's Directory of 1823 was published. They were Jno Pepper and Joseph Cracknoll, druggists. By 1839 there was William Cole, chymist & druggist and Joseph Cakebread Spurgin, chymist, druggist and dentist[7] (dentistry was probably restricted to the pulling of teeth!). Mr Spurgin's shop was at 180 High Street and, by 1845, he had added the agency of Britannia & Clerical Life Offices to his business. This business had changed hands by 1850 to Richard James Chapman and again in 1886 when John Henry Kirby had the shop which he ran until 1912. David Ward was running another chemist and druggist business in the High Street in 1850. The 1851 census indicates that his premises were on the east side of the street, between a blacksmith's and a corn merchant. By 1871 he had taken over the premises at 151 High Street where he remained until he sold his business to J. W. M. Baugh in 1900.[8]

Chemists and druggists in the first half of the eighteenth century were untrained and unregulated. This changed in 1843 when a London chemist, Jacob Bell, was instrumental in the foundation of the Pharmaceutical Society which received its charter in that year. A school of pharmacy was opened and by 1852 the Pharmacy Act had clearly defined the position of chemists and druggists. They were registered and would in future be examined on entering the profession to become pharmaceutical chemists or chemists & druggists. The first of the Ongar chemists to appear in the Pharmaceutical Society of Great Britain's register was John Kirby in 1869, although he did not have premises in Ongar until 1886.[9]

For most of the twentieth century there was only one chemist in Ongar, that of the Baugh family. Mr Baugh opened his shop in 1900. It stopped trading under his name in 1994, having changed its name to Lloyds Chemists. The pharmacy dispensed prescriptions and sold the traditional chemists goods – patent medicines, home remedies, veterinary products, toiletries, cosmetics and photographic goods, and also had a wines and spirits licence.

ASPECTS OF THE HISTORY OF ONGAR

It was a well respected pharmacy. Sir Frank Hartley, a former Dean of the School of Pharmacy, who went on to become Vice-Chancellor of London University as well as the first pharmacist to be knighted for "services to pharmacy", augmented his salary while he was still at university with locum engagements. He particularly remembers *'four weeks spent every year in charge of the fine old pharmacy in Ongar, Essex, owned by pharmacists Dorothy Baugh and her father.'* [10]

John William Mahanoorah Baugh, born in 1870 in Kandy, Ceylon (Sri Lanka), was the son of Rev. George Baugh, a Wesleyan missionary, although he himself converted to Catholicism. He was sent to school at the age of seven in Taunton, Somerset and he never saw his parents again. His mother died at sea, on the Indian Ocean, while returning home. His father remarried and emigrated to California. On leaving school he was apprenticed to Mr Mason in Bexley Heath, and married his daughter, Alice.[11] He qualified as a pharmaceutical chemist (the higher qualification in those days) and registered with the Pharmaceutical Society in 1891. Between 1891 and 1898 he was in Bexley Heath, the following year he was in Taunton and then in 1900 in Ongar.[9]

John Baugh bought the chemist business of David Ward, who had been in Ongar from 1850 to 1900. He took over Mr Ward's premises at 151 High Street and an entry in Kelly's *Directory* for 1902 reads *'Baugh's Chemist & agent for W & A Gilbey Ltd wine and spirit merchants. Dealers in Photographic Materials and apparatus.'*

151–153 High Street is a fine building. It is timber-framed and plastered and dates from the middle of the seventeenth century. It has eighteenth century and modern additions at the back and has been much altered. On both east and west elevations there are three gables, although there is photographic evidence that the front had had a Georgian facade. This was removed in 1880. There is an unusual, original central chimney-stack which has eight octagonal shafts.[12] A recent survey suggests that the building has always been used for trade on the ground floor, with living accommodation on the first and attic floors. This was certainly the arrangement when John Baugh came to live at number 151 with his wife. The chemist shop occupied two-thirds of the building on the south side, with cellars below for stockrooms. There was a kitchen and dining area behind the ground floor dispensary and shop, with a first floor drawing room and master bedroom, and attic rooms above. Mr Baugh inherited a shop front, which dated from the nineteenth century when the premises was occupied by John Wright, an ironmonger. He had this altered in 1928 by Shaw, builder & architect, of Ongar.[13]

The Baugh family lived over the premises, as was usual then. There were four children, three daughters and a son. The Baugh's eldest daughter, Mary, married Mr Lavender. The next daughter, Hilda trained in domestic science and returned home to keep house firstly for her parents and then for her sister Dorothy. The son William went into insurance, and his son is a general practitioner. Dorothy followed in her father's footsteps and studied at the School of Pharmacy, "The Square," in London and qualified as a pharmaceutical chemist in 1929.[9] She is known to have gained experience doing locum work at other pharmacies, but she helped her father and eventually ran the business. Both she and her father became Fellows of the Pharmaceutical Society of Great Britain in 1954.[14]

In the late 1950s the adjoining premises, King's greengrocers, was bought and the pharmacy then occupied the whole building. The Baughs took great pride in the pharmacy, there were the traditional labelled drug drawers behind the counter, and the floor was kept well polished. Prescriptions issued by local doctors for patients living in the town were prepared in the dispensary. Here also customers would have favourite family remedies compounded and records of these would be kept in the pharmacy's own formulary and prescription book. Dorothy was interested in aseptic dispensing and set up an aseptic dispensary in the cellar. There was an autoclave for sterilising and an aseptic cabinet for preparing penicillin eye and ear drops, which could not be sterilised by heat. Distilled water was produced and during the war they supplied the airforce at Willingale who would have needed it for batteries. Dorothy was an involved member of St Helen's church and was active in the business community of the town.[15]

An important aspect of a pharmacy business in a small market town, serving the farming community, was veterinary products. Baugh's bought in proprietary products from Cooper, Macdougall & Robinson, but also made preparations such as udder cream, cow drench and sheep dip on the premises.

Mr Baugh was interested in photography and the shop stocked film developing equipment and chemicals as well as the usual photographic lines. Medicinal snuff was sold in one ounce "powders", small folded paper packages tied up with pink string and sealing wax. Alternatively customers brought in their snuff boxes to be filled.[15]

Away from the pharmacy, John Baugh attended St Helen's church, played cricket for Ongar, and bowls and chess in later life. He set chess problems for a weekly Catholic paper.[14] He died at the age of 87 on 9 October 1956 and is buried in Ongar cemetery. His wife died the following year. So Hilda and Dorothy Baugh lived together above the shop and Dorothy ran the business, until she sold it to D. J. Rees in 1969. The sisters then retired to Rye. Jill Hope, who assisted Miss Baugh in her later years, stayed on to manage the pharmacy under its various owners until her own retirement in 1998. Dorothy died tragically in a road accident while returning home from her brother's funeral in 1980.

The last three decades of this century have seen gradual, but radical change in the profession of pharmacy. Bottles marked mysteriously "The Mixture", "The Lotion" or "The Tablets" have become a thing of the past. Most medication is now in tablet form and patients are encouraged to know about their medicines. Dispensing NHS prescriptions has become the major role of community pharmacies. Advice on healthcare and proprietory medicines has taken over from the traditional chemist's "cough mixture" or "indigestion remedy." Other retailers now sell some traditional chemist goods, such as toiletries, baby products and photographic merchandise.

When Baugh's was sold to D. J. Rees in 1969, this marked the end of proprietor run pharmacy in Ongar. This pharmacy, still called Baugh's, changed premises in 1985 to 205 High Street because of competition from the newly opened Co-operative Pharmacy which was much nearer to the doctors' surgeries. In 1989 the business passed to Day Lewis, who owned it for a few months and then to E. Soares, who in 1994, sold to the pharmacy chain, Lloyds Chemists.[14] There was one other pharmacy during this century, Lacey (Chemist) Ltd. from 1931 to 1943. This was opened in competition to Baugh's by a former apprentice of his at 149 High Street and was managed for a short time by Muriel Grimson.[16] The aforementioned Co-op pharmacy at 198–202 High Street opened in 1983 in the former drapery store which had once been Ashdown's.

References

1. Holloway, S.W.F. *Royal Pharmaceutical Society of Great Britain 1841 – 1991. A Political & Social History.* (1991) Pharmaceutical Press
2. Matthews L.G. *Milestones in Pharmacy.* (1980) Merrill
3. Chipping Ongar parish registers ERO: T/R 76
4. VCH Essex vol 4 (1956)
5. Smith J.R. *The Speckled Monster.* (1987) ERO
6. Brown A.F. *Essex at Work. 1700–1815.* (1969) ECC
7. Pigot's *Trade Directory* (1823), (1832) and (1839)
8. Kelly's *Trade Directory* (1850 to 1912)
9. Annual Register of Pharmaceutical Chemists (1869–1912) P.S.G.B.
10. *Pharmaceutical Journal* vol 253 (13 August 1994)
11. inf. from Dr J.W.D.Baugh. (1997)
12. Royal Commission on Historical Monuments – Essex Central & SW. (1921) HMSO
13. Ongar W.E.A. Survey. ERO: T/P 96
14. inf. from Jill Hope (1998)
15. inf. from Jean Kendrick (1998)
16. Annual Register of Pharmaceutical Chemists (1930–1945) Pharmaceutical Press

chapter 20

Health care and the local hospitals

by Michael Leach

It is difficult to imagine – and no documents have been found to show – what health care was available in Chipping Ongar before the eighteenth century. A few names indicate that there were medical practitioners in the town: Charles Blomer, barber surgeon in 1622;[1] William Godfrey, practitioner in physic in 1679;[2] John Williamson, surgeon in 1682;[2] John Young, surgeon in 1683;[3] and William Porter, barber and surgeon in 1687.[4] Those who could pay would have had access to blood letting, bone setting, basic surgery and the armamentarium of the apothecary. For the rest – who would not necessarily have fared any worse! – there would have been folk remedies, or the "wise woman." It is possible that Elizabeth Thurogood, who was described at her burial in 1708 as '*widdow, midwiffe, a shopkeeper*,' would have given some form of medical treatment.[1]

The parish register very rarely recorded cause of death, though occasionally accidents, particularly drowning, were mentioned. The exception was in 1574 when it notes '*Thomas, a Strangr, Surgeo of London, buryed 28th July, dyed of plague.*'[1] This was a known plague year in London when those who could, would have left the city, sometimes taking the plague with them. The registers of St Andrew's Hertford, for example, recorded many plague burials in this year, some of them Londoners who had fled there.[5] The Chipping Ongar register over the next nine months recorded nine further "plague" burials, a very modest outbreak compared to the well documented one in Eyam, Derbyshire in 1665/66 which killed 267 out of a population of 350.[5] It is not possible to tell if this modest autumn peak of burials in Ongar was plague, or misinformed diagnoses after the sudden death of a stranger from the plague ridden metropolis. There was another autumn peak of burials in 1665 – suggestive of plague – but no increase in the spring of 1666 which was typical of the epidemic both in London and Eyam.[5] Plague in the crowded town of Ongar was obviously possible, but there is no firm evidence to confirm it.

By the eighteenth century, smallpox had replaced plague as the epidemic killer. There is a very striking peak of burials in 1741 in Chipping Ongar: 33 burials, compared to an annual average of just under 13 over the preceding 40 years.[1] In the same year, the rector of Chelmsford noted in his register that smallpox had been rife in the town.[6] However, there was also a national outbreak of a febrile illness with high mortality in this year (probably typhus)[5] and it is not possible to say whether either, or both, of these two were responsible for the Ongar deaths.

ASPECTS OF THE HISTORY OF ONGAR

The parish surgeon

The first evidence for any form of organised medical provision for the poor is found in 1748 in the earliest surviving volume of the vestry minutes – but this is not to say that no provision was made at an earlier date. In some parishes where records are more complete, parish surgeons were appointed from the late seventeenth century onwards. It is clear that the Chipping Ongar parish surgeon in 1748 was being paid on a "per case" basis, as the vestry indicated that no payment for treatment would be made without prior written consent of a parish officer – an early example of trying to contain the costs of health care.[7] In 1752, this was altered to a single annual payment of £4 for looking after the poor, with the three practitioners (John Boodle, surgeon, John Lenham, apothecary, and James Beasing) invited to do a year each in rotation. The payments are comparable with other small parishes in Essex and Kent.[8&9] By 1761, the agreement with John Boodle was much more specific, with an annual fee of £5 5s 0d to cover treatment '*of any Illness Disorder or Accident as may be necessary and wanting in the Several Branches of his Profession as a Surgeon and Apothecary*,' but it was reduced to £4 again from 1770.[7] It had risen to £7 17s 6d by 1809, with extra payments for surgery (rate not specified), midwifery (10s 6d per case) and inoculation (7s per case). The principle of annual rotation remained, the job being shared between the town's three surgeons, Thomas Walker, John Potter and John Peake. By 1821 the fee had been increased to £15 per annum, presumably due to the increased workload, and midwifery was now paid 15s a case.[10] It is difficult to say how assiduously parish surgeons carried out their duties, but an early nineteenth century surgeon recognised a potential conflict of interest, noting '*if he receives a message from a rich patient in one, and from a pauper patient in an opposite direction, it cannot happen otherwise than that the latter will be neglected.*'[9]

Smallpox inoculation

Charles Creighton, writing at the end of the nineteenth century, noted that doctors in the previous century had only three effective forms of treatment: ipecacuanha for dysentery, quinine for fevers and smallpox inoculation. The former two would not be reckoned effective today but the latter was the means of controlling smallpox until its worldwide eradication in 1977. The acceptability of smallpox inoculation suffered from a number of reversals in the first half of the eighteenth century; however, the Suttonian method – devised by his father, but put into practice on a large scale by Daniel Sutton of Ingatestone from 1763 – had very few complications, and rapidly came into widespread use with a significant reduction in smallpox mortality.[11] The Chipping Ongar apothecary, John Lenham, was an active inoculator from January 1765, using a house at Kelvedon Common for quarantining those treated, who were infectious to others. He advertised his services extensively in the *Chelmsford Chronicle*, promising '*just Care and Attendance, with all Necessaries (Tea and Sugar excepted)*' at four guineas, which was the same fee charged by Daniel Sutton.[12] By the end of 1765, '*many hundreds*' had been inoculated by Lenham and '*not one Person has been in the*

HEALTH CARE AND THE LOCAL HOSPITALS

least Danger, or confined a Single Day to their Bed or Room.' He continued, in terms which would seem rather extravagant today, *'great Numbers of them have been in better Health than they had been for Years before, and not one of them in any ways worse.'* The class of person treated is indicated by a footnote *'extreme good Accommodation for servants at Three Guineas each.'*[13] However, vestries quickly recognised that prevention of smallpox saved money on poor relief, and there is slightly ambiguous evidence that Chipping Ongar vestry was inoculating the poor by June 1767, as well as threatening to prosecute anyone who introduced the disease into the town.[7]

As always, there were those anxious to cash in on a good thing. In May 1766, the *Chelmsford Chronicle* carried an advertisement for what amounted to a do-it-yourself inoculation manual, including recipes for *'the Preparative Powder, Repellant Pill and the Physic used in Inoculation.'* The anonymous author made the optimistic claim that *'the Medicine will in great Measure stop the Contagion in those who do not chuse to be inoculated; or if they should catch it, will cause the Effects to be much more favourable.'*[14] John Lenham, perhaps feeling his professional status or his profits threatened, was in print the next week, reassuring the public that he would never sell medicine anonymously, and that he never used a repellant pill or medicine.[15] Two weeks later, the anonymous author inserted the following sardonic and offensive advertisement: *'The nameless Author presents his Compliments and Thanks to Mr Lenham for his generous Declaration that his Nostrum is still a Secret, and that he had no Hand in the Inoculating Treatise. Had this not been publickly affirmed, the World might have supposed Mr Lenham the Author, which perhaps might have injured the sale of the Pamphlet.'* The same paper carried a notice from Daniel Sutton, denying the authorship of what he called *'a catchpenny Treatise'* and stating that he had analysed the medicines and found them to be dangerous.[16] As often happens, the controversy seems to have provided useful publicity, and the "Treatise on Inoculation" ran into a second edition the following week! The author would appear to have been Matthew Porter.[17]

The workhouse infirmary

The Poor Law Amendment Act of 1834 united groups of parishes to form single poor law unions. The workhouse for the Ongar Union was established at Stanford Rivers in 1836 and the building still exists as the premises of Piggott Bros & Co. Ltd. Either contemporarily, or certainly by 1865, there was an infirmary for the sick poor, with two 16 bed wards, one for men and one for women, in a separate block behind the main workhouse building. An isolation block was built at the north end for infectious cases, and there was also a small lying in ward for post-natal patients by the end of the century.[18] The infirmary fulfilled the function of a modern hospital for the poor. In 1897, for example, John Richardson was admitted suffering from a broken leg caused by a kick from a cow, and a few years later two men with broken bones were admitted after a fall from a haystack in Willingale.[19] Eliza Underwood, wife of the last Master, was matron from 1902 to 1920, and was reputed to have been the first workhouse matron in Essex to be fully trained both as a nurse and a midwife.[18]

The Ongar General Friendly Society

The workhouse only provided medical care to those on parish relief – others had to pay. In the summer of 1829, for example, the builder Richard Noble ran up a bill of £16 18s 6d with the local surgeon, John Potter, and in 1834 five consultations with another local surgeon, John Peake, including medicines and '*reducing Hernia by ye Taxis,*' cost £1 11s 6d.[20] Clearly this sort of expenditure was out of reach of the poorly paid, whose lot had been worsened by the recession after the Napoleonic War as well as the 1834 Poor Law Act, which was designed to cut the escalating costs of poor relief. It was perhaps the harshness of the new Poor Law which led a group of local clergymen to establish the Ongar General Friendly Society in 1839. Members were mainly labourers, with a few servants and artisans. The subscription system was complicated, but provided various forms of benefit. Firstly, there were weekly cash payments during periods of sickness. Secondly, death benefits were paid to widows, or directly to the undertaker if there were problems with funeral expenses. Thirdly, the Society paid a local surgeon, Frank Dobson Potter, an annual fee of £7 10s 0d to '*furnish Medicines etc to all Members resident within 6 Miles of his Surgery.*' Fourthly, there were one off payments (usually £2) to surgeons for amputations and setting fractures. This was the beginning of health care provided by insurance, and the success and growth of the Ongar General Friendly Society showed that it was fulfilling an important need. The society continued until the requirements of Lloyd George's National Insurance of 1911 (which combined state insurance with friendly society payments to provide sickness benefit and free access to a "panel" doctor for those on low income) necessitated amalgamation with a larger society. In September 1912, the Ongar Society was absorbed by the Manchester Unity of Oddfellows.[21]

Water supply and sewage disposal

During the nineteenth century, increasing public concern – and the developments of medical microbiology – slowly brought about major reforms of the country's water supply and sewage disposal, with corresponding improvements in public health. The Public Health Act of 1848 (reinforced by a further Act in 1858) allowed the voluntary creation of local health boards. It seems likely that the Ongar board of guardians had established a local health board by 1865, as, on 2 May that year, it appointed Frederic Chancellor (the Chelmsford architect who was actively involved in public health matters)[6] to inspect the drainage of the parishes of Chipping and High Ongar.[22] His report was forwarded to the relevant vestries, and Chipping Ongar vestry summoned a public meeting in August to consider the proposals.[23] However, it seems that the usual reluctance of vestries to incur any expense (and the Chipping Ongar vestry was already facing costs for the new cemetery) prevented any action from being taken. It was not until the replacement of the vestry system in the local government reorganisation of 1894 that any progress was made. In the meantime, the Ongar board of guardians continued to take initiatives on public health, appointing a sanitary inspector (Inspector Charles

HEALTH CARE AND THE LOCAL HOSPITALS

Fox) in June 1866, and drawing up and distributing to every parish in the Union *'directions and regulations'* for the prevention of cholera in July 1866.[22]

Chipping Ongar remained without main drainage, and dependant on shallow wells or the Cripsey Brook for drinking water for the rest of the century. The stimulus for improvement came from the appointment of local medical officers of health in 1891; for the Ongar area this was Dr J. C. Quennell. His series of reports – and pressure from the energetic county MOH, Dr J. C. Thresh – gradually led to the essential improvements in sewerage and water supply described in Chapter 22. It is difficult now to imagine the foul condition of the Cripsey Brook, described by Ongar Parish Council in August 1899 as *'the receptacle of most of the sewage of the town of Chipping Ongar and, during the dry season, most offensive and dangerous to the health of the Inhabitants.'* [24]

The annual Summary of the Reports of the Medical Officers of Health[25] contains much detailed statistical information about death and disease in the Ongar rural district from 1891 onwards. It is instructive to read about diseases now confined to the poorer countries of the world, such as tuberculosis, typhoid and diphtheria. There were deaths from measles and whooping cough, and school closures were used to control the spread of infectious disease. There is a detailed description of the last smallpox outbreak: 12 cases in the Ongar workhouse in April 1904, introduced by an inmate who had been infected while an in-patient in the London Hospital. All residents were vaccinated and quarantined, and there were no deaths, but there were four further cases in Moreton, caused by a discharged workhouse resident. Typhoid largely disappeared after the first few years of the twentieth century, due to the major improvements in water supply and sewerage throughout the Ongar district. Both treatment and control of diphtheria benefited from the use of anti-toxin, first used in this country in 1895 and the first effective therapeutic agent against an infectious disease since the introduction of smallpox inoculation nearly two hundred years earlier.[26] Anti-toxin was being used as a prophylactic by 1900, and in 1906 ORDC agreed to meet the costs of those unable to pay. The fall in both deaths and cases of diphtheria suggest that this policy was successful.

The Ongar isolation hospital

Though the workhouse infirmary had an isolation ward, this was only available for the poor. In every annual report from 1891, Dr Quennell mentioned the need for an isolation hospital for the area.[25] In 1897, ORDC was persuaded by Essex County Council (represented by the County MOH, Dr Thresh, in person) to establish a 26 bed isolation hospital to serve Ongar, Chigwell, Epping and Buckhurst Hill. Attempts to find a site proved difficult – not surprisingly, no one wanted this sort of neighbour! In November 1899, the owner of "Two Acre Shot", a field in Stanford Rivers, was willing to sell for £600.[19] Progress was very slow, and Dr Quennell in his report for 1900 wrote *'erection of an isolation hospital is under consideration, but without powers of compulsory purchase, it seems impossible to acquire a suitable site. The matter is one of urgent necessity, for the isolation of infectious*

ASPECTS OF THE HISTORY OF ONGAR

diseases in small tenements is impossible.'[25] Purchase was not finally completed until 1903, when the vendor held a celebration dinner.[19] However, events had moved faster than plans, and in December 1901, a smallpox contact from Little Yeldham was arrested in a public house in Beauchamp Roding. He was detained overnight in a contractor's hut at the new sewage treatment works, and removed the next day to a tent behind Holly Tree House, Stanford Rivers, for 14 days observation.[19] Pressured to take action, ORDC established the Ongar Smallpox Hospital by purchasing seven tents at a cost of £168. One could accommodate up to ten patients, one was for nurses, another for caretakers, and four for '*sanitary and other conveniences.*' These were pitched on land in Stanford Rivers rented from a council member, but, after local protests, were removed in February 1902 to a remote site near Ongar Park Wood.[19] By this time, several other urban and rural districts in Essex had made similar provision. Chelmsford, for example, had bought a four bedded tent hospital from Piggott Bros in 1883 for £72 9s 4d.[6]

The problem of the isolation hospital grumbled on after the vendor's celebration dinner in 1903. The ORDC Hospital Committee had plans drawn up for a six roomed hospital, the estimated cost being £600, including fittings. There was uncertainty about the eligibility for an Essex County Council grant of £10 per bed, and anxiety about loss of autonomy if such a grant was accepted. The Local Government Board, whose agreement was necessary to sanction the loan, insisted on the addition of a mortuary, a wash-house and a laundry. Unable to resolve the problems, ORDC had decided by August 1905 to abandon the project, and agreed that the tent hospital could be disinfected and used for other infectious cases, if the need arose.[19] There is no evidence that it was ever used in this way, though it was still in storage in 1913. In practice, the few cases needing admission were sent to infectious disease hospitals in Romford and Dagenham.[25]

During the First World War, temporary Red Cross convalescent hospitals for soldiers were established in the area: Blake Hall for officers, the Budworth Hall for other ranks.[27] The workhouse infirmary also took 10 convalescent soldiers '*in pale blue uniforms*' during this period.[18] After the war, it was decided to raise money to build a hospital as a permanent war memorial to those who had died. A local GP, Dr G. R. Wilson, was actively involved in this.[28] However, money was slow to come in, and it was not until 1928 that the site in Shelley was bought.

Ongar and District Cottage Hospital

Either frustrated by the delay or (according to rumour)[27] by the failure to design the building along lines approved by King's College Hospital, another local GP, Dr H. C. C. Hackney and '*a few local gentlemen*' acted unilaterally and opened the Ongar & District Cottage Hospital in September 1928. A bungalow (now 69 Fyfield Road, Shelley) was rented, and adapted to take six beds and an operating theatre. Soon after, '*owing to the long list of sufferers seeking admission,*' the adjoining semi-detached bungalow (now number 71) was added, providing a further eight beds and accommodation for nursing staff. In September 1930, a nearby house (probably the one now numbered 63) was rented for nursing staff, and the vacated space in the bungalow adapted for out-patients. A further house was rented in 1932 for use as a hospital annexe, increasing the in-patient beds to 22. In the first four years, there were 1086 admissions, 708 major operations and 5,122 out-patient attendances.[29] Though there was an impressive list of honorary medical staff, it appears that most of the work was done by Dr Hackney and his assistant, Dr O. F. Barr. The other local GPs were not involved, as they mistrusted Dr Hackney, and were committed to the War Memorial Hospital.[27]

In 1935, the Cottage Hospital was financed by (a) receipts from patients, their benevolent societies, and the Hospital Savings Association (£1,344) (b) a small band of annual subscribers who contributed just over £43 (c) donations from individuals or associations (nearly £128), and (d) a large variety of fund raising events, including dances, concerts, whist drives, local and agricultural shows (nearly £544). There were also food collections – nearly 4000 eggs were collected in "egg week" and 3,200 lbs of groceries on various "two pound" days. In spite of the closure of the annexe (ostensibly due to the difficulty of supervising the four isolated in-patient beds), expenditure exceeded income by nearly £137 in 1935.[30] It is remarkable that the community was able, for several years, to support two rival hospitals within 50 yards of each other, Ongar War Memorial Hospital having opened in 1933 just down the road.

It is not clear when the Cottage Hospital closed. Dr Hackney was arrested in January 1941 for failing to attend court to answer charges of *communicating information useful to an enemy* '[31] and when, in March 1944, he received a 15 month prison sentence for forging cheques stolen from a patient, his name was erased from the Medical Register.[32] It seems likely that the hospital had closed by or before this time.

Ongar and District War Memorial Hospital

The war memorial fund raised £3765[33] and the hospital, built by Messrs Noble, was finally opened on August bank holiday, 1933, by Brigadier General R. E. Colvin, Lord Lieutenant of Essex. That evening, there was a fight in a gypsy encampment at Moreton and the hospital was busy dealing with casualties! The running expenses were met in a very similar way to the Cottage Hospital. There were collections of food from the town and neighbouring villages, money from annual subscribers, donations and house to house collections, as well as the annual garden party at the Wilderness, and the weekly activities of the "Drum and Monkey Club" which toured the district in fancy dress. Between 1932 and 1947, between £30,000 and £35,000 was raised by the community,[33] plus sizeable donations of food (5487 lbs of groceries in 1937 and 5 tons of potatoes in 1947, for example). The hospital finances were sufficiently secure to enable a new wing, costing £1723, to be built in 1939, providing a flat for the matron, as well as new kitchens and staff quarters, and freeing space for four additional beds.[34] In 1944, £760 was spent on additions which included the purchase of the bungalow opposite (now The Willows, number 38) and the adjoining house (now number 59) to provide homes for the nurses. The operating theatre was extended to provide a steriliser and scrub up room.[35]

ASPECTS OF THE HISTORY OF ONGAR

During the Second World War, the government Emergency Hospital Scheme provided a significant subsidy, though there is no record of how many war casualties were treated. After the war, local collections of food were augmented by supplies from the Overseas Food Gifts Board, as well as a donation of Heinz foods from Mr Heinz junior. The "Drum and Monkey Club" was still active in 1947 when it raised nearly £142.[33] However there was a rapid rise in the annual deficit after 1945, and the treasurer's report of 1947 warned that a £500 loan from the bank (with the chairman, Mr D. A. J. Buxton, acting as guarantor) had proved inadequate, necessitating an urgent approach to the Ministry of Health for funds to keep the hospital running. Then – as now – the high cost of new drugs was clearly a problem, and it is interesting to note a separate "penicillin fund" in the 1947 accounts. It has been said that many hospitals were on the point of bankruptcy at the time of the National Health Service takeover on 5 July 1948. Ongar Hospital ended the 1947 financial year with a £1454 deficit and, judging from the treasurer's rather despairing comment, it was proving difficult to maintain, let alone increase, the fund raising efforts with the NHS take over imminent![33] At a public meeting on 23 September 1948, it was resolved to form a League of Friends of the hospital, and this was formally constituted by the election of officers the following month, making it one of the earliest NHS Leagues of Friends (though many similar support organisations pre-existed the NHS).[36]

Over the next two decades, the hospital surrendered various functions to the local district general hospitals. The last major operation was performed by the Epping surgeon, Mr Tony Baron, in 1952.[37] X-ray facilities were withdrawn when the apparatus became obsolete. The maternity beds closed on 1 January 1969 due to the difficulty of recruiting trained midwives. This gradual run down led, on 14 April 1969, to the announcement by the North East Metropolitan Regional Hospital Board of plans to close the hospital on the grounds that the beds were underused, that there were difficulties in recruiting staff, and that there were spare beds at Epping and Harlow hospitals where "better" facilities could be provided.[38] There was a vigorous local protest campaign led by the rector, the Rev. John Vaughan Jones and one of the local GPs, Dr Ted Hatfield, involving television appearances, a protest (complete with patient and bed!) outside the DHSS headquarters at Elephant and Castle, and disruption of a RHB meeting – there was even threat of a libel suit! On 14 May 1970, the Secretary of State agreed in principle to the closure subject to (a) satisfactory arrangements for the transfer of existing in-patients (b) provision of suitably staffed GP beds at St Margaret's Hospital and (c) the existing Ongar Hospital buildings to be put to an alternative health or welfare use.[39] Essex County Council had agreed in principle to use the buildings to provide accommodation for the elderly mentally infirm. Over the next two years, there were various attempts by the RHB to establish GP beds in Hornbeam pavilion at St Margaret's Hospital. Lack of finance prevented their realisation and the facilities at Ongar Hospital were steadily improved in the 1970s by ambitious projects funded by the League of Friends: a large downstairs day room, two upstairs day rooms, and the installation of a lift in 1979.

More ambitious plans to increase the number of beds had to be shelved, but day care provision started in the 1980s and grew steadily. During that decade, it was seen as an excellent example of a community hospital and was shown off to visiting NHS administrators.

However, the market driven NHS reforms of the 1990s were hostile to small hospitals which were increasingly sacrificed to try to solve health authority budgetary deficits. Half of Ongar Hospital's beds were normally used for long stay patients, but the NHS withdrew provision of long term care from 1994. This loss and – in theory at least – better community care reduced the need for in-patient beds. Further reorganisation split Essex into two purchasing authorities, effectively resulting in the hospital being unable to take patients from the southern half of its traditional catchment area. The local GPs made many suggestions for new uses for the underused beds, but nothing resulted and they were left with the feeling that the hospital was being left to wither on the vine. In May 1997, the Essex & Herts Community NHS Trust mounted a consultation exercise on the hospital's future, without disguising its preference for selling the building as a private nursing home. In January 1998, the preference became a decision. The hospital closure was vigorously opposed by local residents, and the Community Health Council lodged a formal objection. In May 1999, the Minister of State for Health refused to agree to the sale to the private sector, and urged further discussions about its future.

Health care in the twentieth century

This differs little from national developments, and is too complex to discuss in detail here. Insurance to cover medical fees, which began with the Ongar Friendly Society in the nineteenth century, was extended by the state in 1911 to cover low income wage earners (but not their dependants). These were called "panel" patients, a name derived from the voluntary panel of GPs who were willing to participate in the scheme. The newly formed local authorities began to take some responsibility for health care provision. ORDC, as already mentioned, was paying for the poor to receive diphtheria anti-toxin treatment in 1906. The earliest surviving ORDC public health committee minutes from 1936 show that payments were being made for admissions to the Chelmsford Isolation Hospital (£1 1s 0d per case, plus £2 12s 6d for every week's stay), as well as hospital ambulance transport at 1s 0d per mile. By 1940 ORDC was paying local GPs to give diphtheria immunisation (which had replaced the anti-toxin as the prophylactic of choice).[11] ORDC was also responsible for local ambulance provision until 5 July 1948, and it is clear that the charges made (1d per mile) came nowhere near to covering the costs.[41] General practice changed little in the first four decades, with single handed GPs working from their own homes (Dr G. R. Wilson and Dr R. Ferguson in Ongar, Dr A. S. David in Fyfield, and Dr H. C. C. Hackney in Blackmore). Though they occasionally covered for each other, GPs normally expected to be on call 24 hours a day, and 7 days a week. Dr David's busiest surgery was on Sunday morning.[27]

ASPECTS OF THE HISTORY OF ONGAR

There were few effective medications, and most came in liquid form. The bottles were wrapped in paper and sealed with wax for private patients, but unwrapped for "panel" patients. Medicines were brown (alkaline gentian mixture, a tonic), bright red (potassium bromide and valerian mixture, a sedative), dark red (containing iron, for anaemia and a tonic), and black (squill mixture, for coughs). In the 1940s, standard charges were 3s 6d for a surgery consultation, 5s 0d for a home visit, and £3 3s 0d for full maternity services. Few patients realised that they were bought and sold with the practice. In 1944, for example, Ongar House (212 High Street) was purchased for £2000 by the incoming GP, plus £750 for "goodwill" (i.e. the list of patients) with a minimal stock of medicines and equipment. The sale of goodwill became illegal after 1948.[27]

The introduction of the NHS in July 1948 was a major revolution, making medical care available at no cost to the entire population. Again, this is a national, rather than a local, story. It is difficult, half a century later, to realise how much this improved the lot of those on low incomes, and how it freed the GPs from the drudgery of account keeping, and debt collection from those barely able to pay. Another major change over the last few decades has been the development of a wide range of effective drugs and vaccines (for example, the sulphonamide M&B 693 in 1939, penicillin in 1944, streptomycin in 1947 and polio vaccine in 1956), and the huge leap forward in sophisticated diagnostic and therapeutic aids. But progress has come at a price to those working within the health service with inadequate funding, and repeated re-organisations in an attempt to spread the jam a little further. Perhaps Petronius Arbiter, writing in AD 65, should have the last word: *'We trained hard, but it seemed that every time we were beginning to form up in teams, we would be re-organised. I was to learn later in life that we tend to meet any new situation by re-organising, and a wonderful method it can be for creating an illusion of progress, while producing confusion, inefficiency and demoralisation'*.

References

1. Chipping Ongar parish register ERO: T/R 76
2. Emmison, F. G. *Wills at Chelmsford 1620–1720*
3. Archdeacon's Act book ERO: D/AEV 11
4. Quarter Sessions ERO: Q/SR/453/6
5. Creighton, C. *History of Epidemics in Britain* (1896)
6. Grieve, H. *The Sleepers and the Shadows* (1994) Chelmsford
7. Chipping Ongar vestry minutes ERO: DP 124/8/1A
8. Brown, A. F. J. *Essex at Work 1700–1815* (1969) Chelmsford
9. Yates, N. et al. *Religion and Society in Kent 1690–1914* (1994) Maidstone
10. Chipping Ongar vestry minutes ERO: DP 124/8/2
11. Smith, J. R. *The Speckled Monster* (1987) Chelmsford
12. *Chelmsford Chronicle* 25 April 1765
13. ibid, 6 December 1765
14. ibid, 9 May 1766
15. ibid, 16 May 1766
16. ibid, 30 May 1766
17. ibid, 6 June 1766

HEALTH CARE AND THE LOCAL HOSPITALS

18 Underwood, V., undated typescript
19 Cuttle collection ERO: T/P 181/15/10–11
20 Richard Noble's account book ERO: D/DU 413/1
21 Ongar General Friendly Society Minutes ERO: D/Q 17/1–3
22 Board of guardian minutes ERO: G/On M5
23 Chipping Ongar vestry minutes ERO: DP 124/8/3
24 Ongar Parish Council minutes (from 1895)
25 Summary of the Reports of the District Medical Officers of Health for the Administrative County of Essex (annually from 1891) ERO library
26 Conybeare, J. J. (ed) *A Textbook of Medicine* (1929) Edinburgh. Also *British Medical Journal* 31 October 1998 p.1243
27 inf from Drs Ted and Sylvia Hatfield
28 *British Medical Journal* vol 315 p. 955 (1997)
29 Ongar & District Cottage Hospital brochure (undated)
30 Ongar & District Cottage Hospital Seventh Annual Report (1935)
31 *Essex Weekly News,* 31 January 1941
32 *News of the World,* 5 March 1944
33 Ongar & District War Memorial Hospital Fifteenth Annual Report (1947)
34 ibid Seventh Annual Report (1939)
35 ibid Twelfth Annual Report (1944)
36 Emrys-Roberts, M. *The Cottage Hospitals 1859–1990* (1991) Tern Publications
37 Ongar War Memorial Hospital operating theatre book (now lost)
38 NE Metropolitan Regional Hospital Board; public statement on Ongar War Memorial Hospital, 14 April 1969
39 DHSS: Mr Crossman's conditions for Ongar Hospital closure, 14 May 1970
40 Ongar Rural District Council public health committee minutes: Loughton library
41 ORDC, *Rural Affairs (1949)*

chapter 21

The railways of Ongar

by Edwyn Gilmour

Part 1: The Epping–Ongar branch

The construction of a railway line to Ongar in the mid 1860s was, when seen against the intense railway activity in the London area during that decade, somewhat unremarkable. It was a period of feverish railway construction and the Great Eastern Railway (GER), which built the line to Ongar, was only one of the thirteen separate railway companies building new routes at this time.[1] However, though most other projects were London based or suburban, the Ongar branch was very much a rural enterprise. It has often been asked why the GER thought it worthwhile to build an extension from Loughton over the steep gradients to Ongar, a market town which, half a century earlier, only had a population of 595.[2]

Understandably, Epping was the more desirable target, as a railway to serve Ongar could have been built at much less cost up the Roding valley. In looking for reasons for the choice of railway routes 140 years ago, it must be remembered that companies invariably took a long-term view with some of their speculative ventures. There was the hope that the presence of a railway would lead to property and commercial development with ever increasing numbers of passengers. Also the carriage of mineral and freight traffic frequently offered companies a better chance of making money than from the transport of passengers.

The origins

Although the GER built the Ongar line, its origins were from an earlier period. The Eastern Counties Railway (ECR) was the first in the field in the east of London and opened their first section from Mile End to Romford on 18 June 1839 with a gauge of five feet.[3] The section from Mile End to a terminus at Shoreditch was completed by 1 July 1840. Three years later, the ECR took over the Northern & Eastern Railway, a struggling enterprise with a line from east London up the Lea Valley to Harlow, Bishop's Stortford and beyond. This had been built to 4ft 8½ in gauge (now referred to as standard gauge). Soon after the takeover, the ECR converted its original tracks to this standard gauge to enable the lines to be linked. In 1849 another connection was made with the Blackwall Railway at Bow Junction, enabling some ECR trains to terminate at Fenchurch Street instead of Shoreditch. As its tentacles spread from the point of divergence at Stratford, the ECR set its sights on Loughton and this extension was completed in 1856.

It was neither the ECR, nor its successor the GER, which first planned the line from Loughton to Epping and Ongar, but an independent concern entitled the Epping Railway Company (ERC). Its chairman was George Parker Bidder, and among the directors was John Chevallier Cobbold MP, a leading citizen of Ipswich who had been instrumental in launching the Eastern Union Railway between Ipswich and Colchester some years earlier. Efforts to promote a line to Epping had been made from the 1830s.[4] But it was not until 13 August 1859 that the ERC obtained the necessary Act of Parliament for the extension from Loughton. The Act allowed two years for the land to be purchased, share capital of £100,000 to be raised in £10 shares, and powers to raise a further £33,000 in loans. However the company was unable to raise the necessary capital.

The ECR was understandably interested in, and unhappy about, the Epping plans. Railway developments were moving fast and ECR were having discussions with both the Eastern Union Railway (EUR) and the more distant Norfolk Railway (NR). All looked on the Epping plan as a good one, but none of them wished to go it alone. There had been friction between the ERC and the ECR, with the latter opposing the passage of the former's bill through Parliament. At one point, the ECR had considered running its own line to Ongar up the Roding valley, bypassing Epping completely. Eventually, the three interested companies (the ECR, the EUR and the NR) agreed to a full scale merger to take over the ERC project which was foundering from lack of capital. And so the GER was born on 7 August 1862, a concern which was destined to become greater that its constituent parts, and to survive up to the grouping of 1923 when it became part of the London & North Eastern Railway.

Soon after the formation of the GER, capital was raised for the extension to Epping and Ongar. The contractor was Thomas Brassey, under the direction of the GER engineer Mr Sinclair, and first turf was cut in March 1863. The work entailed cuttings and embankments through heavy clay. One major constructional feature was the Cripsey viaduct at Ongar, with five 20 foot span arches. Additionally there were three underbridges and five overbridges between Epping and Ongar, and an occupation crossing at North Weald which, in years to come, would have the only level crossing gates on the underground system! After completion of the construction in early April 1865 there was a visit from the Board of Trade inspector, Captain Tyler of the Royal Engineers Railway Operating Division. He expressed concern about the Cripsey viaduct, noting signs of settlement at the southern end. This was remedied by the GER engineer, and permission to open the line was granted without re-inspection.

On 24 April 1865, the whole extension from Loughton to Ongar was opened. Both the *Essex Weekly News* and the *Chelmsford Chronicle* reported that the first train out of Ongar left *'amid the cheers of a huge crowd of spectators, with the cadets of the Ongar Grammar School firing a volley of shots into the air to celebrate the event.'* However, a comprehensive account of the Epping - Ongar branch, published in 1996, states that the event had not been expected to take place until 1 May, and that the date had been moved back at very short notice, giving Ongarians hardly any time to organise celebrations.[5] The townsfolk were alerted to the premature opening by the town crier, and naturally responded by making their way to their new station to witness the spectacle of a new form of transport in

ASPECTS OF THE HISTORY OF ONGAR

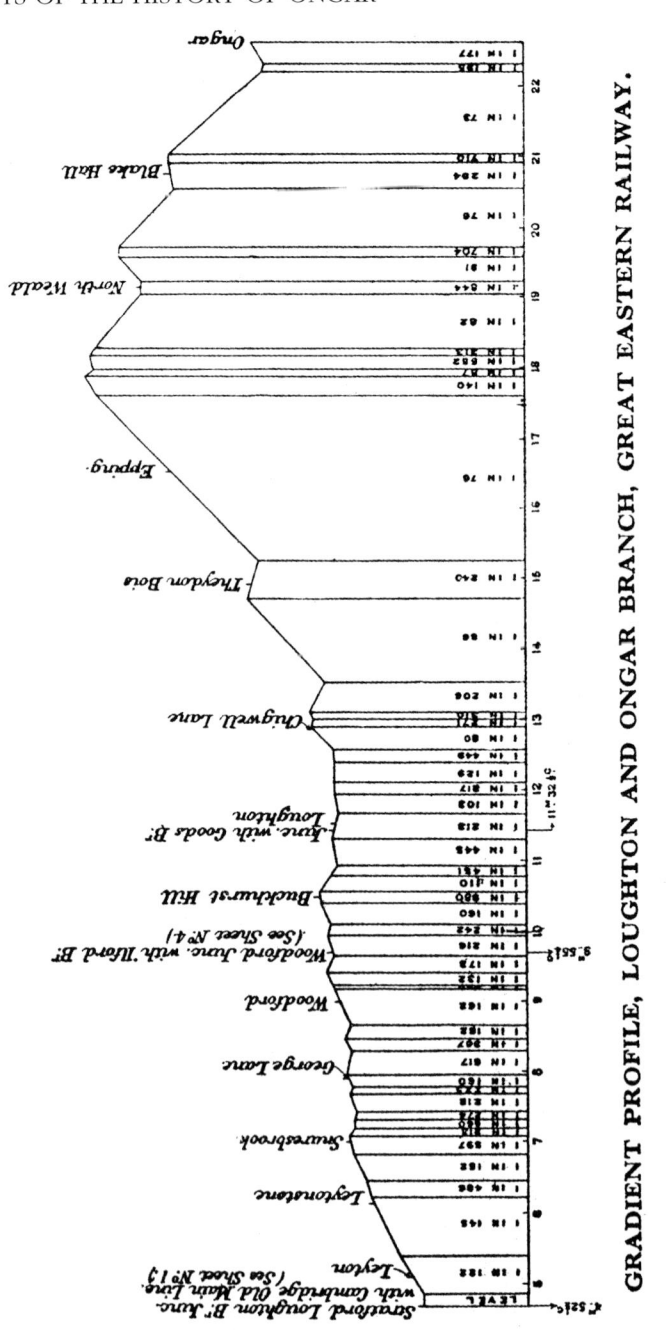

Figure 18   Gradient profile of the Loughton to Ongar branch from *The Railway Magazine* of 1920.

their own back yard. Some travelled on the branch on the first day to enjoy the experience of moving at more than twice the speed of a horse at the trot. The derailment of a locomotive at the end of the day at North Weald took some of the shine off the opening events, such as they were, and the last train finally reached Ongar at about 5am!

Meanwhile, changes were afoot at the London end of the line which ultimately were to affect services to and from Ongar. The Blackwall Railway, which had allowed the ECR to use its terminus at Fenchurch Street, leased this station to the GER for 999 years. The GER renamed their Shoreditch terminus as Bishopsgate, probably to encourage the idea that it was a City terminus. However, Bishopsgate was in every possible way unsuitable for this purpose and in 1865 the GER obtained the necessary Parliamentary powers to build a new terminus in the Finsbury Circus area. The final agreed site was in Liverpool Street, which gave its name to the new station. Ongarians hoping to travel to the new GER terminus had to wait for ten years, by which time the new station was already too small and expansion plans were being drawn up. However, passengers would have found the Bishopsgate or Fenchurch Street journey far more convenient than the mail coach from Ongar to London, which took over two hours, excluding a break at the King's Head, Chigwell, to change horses. The one hour train journey must have seemed dangerously fast!

In the early days, there were three weekday up trains to Fenchurch Street, and one up to Shoreditch. Down trains were of the same frequency. The Sunday equivalent was two and one respectively.[6] This was a marked improvement on the frequency of the coach service which it replaced. Carey's *New Itinerary of the Great Roads* of 1812 shows that the Ongar mail coach arrived in the town at 10am. and departed for London at 3pm. Another option would have been to pick up the Chelmsford Epping London stage coach on the Epping Road.

When the Ongar line opened, it was the terminus of a single track extension from Loughton, and train paths had to be organised to ensure that they did not meet. In order to avoid collisions, a Special Order, number 142, prohibited trains from travelling in either direction between Loughton and Ongar without a train "staff" or "ticket." The winter timetable of 1865 shows that only two weekday trains met on the single track, but these were timed to meet at Epping where the goods train could be shunted into a siding to allow the passenger train to pass. This timetable suggests that it was not possible for two trains to pass anywhere on this section by means of a loop, implying that all stations on the extension would have had single platforms.[7] This was probably the result of the GER's shortage of money at this time, which also necessitated following the contours of the ground fairly closely as well as the use of level crossings, rather than bridges.

The Ongar "branch"

The line between Ongar and Epping has long been referred to as the "Ongar branch", though it does not diverge from a line leading elsewhere at Epping. In the early days, the whole route from Stratford would have been a "branch of the Great

ASPECTS OF THE HISTORY OF ONGAR

Eastern", but it would have ceased to be a branch when it was destined to become part of the underground Central Line under the 1935 London Transport Modernisation Plans. The term branch would have been used again after 1949 when Central Line trains reached Epping, and only the last 6¼ miles to Ongar were steam hauled.

Coaching stock

When the railway first opened, four wheel carriages were common to all passenger trains. These were quite short. The normal pattern of operation was to run 15 carriages to Loughton, where five were detached to be worked through to Ongar. Writing about the GER, C. J. Allen was rather critical of these four wheelers, noting that *'suburban rolling stock was spartan to a degree, owing to the urgent necessity to cram the maximum number of passengers into the minimum possible space…the use of four wheeled vehicles persisted long after other companies were doing all their work with bogie-set trains'.*[8] The shortening of down, and lengthening of up trains at Loughton added between four and nine minutes to the journey, but at least passengers could remain in their carriages, an advantage denied to later commuters.

Towards the end of the nineteenth century, the GER realised that, due to the growing population of the area served by the line, the track between Loughton and Epping should be doubled. This work was completed in 1892 and enabled a much more intensive timetable to be run. Nevertheless, they were still using the archaic four wheeled stock on suburban services. The third class carriages had low dividing walls between compartments, essentially "open thirds" with wooden benches seating five passengers on each side. The second class equivalent were marginally better, with the same layout but upholstered seats. First class had a four a side layout, with one less compartment per carriage to give extra leg room. In 1899, Ongarians would have been impressed by the new carriages which began to make their appearance in that year. Though still four wheeled and gas lit, they provided seating for up to 60 third class passengers per coach in five compartments. This was achieved by building the carriages nine feet wide, making room for six-a-side seating. Another new feature was the slam-door spring-lock system which became the regular form of railway door closure until quite recently.

Extension plans

By the turn of the century, the GER system spread right across Essex into East Anglia. Stimulated by the 1896 Light Railways Act, consideration was given in 1897 to the construction of a light railway from Ongar to Great Dunmow (via the Roding valley) on to Great Yeldham. There would have been an interchange with the Bishop's Stortford to Braintree line at Dunmow. This was one of a number of schemes for extending the line which are summarised at the end of this chapter. In 1910, the GER was working its intensive suburban services at full throttle. Freight traffic had also increased, as shown locally by the enlargement of the goods yard at Ongar with the addition of a new long siding on its southern edge. For Ongar residents using the line in this year, the earliest through train to London was the 7.15am to Fenchurch Street, arriving at 8.26am. A change at Stratford would have connected with a train reaching Liverpool Street at 8.48am. The next trains out of Ongar were the 7.55am to Liverpool Street and the 8.42am to Fenchurch Street. The next three (at 9.39am, 10.30am and 11.33am) went to Liverpool Street, with a 12.38pm train to Fenchurch Street. The afternoon trains were the 2.45pm and the 4.08pm both to Liverpool Street. The evening service was the 5.12pm to Fenchurch Street, the 5.55pm to Liverpool Street, the 6.48pm to Fenchurch Street, ending with the 8.21pm and the 10.30pm to Liverpool Street. The down service was of similar variation and frequency, except for the unusual feature that the last train from Fenchurch Street, due at Ongar at 11.39pm, only went as far as Epping on Wednesdays! The fastest journey was made by the 9.00am out of Ongar which ran non-stop to Epping and reached Liverpool Street at 9.56am. Analysis of the timetable suggests that two trains were stabled overnight at Ongar.[9]

In the early years of the twentieth century, the GER had to face the problem of how to deal with the ever growing numbers of commuters. This was not a problem on the Epping–Ongar section, but the effects of decisions made would affect local passengers. Serious thought was given to wholesale electrification, but this would have cost in the region of £5million and the idea was promptly dropped. Instead the GER looked at other ways of increasing capacity. Carriages with a larger passenger capacity were one answer. The GER's prolonged use of four wheel coaches, long after other companies had abandoned them, has already been mentioned. The GER was also slow to abandon six wheel coaches, on grounds of economy, and even between the wars there were occasional sightings of these vehicles. However, bogie coaches began to enter suburban service in 1911. These were much smoother running than the shorter coaches, and had slightly higher ceilings due to the use of elliptical roofs, rather that the flatter ones on the old stock. These new coaches were allocated to the Loughton line, and would have eventually appeared at Ongar. They were built in the traditional varnished teak and retained the double running boards designed for the very low platforms at certain stations.

In 1919 the familiar teak was being replaced by a dark crimson, not unlike the Midland Railway. But new colour schemes could not solve passenger handling problems, any more than they can today. In 1920, the general manager of the GER, addressing the Institute of Transport, referred to the problems of handling 11 passengers every second between 5pm and 6pm at Liverpool Street. Due to the high cost of electrification and the lack of skilled labour, he thought that the only way forward was the scientific remodelling of their steam suburban service.[8] This policy was successful and increased capacity by 25%. But to what avail? Passenger numbers continued to rise, and at Ongar it is doubtful whether any benefits would have been noticed.

In 1923, with the problem still unresolved, the whole GER system passed into the

ASPECTS OF THE HISTORY OF ONGAR

ownership of the London & North Eastern Railway (LNER) as a consequence of the Railways Act of 1921. There would have been few changes at Ongar, except that the coaching stock reverted to varnished teak and the locomotives lost their familiar blue livery. However there were moves in the corridors of power, and in 1933 the formation of the London Passenger Transport Board (LPTB) enabled the LNER to work towards a coordinated transport policy.

One result of these discussions was the plan to extend the underground Central Line (then called the Central London Line) eastwards from Liverpool Street to Newbury Park via Stratford and Leytonstone. The aim was to take some of the pressure off Liverpool Street mainline station by annexing all LNER lines to the north and east of Leytonstone to the underground network. All these lines, including the Ongar section, were to be electrified to take tube trains. LNER would still continue to operate steam hauled freight trains over these lines, with steam and tube stock sharing the same tracks. These plans were embodied in the 1935 New Works Programme, backed by a £40million guarantee. In March 1937, LPTB published the north east London electrification plan in which there was, for the first time, a hint that Ongar would cease to have through trains to London and would be linked by shuttle trains to Loughton. An electrical substation at Blake Hall station would enable 8 car trains to run to Ongar.[10] However though some tunnelling and other work was done in the late 1930s, the outbreak of World War II put everything on the back burner, apart from one or two projects such as the rebuilding of Loughton station, completed in 1940.

The 1945 Abercrombie plan[11] proposed that Ongar should be expanded as a new town for 60,000 people. Part of the plan was to do what the GER had considered but never done – to extend the railway from Ongar to the main line at Chelmsford. Incredibly, it was intended that this should be administered by London Transport, raising the spectre of a marathon tube journey from Chelmsford to London via Ongar! Ongar station would have changed beyond recognition, the present single platform being replaced by three island platforms. If the Abercrombie plans had materialised, the line would probably have been doubled between Ongar and Epping, and possibly quadrupled from there. Quadruple track from Stratford to Woodford was already under consideration by the GER at the time of the 1923 grouping. With hindsight, it is possible to see that further quadrupling would have enabled fast electric trains to run from Ongar to Liverpool Street, stopping at Epping, Loughton, Woodford and Stratford to connect with the Central Line for intermediate stations.

Electrification was gradually extended after the war, and the steam service was progressively shortened. By 1949, steam only remained on the Epping-Ongar section. In the same year, W. French were given the contract to build a second platform at North Weald to provide a crossing place to allow more trains to run between Epping and Ongar. However, even as the third and fourth rails were being laid on this section, London Transport was having cold feet about full electrification to Ongar.

Changes under the LNER

In 1937, through trains were still the order of the day, but only very early trains went to Fenchurch Street with the majority going to Liverpool Street.[12] The weekday service offered 17 trains each way, increasing to 19 on Saturdays when the last down train left Liverpool Street at midnight, arriving at Ongar at 1.06am. There was a Sunday service of six trains each way.

All this would have come to an end with the war. The first major change was the end of through trains to London at off peak times. For the first time, a shuttle service was run between Ongar and Epping. The presence of an operational airfield at North Weald would have ensured that services were fairly well maintained. Nevertheless, the thorny question of how much – or how little – should be spent on the Epping-Ongar section was under discussion again after the war. The outcome was an improvement programme with upgrading of the signalling system (still semaphore) and a passing loop at North Weald. By far the most important change from the operational point of view was the installation at Ongar of a crossover facing from the loop line, trailing into the platform road halfway along the platform face.

This additional trackwork gave Ongar station the ability to deal with two trains simultaneously on one platform face (inspired perhaps by Cambridge's example). This modification preceded the introduction of push-pull trains (avoiding the need for locomotives to be moved from one end of the train to the other at Epping and Ongar). These two improvements gave Ongar travellers the luxury of a train every 20 minutes, though there was still the inconvenience of the change at Epping. Three trains operated on the single track at peak times. The down train crossed the up train at North Weald, with the former arriving at the street end of Ongar station via the loop. One minute later, the third train, which had been waiting at the signal box end of the same platform, departed for Epping. The newly arrived train then moved up to the signal box, ready for its own departure, making room for the next train coming into Ongar. It was a highly successful merry-go-round arrangement.

Transfer to London Transport

The acquisition of the Ongar branch by London Transport (LT) in 1949 would have been seen as further progress, but this did not herald immediate electrification. In 1952 there was a three week trial of a new light weight diesel multiple unit, suggesting that LT was looking at other options. No definite decision was reached until the end of 1956. Even then, electrification was to be carried out at minimal cost, with no sub-station at Blake Hall and no possibility of running eight car trains on the branch. Ongar was doomed to remain at the end of a shuttle service when steam gave way to electricity. The switch took place on the weekend of 16–17 November 1957, with the two car tube stock going into revenue service from 18 November. Only two tube trains were needed to work the branch, due to their slightly faster speeds. Before this change, the branch was closed for the morning of Sunday 29 September to allow the power cables to be installed.[15]

ASPECTS OF THE HISTORY OF ONGAR

In theory, it was still possible to travel from Ongar to Liverpool Street main line station via the original link between Leyton and Stratford, but this rarely happened. For many years the first two up trains out of Epping on Sundays were diesel multiple units which used this route, as did seasonal excursion trains from Loughton on certain Sundays. Goods trains continued to use the link but were restricted to night time operation. Some Ongar residents, moving into new properties near the station in the 1950s, found their sleep disturbed by over-enthusiastic shunting in the small hours! The nightly goods trains continued until the withdrawal of freight services in the spring of 1966. The goods yard tracks were lifted soon afterwards.

The last steam passenger trains to visit Ongar were specials organised by the Locomotive Club of Great Britain on 7 April and 28 April 1962. These travelled from Liverpool Street to Palace Gates, Chingford, Stratford, Ongar, Stratford, North Woolwich and back to the main terminus. These specials used the connecting link at Leyton, and consisted of two main line corridor coaches hauled by a J15 tender locomotive. It was probably the only occasion when corridor coaches took passengers to Ongar. The platform run around loop was already out of action at Ongar, and the train had to be hauled into the goods yard to use the surviving loop there. An eyewitness reported that enthusiasts *'were milling about all over the place'* in the goods yard, and some strong words were being uttered by railway staff![16] There was reason to be glad of the Leyton link in the bad winter of 1969/70 when heavy snow prevented LT from running electric trains. British Rail helped out with the loan of a diesel multiple unit, and, though this ran from Epping, it did not appear on the Ongar branch. The link at Leyton was finally severed in the winter of 1972/3, ending the possibility of linking Ongar to the main line system.[17]

The first closure proposal

Services began to decline. The first rumbles of trouble ahead came in 1970 when LT withdrew its proposal to stop all Sunday services on the branch, but announced plans to close the line completely. LT gave formal notice of its intentions in the summer of 1970, claiming that the line was losing £100,000 a year. The statutory enquiry took place, and two years later the Secretary of State announced his refusal to the closure on the grounds of potential hardship to users. Despite the closure proposals, Ongar station became important for a very unusual reason in 1972. Previously, all railway distances had been calculated in miles and chains but, with the gradual change to the metric system, LT decided to recalibrate the underground system on a common basis with a single datum point. Ongar, being the most easterly part, was chosen as this datum point, and a low post displaying the legend "0.0" was installed where the track ended. The few who understood the significance of this wondered if LT would be able to close the line, if the whole system was measured from Ongar!

The second closure proposal

In 1979, concerned about the future of the line, a group of individuals formed the

THE RAILWAYS OF ONGAR

Epping Ongar Railway Society (EORS) with a view to running a diesel multiple unit commuter service in the event of closure, supplemented with steam hauled "leisure" trains at the weekend. It registered the Epping Forest Railway Company and made plans while awaiting the next closure proposal. There was not long to wait. In the spring of 1980, LT informed the Greater London Council that it was intending to seek a closure order in view of losses of £600,000 per annum on the branch. Passenger numbers were down to 650 per day, mainly at peak hours. An accusing finger was pointed at Essex County Council which had never provided a subsidy, the LT chairman being quoted as saying *'it is manifestly unfair that GLC ratepayers should meet the whole cost of the deficit.'* As LT had made a loss of £15.7 million in 1979, it was understandable that it wished to rid itself of the loss making branch.[18]

Local authority concerns about the effects of closure led to a passenger survey being conducted in June 1980.[19] Many felt that LT's figures were inflated, the best known story being that two maintenance engineers had been sent out from central London to change a light bulb at Ongar station. Whether this was fact or fiction, a new group, the Epping and Ongar Rail Users Committee (EORUC), was set up to oppose the closure. The arguments became triangular, with EORUC accusing EORS of encouraging LT to abandon the line, and LT defending its costings against EORUC's scepticism. EORS decided to keep its head down while this was going on, but continued to make plans for finances, trains and timetables. The first shares were issued for the Epping Forest Railway Company.

By November 1980, it was reported that 500 objections had been received and a two day public enquiry was duly held at the Budworth Hall. In May 1981, the Minister of State for Transport announced that he had refused closure of the line, but that he had approved the closure of Blake Hall station as well as the reduction of services to peak hours only. This was a somewhat hollow victory for EORUC. EORS, numbering several hundred members, felt that unopposed closure would have enabled them, almost immediately, to bring new life, new hope and new trains to the branch. The society had no choice but to wind up its company, refund its shareholders and disband its membership. The reduced service started on 2 November 1981, and passenger numbers continued to decline.

LT made an attempt to reverse this decline by re-introducing off peak services on 30 October 1989. However, the ever present threat of closure stimulated the formation of another preservation society, the Ongar Railway Preservation Society (ORPS). This was an entirely different body of enthusiasts who seemed unaware that they were on a well trodden path of investigating the viability of running a preserved railway. However there was one fundamental difference between EORS and ORPS. With the former, the agreed and stated aim from the start was the running of a commercial commuter service, whereas with ORPS the main objective was running a weekend steam service with LT still operating its weekday commuter service. Even after the third (and successful) closure proposal in 1994, ORPS gave low priority to running a commuter service. This difference would prove to be crucial.

ASPECTS OF THE HISTORY OF ONGAR

There was never any doubt that the branch could be run successfully as a leisure line. What other railway in the country had a line of optimum length running through pleasant countryside, with challenging gradients, original Victorian stations and an interchange point with a London underground station? This point was well proved when LT celebrated the line's 125th anniversary on 27 May 1990. Running its four car Cravens set between Epping and Ongar, such were the crowds that station staff at Ongar had to give the well known central London shout of *'Let 'em off first please!'*

Successful closure

The third application by London Underground Limited (LUL was the successor to LT) to close the line was successful after another public enquiry on 8 November 1993. The last train, a Cravens set resplendent in red and cream livery (motor driving cars 3906 and 3907, and 1938 tube stock trailer 4927), left Ongar station to the crack of fog detonators on 30 September 1994. One of the conditions for the closure consent was that LUL should find an alternative operator within three years of closing the line. ORPS was the only organisation to submit a tender by the LUL deadline of 6 November 1995, but a request from a potential commercial buyer, Pilot Developments Ltd, for a six week extension was allowed. In due course LUL announced that Pilot were the preferred bidders. A somewhat lengthy wrangle then ensued, involving the two rival bidders, as well as Ongar parish council and Epping Forest District Council. This culminated in representations to the Minister of Transport who, in July 1998, upheld LUL's decision, subject to certain conditions. The main reason for the success of the bid by Pilot Developments was their undertaking to provide a commuter service.

Pilot Developments (subsequently named Epping & Ongar Railway Ltd) completed the purchase of the line in September 1998 and Ongar residents await developments with interest. There is both hope and scepticism. Will the new owners be any more successful than previous operators, and will they have a commuter service running by the promised date of autumn 2000? Time will tell.

Accidents

Serious accidents have been rare on the branch. In January 1864, a navvy was killed during the building of the line. In November of the same year, five trucks of ballast ran away near North Weald, passing through the unopened station at an estimated 70 mph and doing considerable damage before crashing.[13] On the evening of the first day of operation in 1865, as already mentioned, there was a derailment at North Weald.

On Saturday December 5 1903, the rear part of a goods train ran off the line near Ongar station while being shunted to make room for a passenger train. Swift action by the station master enabled a passenger train to be held at Epping moments before it was due to depart. A breakdown gang was called out and it was not until late evening that the line was cleared. Part of the obstruction was reported as "coping", suggesting that the Cripsey viaduct had been damaged. It seems that the signalman may have changed the points before the trucks had cleared because the fog had prevented him from seeing their exact position.[20]

The most serious accident occurred on 19 February 1934 when a down goods train went out of control in icy conditions. The signalman saw the runaway train, headed by a J15 0-6-0, and diverted it into the platform run-around loop. After racing at speed down the loop, the driver and fireman jumped clear before the locomotive demolished the rail stops at the end of the line, and ran up the bank below the High Street. The engine suffered considerable damage, and had to be pulled clear with the aid of a towing locomotive and a steam crane.[21]

On 7 June 1957 a Hunter jet fighter crashed on the line just south of North Weald station, narrowly missing a push-pull unit with an F5 locomotive 67913. On 19 November 1971, snow caused problems, and the 11.28 shuttle from Ongar had braking difficulties on the down gradient into Epping. The train overran platform 1, and was diverted by trap points into the sand drag. This was not sufficient to stop it and the end stops were demolished.[21]

Motive power

Over its 135 year history, the Epping–Ongar line has had the rare distinction of seeing every known form of motive power apart from horses. In the main, steam ruled for the first 92 years and electricity for the 37 years up to closure in 1994, but there were occasional variations. One of these was a petrol driven power unit, said to have been used for a while prior to the First World War. The engine was carefully constructed by the GER to match the coaching stock then in use, and was placed centrally in the train, as a push-pull arrangement with four-wheeled carriages did not recommend itself. No specifications have been found for this unusual unit, but the author has seen a contemporary post card showing a train in Ongar station with an unusual centrally placed, non-standard carriage. There is also an unconfirmed report from the late 1930s of a Sunday rail bus which left the track at Ongar station, taking the road to travel to Moreton and Fyfield.[22]

The second variation was an experimental light weight diesel multiple unit tried out on the line in the summer of 1952. This three car unit, built by A. C. V. Sales Ltd, consisted of two powered cars using a six cylinder diesel engine identical to those in the contemporary Greenline buses. There was a central trailer, and each car was about 40 feet in length. The unit accommodated 129 passengers, and after some trial runs was used for passenger services between 16 and 27 June. The unit was also tried out later on the Metropolitan line at Chalfont Latimer.

Battery locomotives were seen on the line from time to time, including one that was equipped for de-icing. After closure by LUL, a pair of battery locomotives were used to propel an eight-car tube set into Ongar station on 18 October 1996 as part of a publicity venture connected with Pilot Development's acquisition of the line. British Rail's freight service to Ongar from Temple Mills generally relied on a Type 1 Bo-Bo diesel locomotive (D 8200 series) up to the time that freight was withdrawn in 1966.

ASPECTS OF THE HISTORY OF ONGAR

Steam locomotives

In 1865, Ongar had its own locomotive shed, together with a water tank of more than adequate capacity. The importance of the Ongar shed diminished in the latter years of the nineteenth century when a new shed, capable of stabling 10 to 12 engines, was built at Epping.[3] The Ongar shed continued to do minor repairs until after the Second World War when it was closed and demolished.

In 1865, Robert C. Sinclair was in charge of GER locomotive design, and it might be assumed that his sturdy looking Class Y 2-4-0 tender engines were seen on the branch. Within a few years, he was replaced by S. W. Johnson (later of Midland Railway fame) who recognised the importance of tank engines on branch lines. In the early 1870s, he introduced an 0-4-2T (T7) which is likely to have appeared in Ongar. Johnson's successor was William Adams who was responsible for the Class 61 0-4-4T, but precise information on the motive power used to Ongar in the nineteenth and early twentieth century is lacking.

By the 1920s, several sources confirm that 2-4-2 tank engines were used, designed by T. W. Worsdell, nicknamed "The Gobblers" from their heavy fuel consumption. Some later tank engines of similar appearance and the same wheel formation were given the same nickname, but the genuine "Gobblers" were Worsdell's creation. An article in *The Railway Magazine* of 1920 refers to occasional sightings of the *'0-4-4 engines of the 1100 class, and now and then an 0-6-0T.'*[14] The "1100 class" referred to was most probably the S44 (designed by James Holden), the first batch with the numbers 1100 to 1139 being built in 1898. Holden's name was synonymous with good locomotive design on the GER, and his 0-6-0 engines, introduced at about the same time, were extensively used on suburban work. Freight trains on the Ongar line were handled by the well known Worsdell J15 tender engines of 0-6-0 wheel formation.

By 1938 haulage of Ongar trains was firmly under a later fleet of 2-4-2Ts, reclassified under LNER management as type F5. Numbers 7144 and 7147 were on regular duty, but in 1947 fourteen type N7 0-6-2T engines, numbered 9612 to 9625, were moved from Stratford to Epping. This fleet was reduced at the end of the year when electrification had reached Woodford. In 1948 there was an interesting change when the remaining N7s were withdrawn and a new batch of F5s appeared. Numbers 7200–7203, 7209–7011, 7213 and 7214 went to Epping, and 7198 was sent to Ongar.[23] At about this time the quintuple articulated coach sets were replaced by three coach sets of older stock, giving the impression of going back, rather than forward, in time!

On 25 September 1949 a service of push-pull trains started on the Ongar branch, using five modified F5 engines numbered 67193, 67200, 67202, 67203 and 67218 (the last was subsequently replaced by 67213). There were occasional changes. A C12 No. 67363, drafted in from Annesley, appeared at Epping in mid 1953 and worked the Ongar line for about three months. In 1956, there was an unusual development when a J15 No. 65455 appeared on passenger duties, and equally surprising was the arrival of an N2 No. 69546, followed a week later by a Class 4 No. 76401.[26] None of these engines was fitted with push-pull apparatus, so for a while passengers were treated to the spectacle of locomotives using the run around loop at Ongar station. To complete the variety, a Holden type F4 0-4-4, believed to be of North Eastern Railway origin, was brought for use on the Ongar line after being made redundant on the Palace Gates branch. As mentioned above, the last steam train to visit was the special hauled by a J15 No. 65476 on 28 April 1962.

Tube trains

Ongar - Epping **Central Line Table 1**

SHOWING CONNECTIONS TO THE CITY AND WEST END

MONDAY to FRIDAY

ONGAR	05 12	06 13	06 41	07 01	07 23	07 43	08 03	08 23	08 43	09 03	09 39	10 15	10 51	11 27	12 03	12 39	13 15	13 51	14 27	15 03	15 39	16 15	16 49	17 10	17 30	17 50
Blake Hall	16	17	45	05	27	47	07	27	47	07	43	19	55	31	07	43	19	55	31	07	43	19	53	14	34	54
North Weald	21	22	50	10	32	52	12	32	52	12	48	24	11 00	36	12	48	24	14 00	36	13	48	24	58	20	40	18 02
EPPING arr	28	29	57	17	39	08 00	19	39	59	19	54	30	06	42	18	54	30	06	42	18	54	30	17 04	26	46	08
•Leytonstone *LT* arr	53	54	07 23	43	08 07	27	45	09 05	09 26	47	10 23	59	35	12 11	47	13 23	59	35	15 11	47	16 23	59	29	51	18 18	36
•Liverpool St. *LT* arr	06 08	07 09	39	59	24	44	09 02	22	41	10 02	38	11 14	50	26	13 02	38	14 14	50	26	16 02	38	17 14	44	18 06	33	51
•Oxford Circus arr	06 20	07 21	07 51	08 11	08 37	08 57	09 15	09 35	09 53	10 14	10 50	11 26	12 02	12 38	13 14	13 50	14 26	15 02	15 38	16 14	16 50	17 27	17 57	18 18	18 45	19 06

MONDAY to FRIDAY–continued

ONGAR	18 10	18 30	18 50	19 10	19 30	19 51	20 27	21 03	21 39	22 26	23 19	24 00
Blake Hall	14	34	54	14	34	55	31	07	43	30	23	00 04
North Weald	22	43	19 00	22	40	20 00	36	12	48	35	28	09
EPPING arr	28	49	06	28	46	06	42	18	54	41	34	00 15
•Leytonstone *LT* arr	59	19 23	36	59	20 11	35	21 11	47	22 23	23 07	00 05	....
•Liverpool St. *LT* arr	19 14	38	51	20 14	26	50	26	22 02	38	22	20	....
•Oxford Circus arr	19 26	19 50	20 02	20 26	20 38	21 02	21 38	22 14	22 50	23 35	00 32	....

SATURDAY

ONGAR	05 12	06 13	06 45	07 15	07 36	07 56	08 17	08 37	09 17	09 57	10 37	11 17	11 57	12 39
Blake Hall	16	17	49	19	40	08 00	21	41	21	10 01	41	21	12 01	43
North Weald	21	22	54	24	45	05	26	46	26	06	46	26	06	49
EPPING arr	28	29	07 00	30	51	11	32	52	32	12	52	32	12	55
•Leytonstone *LT* arr	53	07 02	27	57	08 18	38	59	09 19	59	39	11 19	12 01	41	13 19
•Liverpool St. *LT* arr	06 08	17	42	08 12	33	53	09 16	36	10 16	56	36	16	56	34
•Oxford Circus arr	06 20	07 29	07 54	08 24	08 45	09 05	09 28	09 48	10 28	11 08	11 48	12 28	13 08	13 46

SATURDAY–continued

ONGAR	12 59	13 19	13 39	13 59	14 19	14 39	15 17	15 57	16 37	17 17	17 57	18 37	19 16	19 51	20 27	21 03	21 39	22 26	23 19	24 00
Blake Hall	13 03	23	43	14 03	23	43	21	16 01	41	21	18 01	41	20	55	31	07	43	30	23	00 04
North Weald	09	29	49	09	29	48	26	06	46	26	06	46	25	20 00	36	12	48	35	28	09
EPPING arr	15	35	55	15	35	54	32	12	52	32	12	54	31	06	42	18	54	41	34	00 15
•Leytonstone *LT* arr	39	59	14 19	39	59	15 19	59	39	17 19	59	39	19 19	59	35	21 11	47	22 23	23 08	00 05	....
•Liverpool St. *LT* arr	54	14 14	34	54	15 14	15 34	16 14	54	34	18 14	54	34	20 14	50	26	22 02	38	23	20	....
•Oxford Circus arr	14 06	14 26	14 46	15 06	15 26	15 46	16 26	17 06	17 46	18 26	19 06	19 46	20 26	21 02	21 38	22 14	22 50	23 35	00 32	....

SUNDAY

ONGAR	06 43	07 21	08 10	08 55	09 37	10 14
Blake Hall	47	25	14	59	41	18
North Weald	52	30	19	09 04	46	23
EPPING arr	58	36	25	10	52	29
•Leytonstone *LT* arr	07 24	08 03	51	37	10 22	59
•Liverpool St. *LT* arr	39	18	09 06	52	37	11 14
•Oxford Circus arr	07 51	08 30	09 18	10 04	10 49	11 26

SUNDAY–continued

ONGAR	10 51	11 27	12 03	12 39	13 15	13 51	14 27	15 03	15 39	16 15	16 51	17 27	18 03	18 39	19 15	19 51	20 27	21 03	21 38	22 37	23 13	23 51	....	....	....	....
Blake Hall	55	31	07	43	19	55	31	07	43	19	55	31	07	43	19	55	31	07	43	41	17	55	....	....	....	....
North Weald	11 00	36	12	48	24	14 00	36	12	48	24	17 00	36	12	48	24	20 00	36	12	48	46	22	24 00	....	....	....	....
EPPING arr	06	42	18	54	30	06	42	18	54	30	06	42	18	54	30	06	42	18	54	52	23 28	00 06	....	....	....	....
•Leytonstone *LT* arr	35	12 11	47	13 23	59	35	15 11	47	16 23	59	35	18 11	47	19 23	59	35	21 11	47	22 23	23 18	....	....	....	....	....	....
•Liverpool St. *LT* arr	50	26	13 02	38	14 14	50	26	16 02	38	17 14	50	26	19 02	38	20 14	50	26	22 02	38	33	....	....	....	....	....	....
•Oxford Circus arr	12 02	12 38	13 14	13 50	14 26	15 02	15 38	16 14	16 50	17 26	18 02	18 38	19 14	19 50	20 26	21 02	21 38	22 14	22 50	23 45	....	....	....	....	....	....

A–Change at Loughton, not at Epping. •–Change at Epping, unless otherwise shown.

Figure 19 London Transport timetable of July 1965.

From 18 November 1957 two 2-car sets of tube stock replaced the steam shuttle. It would have been an unfortunate time of year to make the change, with the doors left open for long periods while waiting at Epping and Ongar, combined with the poor output of the electric heaters. In the early 1960s the old tube stock was replaced by new 4-car sets, built by Metro-Cammell in unpainted aluminium. In the last years, two Cravens sets, painted red, were used on the branch. One of these sets is now in preservation, appearing on special occasions on various parts of London Underground system.

Stations

The three station buildings on the branch have been described as *'ranking as amongst the finest on the Great Eastern system'* and, apart from a few alterations, and a little re-building after accidental demolition at Blake Hall, all are original. They are of the standard GER pattern of the time, with a two storey station master's

ASPECTS OF THE HISTORY OF ONGAR

house attached to a single storey block containing station offices, waiting rooms etc. North Weald has the only surviving GER signal box (albeit on a later brick base), including its original lever frame, though the block signalling instruments have gone. Most of the ancillary buildings on the branch have gone, including the water tower, locomotive shed, goods shed, signal box and station master's wash house at Ongar. The concrete base of the goods yard crane remains at Ongar, as do the loading bays here and at North Weald, both of course without track. Ongar station, although a terminus, was laid out as a through station due to the original intention to extend the line.

Freight traffic

Railway freight offered advantages of speed and cheapness over horse drawn transport, particularly over longer distances. Thus all kinds of merchandise came to Ongar by rail and the yard was often packed to capacity. In 1900, the yard was enlarged by adding a long siding on the south side. Down goods included coal, agricultural machinery, chemical fertilisers, animal feed (including brewer's grains), building materials, street sweepings, sludge from Lea Bridge sewage works and lime from London's gasworks. Traffic in brewer's grains continued all the year as farmers would pit several hundred tons for winter use during the summer months.

Up goods included potatoes, wheat, barley, cattle beans, sugar beet, hay, straw, livestock, timber (some for the Darlington railway works) and milk, as well as all parcels over the Post Office maximum of ten pounds in weight. On payment of an extra 3d, letters would be taken for posting at Liverpool Street. Hay and straw required a lot of work, as each wagon needed two truck sheets and two ropes to secure. This was to protect against the risk of fire from sparks from a locomotive.[25] Milk was particularly good business for the railway, and at its zenith, just after the First World War, 1200 gallons of milk were conveyed from Ongar every week. Full churns arrived twice a day at the loading dock by farm cart or lorry. However, this trade was killed by the General Strike of 1926, when necessity demonstrated that the whole job could be done more simply from door to door by lorry. Coal continued to arrive by train until the closure of the yard in 1966, and in spite of the recent growth in rail freight, it seems very unlikely that freight traffic will ever return to the Ongar yard.

Expansion and economies – Ongar station's rise and fall

Passengers travelling to and from Ongar in the tube era became accustomed to seeing no more than one person on duty at Ongar station and, after the installation of an automatic ticket dispenser, perhaps not even that, in spite of that machine's frequent rejection of legitimate banknotes in good condition! But in the past it was very different when the station staff numbered seven or eight – and more, if the staff in the goods yard, engine shed, signal box and so on were included. In the 1920s, the ticket office was open from 6am to 10pm, and the goods office from 8am to 6pm on weekdays, 8am to 1pm on Saturdays.[25] The growth of staff is reflected by the construction of a detached porters' room in 1887, carefully designed to match the style of the 1865 buildings. In 1896, another building was added – a store shed for foot warmers, an important aspect of passenger comfort in the days before train heating. Four staff cottages were built by the GER in Bansons Way in 1892, with a further seven opposite them in 1912.

Proposals to extend the line

Examination of a map of the railway network prior to 1900 shows that one rural area of the Home Counties was relatively untouched by the long tentacles of the system. This large area lay to the north east of Ongar. Soon after completion to Ongar, the GER considered an extension to Dunmow along the Roding valley, with a subsequent plan to extend to Bury St Edmunds in 1888.[29] The very poor financial condition of the company prevented the realisation of either of these. Other GER suggestions were to extend to the main line at Chelmsford or Ingatestone,[26] a scheme which was revived by the 1945 Abercrombie plan which included freight sidings to serve the industrial estate planned at High Ongar.[11] The GER terminus at Chingford, like Ongar, was built as a through station, and there were plans in 1864 to extend to High Beech and, ultimately, Epping. This would have linked Chingford to Ongar and any station beyond. Just over 100 years after the 1865 opening, the GER idea of an extension from Ongar to Dunmow was revived. Though no details of this proposal can be found, one assumes that it was quickly realised that long journeys by tube train through open country were not likely to be financially viable!

Part 2: Light railways with a terminus at Ongar

By the end of the nineteenth century, most major cities had a railway in or near them. But there were huge areas of countryside without convenient access to a railhead because the potential useage could not justify the financial outlay. By reducing the infrastructure requirements, the 1896 Light Railways Act stimulated the building of new lines by reducing construction and operating costs. Two such light railways were planned with a terminus at Ongar, not necessarily connected to the line from London

The Central Essex Light Railway was planned to run from Ongar via High Easter to Dunmow to connect with the Stortford-Braintree line. After Dunmow, the proposed line proceeded to Great Yeldham via Great Bardfield and Finchingfield, the total distance from Ongar being about 28 miles. At Great Yeldham, connection with the Colne Valley and Halstead railway was intended. The line was authorised to be built in 1901 but for some reason – possibly difficulty in raising funds – work was never started. Extensions to the authorisation were made in 1905, 1907 and 1908. The projected railway was shown on the Clearing House maps for several years but the scheme was dropped at the beginning of the First World War. It last appeared on the Clearing House map of 1917. The promoter was (Colonel) H. F. Stephens, a very active promoter of light railways in Essex and elsewhere.

ASPECTS OF THE HISTORY OF ONGAR

No sooner had the Central Essex Light Railway disappeared than a new company – the Essex Light Railway and Property Company – applied to build an almost identical line, called the Mid Essex Light Railway. The main difference between the two was the name of the company! The railway was authorised subject to the usual provisions that it should be built *'with all proper and sufficient rails, plates, sidings, junctions, turntables, bridges, culverts, drains, viaducts, stations, approaches, roads, yards, buildings and other works and conveniences connected therewith.'*

The plans of the Mid Essex Light Railway showed that it was to start *'in the parish of Chipping Ongar, in the rural district of Ongar, in the field adjoining the Great Eastern Railway, on the northern side thereof immediately opposite the western end of the booking office and fifty yards there from....'* From which it must be presumed that it would have been built on a higher level (where Bowes Drive and Marks Avenue now stand) in order that it could leave Ongar without the need for a tunnel. It would have proceeded to (or near) High Ongar, Fyfield, Beauchamp Roding, Abbess Roding, White Roding, Leaden Roding, Aythorpe Roding, High Roding, Great Canfield and Little Canfield to Dunmow where it terminated *'in a field seven chains or thereabouts west of the centre of the bridge at Dunmow station.'* The promoters were given permission to run either steam or electric trains, and to install their own generating station if necessary. Nothing more seems to have happened after obtaining authorisation, and the scheme joined the great-might-have-beens.

Plans for an Ongar to Shenfield light railway were completed on 23 July 1919. Like its contemporary, the Mid Essex Railway, its station was situated in a field near the GER station at Ongar. It would have gone east immediately, with a level crossing over the High Street, skirting the northern boundary of the cemetery and then turning south towards Kelvedon Hatch, Doddinghurst and Shenfield where it terminated close to the GER station there. It is not known if this application was ever authorised.[27]

While there has been plenty of work for surveyors and solicitors over the years, nothing ever bore fruit. It is doubtful whether any of these plans for railways in rural Essex would have succeeded financially. But there is a revival of interest in railway building at the end of the twentieth century, and the suggested Cross Rail link would connect Epping to Wimbledon with a minimum number of interchange points along the way.

Part 3: Narrow gauge industrial railways

Though not an industrial area, Ongar has had a number of minor industries which used narrow gauge rail for moving materials. There is photographic evidence of such a track at the Hallsford Bridge brickfield, though no route map or technical details have survived. It was probably 15 inch gauge, and the only rolling stock would have been a set of robust trucks to carry quarried material or completed bricks. There is no evidence of the motive power used, but it is possible that it was a simple petrol driven unit with four wheels and one driven axle.

It is said that Ongar gas works had an associated narrow gauge railway, possibly for moving coal or coke between the two sites, or across to the adjoining brickfield in the Greensted road. No photographic or other evidence has been found. In view of the short distances it is likely that such a railway would have relied on human power to propel the wagons!

The best documented industrial railway was built within five miles of Ongar in open countryside in the early 1920s.[28] This belonged to the Rom River Sand and Gravel Pit Company and ran east from the Ongar Brentwood road into Poles Wood to exploit a substantial deposit of sharp sand. The track enabled sand to be carried to the main road. Photographs suggest that it was three foot gauge, using four wheeled side tipping hoppers, each carrying about a yard of sand. The locomotive – it appears that there was only one – was of a most unusual design, probably a Simplex specially built for the company. It had a strongly built base, extending beyond the width of the trucks and concealing its wheels. The driver sat sideways between the fuel tank and the engine, and was protected from bad weather by a flimsy awning behind and above him, supported on insubstantial poles. The hoppers tipped only in the direction faced by the driver, who was presumably-seated sideways in order to oversee this operation. Judy Cowan indicates that the wagons were hauled up from the deepest part of the pit to level ground by a winch, and the unusual design of the locomotive suggests that it may have had some part to play in this.

References

1. Moody, G. T. "London Lines in the 1860s" in *The Railway World* (January 1957)
2. Carey's *New Itinerary of the Great Roads* (1812) 5th edition
3. Farmer, J. *The Great Eastern Railway as I knew it* (1991) pub privately
4. Frost, K. A."One Hundred Years of the Ongar Railway" in *Essex Countryside* (April 1965) p. 276
5. Kay, P. *The Great Eastern in Town and Country* vol 3 (1996) Irwell Press
6. trains to London are termed "up" trains, those from London "down" trains. This notation was introduced by stage coach operators, and is still used.
7. *Keeping Tracks* issues 8 & 9 (Summer & Autumn 1995) Journal of Ongar Railway Preservation Society
8. Allen, C. J. *The Great Eastern Railway* (?1955) Ian Allen Ltd
9. Bradshaw's *Guide* (1910)
10. *N.E. London Electrification* (1935) LPTB
11. Abercrombie, P. *Greater London Plan* (1945) HMSO
12. Bradshaw's *Guide* (1937)
13. Newens, A. S. *A History of North Weald Bassett and its People (1985)* North Weald
14. *The Railway Magazine* (September 1920) vol 47 p. 150
15. "Epping-Ongar Electrification" in *The Railway Magazine* (November 1957) p. 760
16. inf from Frank Hart
17. "Central Line isolated" in *The Railway Magazine* (March 1973) p. 152
18. "Epping–Ongar closure being sought" in *The Railway Magazine* (May 1980) p. 249
19. Epping/Ongar Branch Line Survey Report (Oct 1980) ECC and EFDC
20. *The Railway Magazine* (January 1904) p. 85
21. Newens, A. S. op cit. Also Middlemas, T. "Out on a limb" in *The Railway Magazine* (July 1980) p.321
22. "Ongar Station reflections 1928–1939" (undated) ms notes by V. Owers

ASPECTS OF THE HISTORY OF ONGAR

23 Middlemas, T. "Out on a limb" in *The Railway Magazine* (July 1980) p. 318
24 Kay, P. *The Great Eastern in Town and Country* vol 3 (1996) Irwell Press p. 67
25 details of goods traffic from "Ongar Station and Staff 1917" undated ms notes made by Charles Owers, junior goods clerk; and "Ongar Station reflections 1928–1939" op cit
26 Rumble, J. "Beyond Ongar" in *Keeping Tracks* issue 3 (Spring 1994) Journal of Ongar Railway Preservation Society with information from the Colonel Stephens Society.
27 Rumble, J. op cit, and *The Railway Magazine* (August 1954) p. 587. Also railway records at ERO.
28 Cowan, J. *Kelvedon Hatch – Our Village Past and Present* (1984) Pilgrims Press, Brentwood.
29 *The Railway Magazine* (Nov 1962) *p. 807*

chapter 22

The utilities

by Harry Myles

Gas

By 1815, London had had 30 miles of gas main,[1] but it was some years before other towns decided to have their own gas works. At first, householders were apprehensive about having gas in the house, due to the dangers as well as the unpleasant smell of the product of those early gas works, which lacked proper purification systems. In 1817 in Colchester Harris and Firmin, chemists in the High Street, manufactured gas on their premises to light their own and adjoining shops. By 1819, they were supplying gas for street lighting, and by 1826 growth in demand led to the formation of the Colchester Gas Light and Coke Company with 31 shareholders.[2] Chelmsford formed a gas company in 1819,[3] and Brentwood and Ongar followed in 1836,[4&5] while Epping did not have gas until 1862.[6] Demand grew slowly, but was stimulated by the invention of the gas mantle (which greatly improved the effectiveness of gas lighting), and the domestic gas cooker later in the nineteenth century. The Ongar Gas Company, established in 1836, supplied the town and the immediate area, eventually including Marden Ash, Shelley and parts of Greensted and High Ongar. In July 1837, the quarter acre site was described as '*gas works and garden*,' occupied by Thomas Evans,[7] who was probably the works manager. William Rand, described as a brick maker in 1832,[8] was the first proprietor of the Ongar gas works, and was still running both enterprises in 1845.[9] Whether he, or another local person, was responsible for setting up the company and raising the necessary capital is not clear. By 1859, Frederick Noble (of the local building firm) was the proprietor of both the gas and brick works.[10]

The Ongar gas works was situated on land adjoining the present lorry car park in the Greensted Road. Initially the gas holder was on this site, but at a later date it was sited behind 1 and 3 Coopers Hill (now Shepherd's Galleries) with gas piped to it under the main road, perhaps to make more room for gas production on the original cramped site. This gas holder was a prominent landmark entering the town from the Brentwood direction, and was finally dismantled in 1980. The works manager had his house close to the gas holder, but this was demolished in either 1939 or 1945. He then occupied a flat over the shop which sold cookers, heaters, gas mantles and clothes irons (now Shepherd's Galleries). The building behind (still surviving) was the workshop where fitters repaired appliances, and their two wheeled carts, used for deliveries to customers, were a familiar sight about town.[11]

In the early days, the gas works shared its proprietor with the brick works on the other side of the Greensted road. It is thought that they were connected by a narrow gauge railway track which would have been used for moving coal, as well as the waste clinker from the gas works which was used in brick making.[11&12] Yellow bricks with clinker inclusions, probably made in the local brick works, can be seen at the rear of Central House in the High Street. Coal, the fuel required by both enterprises, presumably came by canal to Chelmsford and then by horse drawn wagon to Ongar. When Ongar was linked to the national railway network in 1865, coal would have been obtained more conveniently from the goods yard

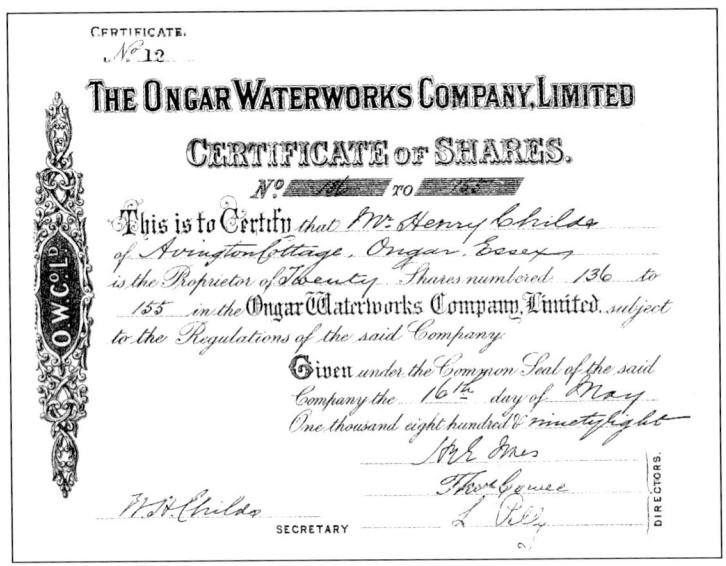

Figure 20   Ongar Waterworks Company share certificate, dated 16 May 1898.

at Ongar station. Demand grew with the acceptance of gas and the growth of the town, and in 1900 the gas works was consuming 677 tons annually, rising to 978 tons in 1910. The price of coal at this time was less than £1 per ton.[13]

By the turn of the century, the gas company was in the hands of the Jones family of Marden Ash House. The directors were Messrs H. E. Jones, T. Cowee, H. E. Brown and W. H. Childs, the company secretary being C. H. Foster. The annual general meetings were held in the Budworth Hall. In January 1910, as the company had little opportunity for expansion, the directors called an extraordinary meeting which agreed to the amalgamation with the larger Bishops Stortford and District Gas Company.[13] However, gas continued to be made at the Ongar works which produced its last batch in 1934. From then on, gas was supplied by pipeline from Epping.

Electricity arrived in the town in 1932 (and much later in the rural areas – Nine Ashes road, Stondon Massey, was not supplied until 1949)[11] but was slow to replace gas. The Budworth Hall was still almost entirely gas lit in 1946,[14] and the odd house in Castle Street, Coopers Hill and St James Avenue was still without electricity and dependent on gas light into the 1970s.[12]

THE UTILITIES

Electricity

Economic production of electricity requires large power stations and a large consumer base as was found in London, Chelmsford and Brentwood. Small towns, such as Ongar, had to rely on gas for lighting and cooking. The costs of providing power lines and installation were high, and money was short in the 1920s and 1930s, so householders were reluctant to invest in an alternative fuel.

It must be remembered that the electrical appliances that we now take for granted were not available. Though radios require electricity, early equipment used accumulators – a re-chargeable battery in a glass container with a carrying handle. These would be taken to a local shop for recharging at intervals.

A landline from Epping was installed in 1932[15] and Ongar finally had electricity. Electrical appliances, such as irons, vacuum cleaners and radios, then became available. Television, refrigerators and freezers did not become popular until the 1950s and 1960s.

Water

Up to the end of the nineteenth century, most of Ongar's water was obtained from shallow wells (20 or 30 feet deep), ponds, the Cripsey Brook and – in some cases – ditches. There were only three deep wells in the area: one at Abridge brewery was 436 feet deep, and the two others were at Stanford Rivers rectory and at Suttons, Stapleford Tawney.[16]

In the mid 1890s, Ongar parish council was campaigning for the improvement of the town's water supply. They failed to persuade both the Herts & Essex Waterworks Co. and the South Essex Waterworks Co. to extend their mains into Ongar. The council then turned to a local business man, Mr H. E. Jones (commonly known as "Gassy" Jones from his involvement in the Ongar Gas Co.) for advice on establishing a private water supply company.[17]

The Ongar Water Works Company was established in 1897 without statutory powers and remained independent until 1907 when it was taken over by the Bishops Stortford Water Works Company. Water for Ongar was obtained from a spring in a field in Shelley and was taken in open jointed earthenware pipes to the pumping station on the bank of the River Roding. From here, it was pumped up to a water tower in Shelley (on the site of what is now Heron Court). The tower was higher than the town, which enabled the water to be fed to households by gravity.[18] Unfortunately, cattle contaminated the spring, and in dry weather there were heavy losses through the open jointed pipes. The supply then had to be supplemented by pumping water direct from the River Roding, which was heavily polluted with Fyfield's sewage! The County Medical Officer of Health stated in 1898 *'the new public water supply cannot be regarded as satisfactory, as the source is dangerously liable to pollution.'*[19] The company solved this problem by fencing off the spring, installing iron supply pipes and filtering the water through several feet of special sand at the pumping station.

ASPECTS OF THE HISTORY OF ONGAR

The Ongar company was reluctant to take water from another company, even though there was a supply piped to North Weald. One reason for their reluctance was the requirement to pay 8% interest on the capital cost of extending the pipeline. However the population and the demand for water continued to grow, particularly with the building of the Hackney Cottage Homes, and it was clear that the Shelley spring could not meet the increasing demand.[18] In May 1907, the Bishops Stortford Water Co., which previously had submitted an application to the Board of Trade for a provisional order for the extension of the company's district by raising £25,000 of capital, was able to absorb the Ongar company. This expansion saw the Herts and Essex Water Co. come into existence. Mr C. H. Foster was appointed an agent for the company in the Ongar district at a salary of £25 per annum.[20]

The water supply was of much better quality, and was pumped from the Hackney Union via the Harlow pumping station. The cost of the necessary pipes was £930, with another £473 for laying them. An iron tank on brick columns was planned at Ongar (costing £1100) but this was postponed. High Ongar was connected to the main water supply in 1913.[20]

Some wells in the town were still in use in the 1930s. In July 1940, Ongar Rural District Council (ORDC) decided that the public well on the east side of Marden Ash Hill should be re-opened to provide a water supply in the event of damage to the mains by enemy action.[21] Analyses by ORDC in the 1930s and 1940s had shown that most of these wells were heavily polluted.[22] One of the main diseases caused by polluted water is typhoid fever, but strangely enough the incidence of this disease in the area was said to be half the average for England and Wales.

Sewage

Before a proper sewage system was built, many households used a small portable structure as a toilet, popularly called a "bumby", or earth closet. This was placed over a hole dug in the garden, and every so often a few shovels full of earth would be put in the hole. When the hole was full, the bumby would be moved to a new hole. After a suitable period, the old hole would be dug out and its contents spread over the vegetable patch. Ongar gardeners were well known for the quality of their vegetables![11] Gut parasite infections were said to be common in houses using earth closets.[23]

Like numerous small towns in Essex, Ongar had no way of disposing of its sewage. Dr J. C. Quennell was appointed local medical officer of health in 1891 and reported in the following year *'the River Roding, receiving as it does the sewage of the villages on its banks and the town of Chipping Ongar, is a possible danger to public health.'* In 1895, he wrote to the newly formed Ongar Rural District Council *'there does not seem to be any system of drainage in Chipping Ongar. What drains there seem to find their way into the river which, especially in dry weather, cannot fail to be thereby heavily charged with sewage. Privy cesspits are common, and in many places are badly covered and dangerously near houses, and, in*

THE UTILITIES

some cases where closets are furnished with pans, there is no proper provision for flushing.' [19] The newly formed parish council was actively involved in trying to obtain proper sewerage for the town, and was applying pressure to the landlords of properties without privies or water closets.[17]

Mr Jarvis, surveyor to ORDC, drew up plans for the sewerage of the town (and part of High Ongar) with a treatment works at Hallsford Bridge. Progress was slow due to the landowner's opposition to the site of the works but by 1902, the new town sewage system was in use and draining 1000 households and the waste material of the Marden Ash brewery. The main sewer followed the course of the Cripsey Brook to settlement tanks at Hallsford Bridge, the sewage flowing by gravity through the open septic tanks into a series of open channels on the six acre site. Purified effluent was discharged into the River Roding. The dry weather intake was 19,200 gallons a day, and the annual cost of labour and maintenance was £60.[24] This site treated Ongar's sewage until replaced by a new works, with a dry weather capacity of 161,000 gallons, built at Stanford Rivers by ORDC in the late 1930s.

The present sewage treatment works on the same site in Stanford Rivers was opened by the chairman of the Thames Water Authority in 1976. It had a capacity of half a million gallons daily, and was also able to deal with sludge from outlying works at Abbess Roding, Epping Green, Theydon Bois, Thornwood and Willingale.[25]

Telephones

The original Ongar telephone exchange was on the first floor of 181 High Street. The post office was on the ground floor with the mail sorting office at the rear. The exchange opened in 1913.[11] Mrs Wilson, who later became chief telephonist, was well known amongst subscribers. She would inevitably recognise the caller's voice and had a good idea to whom they wished to speak. A newly arrived GP received much background information on patients to whom he was about to be connected! [26]

The first telephone to be installed was in the Grammar School (now Central House, owned by the Brighty family) and had the phone number Ongar 1. Brighty Properties still retains this number, though over the years prefixes of 20 and 36 have been added to make it Ongar 362001. Originally, Stondon Massey and Kelvedon Hatch were served by the Ongar telephone exchange.[11]

Ongar had a telegraph service from 1872.[5] Ongar railway station was acting as a postal telegraph agency in 1913 and was able to transmit telegrams on behalf of the Postmaster General.[27] Telegraph boys have long since disappeared, though at one time they were a familiar sight on their bicycles. They wore dark blue uniforms with pill box hats, and had a leather pouch attached to a waist belt for the telegrams.[11]

The automatic telephone exchange in Bansons Lane was opened in November 1960. Before the old exchange closed, every subscriber was rung and asked to test the automatic dialling system, and to check that they were happy with it. The last

ASPECTS OF THE HISTORY OF ONGAR

manual operators were Mrs Railton, Mrs Hatchard, Mrs Whiterod, Mrs Skingsley and Mrs Hillman.[28]

With the arrival of automatic telephone exchanges and the growth of information technology, telegraph boys and local telephonists have passed into our yesterdays.

References

1. Williams, T. I. *A History of the British Gas Industry* (1981) Oxford University Press
2. VCH Essex vol 9 (1994)
3. Grieve, H. *The Sleepers and the Shadows* (1994) Chelmsford
4. VCH Essex vol 8 (1983)
5. VCH Essex vol 4 (1956)
6. VCH Essex vol 5 (1966)
7. Chipping Ongar tithe award ERO: D/CT 262A
8. Pigot's *Directory* (1832)
9. Post Office *Directory* (1845)
10. Post Office *Directory* (1859)
11. inf. from R. Shepherd
12. inf. from M. Leach
13. Ongar Gas Co. minutes. ERO: D/Z 24
14. Budworth Hall inventory and valuation. ERO: D/DU 1786
15. ERO: Q/RUM 1 &2
16. Thresh, Dr. J. C. *Essex Water Supply* (undated) in ERO library
17. Ongar Parish Council minutes
18. Minutes of Ongar Water Works Co. Herts Record Office: PUW 5/1/1
19. Summary of the Reports of the District Medical Officers of Health for Essex (1891 to 1902) in ERO library
20. Herts Record Office: PUW 4
21. ORDC public health committee minutes: Loughton reference library
22. ORDC test results on water analyses 1935–1943. Loughton reference library (now lost)
23. inf. from Dr Ted Hatfield
24. Summary of the Reports of the District Medical Officers of Health for Essex (1903): ERO library
25. *West Essex Gazette* 12 March 1976
26. inf. from Dr Mary Milnthorpe
27. Great Eastern Railway timetable 1 October 1913 to 31 March 1914. I am grateful to Ian Strugnell for this information.
28. *West Essex Gazette* 18 November 1960

chapter 23

Henry Childs of Ongar

by Philip Brooke

Henry Childs was born on the last day of 1828 at Petersfield, Hampshire.[1] His father was a cordwainer, a maker of boots and shoes to order. As the business seems to have flourished for nearly 40 years,[2] Henry probably had a comfortable childhood. His father perhaps saw that he was apprenticed to a draper, and maybe helped him to rent trade premises in London when he first set up in business.

Marriage

On 29 April 1857, at the age of 29, Henry married Jane Spiers at Alresford, Hampshire. She was the daughter of H. Spiers Esq. of Stockbridge,[3] a fellmonger (a supplier of skins, cattle hides etc.). It is not difficult to imagine the young Henry accompanying his father on periodic visits to sort out suitable leather for use in boot and shoe making. He would have had the opportunity to get to know the Spiers' daughters and, eventually, the courage to ask her father for Jane's hand in matrimony, as was the custom in Victorian England.

First business

Henry set up home and his new business as a linen draper in the fashionable district of Hammersmith, London, at Terrace House, 12 King Street West.[4] He employed two people in his sewing workshop. His son William was born there in 1858, followed by his daughter Mary Ellen on 20 June 1860. It seems that Henry sold up and moved soon after that, as his second son Austin was born in Ongar in 1863. Emily Blanch followed in 1867 and Janet in 1869.[5]

Move to Ongar

It is not clear why Henry chose to move his home and business to what seems to have been numbered 4 (now 192–194) High Street, Ongar. Perhaps the pace of city life did not suit him or his wife, or perhaps he found an ideal property at a low rent in a place that they liked. It had good sized living accommodation, a coach house and stables, plus a good sized workroom. There was a twice weekly carrier service to London run by George Bretton,[6] before the railway opened in 1865. Keeping up with London fashions would not have been difficult. Henry would probably have maintained the contacts he had established during his time in Hammersmith. By 1871 Henry was well established with six living in staff. The census of that year tells us who they were: Ellen Ellis, dressmaker; Emily Clark, milliner; Henry Sims and George Holder, drapery assistants, and two domestics, Edith Mood and Elizabeth Clarke, the latter being a nurse to look after young Janet.[7]

ASPECTS OF THE HISTORY OF ONGAR

In the 1860s, Ongar held its petty sessions at noon on Saturdays, the day of the weekly market. Admiral C. H. Swinburne was lord of the manor [8] and the Ongar Union workhouse was under Robert William Low, master, and Mrs Ellen Low, matron. The local auctioneer and insurance agent was Charles Foster. George Edwards, George Pollard and Miss Elizabeth Thimlaby were amongst the drapers in the town. Mr Frederick Miller Noble was a builder, with brick tile and pipe works, a family concern established in 1805. They were also involved as proprietors of the gas works and, like most builders at that time, were involved in undertaking. Henry Childs supplied and fitted the fine linen and lace work for lining out the coffins.

Community involvement

This was to be his home for the rest of his long life and he played a very active part in the community. He appears in the minute book of the voluntary subscription fire brigade (formed in 1840), when he was appointed to the committee for general management of the fire engine.[9] He seems to have been very keen on this venture and was a regular attender at meetings from 1882. In 1883 he subscribed 2s 6d, and the accounts show that he continued to contribute until 1901. A. P. Fenn, secretary in 1883, was also the engineer, with seven men. A fire escape was donated by Henry Gibson in 1889. The parish council did not take over responsibility for the fire service until 1904.

Many towns had a rifle volunteer brigade, and in Ongar it was customary for local businesses to contribute generously to the annual prizes. Henry donated a silk umbrella (won by Private J. Jones). Fred Noble gave a military greatcoat, Mr Barlow an American folding chair and Mrs Barlow bottles of gin, rum and whisky (won by J. Lucking!).[10]

Henry is mentioned in an old press cutting as treasurer of the Ongar Horticultural Society.[11] He was also a director of the Ongar Gas Company. In May 1898, he purchased 20 shares with the Ongar Waterworks Co. Ltd (of which his son William was secretary), adding a further five shares in March 1901. The waterworks was taken over by the Herts & Essex Waterworks but Henry kept his stake of shares in that company for the rest of his life. Henry was an active member of the Congregational Church and was one of the trustees. In 1886 he made a generous donation of three guineas to the Budworth Memorial Fund.

The Ongar home and business

Henry rented his double fronted shop and dwelling house for £60 per annum. On 16 October 1878 the freehold came up for auction, and he was thus able to buy the property which comprised a double fronted shop, 32 ft by 13 ft and 10 ft high. It adjoined to a wine shop, with which it probably shared access to the rear on the other side of the shop. The dwelling house comprised drawing, dining and dressing rooms, a workshop and five bedrooms. There was a kitchen and scullery with a "Kitchener" stove and oven (an extremely efficient cooking range of its day) and spacious underground cellars. Outside there were walled gardens with coach

HENRY CHILDS OF ONGAR

house and three stall stables with loft over, and a yard with sidecart entrance to the High Street. The whole property had a frontage of 34 ft on a parcel of land 49 ft by about 150 ft, backing onto the old castle moat and referred to as 195 High Street.

Henry "played the stock market", as it was called in those days, and very successful he seems to have been with it. Each grandchild was given a share in a local firm, and further shares on subsequent birthdays. Surviving papers show, for example, dividends paid to his grandson Cecil on his sixth birthday.

At the age of 56, Henry retired, giving his shop to his first born son William. From then on, Henry is referred to as of Avington Cottage. This seems to have been the dwelling house part of the original property and, as it had plenty of living accommodation, it seems likely that William and his family also lived there while running the business. However another possibility is that the separate coach house and stabling behind the shop was called Avington Cottage. One old resident told me the cottage was behind the shop after the business was sold.

Sadly, Henry's son William died in 1900 and the Childs drapery closed down.[12] The *Essex Weekly News* printed a report on 29 June and commented that '*Great Sympathy is felt for the deceased widow and the three young children.*' [13] Henry then rented the shop and premises for £110 per annum, firstly to Mr N. H. Wightman and then I think to a succession of drapers over the years. By 1914, Mr T. Castle was leasing it for his furnishing and general drapers business, featuring '*Fine pure wool by Jaegar for day and Night wear, Blankets Sheets etc protect from damp and chill maintaining health and Comfort.*' I think that Henry was aware that empty shop premises were likely to be commandeered by the army during the First World War, and he kept it tenanted until he sold it (perhaps about 1919).

A fascinating book for groceries supplied by H. E. Barnard of the Supply Stores, Ongar, has survived. A week's groceries in October 1919 consisted of margarine, quaker oats, matches, sugar, oatmeal, currants and mustard for 6s 8d. Bacon is noted as costing 2s 6d but the weight is not indicated. These were the days when a box of 12 night lights cost 11 $\frac{1}{2}$d and Monky brand, 2d! Inside the book cover are notes on how to use the new Robin starch for collars, cuffs and shirt fronts and how to polish them with the polishing flat iron. In those times, the heat of the iron had to be judged by the time it took to dry a sharp burst of spit! Other useful tips for housewives' Monday wash day boilings included how to tint the water blue for whites, and information about the new liquid brass cleaner.

Two years after his son William's death, his beloved Jane passed from this life on 20 March 1902. He would have then been on his own, with only daughter Blanch near at hand, although it seems he had a great many friends in the town. Henry's housekeeper at the cottage was Miss Minnie Fogg to whom he gave a salary of £35 per annum. In 1917, when he changed his will slightly, he indicated that Minnie was to receive £50 if she was still in his service at the time of his death. I am pleased to say she was and did get the money, although £5 was deducted for tax. Henry must have thought a lot of Minnie Fogg because after his death she had a backdated increase of salary to £50 per annum.

ASPECTS OF THE HISTORY OF ONGAR

Parish Councillor

On 19 November 1902, a casual vacancy on the parish council arose from the death of Dr Clark. Mr Christie proposed and Mr Rose seconded a motion that Henry Childs should be elected.[14] The stage was set for Henry to serve the parish council for a further 18 years, well into real old age. During this time he was one of the local school managers and, at a later date, superintendent in charge of the cemetery. It is clear that he remained actively involved in local affairs for the rest of his life.

Henry Childs' children

Henry's first son William followed his father's trade and married Edith Mary Hall. They had issue Cecil, Edith and Harry, the latter signed in at the will reading of old Henry in 1920. William, as already mentioned, died in 1900.

Mary Ellen, his first daughter, married Henry Denyer, a master miller of Carshalton Mills, Surrey, who once also owned Catsfield Place, Sussex, and Court Lodge Chepstead, Surrey. They had issue Kathleen, Gordon and Russell.

Austin, his second son, was listed as a warehouseman in 1881,[15] but left home soon after this date to go to South Africa, attracted, perhaps, by the gold rush days there. He wrote home from Durban saying he '*was knocking out forty shillings a week as a boarding agent.*' By the turn of the century he had an outfitters shop at Jeppes in the district of Johannesburg. Henry kept in touch, sending (it is thought) stock, which his son paid him for. Letters have survived, giving an insight into Henry, Ongar and other family history. Austin married Alice Mizen and had issue Harry, Dorothy, Kathleen and Norman. I have traced all the descendants, none of whom knew that Ongar featured in their family history. Austin never returned to this country.

Emily Blanch, his second daughter, married Frederick Miller Noble, the Ongar builder, in about 1892. They had issue Frederick, Austin, Richard, Harriet and Arthur. Austin was killed towards the end of the First World War. I understand there is a memorial to him in Ongar parish church, taking the form of a wooden cross on the wall which had been used to mark his grave in France. Arthur led the Territorial Army battalion in the legendary Fourth Indian division of the Eighth Army in the 1939–1945 conflict. He reached the rank of colonel and was knighted. His obituary was printed in *The Times* on 11 March 1982.

Janet, his third daughter, married Thomas Withers Claridge, a horse dealer, and was probably living in Broad Street Alresford, Hampshire in 1920. They had one daughter, Jan.

Henry Childs' death

The Essex Chronicle of 27 August 1920 reported the death on 19 August of Ongar's oldest inhabitant.[11] '*Henry Childs passed away at his residence in the High Street after a short illness in his 92nd year. He was well known and highly respected, having carried on a drapery business for many years in Ongar.*' His funeral was held at the Congregational church with the Rev. G. F. White and the Rev. A. Goodall officiating. Miss Nellie Korf played the organ. A large number of people from the town attended, including the chairman of the parish council (C. H. Foster) and other members, J. Ashdown (gentlemen's outfitter), H. B. Brown (wine and spirit merchant), J. P. Fenn (bank manager), J. W. M. Baugh (dispensing chemist), J. Gingell (estate agent), P. Channell (stationer), J. Surridge (cycle dealer), H. Korf (tailor), F. Mead (baker), J. F. Kerr (ironmonger), T. N. Lavander (butcher), Dr G.R. Wilson (general practioner) and A. Richardson.[11] Henry was buried in the Ongar Cemetery and the stone is inscribed with the words "The Memory of the Just is Blessed."

References

1. Petersfield parish registers. Hants Record Office.
2. *Trade Directories* 1830, 1844, 1847, 1855 and 1859 in Hants Record Office
3. Marriage certificate
4. 1861 census: RG 925 Hammersmith, London
5. Birth certificates
6. Kelly's *Directory* (1861) in ERO
7. 1871 census: RG/10 Chipping Ongar
8. Kelly's *Directory* (1861) & (1871) in ERO.
9. Ongar Fire Preservation Society. ERO: D/Z 49
10. from an old handbill saved from a bonfire.
11. *Essex Chronicle*, 27 August 1920
12. Death certificate 17 June 1900
13. *Essex Weekly News,* 29 June 1900
14. Ongar Parish Council minutes
15. 1881 census: RG/11/1741 Chipping Ongar

chapter 24

Captain Budworth and the Budworth Hall

by Michael Leach

Captain Philip John Budworth was born on 27 December 1817 and was the only child of the Rev. Philip Budworth, rector of High Laver, to survive to adulthood. The Budworths originated from Cheshire, but had been in Middlesex for several generations, and were connected by marriage to the Cleeve family who had acquired Greensted Hall in 1695.[1]

Captain Budworth was educated by a private tutor, and then followed in his father's footsteps to Jesus College, Cambridge where he graduated B.A. in 1839 (and M.A. in 1843). He kept terms at the Inner Temple, but was not called to the Bar. In 1840, he stood unsuccessfully as a parliamentary candidate for the Borough of Sandwich in Kent. In later life, he believed that the disappointment of this defeat was responsible for the ensuing eight years of travel in Europe, Asia and Africa, during which time he came *'face to face with many of the persons and incidents which occupied public attention during that time.'*[1]

The French revolution of 1848, and the resultant political unrest in Europe, persuaded him to return home. Later, he wrote *'I should probably have resumed my wandering life had I not soon afterwards become acquainted with Blanche Trimmer'*, to whom he was married in 1850.[1] However, he was still sufficiently restless to spend nearly a year on his honeymoon, travelling through France, Germany and Italy.

Figure 21   The Wilderness, Captain Budworth's High Street home from 1851 to 1854, from a pencil sketch of about 1850 by C. Mott junior.

CAPTAIN BUDWORTH AND THE BUDWORTH HALL

On their return to England in 1851, the couple made their first home at the Wilderness (later called the Pleasance) in Ongar High Street, moving to Greensted Hall (which his father had acquired in 1837) in 1854.[2] Captain Budworth now threw his energies into serving the county and the locality in a large number of different ways. He had become a J P in 1850, and was subsequently a senior magistrate of the Ongar Petty Sessional Division. He was High Sheriff in 1878–79, and served on a bewildering array of county committees (including Constabulary, Parliamentary, Additional County Asylum, Highways and Bridges, Records, and Militia Armouries). He was particularly active on the Constabulary committee on which he was responsible for initiating various reforms, and made a practical contribution by offering the site for Ongar's police station and court house in 1853.[3] He was also chairman of the licensing committee for West Essex, and was founder and first chairman of the Ongar Conservative Registration Association. At different times, he was a trustee of the King's Trust school, a trustee of the Ongar Friendly Society, vice president of the Ongar Cricket Club, a member of the Ongar Fire Brigade committee, and was involved in the restructuring of the Ongar Gas Company. He gave practical and financial assistance to the restoration of St Martin's church, Chipping Ongar.[2] As an influential local person, he was lobbied in July 1883 by Thackeray Turner, of the Society for the Protection of Ancient Buildings, which was opposing the destruction of the south wall of Chipping Ongar parish church to build a new aisle. His reply, while agreeing with the SPAB policy of preserving good features in old buildings, indicated that he thought that little of importance would be destroyed, but promised to endeavour to have the south door piscina re-sited.[4] In this, his influence did not prevail.

In August 1872, Captain Budworth found himself dealing with a much more difficult controversy – the petition for the abolition of the annual Ongar fair, which was seen by a group of residents (headed by Mr Henry Gibson, Clerk of the Peace for Essex, living in the White House, Chipping Ongar) as a serious cause of drunkenness and immorality. As chairman he had to give the impartial decision of the bench, which was to support the petition to the Home Secretary for the abolition. However, he made it clear that his own view was that the public should not be deprived of such a long established traditional entertainment.[5] The Home Secretary was apparently not impressed by the petitioners' case on this occasion, and the fair took place as usual in October that year. Captain Budworth, having been spotted in the crowd, made an impromptu speech for the working man's right to enjoyment, and urged them to good behaviour as a defence against future attacks by the petitioners. Someone shouted '*three cheers for Captain Budworth*' and the band struck up "For he's a jolly good fellow." [6] By 1881, he was chairman of the Ongar Fair committee.[7]

His wife's death in 1862, within a few days of giving birth to their first child, was later described by him as the greatest calamity of his life. He re-married four years later, and had four more children. Later, he wrote '*my life has been of a varied and interesting character, and I am thankful to own that, with one great exception, it has so far been as pleasant as the fitful chances of human existence generally permit. Among many Nations whose languages and customs I have studied, I have seen the brighter and darker side of great events, and been a witness of triumphs and pageants, as well as of war and revolt...'*[1]

Though in failing health, he remained involved in public life until shortly before his death, which came swiftly at the evening meal at Greensted Hall on 9 January 1885. The funeral, five days later at Greensted church, was a sombre affair with tenants acting as pall bearers, window blinds drawn, and the shops of Ongar closed. The large number of mourners, including 40 members of "G" Company (Ongar & Epping) 1st Volunteer Battalion Essex Regiment, could not be accommodated inside the tiny church.[2]

The Budworth Memorial committee

A public meeting was held in the Town Hall on 3 June 1885, with the Rev. E. J. Reeve, rector of Stondon Massey, in the chair. Henry Gibson, Captain Budworth's old adversary over the Ongar fair (and the architect of its final suppression in 1892), significantly commented that *'there are many things on which he and Captain Budworth might and did differ very materially.'*[8] He suggested that a " coffee room and tavern" might be a very fitting memorial. The Rev. F. A. S. Fane, rector of Kelvedon Hatch, explained that he had been given a sum of money to be spent as he thought fit, and he had already considered building a coffee room near the railway station for the benefit of the whole neighbourhood. He estimated that, after purchasing the site, he would have £300–400 in hand towards the cost of the building. The report contains no reference to the temperance movement, but coffee rooms were a favoured Victorian antidote to the evils of alcohol. In his account of Ipswich, John Glyde wrote *'the charge for a cup of this wholesome beverage is three halfpence; and the avidity with which it is taken, in preference to ale, by numbers of porters and others employed at hard labour, is in our opinion strong testimony as to the beneficial influence which has been exercised by the advocates of temperance principles.'* [9] Knowing Henry Gibson's views on alcohol, it seems most unlikely that his proposed "tavern" was intended to sell intoxicating liquor! However informally rooted, the temperance influence lingered a long time, for in 1928 an attempt to establish a bar was rejected unanimously by the committee on the grounds that the sale of alcohol was not a function specified by the trust deed.[10]

The meeting agreed that (a) a substantial memorial to the late Captain Budworth should be provided, (b) the memorial should be a building, named the Budworth Hall, providing a large room for public meetings, as well as reading and recreation rooms (and other such rooms as might be necessary) for the young men of the town, and (c) a committee should be appointed to obtain plans and estimates from an architect, and to have powers to raise money and purchase a site when funds allowed. The meeting may have been more controversial than was reported, as the next edition of the *Essex County Chronicle* published a ferocious attack written by Mr W. Scruby, the Ongar postmaster, suggesting that Captain Budworth would

CAPTAIN BUDWORTH AND THE BUDWORTH HALL

have disapproved of the whole idea, and that it would be an insult to his memory![11] The appointed committee was heavily weighted with local clergy (including the Rev. F. A .S. Fane, the originator of the coffee room idea), as well as Henry Gibson, the leader of the anti-fair faction.

Figure 22 The architect's drawing from the Budworth Memorial subscription list. The existing building differs in various details. The proposed Budworth coat of arms can be seen above the main porch.

The next public meeting, on 25 August 1885, was informed that the Rev. Fane had bought the land near the police station, measuring 50 ft by 100 ft, from Captain Budworth's trustees and had donated this, as well as the unspent surplus of £400, to the committee. Plans prepared by Mr Fothergill Watson, architect of Nottingham, had been agreed after certain alterations. The total estimated cost of the building, including furniture and fittings, was £1400. The committee had decided that the Budworth coat of arms should be displayed in a conspicuous position on the new building.[12] This decision was probably a casualty of subsequent economies, as the final cost was £200 over the estimate. One engaging quirk that did survive can still be seen in the stonework on the High Street side of the clock tower – the inscription "F. W. ARCH" (i.e. Fothergill Watson, architect) on the scroll between "BUDWORTH" and "HALL." The first trustees were Rev. F. A. S. Fane, Sir Charles Cunliffe Smith, Henry Edward Jones, Tyndale White and Josiah Gilbert.[13]

The reason for choosing a Nottingham architect was not explained. However, Josiah Gilbert, grandson of the Rev. Isaac Taylor, was actively involved in the project, and was one of the first trustees.[12] It had been probably through his influence that, in 1865, his brother Isaac Charles Gilbert of Nottingham gave his services free of charge to design the Congregational Church Sunday school.[14] Fothergill Watson was briefly in partnership with I. C. Gilbert, so it is not surprising to find both names as architects of the Ongar cemetery chapels in 1866.[15] I. C. Gilbert died in March 1885,[16] and it seems likely that Josiah Gilbert recommended his brother's former partner. Watson had, by then, designed a number of robust high Victorian public buildings in his home town and had the reputation of being a stickler for good workmanship. His involvement with the Temperance Movement in 1884, when he designed an institute and coffee tavern in Hucknall, may also have recommended him to certain members of the committee![17]

Financial problems seem to have dogged the building from the beginning. Money was slow to come in, and it appears that Henry Gibson made up the deficit from his own pocket before the Hall was opened, as well as personally paying for the furniture and fittings.[18] The builder was the local firm of Frederick Noble, with stonework by J. H. Wray of Chelmsford. The Budworth Hall was opened on 9 February 1887 by the Rt. Hon. Sir Henry Selwyn Ibbetson MP, who gave a short eulogy to Captain Budworth. Henry Gibson also spoke, a little defensively perhaps, denying that '*the hall was an institution which would not have met with the hearty approval of Captain Budworth, expressing the hope that it would prove a temple of peace, concord and harmony.*' [19] The speeches were followed by an impromptu concert organised at short notice by the Ongar Glee Club.

The first twenty five years

The completed building provided a public coffee room (with its own entrance under a small porch directly off the High Street on the southeast side of the building), with a kitchen behind. Beyond that was the billiard room. To the north of the central corridor, from front to back, was the main staircase, and a large reading room (which over the years acquired books, stuffed birds, a microscope, a German shell case, portraits and paintings, and various other objects). There were two small living rooms at the back for the caretaker with a narrow staircase leading to a small bedroom. Upstairs, in the main body of the building, was a large meeting room with galleries (seating 300 people), a large committee room and a smaller room in the tower (later known as the north committee room).

A public meeting was held in the Budworth Hall on 22 March 1887 to consider how to celebrate Queen Victoria's jubilee. It was agreed that a clock would be a fitting memorial, and every householder in the town was invited to subscribe. By October, the committee was in a position to order a single dial clock, but, after appealing for further funds, a striking clock with three faces, internally illuminated by gas, was installed by Messrs Gillett of Croydon at a total cost (including the necessary building work by Frederick Noble) of just over £108.[20] The outspoken Mr Scruby had not approved, and had written earlier to the jubilee committee, promising '*two guineas towards any local object, except a clock in the Budworth Hall.*'[21] The clock was started by Gertrude Fenn, daughter of the local bank manager who was honorary secretary to the jubilee committee, at 4 minutes past 4 o'clock,[22] and was commemorated by eight verses of doggerel. The first verse gives the flavour, with its laboured reference to the local builder:

> 'The Budworth Hall Clock is now fixed in the Tower
> Of that "Noble" and excellent Hall
> To give correct time – and so chime the hour
> That each sound may be heard by us all.' [23]

The Budworth Hall then settled down to its function as a club for the young men of the town (it is not clear when women were first admitted), and as a meeting place for local societies (such as the Black and White Minstrels and the annual Chrysanthemum Show) and various public functions. At election time, there was considerable rivalry between the Conservatives and the Liberals to get the first booking for a public meeting.[22] The coffee tavern was probably run in the early days by the resident caretaker (as it was after 1920). Its first big commission was on 21 June 1887 when it supplied 18 gallons of tea (at 1s 4d per gallon) and seven gallons of coffee (at 1s per gallon) for the open air jubilee dinner.[20]

On 1 July 1911 the trustees of the Budworth Memorial Hall leased land at the rear of the Hall to the directors of the Ongar Assembly Rooms Ltd. The lease was for 14 years at a rent of £1 per annum, '*if demanded,*' and refers to a building '*thereon recently erected to be known as the Ongar Assembly Rooms.*' There were clearly very close links between the two as the two directors of the company (H. E. Jones and Tyndale White) were also trustees of the Budworth Institute and the secretary was J. P. Fenn.[24] The building is said to have cost £700.[25 & 26] At the end of the lease, the building was to revert to the lessors, on condition that the Essex Hunt Club committee should have use of the Assembly Rooms (together with the public rooms in the Budworth Hall) once a year.[24] The room (now called the ballroom) was reputed to have the finest dance floor in Essex, and was used by the Essex Hunt. An elderly resident recalled hours spent waxing the floor, and the spectacle of large numbers of carriages setting down guests on ball nights. There was no bar, but claret cup was served made to a special recipe using locally grown herbs.[22] The lease was surrendered prematurely to the lessors in September 1919.[24]

The First World War brought about a major change in the use of both buildings, which were taken over as a Red Cross hospital, staffed by local VAD nurses, with Miss E. M. Jones as commandant.[26] An oil painting by the local artist, George Rose, shows the ballroom laid out as hospital ward, and contemporary photographs show groups of soldiers (many were said to be Belgian) posing with the nurses under the front porch. It is likely that some form of temporary link was formed between the building at this time (probably with the corrugated iron roof which required repair in 1926).[27]

Between the Wars

This was a difficult time for the Budworth Hall Institute which had by now acquired the adjoining ballroom. In 1923, the caretaker's wages were reduced from £2 to £1 10s per week, and, as the coffee tavern was making a loss, he was instructed to open it on Sundays. By 1926, there was concern about the external condition of the building, the ballroom annexe roof was leaking and the coffee tavern was still making a loss (as it was also in 1928). The only visible change to Fothergill Watson's building was made in 1924 with the addition of a bay window to the coffee tavern. In 1931, installation of electric lighting was considered, but the estimate of £70 from the London Electric Supply Company was considered beyond the means of the Institute.[27] Surviving accounts from the 1930s show losses exceeding profits by a considerable margin,[28] and there is a later reference to *'the personal generosity of the President, Mr Stanley H. Jones, saving the Institute from being in the red'* during this period.[29]

The Second World War

This probably insured the building's survival, due to various essential new uses, and an assured income. On 23 May 1940, the concert room, committee rooms and ballroom were requisitioned for billeting troops. The schedule of condition at that time gives a depressing picture of a shabby, badly worn interior.[30] In a further requisition dated 10 February 1941, Ongar Rural District Council evacuation scheme took over the upper floor as a rest centre for evacuees. Lettings and individual membership continued till the following year, but ORDC requisitioned the remaining areas on 1 February 1942.[31] The British restaurant moved into the ballroom, and the services canteen, run by the WRVS and previously in cramped accommodation in the adjoining school hall, took over the concert room.[32] The building was returned to the Institute on 1 April 1946, and £493 was received for compensation claims.[28] An inventory, dated 4 April 1946, shows a surprisingly well-furnished building with partial electric lighting in the ballroom, kitchen and café (the former coffee tavern). The reading room still contained two cases of stuffed birds, a quantity of geological specimens and curios, ten portraits and pictures and 45 books. There was a three quarter sized billiard table and two grand pianos in the ballroom, the Ibach being valued at £100.[33]

The last fifty years

The Institute's finances benefited in 1946 from the payment of £493 for compensation and breakages, but the cost of neglected maintenance quickly took its toll and annual profits had dwindled to a loss by 1949.[28] Faced with the imminent problem of expensive repairs to the roof, the 1949 AGM agreed that the Budworth Hall and all its assets should be transferred to the Ongar Rural District Council to be run as a community centre. ORDC agreed to this offer, but asked the Institute to clarify its charitable status. This proved a major stumbling block, as the Charity Commissioners stated that the Declaration of Trust, dated 30 December 1886, could only be varied after financial failure of the trust, and that, as the Institute was still solvent, no variation could be allowed. The committee considered that there *was* de facto financial failure, as £2000 needed to be spent on the roof, and legal opinion was sought.[27] It is not clear why, but the proposal had been dropped by June 1950, as had, it seems, any plans to deal with the roof. The accounts show relatively small sums spent on repairs and maintenance through the 1950s (totalling £850 in that decade) but costs rose rapidly in the 1960s (£4653 over seven years).[28] In 1962, the Hall was closed for two months for re-roofing the whole building, as well as various internal alterations including the conversion of the reading room to a ladies' powder room.[34] The portraits which had hung in the reading room (including those of Captain Budworth, Henry Gibson and others) were moved to the south committee room, and that of the Rev. F. A. S. Fane was sold to a descendant. Subsequently all the remaining portraits disappeared, and recent attempts to trace them have been unsuccessful.

The financial problems continued. Though income from lettings increased nearly four fold over the two decades and various grants had been obtained from the Carnegie Trust, the Ministry of Education and Essex County Council, things came to a head in 1967 with lightning damage and a serious outbreak of dry rot and furniture beetle infestation. A sense of despair entered the minutes, which noted that, with almost full bookings, there were no means of increasing income, and the option to sell or demolish the building was discussed. A new building on the Pleasance site was suggested. In 1968, the County Architect considered that the building had reached the end of its useful life.[27] In 1969, there was an unsuccessful application to use part of the empty house on the Pleasance site which had been acquired by Epping and Ongar Rural District Council.[10]

However it was the Institute, rather than the building, which had reached the end of its life. An important change had already been made in 1963 when the Budworth Hall charity was reconstituted with a committee of management of nine elected members, plus a further six representing local clubs and organisations. In 1968, it was decided that the Budworth Hall should become a community association. This would make it eligible for grants from the Department of Education and Science and local authorities, and the cost of a full time warden would be met by the County. It would also reflect an evolutionary change which had already occurred, as the accounts show that there had been no individual members of the Institute since 1956. Also the number of clubs and organisations using the building had grown significantly and many were not represented on the committee. The inaugural meeting of the Ongar and District Community Association was held on 28 June 1968, and the final meeting of the Budworth Hall Institute on 2 October 1968.[27&35]

The CA thrived. In 1972, there were plans for converting the concert room into a 178 seat theatre with raked seating, and forming a new entrance on the north side of the building at an estimated cost of £15,000. The architect was John Amor.[36] By 1974 there were modified, but no less ambitious, plans (by the Bright Freeman Partnership of Loughton) for improvements, with a permanent bar, a new entrance and porch on the north side of the building with adjacent warden's office, and conversion of the concert room to a 120 seat theatre with projection room. The estimated cost was £37,000.[37] Work on the bar and the new entrance and warden's office was started soon after, and was completed by 1976 at a cost of £12,000.[38] Anyone remembering the original gloomy entrance off the High Street, with the gent's toilet as the first welcome, will appreciate what a huge improvement this was. However, raising money – as ever – was a problem, and by 1978 the CA was £2000 in debt. Thanks to the energy of the new chairman, Ron Barnes, this was cleared, and much outstanding work to the interior was completed voluntarily by members of the CA.[35]

In October 1980, a new chairman, George Brown, was elected and for the next two years the Ongar Christian Fellowship (OCF) was heavily involved in the CA. In 1981, it became evident that re-roofing and a further assault on the dry rot would be needed, at an estimated cost of £15,000. There were further problems at the end of 1982 when OCF ended their involvement in the CA, and both the bar and the café were closed for a time. The new chairman, Kenneth Bird, was successful both in attracting new volunteers and in improving the financial situation, and the necessary repairs were done. In 1986, the Budworth Hall celebrated its centenary with a Victorian town day on 5 July, a colourful parade in the High Street (with shop windows, as well as residents, dressed appropriately) and a commemorative lunch.[35] Time continued to take its toll on the structure, however, necessitating the rebuilding of the four main chimney stacks from 1990 onwards, at a cost of £20,000. The clock had a thorough overhaul in May 1990.[39]

The hall is still used on a daily basis by a large variety of local organisations and family functions, and provides a vital focal point for the community. It is maintained to a high standard, and is being improved continually to meet the ever changing requirements of a public building. Any organisation of this sort depends on the enthusiasm and the sheer hard work of the committee members themselves. The CA, occupying a large flamboyant listed building constructed at a time when maintenance costs were not a consideration, has always needed generous amounts of both qualities, particularly as it receives no public funding, apart from a grant from the Parish Council (who also maintain the clock). As this account shows, the CA (and its predecessor, the Budworth Institute) has had many struggles to survive, but with the growth of the town and the increasing appreciation of the qualities of Victorian architecture, its survival is probably more assured now than at any time in its history.

References

1 Budworth P. J. *Memorials of the Parishes of Greensted-Budworth, Chipping Ongar & High Laver*, (1876) Ongar
2 *Essex County Chronicle*, 16 January 1885
3 Essex Constabulary minutes. ERO: Q/Acm 15
4 letter of 14 July 1883 from P. J. Budworth to Thackeray Turner: SPAB Library
5 *Essex Weekly News*, 16 August 1872
6 ibid 18 October 1872
7 VCH Essex vol 4 (1956) p.167
8 *Essex County Chronicle*, 5 June 1885
9 Glyde J. *The Moral, Social and Religious Condition of Ipswich*, (1850)
10 *West Essex Gazette*, 24 January 1969
11 *Essex County Chronicle*, 12 June 1885
12 *Essex County Chronicle*, 4 September 1885

CAPTAIN BUDWORTH AND THE BUDWORTH HALL

13 undated typescript referring to Indenture date 24 June 1886
14 VCH Essex vol 4 (1956) p.165 (where he is incorrectly named as J. C. Gilbert)
15 Burial Board minutes 4 January 1866
16 inf. from Robin Gilbert
17 Brand K. *Watson Fothergill, Architect*, (1981), Nottingham Civic Society
18 letter of 8 December 1886 from Henry Gibson, ERO: D/P 124/28/6
19 *Essex County Chronicle* 12 February 1887
20 Ongar Jubilee Committee minutes. ERO: D/P 124/28/7
21 *Essex County Chronicle* 25 March 1887
22 inf. from Mrs Rose
23 *The Budworth Hall Clock.* ERO: D/DU 1786
24 lease dated 1 July 1911, surrender dated 10 September 1919
25 Ongar and District Chamber of Commerce Guide 1961–62
26 *An Appeal for Funds* 1965
27 Ongar Institute minute books 1919–1936 & 1941–1968: Loughton reference library
28 Budworth Hall Institute and Coffee Tavern annual accounts 1935, 1936, 1938, 1942, 1946–1968: Loughton reference library. Ditto for 1934, 1937: ERO: D/DU 1786
29 *West Essex Gazette*, 8 May 1959
30 schedule of condition. ERO: D/DU 1786
31 requisition orders. ERO: D/DU 1786
32 inf. from Eleanor Elstone
33 inventory and valuation. ERO: D/DU 1786
34 *West Essex Gazette* 3 August 1962
35 inf. from Marion Slade
36 *West Essex Gazette* 4 August 1972
37 Ongar & District Community Association "The Centre Project" 1974
38 *West Essex Gazette* 27 February 1976
39 inf. from Edna Treadwell

chapter 25

Primrose McConnell and Ongar Park Farm

by Sandra Kerr

Agricultural students everywhere (including my sons!) look upon a copy of Primrose McConnell's *Agricultural Notebook* as their agricultural Bible. When McConnell was a student under Professor Wilson at Edinburgh he *'oftentimes felt the great want of a book containing all the data connected with the subject he was studying.'*[1] The first edition of his *The Agricultural Notebook* was published in 1883 whilst a tenant farmer of Ongar Park Hall. It has been updated ever since, with the twentieth edition published by Messrs Blackwell in 1992. Only Fream's 1892 *Elements of Agriculture* (with its most recent edition in 1992 renamed *Fream's Principles of Food and Agriculture*) can claim as long a period in print as an agricultural textbook. How many agricultural students, farmers, lecturers, and advisers have wondered who McConnell of Ongar Park Hall was?

Primrose, named in the family tradition from the time when his ancestors were connected with the Primrose family estates near Edinburgh, was born on 11 April 1856 into the farming family of Archibald and Agnes at Lessnessock Farm near Ochiltree in Ayrshire. Originally intending to become an engineer on leaving Ayr Academy, Primrose was apprenticed to a Glasgow engineering firm but transferred to the University of Edinburgh to study scientific agriculture, in which he was eminently successful, obtaining the Highland and Agricultural Society of Scotland Diploma and BSc. By 1882 he was professor of agriculture in the Glasgow Veterinary College.

By the summer of 1883 Primrose had persuaded his retired father to return to farming and together they became tenants of Ongar Park Hall. As such, they were the beginning of the migration of Scots farmers to 'derelict Essex.' In the early 1880s McConnell wrote *'reports and advertisements of vacant farms in the south of England appeared in the papers – notably in the* North British Agriculturalist *and* Ayr Advertiser *– land actually going begging for tenants; so we turned our eyes southward. First one or two came, and finding the taste good, sent back a satisfactory report to their friends. When these latter came, they in their turn sent for other friends, until now the country is overrun with us.'*[2] This is possibly the connection with McConnell and the present Kerr family at Ongar Park Hall, both of whose ancestors came from Ayrshire. The Kerrs travelled down from Scotland by train to Blake Hall Station with all their goods and chattels (including livestock) to Wardens Farm in 1889, and moved to Ongar Park Hall when Primrose McConnell left in 1905.

At the age of 27, having made a start in farming, Primrose returned to Scotland and married the minister's daughter, Katherine Anderson, on 10 January 1884 at the Free Church Manse, New Cumnock. Later that year their daughter Anna was born. Archibald arrived three years later, to be followed in 1890 by their second son, Primrose. The family lived in Ongar Park Cottage on the farm until 1893, when Archibald McConnell senior returned to Scotland, and they moved into the farmhouse. *'The farm we took was partly derelict; the previous tenant had held it for four years and it was afterwards farmed by the landlord for two years, as no tenant was forthcoming. It was not in a very flourishing condition when my father and I took hold'.* [3]

Primrose took over the tenancy of Ongar Park Hall from his father in 1893. The farm consisted of 636 acres which he described as *'a dairy and mixed husbandry farm'* – the policy with which most of the Scots immigrants were successful. With cereal prices falling in the 1880s and cheap grain being imported from North America, he grassed down about 200 acres and made his living from eighty dairy cows (sixty of which were in milk at any one time), and by rearing sixty calves annually to two or three year olds.

The period from 1750 to 1880, when British farming was the most progressive in the world, then began to decline. This was particularly due to exploitation of new lands overseas (and to the development of cheap and reliable means of bringing their products to Britain), and it brought a sudden and serious depression to British agriculture. This depression continued until 1939. One long term remedy was liquid milk development. McConnell developed his own system of milk recording for which he was awarded a gold medal and kept a Gerber fat testing machine in his own dairy. He was also one of the founders of the Eastern Counties Co-operative Dairy Farmers Association (subsequently United Dairies) and a regular attender at the Dairy Show in London, as well as a member of the Council of the British Dairy Farmers' Association.

He was a great believer in large fields and the use of machinery and, with the help of Mr. Cottis of Epping, McConnell was successful in adapting the American hay sweep for use in this country. *'This labour-saving implement is of American origin and was first adapted to work in this country in 1894 by the author of this handbook. It took him two years of experiment and development to get it to handle an English crop satisfactorily but it is now a recognised adjunct of the hayfield and many thousands with many different modifications introduced by different makers are now in use in the South of England.'* [4] He was taken to see one being pulled by a tractor a fortnight before his death. [5]

In order to supplement his living at Ongar Park Hall, McConnell lectured, wrote and travelled extensively. He visited Canada in 1890 and 1891 and was associated with the late Lord Brassey who had set up the "Sunbeam Farms" for native American Indians near Indian Head, Saskatchewan, meeting some of the Sioux Indians who took part in the Little Big Horn massacre of 1876. He also wrote sections of some of the encyclopaedias which were popular at the beginning of the twentieth century (including the article on agriculture for the *Encyclopaedia Britannica*), as well as articles for the major agricultural journals. From 1905, he edited and wrote for his own magazine *Farm Life*. Its aim was to provide news and practical information, all illustrated with photographs, as it was considered that country people were *'particularly susceptible to pictorial teaching.'* As with his writing, McConnell's involvement with education was carried on in parallel with his farming. All his appointments, with the possible exception of the Glasgow chair, were part time. He taught agricultural science at Balliol College, Oxford from 1886 to 1893 and subsequently at the Essex Technical Laboratories at Chelmsford (the forerunner of Writtle College) which was congratulated on securing the services of *'one of the best known agricultural authorities in the country'* as lecturer at their nine week winter school.[6] The close proximity of the laboratories to both the cattle market and the corn exchange in Chelmsford enabled them to arrange instruction for local farmers. Market day lectures were held on Friday afternoons and one such lecture entitled "Exhaustion of land by dairying" was given by Primrose McConnell on 18 December 1903. It considered the relative merits of cow and bullock manure! [7]

In December 1898 there was a serious fire at Ongar Park Hall, in which a barn and sheds were gutted.[8] The alarm was raised at 2am, and McConnell's 13 year old daughter was sent on foot to Ongar for the fire engine, which arrived at 4.30am. By this time, the fire, which at one point had threatened the farmhouse itself, had been brought under control. Primrose McConnell had remodelled the farmstead as a dairy farm, building the dairy himself. The barn and old cowhouse were rebuilt after the fire. In June 1899 McConnell took part in a European Study Tour, and with a group of 46 farmers visited Rotterdam cattle market, a cheese market, an agricultural analysis station, a condensed milk factory, the Agricultural Winter School at Goes, and arable and dairy farms – all in five days.[7]

In February 1904 McConnell, exasperated by his landlord's agents, gave notice of his desire to quit Ongar Park Hall. What began as a minor disagreement over valuations escalated into a major legal battle in which claim and counterclaim about permissible rotations, dilapidations, sales of hay, purchases of manures and feeding stuffs, ploughing of meadows and maintenance of buildings were traded backwards and forwards between agents, solicitors, valuers, arbitrators and eventually a judge in the Essex County Court. Although McConnell felt that he had the better of the argument, he clearly resented the waste of time, energy and money on legal costs. He was spurred to write an 84 page report on the whole affair containing every relevant letter and legal document, and to have it privately printed.[3] In the introduction he explained that the case had so many unique features and that many of his friends were interested in the details, especially of the valuations, *'that I consider it desirable to set these forth herein.'* It may have been as simple as that. It might also be that he had his reputation to consider. What would have been the effect on his career as a writer, lecturer and generally accepted agricultural expert if the story that he had been taken to court by his landlord for what might be construed as bad husbandry went unchallenged? He had to demonstrate not only that he won the case, but also it had arisen in the first place from the inability of a traditionally-minded landlord (and his agents) to accept McConnell's modern methods of dealing with low prices for the traditional products of the district. By the time the case ended, McConnell had moved to a new farm. In the autumn of 1905 he bought North Wycke, 500 acres of the flat land between the Crouch and Blackwater estuaries. He remained at North Wycke for the rest of his life, gradually becoming less involved in the physical work of farming, but remaining active as a writer. His granddaughter[9] remembers that he was always surrounded by piles of manuscripts and proofs. His daughter Anna married the son of the farmer from Waterend Farm, Ongar, in 1910 and returned to live at North Wycke in 1928 when her husband James Milroy Kelly became farm manager there. Primrose's first son, Archibald, was an invalid with tuberculosis from 1922 and died in 1935. His younger son, Primrose, fought through the First World War as an artillery officer and was killed in action on the Salonika Front on 18 September 1918.[10] The effect on his father must have been severe, particularly as McConnell had lost not only a son but also a colleague in farming and writing. In July 1931, at the age of 75, he died and was buried in the Congregational burial ground at Southminster. North Wycke remained in the family until Anna Kelly died in 1943.

If this long list of productions and achievements suggests a dour workaholic, it is misleading. Rather, it is evidence for his enormous energy and endless interest in the world around him. It was no dilettante interest. He believed in dealing professionally with the questions that puzzled him. Faced with a new plough, he would fit it with a dynamometer and use it himself for a day.[11] When he realised that he did not know when calves began to ruminate, he got his cowman to observe them, as well as making observations himself. When they compared notes, they agreed that the process began at about three weeks.[9] He tried out a new milking machine for several months, but found that it resulted in decreased yields and went back to hand milking. He then wrote an article for the *Agricultural Gazette*, setting out the figures and probable explanations for the poor yields. Though he may have found against a particular machine, he was too wise to write off the whole idea: '*we do not know what mankind may accomplish in another generation. We may, therefore, see a successful milking machine but it has not arrived yet.*' Bus loads of visitors would come to see his hundred cow cowshed.[9] His granddaughter described him as one of the first modern farmers. He operated a specialist enterprise on a large scale in response to the market forces of the time, and adopted whatever innovations passed his critical evaluation. Friesians, for example, did, and silage did not. He was, as she said, '*a pioneer in everything.*' [9]

Acknowledgement

The author gratefully acknowledges the assistance that she has received from 'A Pioneer in Everything: Primrose McConnell 1856–1931' by Paul Brassley, published in *The Journal of the Royal Agricultural Society of England* (Autumn 1995)

ASPECTS OF THE HISTORY OF ONGAR

References

1. McConnell, P. *The Agricultural Notebook* (1883) Crosby, Lockwood & Co
2. McConnell, P. 'Experiences of a Scotsman on the Essex Clays' in *JRASE* vol 2 (1891)
3. McConnell, P. *Report on the valuations at Ongar Park Hall, Ongar* (c. 1907) published by the author
4. McConnell, P. *The Complete Farmer* (1911) Cassell
5. *The Advertiser*, 11 July 1931
6. *Journal of Royal Agricultural Society of England* (1995)
7. Beale, C. & Owen, G. *Writtle College – The First Hundred Years* (1993) Writtle
8. Cuttle collection of newspaper cuttings ERO: T/P 181/8/29
9. interview with K. Kelly by P. Brassley in 1995
10. *University of Edinburgh Roll of Honour 1914–1918* (1921) Edinburgh
11. McConnell, P. *Diary of a Working Farmer* (1906) Cable

chapter 26

Ongar Cricket Club

by Bernard Shuttleworth

Ongar Cricket Club can be proudly numbered amongst the oldest clubs in the county, having celebrated its sesquicentennial birthday in 1995. It was formed at a public meeting held in the Town Hall on 17 June 1845. Most of the founders were local tradesmen and professional men, and were headed by Henry Bullock, himself a businessman. Twenty-seven members were enrolled on that first evening.

The committee consisted of president, Henry Bullock; treasurer, Rev. P. W. Ray; secretary, T. S. Richardson and six other members. Applications for membership were dealt with by a sub-committee of ten, and certain criteria had to be met, two black balls to exclude. Rules were formulated for the administration of the club. Thursday was to be the official match day, with play to commence at 3pm. Any late comer was to be fined the sum of 6d, the fine to be doubled if not paid before the culprit's next appearance on the ground. The annual subscription was 10s 0d and honorary members could be admitted for the handsome sum of 1 guinea.

The season commenced on the first Thursday of May and ended on the last day of August. Punctuality at that time was obviously of the essence. A rule specifically mentioned that the secretary was to bring the time, regulated by Mr Johnson's clock, to the ground on match days to ensure punctuality and to govern the playing time. Mr Johnson may have been the local clockmaker, though no such name appears in the trade directories of the period.

Unfortunately the document recording the inaugural meeting fails to indicate the location of the ground. It is known that four different grounds have been used during the club's history, namely at Marden Ash (near the Stag public house), Greensted Road, Bowes Field and the present home at Love Lane. A fine timber pavilion graced these grounds, and it was dismantled and reassembled with each change of ground. It provided changing facilities up to the 1960s when it was finally demolished by the members. Local knowledge confirmed that the building was well over 100 years old by this time. The old bat, originally placed on the top of the old bell tower as a weather vane, is still passed on to each president when they assume office. Another feature of the tower was the Essex shield with three seaxes carved on it, the only other relic to have been preserved.

In 1874, it was decided to increase the committee from six to ten. It was also agreed that the club colours should be amber and black. A new rule was introduced regarding the use of obnoxious language on the ground and any member found guilty was liable to exclusion. The annual subscription was reduced to 2s 6d and was to be paid by 25 March (instead of 1 January as laid down by the 1845 rules). Players who promised to play but failed to turn up were to be fined 2s 6d for each offence. This seems a harsh penalty, equal to the annual subscription at that time! Members could use the club equipment when necessary and such equipment was to be stored at the treasurer's residence. That particular rule would be met with some hostility today. Unfortunately the records of the club after 1874 have been lost, apart from a couple of photographs from the turn of the century. Most of the players shown are unknown, though the familiar figure of the late Bill Sammes can be recognised amongst his team mates.

After the Second World War, the club slowly got into swing again. Stalwarts, such as George Hadley, a past president, were coming to the end of their playing days while others, such as J. W. M. Baugh and Dr G.R. Wilson, had long since played their last game. The oldest records of matches played go back to about 1905 and, on the evidence available (including press cuttings in the club's records), it appears that Bill Sammes was the highest scorer for many years on the Ongar ground with 135. That record, of course, no longer stands, having been broken several times since. Just prior to Bill Sammes' death in 1949, his youngest son Frank completed the unusual feat of the "cricketer's double", scoring 1000 runs and taking over 100 wickets in one season. This event is so rare in club cricket that it was reported in the *Essex Chronicle*.

Annual dinners were held quite regularly in the early 1950s, usually at the King's Head in Ongar, costing 7s 6d a head. These were always well attended events, giving members a chance to bring along their wives or girlfriends, as well as to enjoy the company of their playing colleagues once again during the long winter months. At this time, a local enthusiast, the late Cyril Gould, organised club matches against the Essex Club and Ground 11. The Essex team was made up of two or three local players from teams such as Wanstead or Walthamstow, the rest being mainly first team county players. The Ongar side also had invited guest players to make the match a little more evenly balanced. These matches against the Club and Ground would never have been possible but for the kind generosity of Cyril Gould, who not only arranged the fixtures but also met the bill for the hire of a marquee, and the lunches and teas for all concerned. Mr Gould benefited the club in other ways, too. He funded the building of the outside toilet block which served the club for many years until its demolition in the 1990s after having suffered from the hands of vandals. At his death, he left a legacy of £500 for the benefit of the club.

Another local personality, Dr Derek Milnthorpe, was extremely active in the club, holding the offices of chairman and treasurer in spite of having the heavy commitments of a local GP. He also organised the cricket teas, attended the weekly ritual of wicket preparation and generally got involved when any work was required. Though he sadly died far too early in 1969, he left behind the drive necessary for running a successful cricket team, something which is essential in modern times. Another well known Ongarian, JP and local councillor, Jack Coles, worked very long hours on the ground for the club, from immediately after the war until his death in 1983. Local politics and sport were his life, and the tireless effort that he put into the club during that period are sadly missed. He was also a past president of the club.

Unlike football, club cricket was played on a friendly basis throughout England (with a few exceptions) and it was not until the 1960s that the game became more competitive. After years of discussion, leagues were established and in 1976, Ongar tasted their first season of competitive cricket in the Senior Essex League. During the next year or so, the organisers decided to branch out into sponsorship, and in 1979 the league became known as the Lillywhite-Frowd Essex League. Over the next ten years the club enjoyed playing competitive cricket against teams in the southern part of the county.

During this time the club staged several benefit matches for county players Ken McEwan, Graham Gooch (then the England captain) and Keith Pont (who was later appointed both coach and captain of the club's first XI). These matches were played on the Love Lane ground and attracted quite large numbers of spectators. It was during the Gooch match that the club was visited by ITV television cameras anxious to interview Graham about a forthcoming tour with the England team. His decision by phone from the ground meant that the club played a very small, but significant, role in Graham Gooch continuing as the England captain. Television sports news made the announcement that evening, and showed a small clip of the match at Ongar.

After the last benefit match for Keith Pont, it became more acceptable to both parties to play a golf match between the beneficiaries and the club. The star of the day would bring along two or three of his county colleagues to give support, and at the end of the day everyone enjoyed an evening dinner where the day's prizes were distributed and many cricket tales told. Golf matches were arranged for Neil Foster, Derek Pringle, John Childs and, once again, Graham Gooch. All were played on local courses. Each of these events brought in considerable revenue, always vital to a small club. Inflation was making itself felt, and the money was quickly used in machinery maintenance, ground improvements and so on. Sight screens were purchased and the club's main sponsor, Travis Perkins, provided the materials for a new score box to be built. Other businesses who helped in providing club shirts for both senior and junior members were J. Brace & Sons (local timber merchants), Raggett, Tiffin & Harries (solicitors) and James Capel Associates.

In the 1980s, the club did several tours in north Devon. These events were extremely well supported and great fun, and some memorable cricket was enjoyed by all taking part. Unfortunately these tours have ceased, but the juniors carry on the tradition, touring the Isle of Wight over the Easter Bank holiday with the support of one or two dads.

In 1989, the sponsorship of the league changed again, and it became known as the

ASPECTS OF THE HISTORY OF ONGAR

Morrant Essex League. With reasonable success in their league matches, and ambitious to play on better grounds, the club applied to join the major county league, the Colour Assembly Essex League. This application succeeded in 1994 and the club was placed in division 2, playing their first full season in 1995. In 1998 the league sponsorship changed hands and became known as the Shepherd Neame Essex League. Though the club is still waiting to gain league honours, it has won the Vernon Cocking Cup and the Max Taylor Trophy on several occasions, together with the Proudlock cup. Recent years have seen the club entertain an MCC XI to mark its 150th anniversary, together with the extremely popular president's match which takes place every August.

I cannot let this opportunity pass without making reference to the support and encouragement given to junior members of our club, and to record their tremendous part in playing and providing a pool of up and coming youngsters on whom the future of the club will depend. The people behind this part of the club are Paul Kelly and Pat Bolden. One of their successes is that three members have played for the Essex Under 15s against other county sides, gaining considerable experience along the way. The coaching and expertise provided by the former Essex cricketer, Keith Pont, was extremely valuable in attracting large numbers of boys to the grounds on Monday evenings. Regrettably, Keith is no longer able to coach due to other commitments, but qualified members of the club continue to offer this service.

The junior section of the club was started many years ago, but the chief organiser, who really got it going in earnest, was the late president and chairman, Philip Page. He not only undertook this task, but was also the county's youth organiser at the same time. It is very different from the early days, when juniors had to arrange their own matches, prepare their pitches and get themselves to away matches, sometimes on bicycles. One of the clubs regularly played was Hutton CC, which included a young lad called Paul Pritchard. Even at the age of ten, it was obvious that he was destined to go on to greater things, and he later become a prominent batsman at county and national level, as well as captain of Essex.

In the 1998 season, the club recorded another first by engaging the services of an Australian cricketer, Adam Williams, who plays for Tasmania. A forceful batsman, and a more than useful medium pace bowler, it was no surprise to find that he was an excellent and inspirational fielder. He thoroughly enjoyed coaching junior members and quickly became a most popular player amongst the seniors. Being accustomed to dry hard pitches back home, he gradually adjusted to the soft pitches in that wet season. He has since become the first honorary member of the club in recent years.

Today the club is still headed by a president and run by the officers listed below. All these offices require considerable enthusiasm and hard work, and the club is fortunate in having a splendid team to undertake these various tasks. The club's AGM is usually held in October.

ONGAR CRICKET CLUB

A final mention must go to the club's supporters and vice presidents, all of whom have given a considerable amount to make this a happy and progressive club. Those who are numbered amongst this band of stalwarts are Rob and Laurie Coles, Den Hutchings, Colin Nicholls and George Finbow (both former chairmen), Bob Brown, Trevor and Hazel Powell, Frank Collins, John Thurgood, Graham Francis (representing Travis Perkins), Roger Timms, Ray Harrop, Bob Dick, Bernie Brace, Terry Leigh, Mike Walker, Keith Pont, Maurice Moore, Paul Dick and the wives of the late Wilf Smith, Dick Arnold and Phil Page.

As a lasting reminder of the association that Wilf had with the club, two bench seats were kindly donated by Mrs Doreen Smith. Mrs Phil Arnold donated a silver salver, known as the Dick Arnold Trophy, to be awarded annually to the member considered to have contributed most to helping the club. Another trophy, the First Team Player of the Year, was donated by the late Mr Wood and is awarded annually. To all of these people, the club owes a sincere *thank you*.

Sources

1. record of Ongar Cricket Club inaugural meeting (1845)
2. *Laws and Regulations of the Ongar Cricket Club* (1845) printed in Ongar by T. S. Richardson
3. *Rules of the Ongar Cricket Club* (1874) printed in Ongar by C. Slocombe
4. inf and assistance from the current committee: Bernard Shuttleworth (president & treasurer), Michael Wood (chairman), David Powell (vice-chairman & ground manager), David Spennock (assistant treasure), Nigel Shuttleworth (secretary & club representative)), David Coles (fixture secretary), Paul Kelly and Pat Bolden (youth organisers).

chapter 27

Scouting in Ongar

by Peter Evans

The early years

From Robert Baden-Powell's first experimental camp in 1907, the Scout movement spread rapidly, both in this country and worldwide. Growth was so rapid that Scouting often started in a town before it had been officially registered with the Boy Scouts Association. This seems to have been the case in Chipping Ongar where the earliest evidence comes from two postcards of a Scout parade dated 1912, though no written records survive. Normally each Scout group is identified by a four or six digit number, with an order number to show whether there is, or has been, another Group in the area. Over the years, two "1st Ongar", two "2nd Ongar", two "3rd Ongar" and one "4th Ongar" Groups have been registered.

The earliest official records of a local Group is found in the Essex County Scout office which shows that, in 1921, 14 boys were meeting in the Congregational church under the leadership of the Rev. G.F. White (Scoutmaster), assisted by Mr R. A. W. Comber. No Wolf Cub Pack was registered. A copy of an entry in an autograph book, dated 29 March 1922, describes a presentation made to the Assistant Scoutmaster of the 1st Ongar Troop on leaving the district for New Zealand, and subsequent pages list 10 committee members and 47 Scouts. Many of the surnames are still found in Ongar. An undated press cutting gives a full account of the farewell party.

> 'Assistant Scoutmaster R. Comber was the recipient of a parting gift from the officers and members of the Ongar Troop of Boy Scouts on Wednesday evening. He had for over two years acted as Assistant scoutmaster, and generous tributes to his services were made by Scoutmaster Fisher, who presented him, on behalf of the Troop, with the Scouts' badge of thanks (the Swastika). The gathering took place in the Congregational schoolroom, and Mr H. Childs, who was the life and soul of the proceedings, presided over a good attendance. The first part of the evening was given over to a varied programme of displays, songs, recitations etc. provided by the Scouts themselves. They were greatly applauded in their display of signalling, given under the direction of Signalling Instructor, Mr E. Tagell. Scoutmaster Fisher gave a skilful exhibition of club swinging. Scouts C. Bryant and W. Pearson recited very effectively, and songs were nicely rendered by Assistant Scoutmaster Coles and Scouts Sitch and Camp. Troop choruses were sung and received great applause. The Cubs, looking very smart and business-like under Cubmaster Lacey, gave their Cub howls, that could be heard at Ongar

Railway Station. The Girl Guides, with their Captain Miss Baugh, and Miss Brown (Lieutenant) were in attendance and helped to make this farewell social to Assistant Scoutmaster Comber a glorious send-off. Refreshments were dispensed, this part of the proceedings being looked after by Mrs Knight, Mrs Jenkins, Mrs Long, Mrs Smith and Miss Waters. The singing of the National Anthem ended a very enjoyable evening.'

The application to register the 1st Ongar Cub Scout Pack (referred to above) was made by Mr J. E. Lacey on 4 March 1922. The open pack (i.e. any eligible boy could join) had 26 Cub Scouts and two leaders, and met in "The Den" at the Congregational church. County records show that, in 1923 and 1924, the troop was led by Mr A. Fisher, assisted by Mr T.V. Nickelson. Messrs J.E. and E.F. Lacey were in charge of the Wolf Cub Pack. Four years later, the county record noted *' 1st Ongar are to be complemented on being 60 strong, the largest in the County, and are now founding a new Scout Troop.'* This was registered as the 1st Ongar Scout Troop on 1 December 1926 under Mr Lacey, acting Scoutmaster and Mr C. Bryant, assistant, with 24 scouts, two Rover Scouts and two leaders. It is thought that this was in addition to the existing Troop. The last census figures were received by the Scout Association Headquarters in 1931, and it is presumed that the group closed soon after. County records show no Group in Ongar after 1934.

However, what is curious is that a controlled Group (i.e. one with restricted membership), called the 1st Ongar, was registered at the Chipping Ongar senior school in May 1937 under the leadership of John G. Gomer (registration number 18650). This had 20 Scouts and one leader. There is a postcard showing a gathering of young people, marked on the back *'Visit of Baden-Powell to Forest Hall 1937,'* but the association's archivist has been unable to verify from the founder's diaries that he did in fact visit Scouting in the town. County records of 1940 and 1947 show a 1st Ongar Group in existence, suggesting that two separate 1st Ongar Groups were registered before the Second World War, and that the second one existed throughout the war.

In 1942, the county Scout Council archives reported the formation of the 2nd Ongar Scout Group (registration number 21402) at the London County Council's "residential school for mentally defective boys". This was the school later known as Great Stony. In 1943, this Group had 24 Wolf Cubs, 24 Boy Scouts and three leaders. The Group leader was Mr W. Uden, the headmaster of the school. No further censuses appear and the last county entry for this Group is in a District return dated 1957.

Post-war re-emergence – establishing Scouting to last the millennium

A 3rd Ongar (St Martin's) Scout group was first registered on 9 July 1947 as a church controlled group (registration number 252258), led by Lewis Walker, the verger, with a membership of 12 Scouts. There was also a Wolf Cub pack of eight boys, led by Mrs Uden, the wife of the headmaster of Great Stony school. In the following year, a 4th Ongar (Congregational) Scout Group was formed (registration number

ASPECTS OF THE HISTORY OF ONGAR

26085) with 22 Scouts led by the Rev. W. H. Walker. Nothing more is known about this Group.

The activities of the 3rd Ongar Group are noted in the church magazines during the incumbency of the Rev. John Vaughan-Jones. In May 1949 *'with nearly 40 Scouts and Cubs and Mrs Avery to help with the Cubs, the Group is second to none in the District, but could do with a young man or two to help.'* In October 1949, new Troop Colours, given by Mrs W. Uden, and new King's Colours, given by Flying Officer L. Walker, were dedicated in St Martin's and the District Commissioner presented First Class badges to John Hart and John Anderson, and Second Class ones to Robert Geary, Arthur Thurley and John Frost. In March 1950, Cubs were meeting in the parish rooms under the charge of Mrs Barbara Avery after the service. In September 1950, the rector wrote *'once again this year, I was able to spend some time with the Scouts in camp at Highwood. There were 16 boys under canvas....'* There was an organised bonfire on the Rectory field on 6 November 1950, and in September the following year, the rector was again under canvas at a Scout camp near Lambourne church. In July 1952, the church magazine reported *' the June issue of ' The Scout' announced the award of a portrait of the Chief Scout to St Martin's Scouts for the best report of recent activities by a Troop. The report was sent in by Patrol Leader Alan Laggett. A similar award was won by the Troop in November 1947 by John Hart.'*

In 1953 the Troop was suddenly left without a leader and had to close, followed a few years later by the Cub Pack. In April 1957, the *Church Magazine* reported *' The 3rd Ongar (St Martins) Cub Pack had to close owing to the resignation of Miss V. M. Prior*, the Cub Mistress. *She had carried on single handed for 3 years. No one could be found to take her place.'*

Scouting was restarted in Ongar after a meeting convened on 18 April 1957 by the Rev. John Vaughan-Jones. The meeting was attended by the rector, Mr A. Simpson, the Assistant District Commissioner, Mr R. C. Rogers, prospective Leader and 10 boys (Bernard Brace, Stuart Cullum, Christopher East, Roger Emberson, Martyn Everett, Roger Ludlow, Malcolm Ludlow, Terry Neil, Colin Rogers and Tommy Humphreys). They can be regarded as the founder members of the present 3rd Ongar Scout Group. An explanation of Scouting was given, and those interested were invited to a meeting the following week. If six turned up, a Troop would be formed. All ten, plus a newcomer, Michael Roberts, returned, and were divided into two patrols. For a short time meetings were held at "Brookfield" in Bushey Lea, but soon moved to the church rooms in Castle Street when membership had increased to 19. On 25 June 1957, the Scout District Commissioner attended a ceremony where the boys made their Scout promises and became invested Scouts. The Group then settled down to passing Tenderfoot tests and attaining Second Class standard badges.

By July 1957, increasing membership necessitated the division of the Troop into four patrols. Due to lack of equipment and experience, it was not possible to hold a summer camp, but six of the Troop joined the 1st Nazeing Scout Troop's camp in the Lorna Doone valley in North Devon. All six were elected honorary members of the Nazeing Troop. In August, the Troop undertook its first public service and sold all the available programmes for the Ongar Show – to the consternation of the organisers! A Cub pack was being run by Ian Rogers, after the resignation of its first leader Miss Prior. In August, Mr R. C. Rogers became Scouter in charge and the Group was officially registered with the Scout Association in October 1957 (registration number 33514). A new Scouter took over in January 1958, allowing Mr Rogers to become Group Scoutmaster. In the autumn, a new Assistant Scoutmaster, Mr R. Sutton, joined and was assisted by two senior Scouts, David Peck and Warwick Latin. An active group supporters committee was in action (led by Mr T. Humphreys with Mr M. Everett as the first treasurer), and two other Assistant Scoutmasters, Kim Footer and Michael Scott, were also recruited. The reason for mentioning all these names is that, without their enthusiasm, the following 40 years of service to young people might not have been possible.

There was a growing list of activities, with a variety of visits including one to the 40th Chingford Scout Group, recorded as *'in my view, the most happy outing that the Troop has enjoyed so far, bar none, despite the unhappy accident to Graham Getgood and the seat of Colin Roger's uniform trousers!'* By the end of 1957 the Group had outgrown the church rooms, and moved to the upper assembly room in the Budworth Hall. A camp was run at Easter 1958 for the 12 Scouts who had passed their Second Class badge, *'a most successful camp and, but for the fact that it became bogged down under 11 inches of Kentish snow at Downe and had to be abandoned on Easter Sunday, would have been an unqualified success.'* Group fund raising using the traditional Scout methods of bob-a-job, rummage sales and sale of work enabled the first tent and other camping equipment to be bought.

By April 1958 recruitment was such that admissions had to be closed. The problem, still common to Scouting, was that there were too many lads and too few helpers. Mr Rogers had to resume the leadership of the Scout Troop, leaving the position of Group Scoutmaster vacant. This was filled by the arrival of an experienced Scouter, Mr Paul Allmen, who had previously been Scoutmaster of the 2nd Ongar Scouts at Great Stony school. It is assumed that Mr Rogers left the Group in the latter half of 1958, as this is the last date that his name appears on a Group document. Fund raising activities continued enthusiastically, and the Group's funds began to accumulate.

At the AGM in March 1961, there were discussions about a permanent home for the Group. In May two huts which had been the garrison engineers' offices at Warley Barracks were purchased. The next problem was how to get them to Ongar and where to put them. Volunteers dismantled the hut interiors, and wives and boys came to pull out nails. It then took a team of skilled builders a week to dismantle the huts. The search for a site ended happily when Ongar parish council leased a plot of land in the corner of the sports field to the Scouts for 21 years at a peppercorn rent of £1 per annum. An access track was provided from

ASPECTS OF THE HISTORY OF ONGAR

Love Lane, as well as a path with a footbridge into what was then the rectory garden (now the Shakletons estate).

From this point onwards, the story of the 3rd Ongar Group's headquarters becomes a magnificent saga of enthusiastic cooperation between devoted volunteers, expert scroungers, generous donors, eager helpers, and professionals working on a largely non-profit basis. Foundations, brickwork, erecting, roofing, felting, lining, partitioning, flooring, painting, papering, decorating, furnishing, laying the path, erecting the fence, levelling off the site, and making everything spick and span for the official opening – these tasks consumed hundreds of man hours of dedicated work. The whole enterprise was a vivid and rewarding example of what a community can achieve when inspired by a few firebrand enthusiasts. The new headquarters were opened on 29 September 1962 by Major G. Capel-Cure, vice lieutenant of Essex, accompanied by Lt-Col. D. P. Papillon, county commissioner of Scouts in Essex and the official programme listed the group officers, leaders and supporters who helped to give the group its own home. While it would be wrong to single out individual contributors to the successful provision of a permanent home for Scouting in Ongar, the person universally acknowledged as the prime motivator and enthusiast was Dr Ted Hatfield, an Ongar general practitioner. As a result of his commitment, he was appointed president of the Scout Group, and awarded the Association's merit award, the Silver Acorn.

In 1963, the Group achieved a milestone when Rob Williams achieved the highest training award possible, the Queen's Scout award. Rob also represented the Scout District at the world Scout Jamboree in Greece that year. In 1964, David Clare was recruited as a new Scouter, and he (and his wife Doreen, who became Cub Scout leader) were to be a driving force in the Group for the next 22 years. In the same year, the 2nd Ongar controlled Group was formed at Great Stony school (registration number 37055) by the headmaster, Ron Barnes. It started with 14 boys and one leader, and continued until the school's closure in 1994. The 3rd Ongar Group continued to grow, and in 1966 Mr Jack Osborne superseded Mr Allmen as Group Scout Leader. Mr Osborne was to have a strong impact on Scouting, both in the Group and in the Epping & Ongar District.

The Scout Movement underwent a major review in that year. The Boy Scouts Association became the Scout Association, and the traditional uniform of bush hats and shorts was changed to something more appropriate for the young people of the day. The training programme was updated, and most of the section names were changed, as well as the age range and eligibility. It took the national press 30 years to catch up with these changes! Wolf Cubs became known as Cub Scouts. The two senior sections (Senior Scouts and Rover Scouts) were formed into the Venture Scouts for 16 – 20 year olds. In 1968, David Clare and Geoff Davies opened the first Venture Scout unit in the town.

The 1970s – activity and diversity

At the beginning of the decade, the author (known as "Snowy") joined the Group as an Assistant Scout Leader to David Clare ("Stag"). Both were to give over 25 years service each to the Group and to hold the post of Group Scout Leader. Scouting is an organisation with many traditions, but these are only retained as long as they are relevant. During the 1970s, a number of new traditions evolved. The annual renewal of promise at the St George's day parade grew larger with the expansion of the Group. Members were encouraged to keep their promise to develop a faith by attending regular youth services. An annual carol service was held with a toy collection for homeless children. During the late 1960s, the Group held its own bonfire and fireworks party at the headquarters. During the 1970s, this was opened to the general public. Over the next two decades, due to its very high standards, it became the principal public display in the town, as well as a major fund raising event for the Group. To accommodate its growing popularity, this event was moved to the sports field in the 1990s in association with the Ongar Sports and Social Club. Another popular and successful fund raising activity since the 1970s has been the annual spring sale of bedding plants at the Budworth Hall.

Annual events such as camping, sports and swimming became traditional activities. The annual patrol leaders' dinner was started in the 1970s, a five course formal dinner served to 50–60 parents, leaders and friends in the headquarters, decorated to illustrate a particular theme. Troop leaders were guests, and banned from the kitchen. In 1972, the group built and equipped a small fleet of canoes and "Slack Alice", "Green Streak", "Ever'ard" and "Grasmere" were taken to the 1973 group camp at Grasmere. The fleet was expanded over the next 20 years. In 1972, the Group provided home hospitality to a Troop of Swiss Scouts attending the international Jamboree in Essex, and this hospitality was returned when the troop had its summer camp in Switzerland in 1974. This was the first of a number of overseas camps and visits, the next being in 1978 when 50 members camped at Wiltz in Luxembourg.

From the beginning of the 3rd Ongar, the Group relied on (and was very grateful to) Dr Ted Hatfield for the use of his Land Rover for transport, even after it was accidentally set on fire (full of fireworks) at one of the bonfire parties! It became clear that the Group needed its own more suitable transport. In 1976, Cub Scout leader Francis Hoffman enlisted the support of the CO of the King's Troop, Royal Horse Artillery with a fund raising event on Bowes Field on 8 May. The centrepiece was two horse drawn field guns and limbers of the King's Troop performing their well known routine and charge. Within two months, the Group had its own van and has had its own transport ever since by regularly upgrading. The present vehicle is a modern minibus which complies with all the legislation introduced since boys were first transported in the back of a Land Rover!

In 1977 the town celebrated the Queen's silver jubilee. The Group was represented on the town's celebration committee, a Venture Scout working party supported events on the sports field and a barbecue was run by Rotary in the Scout grounds. During this decade the Group regularly entered a float in the comprehensive school's carnival parade, and scooped several first prizes. Membership continued to grow. A third Cub Scout Pack (the "Castle") was formed in 1976 to supplement the existing "Motte" and "Bailey" packs. The troop was divided into two, "Viking" and "Saxon". The author re-established the Venture Scout unit, the original unit formed in 1968 having lapsed after three years.

The 1980s – consolidation of the past and foundations for the future

Membership remained healthy, at around 125, for most of this decade. In 1985 the 15th Blake Hall Sea Scout Troop was formed, led by Colin Eaton with 15 members (registration number 251158). Soon after a Cub Scout Pack and a Beaver Scout Colony were formed, the latter being one of the first in the District. The Group placed emphasis on water and sailing activities, using Royal Yachting sailing courses annually for eleven years. Many boys obtained the RYA qualifications, some eventually owning their own dinghies.

In 1987 a plea was made for leaders to start a 3rd Ongar Beaver Scout Colony for 6–8 year olds, and by 1988 Brenda Ray, Dee Costigan and Marilyn Harvey had been invested. With the wider Scouting provision, overall membership rose to 163, showing that the needs of the younger boys were being met. By this time there were 18 leaders and six sections, mostly full (and the Beaver Scouts with a waiting list). The Venture Scout unit, with up to 20 members, emulated their 1970s predecessors by walking the 196 mile coast to coast footpath in the north of England. In 1986, there was a sponsored climb of the three highest peaks in the Great Britain in 44 ½ hours.

The community has been very supportive of the Scouts in many ways, particularly in providing training support and in fund raising. For a number of years the local firemen ran a "fireman's badge" course. A parent presented a wooden trophy in the shape of a bell (made from timbers from the old Stock Exchange) to the watch running the course. On one occasion the Venture Scouts held an investiture at the top of the greasy pole in the fire station, with those invested sliding down to the floor below! The police station has given tours, as well as practical talks on subjects ranging from road safety to drugs awareness. Roger Spearman, of High Ongar garage, regularly ran a mechanics badge course. Schools have allowed use of their sports fields, farmers permitted access to their land and much more.

In return, the Group has tried to support the community in a variety of ways, such as chopping wood for the elderly, litter picking, snow clearing and fund raising for Ongar hospital, Community Care and Finch Court.

The 1990s – the pinnacle of expansion

In 1991 the first girls were invested in the Venture Scouts, on a raft in the middle of Skreens Park lake, Roxwell. The 3rd Ongar group had become a registered charity with an annual turnover of £19,000 from subscriptions, fund raising and camp fees. The parents' committee had paid for the re-roofing of the hut and a new minibus. However the youth programme was becoming a victim of its own success, having difficulty in recruiting enough volunteer leaders to meet the demand. The problem was solved by the merger of the 15th Blake Hall and the 3rd Ongar Groups in 1990. The new Group retained the 3rd Ongar name, but the new blue and green scarf symbolised both land and water activities by combining the colours of the two former groups. In 1992 there were eight separate sections, each (apart from the Venture Scouts) with at least 20 members. Some had a waiting list and the Group had the highest ever recorded membership of 178, with 24 warranted adult leaders, all trained or in training. The hut was in use five nights a week, some nights one section following another. However the momentum could not be maintained due to the difficulty in obtaining enough adult volunteers. In 1994 the Motte Cub Scout Pack closed, its members being divided between the two remaining Packs.

In 1994 the Venture Scouts joined 4,500 others in their biggest ever national event. This was a four day mystery tour to a number of sites in Europe, ending with three days in Paris and including EuroDisney! In 1995 a contingent went to the Scout training headquarters at Gilwell Park to greet the Queen on her official visit to open the refurbished premises. In 1997 there was a change of leadership in the Blake Hall Scout Troop which resulted in a return to land based activities under the name of Saxon Troop. In the last years of the decade there was an annual weekend camp for members led by Scouter David Green. There were over 100 campers on these weekends.

The impact and achievements of Scouting in the town

The aim of the Scout Association is *'to promote the development of young people in achieving their full physical, intellectual, social and spiritual potentials as individuals, as responsible citizens and as members of their local, national and international communities.'* Over two thirds of the twentieth century, hundreds of young people in Ongar have experienced the fun of Scouting, as well as achieving their individual and collective goals. Some have been involved for a short time, others have progressed from section to section to complete the Venture Scout training programme and gain the prestigious Queen's Scout Award. In 1995 the first female Queen's Scout, Lisa Portman, was invited as a delegate to the Russian Scout federation conference in Moscow, marking the re-introduction of Scouting in Russia after the collapse of Communism. Over the years Scout awards have helped their holders to further their careers, or to go on to further challenges such as Duke of Edinburgh awards, "Camp America" or "Operation Raleigh". One Cub Scout, who saw the charge of the King's Troop in Ongar, would eventually lead the charge himself. The best memories for most Scouts are the camps and expeditions, times of real independence, activity and fun. For the leaders, these were the most responsible as well as the most rewarding times, particularly the overseas camps in Switzerland, Luxembourg, Belgium and France in the 1970s and 1980s.

ASPECTS OF THE HISTORY OF ONGAR

Ongar Scouts have regularly attended the four yearly Essex International Jamboree with between 2000 and 4000 Scouts and Guides from around the world. The pinnacle for international experience is the World Scout Association Jamboree which is also held every four years. It is to the credit of the 3rd Ongar that, since its formation, 16 members have been accepted as part of the County Troop to represent the UK, three as leaders.

Involvement with local and national charities has already been mentioned. A variety of national charities have benefited from the group's efforts, both financially and practically. The annual sponsored walk has been a regular fund raising event and for several years the group pre-sorted 25,000 envelopes for the Leprosy Mission's Christmas appeal. The Castle Beaver Scouts regularly raised money to help the education of Marhesh, a child adopted by the "Save the Children Fund" in India. A number of other local fund raising activities have benefited from practical assistance from the Scouts, with the redoubtable marquee being erected at many events.

The Ongar Headquarters have welcomed a number of VIPs. In 1994 Gabriel Amori, national executive commissioner for Ugandan Scouts, came to collect the Group's cheque for the charity "Unite", and explained how this would be used to help Scouting in Uganda. In 1988, when the Venture Scouts were raising money towards a school in Nepal, two sherpas (in the UK as part of this project) were brought here to see a Scout Troop in action. The Patrol Leaders dinners have had many guests, including Alexander Bonder (who was involved in the re-introduction of Scouting to Russia), two County Commissioners, most of the Assistant County Commissioner's team, and the editor of the "Scouting" magazine. Other Scout Groups, and police cadets walking the nearby Essex Way, have camped here. All are recorded in the group visitors' book.

All adult Scout leaders undertake the appropriate training programme, leading to the award of the coveted "Wood Badge". The last three Group Scout leaders of the 3rd Ongar have all taken roles in district Scouting. Jack Osborne became District Commissioner, David Clare, Assistant District Commissioner, and Peter Evans, Deputy District Commissioner. The latter became a member of the Association's paid staff, as Programme and Training Adviser at Gilwell Park. Ron Barnes became a National Commissioner with special responsibility for the handicapped, and another Ongar resident, Mick Berry, who did his Group Scouting at North Weald, was also to be appointed District Commissioner. All five received the Silver Acorn, the second highest merit award of the Scout Association, for distinguished services to Scouting.

The final word on the impact of Scouting comes from Steven Richmond, a Patrol Leader in the 1980s. Steven went on to Sandhurst army officer training college, graduated and eventually served in the Falklands campaign. On his return, he was asked if anything he had done in Scouting had been helpful in his chosen career. He replied *'at Sandhurst, I realised that my opportunities of working in a team –*

and, as Patrol Leader, leading a team – gave me an understanding of team work and getting on with different types of people, and as such gave me an advantage over the other cadets who hadn't had this experience.' Evidence indeed that Ongar Scouting has had an impact and achieved its aim.

Some thoughts on the future

Scouting has succeeded by its ability to change and from the support it has received from the community, particularly from the generosity of adults giving their time to lead the Scouts and raise funds to ensure that they were properly equipped. As the second millennium draws to a close, Scouting is well placed to continue to serve the young people of Ongar. Change will continue. In the late 1990s the Scout Association is conducting a major review of its youth programme to ensure its continuing relevance in a changing society. Since 1991, Scout Groups have been able to agree to admit girls of all ages. This has not been possible in Ongar due to the heavy usage and lack of appropriate facilities at the headquarters, as well as the fact that Guiding also has a strong presence in the town. However, girls have been members of the Venture Scout unit since 1991. Perhaps in the future girls will be admitted to all sections. The headquarters, still housed in an ex-army wooden hut, will have been in use for 40 years by 2002, a tribute to all those parents who have kept it maintained. But it must surely have a finite life, and its replacement will be a challenge for the next millennium.

Certain milestones beckon. The first will be a millennium celebration at a camp in May 2000. The first centenary of Scouting will be in 2007, and Ongar Scouting will want to be involved in that celebration. There is also a strong possibility that the centennial 21st World Scout Jamboree will be held at the nearby Hylands Park, and in April of the same year, the 3rd Ongar Scout Group will reach its own golden jubilee.

This record is written at a time when statutory provision for the young is in decline. Nationally youth services are targeted to areas of greatest need. Ongar's population is growing with the potential for much new housing development. Scouting must be able to respond to these challenges, if necessary by increasing its provision. Whether it is able to do so will depend, as it always has, on sufficient volunteer adults to give time to meet the needs of successive generations of young people. Let us hope they will.

Sources

1   3rd Ongar Scout Group archives
2   inf from Paul Monyhan, Scout Association archivist
3   inf from Graham Greaves, Scout Association records dept
4   inf from Ron Barnes, Colin Eaton, Dr Ted & Sylvia Hatfield, Mrs. Kerrish (daughter of A. S. M. Comber), Peter Markwick, Gerry Reeves, Ian Stern, Malcolm Tretcher, Rev John Vayghan Jones, Dr. Robert Williams and past and present members & supporters of 3rd Ongar Scout Group.

chapter 28

Ongar and District Horticultural and Allotment Society

by Tanya Welford

The Society has been in existence for at least 100 years, although no early records have survived. A surviving newspaper cutting shows that an AGM of the Ongar Horticultural Society was held in the Budworth Hall in about 1896, chaired by the rector, the Rev. Tanner. There was a large attendance. A summer show had been held that year, and a vote of thanks was proposed to the member who had made his ground available for the event. That year was said to have been the hundredth anniversary of the introduction of chrysanthemums to England, and in celebration two silver cups (valued at about 10 guineas) were to be presented for the best chrysanthemums at the autumn show.

Exisiting records show that the Ongar Allotments Society was active in 1941, with 121 members paying an annual subscription of 1s 0d. Affiliation fees were paid to the Essex Federation of Allotments and the National Allotments Society. After the Second World War, the Ongar and District Horticultural and Allotments Society (ODHAS) was formed. There were allotments at the bottom of Cloverley Road on the area now covered by the houses of Longfields. There were further allotments in the area of Green Walk, and below Castle Street – and, at a later date, in Shelley on the site of the cycle speedway, and in Bansons Lane.

The Longfields allotments were prone to thefts of fruit and vegetables, as well as damage from cows getting into the area. Trespass notices were erected and barbed wire was added to the plain wire fence. Allotment wardens were appointed, and there was concern that the Longfields area was to be developed for housing. In 1952, during one of the fencing ventures on the Longfields allotments, a member of the society, Wilf Stokes, lost the sight in his eye from an injury caused by a flying staple. The society set up an accident fund for the victim, and raised a substantial sum of money for Wilf. He was a committee member from the 1950s to 1992 when the society activities ceased. At the 1983 AGM he, together with Len Jones and Arthur Shuttleworth, was presented with an RHS medal for over 100 years service to the society between them. He won many cups at the annual show for his vegetables, dahlias, sweet peas and chrysanthemums.

A further task for the society in the 1940s was the distribution of lime at various sites round Ongar for sale to members. This was part of the national lime subsidy scheme whereby registered horticultural societies could claim a subsidy from the Ministry of Agriculture. This scheme continued into the 1960s. In 1956, 9 $\frac{1}{2}$ tons of

ONGAR AND DISTRICT HORTICULTURAL AND ALLOTMENT SOCIETY

lime was delivered to Ongar for distribution in Ongar, Shelley and Kelvedon Hatch. It was sold at this time for 2s 6d per cwt, but it was thought that a profit margin of 9d per cwt was too high, so purchasers received a 6d per cwt refund. Members were also entitled to a discount on horticultural goods from local shops on production of a membership card. This practice continued for many decades.

In the early 1950s, meetings of ODHAS were held in the Congregational Church hall, moving to the Red Cow pub in Shelley in the mid 1950s. Meetings were often preceded by a short talk on a gardening topic, followed by a lively discussion. The 1957 AGM was held in the Tudor Room in the King's Head. The following year the monthly meetings were held in the offices of Messrs Sworder, Son & Gingell in the High Street, and from 1961 to 1981 in a room at the back of the Bell pub. The AGM in December was followed by a cheese competition, then by cheese and wine, and ended with showing a film of that year's Ongar show.

The society was affiliated to the National Chrysanthemum Society, the National Dahlia Society, the National Rose Society and the Royal Horticultural Society. The society took part in the annual Ongar Show which was started in 1949 and ran until 1963, and was organised by the Ongar and District Agricultural Society. The society had a one day flower show on August bank holiday Monday on the Ongar sports field, with a large marquee full of stunning blooms, fruit and vegetables. There were domestic produce and handicraft classes, as well as entries from beekeepers. It was not unknown for exhibitors to bring a camp bed in order to guard their exhibits overnight! After the demise of the Ongar Show, the society staged its own autumn show in the Budworth Hall.

The society staged a spring or summer show, with an autumn show for chrysanthemums and dahlias. By the 1980s there was less support for these events and only the autumn show was held. This took more the form of a community show and extra classes were included in the schedule to include the Ongar Flower Club and the Ongar Photographic Club. There were children's competitions, such as "a decorated vegetable" or "a sink garden." Local schools were involved and the Autumn show in the Budworth Hall was a great local event, organised by the committee members for the community. After judging, it was open to the public to browse round the exhibits, and enter into the spirit of the occasion. At the end of the day, silver cups and prizes were presented, and finally the auction took place.

The trading post was opened in 1965 in a moderate sized air raid shelter at the back of Carter's the butchers. The society purchased stock in bulk, and was able to offer its members goods at reduced prices. This was a great asset as there were few nurseries or garden centres at that time, and none near Ongar. The trading post was manned by a rota of members every Sunday, and for many years on Friday evenings as well. Members could then spend the weekend working on their gardens or allotments. Subscriptions were collected by district representatives, who were also able to deliver small quantities of goods such as seeds and seed potatoes. This was of particular benefit to members living in the outlying villages who had difficulty in getting in to the trading post. The trading post gradually declined in the face of competition from the increasing number of garden centres in the area. In 1988, the air raid shelter was demolished when the site was sold and new buildings were put up. No suitable new site could be found for the trading post which was no longer able to compete with the prices of the new garden centres.

The closure of the trading post was a great loss to the society as many had joined in the 1970s and 1980s to benefit from the discounts available. Membership had fluctuated over the decades, from 151 in 1961/62 to 422 in the late 1970s. Numbers declined after that, and were down to 113 in 1988 when the trading post closed.

There were other events in the social calendar. A very popular annual dance was held in the Budworth Hall and it was necessary to secure a ticket well in advance to avoid disappointment. There were coach outings to various places, including the RHS gardens at Wisley, and the gardens of Syon Park and Bressingham. There were monthly meetings in the church rooms in Castle Street in the 1970s and 1980s with speakers from horticultural organisations. However much of an experienced gardener you considered yourself to be, there was always more to be learnt on the subject.

The society rents allotments below Castle Street from the local landowner for the benefit of its members. These were (and still are) let out at a favourable rent, and the society remains responsible for their administration. In July 1982, vandals savagely attacked vegetables on these allotments, and six out of eighteen of the plots were damaged. The plots are behind a hedge and out of view of the general public passing on the nearby footpath.

In May 1974, the Ongar Hospital league of friends invited the society to run a stall at their annual garden fete (now the annual autumn Fayre). Members responded, a newsletter requesting items was sent out and money was raised for the league of friends. The stall sold home grown produce, pot plants, beautiful begonias and so on, and was run by Len Jones with the assistance of Bert King and John Francis. Sadly Len Jones died suddenly in 1988 while working on his allotment, after over 30 years of service to the society. The writer then took over the running of the stall, assisted by Bert and his wife Floss, and has succeeded in making a good sum of money every year to hand over to the league of friends.

The society, although not active, still has funds and equipment for the show, and it is hoped that it will be revived in the twenty first century. The existing committee members are few, but with a little extra help and local support, the society could once more flourish.

Sources

1. Society minute book 1956 to present
2. various newspaper cuttings in the Society records
3. Society account book 1941 to present
4. information from Wilf Stokes, Bert King and Frank Hart
5. personal knowledge

chapter 29

The development of Cloverley Road

by Wendy Thomas

with illustrations by Jane Whaler

Introduction

Cloverley Road, on the southern edge of Ongar, is an interesting road, full of character due to the way it was developed. The land was sold off in small plots and bought by people wishing to build a house for themselves, or by local builders or businessmen planning to build cottages or houses to rent. Some plots were developed quickly, others lay vacant for years, often being used as allotments. The first cottages were built in 1904, but the last houses were not completed until the end of the century. This has resulted in considerable variety in the size and style of houses, not normally seen in modern housing developments. Most houses were built before the general availability of motor cars, so that space for driveways and garages was not considered necessary. This was not a problem until this quiet cul-de-sac was opened up in 1960 by the construction of Longfields at the northern end.

The origins of the land

In 1886, Henry Edward Jones of Marden Ash House bought four fields between the Cripsey Brook and the Brentwood Road. One of these fields, five acres in area, was later to be developed into Cloverley Road. It had been called Upland Mead (and later Malting Mead), variously described as meadow, pasture and arable land. At one time it was farmed by Henry Alexander Johnson and later by Charles Foster.[1] The 1848 tithe assessment gives the executors of Major Ord as owners.[2] Major Ord's will has not been found, but in 1855 the members of the Ord family who had inherited the five fields sold them to Edward Cleeve.[3] Mr Cleeve of Abbotsford, Dean Park, Bournemouth, twice raised money on the land, and when it was bought by Mr Jones in 1886, the conveyance included the mortgagees Henry Gibson, solicitor of Chipping Ongar, and Thomas Harvey, farmer of High Ongar.[5]

The sale of the plots

Although Mr Jones bought the land in 1886, he did not begin to develop it until 1903. Initially there was no entry from the Brentwood road,[5] and part of a building had to be taken down to form an access for vehicles.[6] The new road was begun in 1903, but not finished with tarmac until the 1920s when residents had to pay towards the cost.[7&8] It was first referred to as Clover Ley, then Clover-Ley Road and finally Cloverley Road. In October 1903 Mr Winch, a builder from Harlow, submitted drainage plans to the Ongar Rural District Council (ORDC) for the eight cottages that he planned to build. ORDC noted *'this is satisfactory, Mr Jones is laying a 6 inch main to be connected with the council's 9 inch main on his estate, and this and other properties will drain into it.'*[9]

The land was divided into 76 small building plots and the whole site known as "The Elms Estate". When the first public sale was held at the King's Head Hotel in August 1903, ten plots had already been sold and two reserved.[6] The sale particulars described the land as *'well situated on high ground at Marden Ash in the parish of High Ongar just outside the town of Chipping Ongar within 15 minutes walk of the Railway Station and particularly suitable for the erection of good class cottages for which there is a great demand.,'*[10] Lots 7 to 10 were sold to Mr Winch of Harlow at £20 each, lots 12 to 15 to Mr H. Barlow of Ongar at £21 each, lots 20 and 21 to Mrs Gann of Stondon at £20 each (together with lots 24 and 25 at £19 each), lot 22 to Mr Wheal of Epping, and lot 23 to Mr Fisher of Ongar at £20. Lots 27 to 30 were withdrawn.[11]

Further sales took place in August 1904 (when plots 32 to 60 were sold) and in September 1905 when plots 64 to 74 were offered, with 75 and 76 reserved. The 1905 sales catalogue shows that Mr Jones was hoping to extend the road northwards into the next field towards the Cripsey Brook and new plots were marked out on the plan. It is not known why this was not carried out; it was another half century before the area was developed as the Longfields estate.

One of the terms in the conveyance of 1903, contained in the deeds of some of the Cloverley Road houses, stipulates that *'no noisy, noxious or offensive trade, nor any manufacture'* should be carried on, and that none of the land or buildings *'be used as a place of public worship, nor as a public house, inn, tavern or beershop'*. Manufacture of bricks or tiles, and excavation for *'clay loam gravel or soil'* (other than for foundations) was also forbidden.[12]

The houses and the people

Eighteen houses were completed in 1904. One of the first to be built was number 33, The Lodge. Before the sale of 1903, Henry Jones had reserved this plot, and the small "V" shaped one opposite.[6] In 1904, he built a small cottage for his butler, Mr Thorpe and his family. It has been suggested that the spare plot opposite was used as an exit from the road.[13] Another source has suggested that Mr Jones' pony and trap was driven down the side of the house and through the garden. There would have been room for this, and the find of a layer of compacted hoggin under the present drive gives some credibility to this idea. When Mr Thorpe was not on duty at Marden Ash House, he was expected to open the gate to let the trap through, but the exact route taken is not clear.[14] He used to walk up Cloverley Road to work in his dark butler's suit and bowler hat.[8] After Mr and Mrs Thorpe died, their daughter Amy continued to live there for several years. When Eric and Kath Wingar bought the lodge from Mr Jones in 1957, it had been empty for some time and needing renovating and enlarging to accommodate their growing family.[14]

THE DEVELOPMENT OF CLOVERLEY ROAD

Numbers 19 to 31 were built in 1904 by Walter Winch of Harlow, and were called Alpha Cottages. His original plan was for eight cottages, but two terraces of three and four cottages were built.[9] In 1921, Mr and Mrs Lay moved into 2 Alpha Cottages (now number 21). Mr Lay worked as a saddler for G. Stokes & Sons in Ongar High Street.[8] Len Jones, a plumber working for Noble's, and his wife Mary, a cook at Greensted House occupied number 29 from 1948.[15] On the other side of the road, the terrace of four cottages with an inscribed stone reading "Fairview Cottages – 1904" was built by Messrs Wheal and Fisher.[9] They are now numbered 12 to 18. There is a tradition that both sets of cottages were put up to house the workers building the Hackney Homes at the other end of the town. The contractors for the Borough of Hackney, McCormick & Son, came from east London, and would indeed have needed accommodation for their men for several years. However it is clear that this firm did not build any of the Cloverley Road cottages, although it is possible that McCormick rented them after completion.

Later in 1904, numbers 15 and 17 were built for Walter Jackson, a local coal merchant who lived in Greensted Road. By the 1930s, Mr Smith lived in number 15 and kept cows in the field by the Stag public house. He had a cooling shed for the milk in his garden, and delivered daily by pony and trap, ladling milk from his churn into his customers' jugs. Close neighbours dropped in to collect milk themselves.[8]

In 1904, two pairs of semi-detached houses, numbers 43 to 49, were built by Ernest Winch. Five years later, he sold Bush Hill, number 49 (and possibly the other three) to his brother Walter. There was a piece of spare land behind numbers 33 to 55,[16] and in 1924 Walter Winch bought the piece behind number 49 from Mr Jones for £9 2s. All this spare land was subsequently incorporated into the back gardens of the corresponding houses[17] Mr Winch died in 1943 and number 49 passed to Richard Winch who sold it to Leslie and Florence Cracknell in 1959.[28]

Figure 23 65 Cloverley Road, built in 1905, before the extension was added. The railings were removed to St James Lodge, St James Avenue.

ASPECTS OF THE HISTORY OF ONGAR

In 1905 Harry Barlow built Ashlings, numbers 39 and 41. Both properties passed to Miss Carlick who lived in number 41 until 1970. From 1934 she rented the adjoining house to the Kinzetts, whose son Rodney still lives there.[19] Number 65 was also built in 1905 and was the only house at the bottom of the road for many years. Mr Hadler built a single detached house on plots 61 and 62. The name "Marden Villa" can still be seen carved on the front. In 1908 he sold this house to Mr H. W. Mihill, grocer and provision merchant in Ongar High Street. In May 1922 it was bought by Mr H. D. Rainbird, an engine driver of Rosebery Villas in the High Street, who died in 1948.[4] The present owners John and Angela Root bought the house, greatly in need of modernisation, in 1964.[20]

In 1907 numbers 8 and 10 were built for Walter Jackson on land bought by Mr Gann in the 1903 sale. They are directly opposite the houses built for Mr Jackson in 1904. The great granddaughter of Mr Jackson now occupies number 8.

In 1910 Mr W. Fisher built two terraces, each of three cottages (now numbers 26 to 36).[9] In the same year the local firm, F. M. Noble, built numbers 55 and 57. These houses were timber framed on brick foundations and expanded metal was used for the first time in place of lathe and plaster. This technique is still used though the metal is now galvanised to prevent rust. The roof tiles are the original ones made in Noble's brickyard. Eddy and Mavis Cracknell, who started married life in number 14 in 1961, bought number 57 from Noble's in 1971.[13]

Figure 24   53 Cloverley Road, built in 1911, by Messrs Noble, with stables and coach-house to the rear.

In 1911 Noble's built Oak Lodge, number 53, for John Ellington Cowee. This is a detached house, with a stable block to the rear with accommodation for two horses, hayloft, coach house and saddle room. At some point ownership passed to Frank Ward who sold it to H. E. Jones of Marden Ash House in 1923. For a time Mrs

Jones' sister, Mrs White, lived there with her three sons. The present owner David Manning bought it in 1962. Part of the stable block was converted to a two bedroom dwelling in 1964 but the upper floor had to be demolished in 1986 as a planning condition for the construction of a new bungalow (Garden Cottage, number 53a) on land behind numbers 57 to 61.[21]

In 1912 Mr Gann built Cedar Villas, numbers 20 and 22. The former became the home of the family of Mr Frederick Dicker, a builder and undertaker. Fred Dicker had died by 1938 and his son Leslie continued the business. Fred's daughter in law, Lilian Humphreys, still lives there.[22] Arthur and Dorothy Marriage moved into number 22 in 1934. Mr Marriage was a local man from Willingale but his wife's family came from Suffolk, moving to Ongar in the 1920s when her father came to work in Matthew's Mill on Ongar High Street.[23]

In 1914, H.E. Jones converted a stable in the north west corner of the field into a cottage to provide accommodation for his groom, Mr Trundle and his family. This is now known as Elm Cottage and was occupied by Mr Trundle until the early 1960s.[7]

It is not known when Marigold, number 50, was developed. In 1904, Mrs A.F. Price bought two plots of land and at some point put a caravan on the site. This was gradually added to, and in 1925 she bought an adjoining plot. In the same year Spearman & Sons made an application for drainage to a proposed addition to a dwelling at number 50.[9] By 1926, Mrs Price and her son were living in the bungalow which had a veranda across the back overlooking the fields.[7] Mr and Mrs Bass purchased it in 1934 and much work over the years was done to make it more habitable. An extension for a bathroom and kitchen was built after the Second World War.[24]

No early records exist for number 51 and it is not clear when it was built. It is, however, shown on the 1920 Ordnance Survey map, so it may have been developed before the First World War.

Building restarted in 1925 after a break of ten years due to the First World War. In this year H.E. Jones sold either the house (number 54), or the land on which it was built, to Reginald Knapman.[25] Mr Acres the builder put up numbers 67 to 73, probably for Henry G. Ashlyn. Number 73 was the first to be occupied by Mr and Mrs Faux with their two sons and their seven year old daughter, now Rene Ridgewell, who still lives there. The house was called Willowcote because of a large willow tree on the adjoining plot.[7] Number 69 has had a long association with the Smyth family who moved there in 1931, when Mr Smyth was stationed with the RAF at North Weald. Their daughter Helen married Raymond Flesher in 1956 and brought up their family of six there.[26]

The willow tree adjoining number 73 was soon cut down to make way for number 75, a bungalow built by Leslie Dicker for Walter Jackson in 1926. The first occupant, Mrs Price, was a relative of Mr Jackson, and, as her husband had been a

ASPECTS OF THE HISTORY OF ONGAR

horseman at Great Myles Farm, the bungalow was called Myles. Mr and Mrs Offley, who were evacuees, lived there in the 1940s, and Charles and Ingrid Kellam bought it from Mr Jackson in 1964. They still live there.[27]

Figure 25   Mr Frederick Dicker (right) undertaker and builder of Cloverley Road.

Mr Noble and Mr Jackson were quite friendly, and the former expressed his surprise that he was not given the job of building number 75. Mr Jackson replied that he could have the next contract if he could do it at the same price. Later in 1926 Noble's built the bungalows, numbers 44 and 46.[28] Marie Korf has lived in number 46 since 1955.

In 1937 number 63, Tideways, was built by J. W. Seager for Mr H. C. Phillips who was surveyor to the Ongar Rural District Council. By 1940 the house was too large for him and he had started to build a bungalow (number 56) for himself on the opposite side of the road. This stood partly built for some years, probably due to shortage of materials and manpower during the Second World War. Mr Phillips did not move in until 1945.[7 & 8]

In the late 1930s Nobles built a pair of semi detached houses, numbers 4 and 6. The former is still occupied by Jean and Jim Perry who moved into number 4 in 1958.[29]

Other plots remained undeveloped for a surprisingly long time. Mr Barlow had bought plots 12 and 13 in 1903[11] but ownership reverted to Mr Jones in 1923. They were then sold to Miss Lottie Pearce of 17, Cloverley Road, and were used by her lodger as allotments and an orchard. Finally in 1939 Mr Leslie Dicker built a pair of semi detached houses (numbers 35 and 37) in the "sun trap" style so popular in the 1930s. On Sunday 3 September 1939, while cleaning the windows of the newly

THE DEVELOPMENT OF CLOVERLEY ROAD

completed houses, Lilian Humphreys heard the news of the declaration of war.[22] Lemay, number 35, was sold in 1943 to the trustees of the Congregational Church and was used as a manse for the next 20 years.[12] The new owners after 1963, Mike and Jean Edwards, made extensive alterations in which the house lost its typical curved Crittall metal windows. David and Wendy Thomas have lived there since 1988. But the other half, number 37, has retained its original frontage. Mr and Mrs Torrance were the second occupants in 1940, and their daughter lived there until 1988 when the present occupants, Pete and Jan Marchant, moved in.[19]

Windermere, number 38, was built in 1939 by Mr Tom Sitch and rented to Richard King (then owner of the Bridge Garage, Ongar) until Mr Sitch needed it himself in 1955. Mr King liked the house so much that he persuaded Mr Sitch to build a similar house for him next door at number 40. And when the Kings needed a smaller house in 1970, E. M. Taylor built a bungalow (number 42) for them on the adjoining plot bought from Mrs Cynthia Jones.[30]

Building ceased until after the Second World War. The first post war house to be completed was Dunelm, number 48, in 1951. The land was bought from Fred Noble and the house built by Leslie Dicker for Doreen and Wilfred Smith of number 21. Doreen lived there until 1999.[8] In the late 1950s a pair of semi detached bungalows, numbers 59 and 61, was built on land owned by Noble's.

The road ceased to be a cul de sac in 1960 with the construction of Longfields. There was a rush by the allotment holders to gather in their produce before the bulldozers moved in.[26] Two pairs of semi detached houses, numbers 58 to 64, were built in 1964 on the site of the old gravel pit at the north east corner. It was necessary to drive piles deep into the ground to provide adequate foundations, an event remembered by many residents of Cloverley Road and Longfields. In 1968,

Figure 26   35 & 37 Cloverley Road, built in 1939 by Mr Dicker.

ASPECTS OF THE HISTORY OF ONGAR

Roy Webb built a bungalow on land behind numbers 65 and 67, bought by Edwyn and Dorreen Gilmour in 1970. Although now numbered 29 Coopers Hill, the land was part of the original Elms Estate.[31]

Number 11 was built in 1982. The land had been part of the kitchen garden of Greyend on the Brentwood road. John and Jean Woodward organised the building work themselves, using bricklayers, electricians and joiners when necessary. The house is timber framed with a plasterboard lining inside, and four inches of insulation between that and the external brick skin.[32]

Mr Spearman had bought a vacant plot of land, between numbers 11 and 15, in 1979. Foundations were put in, but it was not until 1997 that the house was built by Scanlon & Co of Brentwood. Mr Alan Jones moved into number 13 in July of that year.[33] In 1999 Mary King sold number 50 with planning permission for a pair of semi detached houses. It was bought by Jean and John Woodward's three sons who, following their parent's example, plan to arrange all the labour for building two timber framed houses on the site, thus bringing to an end a century of housing development on "The Elms Estate".

Acknowledgements

I would like to thank the residents of Cloverley Road who contributed to this short history, and especially Angela Root for editing and typing, and Jane Whaler for the drawings.

References

1. abstract of title, deeds of 65 Cloverley Road
2. High Ongar tithe map ERO: D/CT 263
3. conveyance, deeds of 49 Cloverley Road
4. conveyance, deeds of 65 Cloverley Road
5. 25" O. S. map (1896) at ERO
6. sale catalogue and map (1903) ERO: B1749b
7. inf from Rene Ridgewell
8. inf from Doreen Smith
9. record of plans submitted to ORDC sanitary committee (1901 to 1929) ERO: A7547part
10. sale catalogue (1905) ERO: B1749b
11. Cuttle collection of newspaper cuttings ERO: T/P 181/8/29
12. deeds of 35 Cloverley Road
13. inf from Eddy Cracknell
14. inf from Eric Wingar
15. inf from Mary Jones
16. 25" O.S. map (1920) at ERO
17. 25" O. S. map (1995) at Ongar Library
18. inf from Leslie Cracknell
19. inf from Rodney Kinzett
20. inf from John Root
21. inf from David Manning
22. inf from Lillian Dicker
23. inf from Dorothy Marriage
24. inf from Mary King

THE DEVELOPMENT OF CLOVERLEY ROAD

25 inf from Mark Wreford
26 inf from Helen Flesher
27 inf from Charles Kellam
28 inf from Alan Sawkins
29 inf from Jim Perry
30 inf from Tom King
31 inf from Edwyn Gilmour
32 inf from John Woodward
33 inf from Alan Jones

chapter 30

Living history – eye witness accounts

by Felicitie Barnes & Christina Thornton

Our lives are ordered so that we all have a present, a future and a past. As we get older, our past is longer and our future shorter. We live in the present, but when tomorrow comes, today is our past. In a town such as Ongar, we can look at the buildings and know that they have a past. They cannot tell us of their experiences, but those who lived or worked in them, or even walked past them, can do so. People are inextricably involved in the past, and can tell us what went on in their lifetimes and recreate the past by sharing their experiences with us. In the words of the oral historian, Paul Thompson:

> '...the immediate environment also gains, through the sense of discovery in interviews, a vivid historical dimension: an awareness of the past which is not just known, but personally felt. This is especially true for a newcomer to a community. It is one thing to know that streets or fields had a past before one's arrival; quite different to have received from the remembered past, still alive in the minds of the older people of the place, personal intimacies of love across those particular fields, neighbours or homes in that particular street, work in that particular shop.'

Artefacts help us to understand the history of a town. Photographs, drawings and books give us an idea of what happened, and how and why it happened, but nowhere can we listen to the rhythms and sounds of life as we can in an inflection of tone in a raconteur's voice when relating a particular experience. It takes the human voice to infuse words with a deeper meaning. Our privilege has been to talk to a number of Ongarians who were born in the first half of this century, and to record their reminiscences of life in the area up to and including the Second World War. Memories can be transient or nostalgic – most are happy, but some of course are sad. Some are very personal and painful to recall, as the passage of time does not always dull the senses. It has been very touching to have the trust of these people (who perhaps we can call our friends) and to see their wonder at what they can remember. Several have said that they cannot remember much, but then find that one memory leads to another. We leave them with other names to follow up, and promises of photographs that are hidden away in an attic or a drawer. We are extremely grateful to all of them.

This chapter will look at Ongar as it was between the two World Wars, and will compare the town as it was then to what it is now. Ongar was described as:

> 'an awfully nice little town, very self contained, and had all the sorts of shops you could possibly want. A very good chemist, two butchers, Mr

LIVING HISTORY - EYE WITNESS ACCOUNTS

Ashdown the draper, a clock shop, a fishmonger, Barclays Bank, a very nice self contained town with no problems with parking. You could park your car in great comfort anywhere along the main street, which was wide and uncrowded and had several nice pubs. A good railway station which was the end of the line. This was one of its salvations, as it didn't go anywhere, unlike Brentwood or Ingatestone. Ongar remained very unspoilt with a lot of old buildings.'

The patterns of life were well ordered, and the rhythms slow. The sounds were gentler and softer, of horses' hooves and cattle, and the smells were of a small rural town.

Parents and grandparents

My friends have often returned to their childhood, and talked of their parents and grandparents. Many said that their forebears came to Ongar for reasons of trade or commerce, and others because they were in service. Les Cracknell's grandfather came to Ongar through his work as a platelayer on the railway. They came from various parts of the country, which gave their children the opportunity to leave the confines of Ongar by travelling to visit their grandparents. Those with both grandparents in the town never had the same chance to travel, and the annual outing was their only experience of the world outside. Many met their future partners in Ongar and settled here, so that their children grew up in the town.

Outings

The one big occasion for the children was the Sunday school outing to Maldon or Thorpe Bay, or even to a farm in Stanford Rivers. They have such happy memories of the big day each year. They would go in a charabanc. They would take sandwiches. They would sing and laugh, and the driver would quicken speed as they approached a bridge, and they would scream. They recalled the exhilaration 70 or 80 years later. Now, being grandparents themselves, they talk of the wider horizons of the younger generations, and of their own children scattered around the world.

Health and sickness

There are tragic memories of the loss of uncles and grandparents in the First World War, and the separations caused by war. One of our oldest residents, Miss Korf, remembers the arrest of her German father when she was 11 years old. He had had a telephone installed for business purposes which probably increased the suspicion of the authorities, who regarded anyone of German origin as a security risk. He was interned on the Isle of Man. Other sad memories were of those who died prematurely of disease. A very dear friend died of consumption in her teens, and spent her last year lying out of doors in the garden. There were epidemics of diphtheria and scarlet fever, which spread among the children at the Trust school. Some children were removed from there, if the parents could afford it, and sent to private schools in the town. Others spent all their school years from five to fourteen at that school. Scarlet fever victims were taken to Rush Green isolation hospital by horse drawn ambulance, and kept for six weeks. Visiting was forbidden, and any toys sent in had to be left there for fear of spreading the disease.

Ongar had two hospitals between the wars, the first to open being the Cottage Hospital in the Fyfield road, just past where Ongar War Memorial Hospital now stands. The Cottage Hospital closed at the beginning of the Second World War. Both were self-contained and each had an operating theatre. Only the most severely ill or injured were taken elsewhere for treatment, occasionally to London hospitals. The youngsters were mainly treated for adenoids and tonsils. Sometimes these operations were carried out on the kitchen table at home, and sometimes in the hospital. One still cannot forget the smell of ether, strongly reminiscent of walking into the operating theatre. Another recalled running away from the hospital after failing to be put out by the anaesthetic, and then being found in the fields and being brought back to face the ether mask again.

The doctors at that time charged for their services, and one had to be really ill to justify the call out. A home visit cost 2s 6d, but sometimes the doctor would not charge because of the poverty that was apparent in the home. District nurses worked with the doctors, and it was their responsibility to attend women in labour in their own homes. The nurses worked a "district" which included the neighbouring villages. One district nurse spoke of the terrible conditions that they had to face in some of the cottages where they attended a birth. There would be no running water; all that was needed had to be carried in buckets from the well to be heated on an open fire. The cottages were old, and often flea and bug ridden. There would be no clean clothes for the new baby. There were no drugs or "gas and air", and sometimes the labour would go on for two days. The arrival of a new baby was one of the happiest experiences for this nurse. On occasions, she had taken her own daughter's dolls clothes to put on a new born baby who had nothing to wear! Some of those we talked to were mothers in the Second World War before the NHS came into being, and paid into a "club" which helped with medical charges when the need arose. They were overawed at the thought of a free health service.

School

The earliest memories are often of school. There were no play groups, so starting school was a very big happening in their lives. Usually an older brother or sister, or cousin or neighbour would take them when they were five years old. There were no school dinners until the Second World War, so they all went home at dinnertime. Mum was always there, she did not go out to work. There were no problems about picking children up from school. With very little traffic and no strangers about, it was safe for children to walk home. Some walked considerable distances, and Emily Taylor recalled the five mile walk to her school in Stanford Rivers at the age of five. Children respected, and sometimes feared, their teachers.

Mr Tilson, the headmaster, was very strict, and children did as they were told. If not, there was the cane to remind them. The girls remembered the pranks of the boys, flicking ink wells up with a ruler when one of the double desk lids was closed with a bang.

The name of Barker was synonymous with the council school. Fred, and his sister Ann, were pupils at the school in the 1920s, and both stayed on as pupil teachers. After training, Fred returned as a teacher and both he and his sister worked in the school until retirement. No story about schooldays failed to mention Mr or Miss Barker. The pupils stayed until fourteen, and during the last years the boys had lessons in woodwork, and gardening on the allotment. Girls were taught cooking and laundry. One lady remembered that her teacher brought in her own things to be laundered by the girls, and had to reap the consequences of scorched clothes when the iron was too hot! There was a combustion stove in each classroom for heating. Those who were nearest were too warm, those further away were too cold. Everyone got chilblains. Classes were mixed, but there were separate playgrounds for boys and girls. The caretaker would throw buckets of water down when it was very cold to make ice slides in the playground. Those who went to private schools wore a uniform, but, as it was expensive to buy, it had to be worn out of school as well.

Some children, who had been entered for the scholarship at the council school, were selected for secondary education at one of the single sex selective schools at Loughton. Ongar secondary school did not open until September 1936. The only local alternative was the private Ongar Grammar School which had a very good reputation, taking pupils from abroad as well as from many parts of the British Isles. Though it was less expensive to send boys to school in Loughton, there were a few day boys from the local community at the grammar school. They were expected to go to school on Saturday, but were excused the Sunday church parade when the boarders walked to the parish church in crocodile, wearing their boaters. Another memory was of the girl pupils boarding at Bowes School with their distinctive yellow and brown uniforms.

The railway

Though the roads were quiet (except at certain times), the railway station was always bustling. The London and North Eastern steam trains ran out to the terminus at Ongar. Commuters could reach Liverpool Street in about an hour, paying 1s 6d for the privilege. Trains were fast, comfortable and warm, and frequent enough not to be crowded. Taxis were a common sight in the station yard, bringing commuters to and from their trains. Very few people had cars in the 1920s and 1930s, even though there was no driving test and petrol cost about 1s 0d a gallon. There were four or five taxi firms in the vicinity of Ongar. Everyone else walked to or from the station, and the paper shop was always busy from 7.30 am as commuters called for their morning papers. Miss Korf worked for the local solicitor, and would be sent up to London by train with letters and documents, as part of her work. She often returned late at night, but had no fear of

ASPECTS OF THE HISTORY OF ONGAR

travelling on her own or walking home through Ongar. Up to the General Strike of 1926, a milk train left the station at 8am. Local farmers brought in their milk, as well as their sons and daughters who would be travelling to school in Loughton. The driver of the milk train was flexible enough to take anyone who had missed their usual train, so that children would not be late for school! Passenger trains were cheap for local travel too, and were used for a trip to the cinema in Epping, or an evening date at a local dance.

The station was very much an integral part of the town and had an important part to play in its commercial life. Farmers brought their crops of potatoes and sugar beet for transport to London, and collected goods sent out from the city. Delicacies such as strawberries would be sent from the local nursery. The goods yard had designated areas for the delivery and collection of certain items, and the noise and bustle would be going on all night. The staff appointed to oversee these tasks were accommodated in houses built for them in Banson's Way. The four or five local coal men would pick up their deliveries from the yard, ready for their rounds the next day. Fish, ordered by telegraph the day before, would arrive in the early hours of the morning. Pigs and cattle came into the town via the goods yard and would be driven out into fields in the neighbourhood, until they were ready for the slaughterhouses of the local butchers. Wood for the local wood yard, goods from London shops and newspapers all came by train. A less savoury arrival was horse manure from the streets of London on its way to fertilise the surrounding fields.

Local employment

Many school leavers at fourteen already knew where they were going to work. For those who did not, there was an unemployment office in a private house on Marden Ash Hill. Many girls went into service in the big houses in the area, or further afield to Woodford or Wanstead. This was a chance to find out how other people lived, but they usually found it very hard physical work. Other young ladies worked at Ashdowns, other local shops or the egg packing station along the Epping road. The Ness sisters had their own bespoke tailoring business in their house in Castle Street. One man told me how his grandparents, who were publicans at the beginning of the century, decided that the four sons should be taught a trade, and that the two daughters should be brought up as ladies. One young lady wanted to be a hairdresser, and her father paid for her to go to college in Loughton. The course cost £100, as well as the train fares. After training, she went into partnership in the town, working under difficult conditions with no running water or electricity in the shop. There were no rollers, and "finger waving" cost 2s 6d. Perms took three hours, as the hair was steam clipped to a machine which dripped hot water over the client! This cost £1. Tips, which could be threepence, were used to buy stockings.

Many of the young men had already worked part time for local tradesmen, and had jobs waiting for them. Len Stokes tells how he had been working for the local fish merchant as a delivery boy, so he was allowed to leave school at 13 $^{1}/_{2}$ to take on the job permanently. He was not very big, but had to deliver fish on a trademan's bike. He was unable to cycle as the load was too heavy for him. He was out of Ongar all day, delivering to large houses and villages in the vicinity, each day a different round. He would pick up the orders for the following week. Another job was to deliver ice, and he remembers taking a load out to Dudbrook Manor after returning from his daily fish round. The ice was needed for a cocktail party. His day started at 7.30am, collecting the fish sent from Billingsgate to the railway station. The fish then had to be displayed and packed with ice, all outside, whatever the weather. The ice, which was delivered twice a week from a firm in Romford, had to be broken up with an axe.

The butcher's boys were also doing their rounds of the villages, many by pony and trap, but Fred Powell remembers driving a motor van when he was only fifteen. His round was long and he often finished after dark, people coming to the door with candles. He would collect the money, and they would go to the van to choose the meat. The butcher's boys also had to make the sausages, and to help in the slaughterhouse. At fifteen, they were doing a man's job. The conditions of work were not good, with three days holiday a year. It was supposed to be a week, but the other days were bank holidays. There were no union rights.

Local tradesmen

"Granny" Searle had a greengrocers shop, supplied by the nursery run by her husband (and later her sons) next to the Budworth Hall. The saddler, on the other side of the Budworth Hall, made everything for the farm and employed three or four people. Many remember the smell of the leather. Harnesses had to be made to order because they had to be fitted, and padded items were sewn by hand, clamped to the leg while they were being stitched. There were two tailors in Ongar. Mr Rose was well known for the quality of his work in making riding clothes for the gentry. Mr Korf worked in the Chapel Cottages and made riding habits for ladies. He was very well known, and clients came from as far away as Brighton for their riding attire. His daughter remembers the noise of carriages drawing up at the door before the First World War, and the ladies being fitted for their costumes. Her mother was always present as a chaperone. There was a wooden horse in the front room so that her father could see that the habit hung correctly.

Further down the High Street was Matthews and Barker, the carriage makers. They had a thriving business in the days before motor vehicles, and employed as many as a dozen men. They made carriages for the gentry, farm vehicles and ambulances, dog carts and broughams. Vehicles were made entirely from scratch with only timber, metal and other raw materials being bought in. They required the skills of wheelwrights, upholsterers and sign writers. Mr Surridge sold motor vehicles and motor bikes, and also ran a taxi business. His son Victor was well known, having broken the record at Brooklands by exceeding 60 mph over one hour when only 19 years old. He was killed soon after in the Isle of Man TT races.

ASPECTS OF THE HISTORY OF ONGAR

Another untimely death was that of Father Byles, the Roman Catholic priest, who was drowned in the sinking of the Titanic. One Ongar resident remembers him because, if he met her in the town, he would hold out his arms and twirl her round.

In 1919, the parents of Mr Raggett, on their visit to Ongar, walked from the station into the town and did not see a soul. Mrs Raggett said that under no circumstances was she going to live in such a dead place, but her husband thought otherwise and established himself in the community. He fulfilled, at various times, the roles of town clerk, billetting officer and food officer.

Next to "Granny" Searle's shop was a sweet shop, and the proprietor, Mrs Atkinson, made lovely ice cream. She kept it behind a curtain, and supplied a bench in the shop for her customers to sit on, as it was not the done thing to eat in the street. The milkmen delivered by horse and cart. The horses knew where to stop and customers brought their jugs out to be filled from the churn. Coal merchants delivered too, to supply the fires that belched their fumes into the atmosphere causing fogs that were so thick that people could not see more than ten feet in front of them.

There were several butchers in the town, one of which was Carter's. This had changed hands since being in the family in the eighteenth century, but had been bought back by Peter Carter's father in 1929. Butchers' shops were always on the shady side of the street, and many had slaughter houses to the rear. Effluent from these was discharged into the Cripsey Brook. Bones went to the glue makers, fat to the soap makers, hides to the tanners and local gardeners barrowed away the strained blood to fertilise their gardens. Nothing was wasted!

Housewives were able to shop in the town on a daily basis, or send their children to buy odds and ends, but their weekly order would be delivered. The next week's order, written out in a book, would be collected when the delivery was made. In the International Stores at the centre of town, everything on the provision counter was cut up and weighed by hand. Nothing was pre-packed. Ashdown's, the ladies' outfitter, stocked haberdashery, and had a separate shop as the gents' outfitter. There was a market once a week at the Kings Head, selling rabbits, chickens and geese. Those who felt the need to go out of Ongar could catch the train to Stratford (where there was a good shopping centre) or the Green Line bus to Brentwood, Chelmsford, or Romford. In the 1940s, there was an hourly red double decker bus from the Red Cow in Shelley to Romford. The fare into Ongar was 1d and children went free.

Church and social life

The churches played an important part in the life of the town. Even the children of non-believers went to Sunday school. Several men said that they had been in the church choir, and their fathers before them. Mr Barker and his sister played the organ at St Martin's for many years. The Congregational church organised a lot of social activities and had a tennis court behind the chapel. The sports club, started

LIVING HISTORY - EYE WITNESS ACCOUNTS

by Mr Barker and Mr Myson, also had grass courts and matches were played against other clubs. All the big houses in the area had their own tennis courts, extensively used for social occasions. Social life often centred round the family with relations visiting and singing songs round the piano after Sunday tea. The radio was much appreciated and used, and it was usually the children's job to take the accumulator to the shop to be charged up.

There was also a cycling club, and the cycle shops of Mr Wingar and Mr Surridge did a good trade. The young men looked dashing in their plus fours, and the young ladies were able to participate as well. They cycled all over the south east, sometimes on tandems, going into Kent or Suffolk, as well as taking part in competitive trials. The Territorial Army had a base at Ongar which attracted young men, and introduced them to boxing. The Ongar team competed in area competitions and produced some promising boxers.

The Hackney children's homes were opened in 1908 and brought employment for many local people. Staff houses were built along the Fyfield road which the occupants were allowed to buy on a mortgage of 2s 6d per week. The Hackney Homes were self contained, but many of the staff came from the town and were encouraged to participate in whist drives and dances. The children had a band, which raised money for charity. The annual fete, which was much enjoyed, took place on the Oval, the central grassed area around which the homes were built.

The appearance of the Budworth Hall has not changed much, apart from the addition of the ballroom at the back, built for the Essex Hunt balls which were held there once a year. This was a fashionable occasion for the local gentry and catering for it was in the hands of the landlady of the King's Head. The ballroom had a special sprung floor and was used for other dances too. The Essex Hunt would sometimes meet in Ongar at the King's Head, and there were also otter hounds and beagles in the area. These were good occupations in the winter. During the First World War the ballroom was used as a recovery centre for injured soldiers. Charlotte Marles remembers the men in their distinctive blue and red uniforms, getting used to the loss of limbs. The children were sent to entertain them with recitations and songs.

The fire service

Ongar, then as now, had a fire station. At first, it was situated on an island in the road outside the Two Brewers pub. It was manned by part-time firemen, who were summoned by bells in their homes or workplaces. The problem was that it was horse drawn, and the animals had to be caught in the fields where they were put out to graze. The saying was *'Keep the fire going until we've caught the horses.'* The firemen became full time during the Second World War, moving to a building behind the Lion pub (which, after its demolition, provided the site for the present purpose built station). Many stories are told about the Lion yard, used for overnighting 30 bullocks on their way to Epping market, driven by one drover and his dog. Another visitor was a special stallion, taken round to service mares on the local farms, *'led around with trimmings and stuff on it.'* Thrashing machines and steam ploughs also went round the farms in the winter months, and the Lion was a favourite stopping place for refreshment. It had the only ostler in town, and when the circus came, the elephants were stabled in the Lion yard.

Ongar and the countryside

At the turn of the century, housing in Ongar was confined to the centre of the town with ribbon development on Marden Ash Hill, Brentwood road and Greensted road. The first big growth was the Fairfield Road estate, built for the Green Line workers, on the area where the fair had always been held. A Green Line depot had been established in Ongar at the end of the 1920s. Some houses were built along the Fyfield and Moreton roads but the town was surrounded by fields in the inter-war period. Boys would be out rabbiting, as there was a market for rabbit skins. The atmosphere was of tranquillity, children running in the fields with no cares, their parents willing for them to be away all day with sandwiches and a bottle of cold tea. Families would walk together on Sundays, while children picked bluebells and primroses. A favourite walk was the Long Walk from the Budworth Hall to Greensted. There were seats scattered along the way, and shade from the trees when it was hot. This was the favourite venue for visitors from Leyton who came in topless buses, two at a time, loaded with picnickers to spend a day in the country.

There was a gate between the houses in the Fyfield Road which children could go through to play in the fields. One lady remembers gleaning for corn in these fields after harvest, using a little wooden cart that her father had made. Another lady looked out over the same fields from a house called "Meadow View" which now overlooks the Shelley estate. A Marden Ash resident recalls *'Ongar was a lovely place to live in. We had a lovely childhood. We were able to go over into the fields when it was hay making time and take picnics and throw hay at each other. It was wonderful. We used to be able to play out on the pavement with our tops and whips. We used to have such cheap things, nothing was expensive. We used to go out for walks over the fields and pick bluebells. There used to be a bluebell wood where the school is now. We played cricket on the Stag field. It was really lovely. We knew practically everyone in Ongar. Everybody knew each other.'*

Aukingford Gardens, with 16 houses, was built in the 1920s by Mr Lee. He was allowed to do this on condition that he dug a well, and maintain the water in it for 48 hours. It was built along the footpath that ran from Ongar to Moreton, and the most direct way to get into Ongar was to use the footpath that came out near the railway station. These fields were farmed by the farmer at Bowes Farm and cattle were kept on them. Near the station was the sports field with a cricket pavilion. This field was used for the Ongar show.

The utilities

The houses did not have much in the way of services. Each group had a well or a pump. The sanitation was a privy down the garden which had to be emptied into a trench, and covered over with soil in a prescribed way. The trench could be used again after three months. Chamber pots were used at night time. Lighting was by gas lamp, and the mantles used downstairs cost sixpence a time. Upstairs the lighting was more primitive. One gentleman remembered an open gas jet in two of the bedrooms, with the third having no lighting at all. Girls slept in one bed, boys in another. Few houses had a bathroom, and the only form of bath available to most was the tin bath filled with hot water from the copper. This always happened in the scullery, or in an outhouse where there was no heating, and the whole family took turns to bath in the same water. This happened no more than once a week, but on other days their mothers would sit them on the kitchen table and wash them down.

It was not until after the Second World War that most of the housing estates were built in Ongar, and that people began to have a better way of life. Most of the older houses were rat ridden and water would seep into the cellars. The road near Ongar bridge would flood easily, and children had to paddle through the water to get to school. The cottages behind Matthews and Barker had to have the cellars pumped out every day. Children would catch fish in the river and keep them there.

Wartime

The Second World War was the beginning of change in Ongar. Many evacuees arrived from East London, escaping mainly from the bombing of the London docks and Silvertown. The evacuation office was at 96 High Street. Some evacuees, such as the Clark family, stayed on and were eventually re-housed in the town. The schools were hard pressed to cope with the influx of pupils and Mrs Marles remembers a "shift" system operating at the newly opened Ongar secondary school. The local children had their lessons in the morning, followed by the evacuees with their own teachers in the afternoon. She talked of the difficulties of teaching children in the poorly lit air raid shelters and of the ingenuity of word games and story telling to keep them occupied. The children accepted the restrictions of war and enjoyed the freedom of Ongar. There were special activities just for the evacuees, but these were opened to Ongar children when the evacuees left. The staff at the Hackney Homes put on film shows on a Saturday. *'We would give our names in at the lodge. It cost one penny. They were dreadful and always breaking down, and black and white, and flickering, but we thought they were wonderful. They were old Will Hay and Charlie Chaplin films. That was the only entertainment we had.'*

The war also brought service men and women to Ongar, some Americans but mostly RAF and WRAF stationed at North Weald. Some were billeted in this area, at Blake Hall, Bowes House and the White House. The Congregational church became a rest and recreation centre with a canteen run by local ladies. Inevitably romances occurred! There was some bombing, mainly directed at North Weald airfield, and people sheltered under tables, under the stairs or in cellars. There was only one direct hit, on 12 February 1945, when St James' church was destroyed and

ASPECTS OF THE HISTORY OF ONGAR

adjoining houses damaged. Fortunately no one was killed, but a certain goat was never seen again!

The way of life in Ongar changed. The young men and women had grown up and were fighting a war, or in the land army, marrying and having their own children. At least one Ongarian was enlisted as a "Bevan boy" and was sent to work in a Midlands coal field. After the war, the Mill Lane brick works returned to brick making after making pipes for field drains, necessary to increase agricultural productivity. Materials for re-building or renovation were in short supply, and paint was mainly green or cream. Innovative sponging and stippling techniques were used to personalise décor. What wallpaper was available had plain borders which had to be cut off by hand. Emily Taylor remembers spending her evenings doing this in readiness for the next day's work. Nothing could ever be the same again.

Paul Thompson wrote '*oral history is a history built around people. It thrusts into history itself. It gives history back to the people in their own words.*' We have enjoyed the privilege of being allowed into the private world of others, and sharing their joys and fears.

Sources

1. Thompson, P. *The Voice of the Past* (1988) Oxford University Press
2. Interviews with John Barker, Rosina Broom, Peter Carter, Cliff Coles, Les Cracknell, Jim Dearman, Jean Easter, Gilbert Gemmill, Rene Getgood, Bert Hadsley, Sylvia Hatfield, John Hough, Rodney Kinzett, Marie Korf, Hilda Lacey, Joe Lee, Zoe Lee, Enid Linney, Em Mabon, Charlotte Marles, Beryl Martin, Eileen Nagle, Fred Powell, Colin Raggett, Phyllis Searle, Joan Stokes, Len Stokes, Emily Taylor, Geoff Waller, Ron Wingar and John Witt.

Editor's note.

The tape recordings from which this article was written have been deposited in the Essex Record Office's Sound Archive. It is also intended that copies will be avaliable at Ongar Library.

Chapter 31

Landmark trees

by Bob MacDonald

illustrations by David and Ann Manners

Landmark trees are not too closely defined; they are simply any "special" trees. They may be special for a variety of reasons – aesthetic, cultural, social or historical. Landmark trees are usually in prominent places and some are associated with special events. The only specific criteria to be observed is that such trees are in a public place, or at least capable of being substantially seen from a public place. The idea of Landmark trees was first mooted by the Tree Council in 1997 and since that time many groups throughout the country, notably tree warden groups, have identified trees "special" to their particular parish, town or village. This process not only contributes to ensuring the future well-being of the trees, but also acknowledges a living, tangible connection with the past history of the community. During 1998 Ongar tree wardens carried out their own parish wide audit of special trees and sought local opinion at the Ongar Millennium History Project Fayre. The following list of Ongar landmark trees represents the results of that endeavour.

1. English or pedunculate oak (*Quercus robur*)
Location: Toot Hill Road, footpath running northwest from Little Thorbens.

One of a number of fine hedgerow oaks, estimated to be at least 300 years old, marking the parish boundary. Chosen for its position adjacent to a public footpath at a point where it enters the parish from the adjoining parish of Bobbingworth. A true landmark tree for walkers. [p.317]

2. Weeping willow (*Salix babylonica*)
Location: Greensted Road, rear garden of Tudor Cottage.

This fine, mature willow is visible from both Greensted Road and Pensons Lane. (Please note that it ison private property.) Although it is doubtful whether this particular tree existed in the mid nineteenth century, it being aged at somewhere between 120 and 140 years old, it nevertheless stands as a very visible landmark to Tudor Cottage's historic association with the Tolpuddle martyrs. [p.317]

3. English or pedunculate oak (*Quercus robur*)
Location: Essex Way, north west of Hall Farm and Greensted Church.

One of the oldest and finest oaks in Ongar. Immediately alongside the Essex Way as it approaches Greensted Hall, this magnificent veteran has been witness to close on 400 years of local history and may well be a descendant of the "cloven" oaks found in the walls of nearby Greensted church.

4. Common lime (*Tilia europaea*) and common yew (*Taxus baccata*)
Location: Greensted churchyard .Many fine trees are to be found in and around Greensted churchyard.

The lime(s), complementary to the tower and the yew (the tree of immortality) adjacent to the chancel (St Andrew's window) have been chosen to represent the rest as they are ever present in the many photographs and paintings of this world famous local church. [p.318]

ASPECTS OF THE HISTORY OF ONGAR

5. English or pedunculate oak (*Quercus robur*)
Location: Millbank Avenue

Another fine oak, this time in a more urban setting. Obviously pre-dating the surrounding housing development by many decades, this single tree is a survivor of the once vast tracks of woodland that covered the Ongar area. A very significant amenity tree in this rather treeless corner of Ongar. [p.318]

6. Three giant redwoods (*Sequoiadendron giganteum*)
Location: Coopers, Coopers Hill, Marden Ash.

First discovered in 1852, it was originally intended that these natives of the west coast of America would be named after the Duke of Wellington who died in September of that year. A '*giant amongst trees named after a giant amongst men.*' However, botanists of other persuasions had different ideas (although the name Wellingtonia does seem to have survived here). They decreed that the giant redwood would take its family name from the local indigenous people, the Sequoia Indians. Either way, these magnificent trees, planted sometime in the second half of the nineteenth century and visible from almost every point of the town are as much a part of the history of Ongar as the house in whose grounds they stand.

7. Horse chestnut (*Aesculus hippocastanum*)

Location Coopers Hill, front garden of No23.

A "naturalised" rather than a "native" tree, the horse chestnut was introduced into this country around 1600. Now established as one of our most popular trees, this particular specimen can be identified in a number of old photographs pre-dating the change from a rural to a more urban setting at the southern end of the town. [p.318]

8. English or pedunculate oak (Quercus robur)
Location: Roundabout on Coopers Hill, Brentwood Road,

A true landmark tree, certainly well over 200 years old, closely associated with the history and development of Ongar, situated as it is at the major junction to the south of the town. It is interesting to note that the wooden seat conveniently provided at its base bears the inscription "High Ongar Parish Council", a reminder of the changing parish and ecclesiastical boundaries. [p.318]

9. Field maple (*Acer campestre*)
Location: Field to the rear of Bushey Lea (Cripsey Brook).

Included as a reminder of the many hedgerow trees that have now disappeared as a result of the changing patterns of land use in and around Ongar. The ditch and raised bank upon which these two delightful little trees reside provides possible evidence of an earlier hedgerow boundary. [p.318]

10. White willow (*Salix alba*)
Location: Ongar Bridge, north bank of the Cripsey Brook.

The taxonomy of willows is very difficult, there being over 20 different species found in the British Isles. Ongar tree wardens are confident that this particular example, in spite of its pollarded branches and starburst-like later growth, is a white willow. White or otherwise, this landmark tree provides an important and attractive complement to two local geographical and historical features – Cripsey Brook and Ongar Bridge. [p.318]

11. Cedar (*Cedrus libani*)
Location: Rear garden of No. 114 High Street, Ongar.

Although on private property, this particular tree is as notable a feature of the Ongar skyline as the

LANDMARK TREES

nearby spire of St Martins church, particularly when viewed from one of the southern approaches to the town. Close up, it is best seen from opposite 10 Castle Street, the former home of the Rev. Isaac Taylor, whose daughter Jane gained a considerable reputation as the author of "Twinkle, twinkle Little Star", and other verses and books for children. [p.318]

12. Beech (*Fagus sylvatica*)
Location: St Martins churchyard.

A magnificent tree, perfectly complementing the spire and famous weathervane of St Martin's. Again best seen from the open space opposite 10 Castle Street.

13. Cherry (*Prunus*)
Location: St Martin's churchyard.

Planted in 1994 to commemorate the thirtieth anniversary of the Ongar Flower Club.

14. Walnut (*Juglans regia*)
Location: The Pleasance garden.

L'arbre d'amitié – the tree of friendship. Donated by the Mayor and Council of Cerizay, Ongar's "twin town", this tree was planted by M. Bernard Mimault, adjoint au Maire de Cerizay, and Councillor Keith Tait, chairman of Ongar Parish Council, as a symbol of the friendship between the two communities of Ongar and Cerizay in May 1989. It now stands as part of the Pleasance garden, an informal open space in the town centre created in 1998. [p.318]

15. Copper beech (*Fagus purpuria*)
Location: The Pleasance garden.

Everybody's favourite. The most commonly mentioned tree at the Ongar Millennium History Fayre, held in April 1998. This beautiful tree also provides one of the most specific links with Ongar's past. It was referred to in "The Wilderness", a poem penned by the Rev. E. W. Sergeant, M.A., assistant master of Winchester College whilst a guest at the house, from which the following is an extract:

> *Beneath the shelter of the spreading beech,*
> *Whose russet foliage, soft and sumptuous, breaks*
> *The rich monotony of the zone of trees,*
> *Forest or fruitful, carelessly combined*
> *Which shield the pleasance from the intemperate east.*

16. Mulberry (*Morus nigra*)
Location: The Pleasance garden.

Although not a native of these shores, this black mulberry is not only a somewhat hidden reminder of our Victorian forebears' passion for introducing "exotic" varieties, but also a reminder of yesteryear when the area now occupied by the Library was in fact the site of a fine town centre house, "The Wilderness." Perhaps this particular tree was indeed one of the "fruitful" mentioned by the Rev. Sergeant.

17. English or pedunculate oak (*Quercus robur*)
Location: The Library car park.

The fifth and one has to say the saddest oak on the list. Surrounded by tarmac and hemmed in by motor vehicles, this very well known landmark continually shows signs of distress (yellowing, decay etc), in spite of the efforts of EFDC and others. Like the former trees so dominant in old photographs of Ongar High Street, this oak should stand as a reminder of the folly of taking our natural heritage for granted. How far into the next millennium will this landmark survive? [p.319]

ASPECTS OF THE HISTORY OF ONGAR

18. Cherry, the "Memorial Tree", (*Prunus*) and Yew (*Taxus baccata*)
Location: Both removed in 1998 from Sainsbury's car park, Banson's Lane.

As part of the ongoing development of the town, 1998 saw the arrival of Sainsbury's at the rear of the Budworth Hall, on the former site of the Chipping Ongar County Primary School. Although rather derelict, the site did contain a number of significant trees, including the memorial tree dedicated to the memory of a young pupil of the former primary school killed in a road accident, and a substantial yew. Both trees were removed as part of the redevelopment. Completion of the redevelopment in December 1998, however, revealed considerable replanting and landscaping of the area. This replanting includes at least sixteen yew trees and, more importantly, the rededication of a new memorial tree, a **Cheals Weeping Cherry (*Kiku shidare Sakura*)**. This will be a truly landmark tree in all respects. A sad reminder of times past, an association with perhaps the biggest single change to Ongar for many a year and a hopeful sign for conservation into the next millennium.

19. Horse chestnut (*Aesculus hippocastanum*)
Location: Shakletons.

An old photograph entitled "Sunday School Treat", bearing a date "30.7.08" shows a large horse chestnut tree in the background. As most of the treats took place in Rectory Field, it is perhaps not unreasonable to assume that the large horse chestnut tree dominating the centre of Shakletons and the tree in the old photograph are in fact one and the same. Certainly this particular tree and its close relatives abutting onto the High Street are true Ongar landmarks, providing as they do a leafy perspective as one approaches the town centre from the north.

20. Scots pine (*Pinus sylvestris*)
Location: Banson's Yard.

This native pine, although only truly wild in the Scottish Highlands, was and is commonly planted across Britain. The exact provenance of these particular local examples is unclear. What is clear is that they considerably enhance the landscape views on the western side of the Cripsey Brook. [p.319]

21. Red horse chestnut (*Aesculus x carnea*)
Location: Ongar cemetery.

Sown from a conker collected from a tree in Moreton just prior to the hurricane in October 1987, this tree was planted at 7.20pm on 27 March 1990 by Graham Gassor and Tony Blyth, then clerk to Ongar Parish Council. Ten years on, the tree stands as a timely reminder that although the vast majority of our trees regenerate naturally, occasionally a sensitive helping hand is appropriate. [p.319]

22. Giant redwood (*Sequoiadendron giganteum*)
Location: Ongar cemetery.

One of a pair, this fine example of the largest tree in the world not only stands as a northerly counterpoint to the Wellingtonias at Coopers Hill, but also serves to remind us of a number of interesting conifers traditionally associated with burial sites such as the yew, the cedar and a fine Scots pine, close to the High Street. [p.319]

23. Horse chestnut (*Aesculus hippocastanum*)
Location: Recreation ground (near Scout hut).

A truly magnificent example of this most popular tree. Large, spreading, easily accessible with a plentiful crop of conkers (from "conqueror" or "conche" – an earlier game played with snails), this particular tree has no doubt provided countless hours of pleasure to the many thousands of residents and visitors who flocked to the agricultural show held annually on this site during the early years of this century. Long may it continue to give pleasure! [p.319]

LANDMARK TREES

24. English or pedunculate oak (*Quercus robur*)
Location: Open field to the rear of Castle mound.

This single tree, very visible, stands as a stark reminder of the changing pattern of land use around Ongar during the last century. Looking across open country toward our neighbouring parish of High Ongar, we might ponder on what has happened to our woodland heritage over the last hundred years and what this same scene might look like at the time of the next millennium.

25. English or pedunculate oak (*Quercus robur*)
Location: Bowes Field.

Another fine English oak with local historic ties to that most English of games – cricket. An old photograph of Bowes field, taken at the turn of the century, shows Ongar Cricket Club pavillion surrounded by a number of substantial trees. Although our present landmark oak may well not have been one of those recorded for posterity by the photographer, it is so close to the site that it must have proved a popular, welcome and shady spot to enjoy the sound of leather on willow during a warm Edwardian summer.

26. English or pedunculate oak (*Quercus robur*)
Location: Great Lawn.

Much loved by local residents, this hedgerow and its attendant standards is another "green" link to times gone by. Old photographs looking south from what is now the Four Wantz clearly show the west side of the High Street, opposite Great Stony Park, to be tree lined. In spite of much development to this part of Ongar, the hedgerow and trees continue to survive and provide a much needed barrier against the incursions of the motor car. [p.319]

27. Common walnut (*Juglans regia*)
Location: Queensway. Front garden of No.109.

A fine tree brought to notice at the Ongar Millennium History Fayre by the occupier of No. 109 and included as an Ongar landmark tree for its amenity value to the residents of Shelley.

The above list is not final. Hopefully, it never will be. It should form the basis of an ongoing audit into the next millennium. Many of the trees listed above are already the subject of tree preservation orders. Further classification of those and others as landmark trees, whilst not attracting greater legal protection, does at least ensure that they are recorded at both district and county level. As important, however, as the protection from arbitrary destruction and/or indiscriminate development, is the need for our trees to be seen as much a part of Ongar's history as its castle, its churches and otherfine buildings. After all, most of them lived here before us, and many will be living here long after we have gone.

1. English or pedunculate oak (Quercus robur)

2. Weeping willow (Salix babylonica)

ASPECTS OF THE HISTORY OF ONGAR

8. English or pedunculate oak (Quercus robur)

7. Horse chestnut (Aesculus hippocastanum)

5. English or pedunculate oak (Quercus robur)

4. Common yew (Taxus baccata)

14. Walnut (Juglans regia)

11. Cedar (Cedrus libani)

10. White willow (Salix alba)

9. Field maple (Acer campestre)

LANDMARK TREES

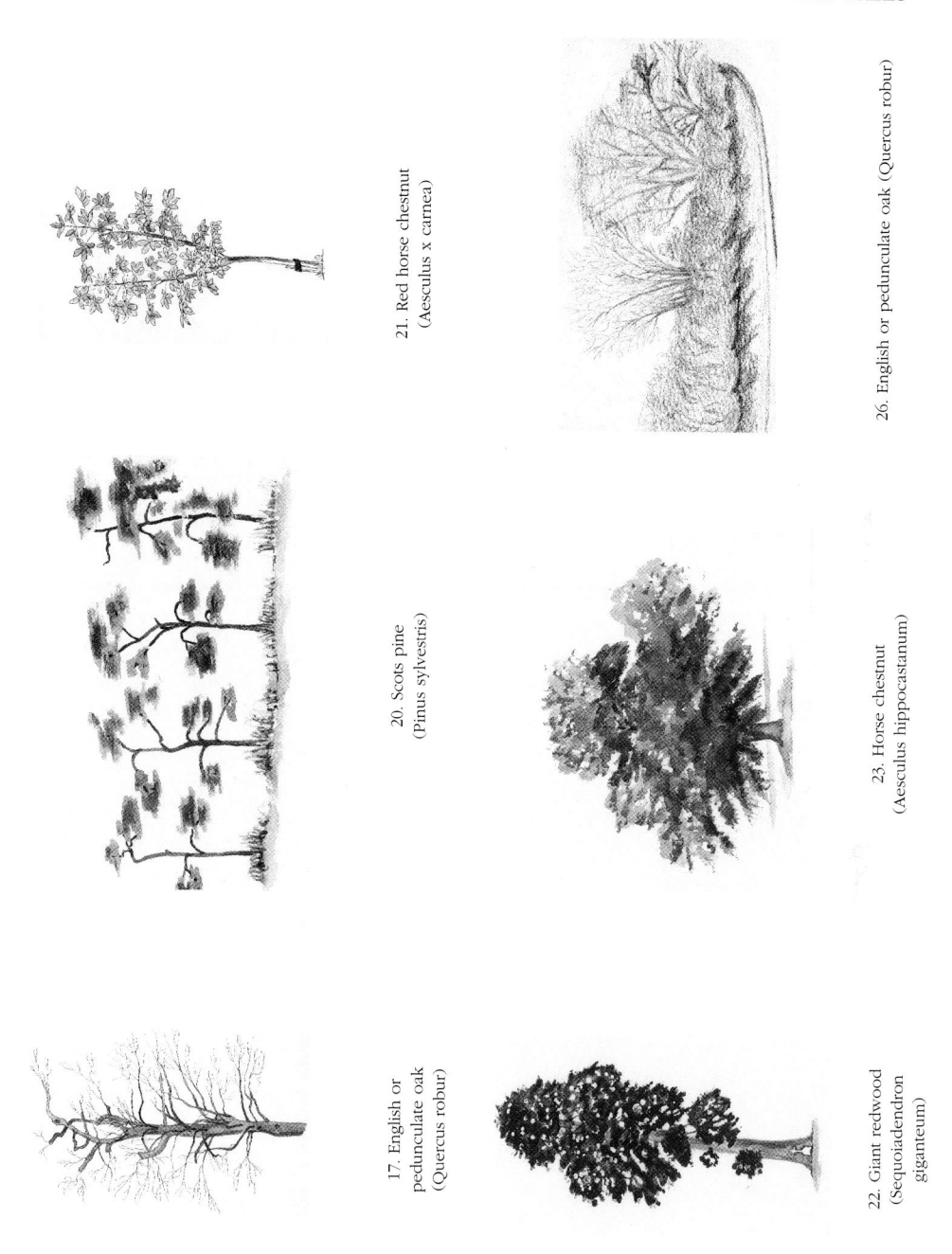

21. Red horse chestnut (Aesculus x carnea)

26. English or pedunculate oak (Quercus robur)

20. Scots pine (Pinus sylvestris)

23. Horse chestnut (Aesculus hippocastanum)

17. English or pedunculate oak (Quercus robur)

22. Giant redwood (Sequoiadendron giganteum)

APPENDIX

Measurements and currency

A variety of units of measurement and currency are used in this book, some of which are archaic. Others are rapidly becoming obsolete and will be equally obscure to future readers. This appendix defines these units and their abbreviations.

Weight
- ounce = oz = 28.3 grams
- pound = lb(s) = 16 oz = 454 grams
- hundredweight = cwt = 112 lbs = 50.8 kilograms
- ton = 20 cwt = 1017 kilograms
- fother (of lead) = $19\frac{1}{2}$ cwt

Length
- inch = in(s) = 2.54 centimetres
- foot = ft = 12 inches = 30.5 centimetres
- yard = 3 feet
- chain = 66 feet = 20.13 metres
- mile = 1.61 kilometres

Area
- acre = 0.41 hectares

Volume
- cubic foot = cu ft = 28.3 litres
- cubic yard = 9 cubic feet
- yard of sand = 1 cubic yard
- pint = 0.57 litres
- gallon = 8 pints = 4.54 litres

Money
- pound (sterling) = £ = 20 shillings = (approx) 1.5 euros
- shilling = s = 12 pence
- penny = d
- guinea = £1 1s 0d
- mark = 13s 4d

Abbreviations

In general, the full name is given when first used in the text, followed in brackets by the abbreviated form used subsequently. There are a few exceptions.

- am = time between midnight and midday
- ERO = Essex Record Office
- ECC = Essex County Council
- GP = general medical practitioner
- GPO = General Post Office
- JP = justice of the peace
- MP = member of Parliament
- NHS = National Health Service
- ORDC = Ongar Rural District Council
- OS = Ordnance Survey map
- pm = time between midday and midnight
- PRO = Public Record Office
- VAD = Voluntary Aid Detachment
- VCH Essex = Victoria County History of Essex

INDEX

A superscript number indicates the endnote number on the page with which it is linked. For example, 99[33] refers to endnote 33 on page 99. The names of books, publications, paintings etc are in italic.

Acres, Mr, builder, 297
Adams, Thomas, baker, 192
advowson of Greensted 41; of Chipping Ongar 19, 37, 42
Agricultural Gazette 273
Agricultural Notebook 270
Ailida 2
Ainsworth, William 138
Alexander, Edward 37; Nicholas (d.1714) 14
Allen, George 145
Allmen, Paul 283
allotments 124, 293, 299
almhouses 106
Alsop, Rev George 19
altar rail 81
Amor, John, architect 267
Amori, Gabriel 288
Anchor Inn, Ongar 207
Anderson, John 282
Anger, Thomas junior 190
Angier, Katherine 145
ankerhold 14
antinomianism 73, 99[33]
Anzer, Thomas 190
apothecaries 214, 219, 220
apprentices 129, 134
arbre d'amitié 315
archdeacon's court 20, 23, 24
Archer, John 190
architects 16, 32, 52, 53, 97[7], 154, 183, 216, 263, 267
Arnold, Dick 279; Mrs Phil 279
Ashdown, John Alfred 143, 259; store 195, 196, 218, 306, 308
Ashlyn, Henry G 297
Assassination of Rizzio 60, 64
Atkinson sweet shop 197, 308
Attlee, William 160
auctioneers 256
Audrey Ruth, clothes shop 196
Auger, James 210
Aukingford Gardens 310
Avery, Mrs Barbara 282
Avington Cottage 257

Badcock, Inspector Doug 140
Baden-Powell, Robert 280, 281
Bainham, James 36, 39
Baker, William 133, 202
bakers 192
Balgarius, Dr Charles 214
Balls, Mr E G 169
banks 201-202
Bansons Lane 290, 316; Way railway cottages 245, 306; Yard 316
barbers 219
Barclays Bank 191, 201
Barker, Miss Ann, teacher, 305, 308; John 312[2]; Fred, teacher, 305, 308, 309
Barlow, Dr 153; H 116; Harry (d. 1920) 203, 294; Henry, builder, 203; James 209; Miss 146; Mr & Mrs 256, 298; Walter 153
Barltrop, Ammon, blacksmiths 200
Barn field 7, 107
Barnard, H E 257; Ralf 2
Barncroft 203
Barnes Mr R 186, 268, 284, 288; Mrs 186
Baron, Tony, surgeon 226
Barr, Dr O F 225
Bartolozzi, Francesco 56, 57
Bartons bakers 193
Bass, Mr & Mrs 297
Baugh, Dorothy (d. 1980) 216, 217; family 32, 217, 218; Rev George 216; Hilda 216, 217; J W M 215, 216, 259, 276; Mary 216; shop 195; William 216
Baynes, T M architect 154
beadle 21
Beadle, Rev Joseph 19, 20, 23
Beard, Joshua, grocer, 191
Beasing, James 108, 220
Beaufort, Lady Margaret 34, 35
beech 315
beekeepers 291
beerhouse 210
beggars, see poor relief; vagrants
Bekesbourne, Kent 35
Bell public house 207, 291
Bennet, R 188; Richard 208
Berry, Mick 288
Bewick, Thomas (d. 1828) 54, 98[12]
bicycles 120, 253, 278
Bidder, George Parker 230
Bingham, Rev Thomas 28
Binckes, Samuel 138, 208
Bingley, Mrs 165; Percival Hubert 160, 165
Birchall-Scott, Mr, architect 32
Bird, Kenneth 268
Bishop, Amy & Edith 158
Bishop Compton's survey 24
Bishops Stortford & District Gas Co 250; Waterworks Co. 251, 252
Black & White minstrels 265
blacksmiths 199, 200, 215
Blake Hall 311; convalescent hospital 224; station 236, 237, 243, 270
Blakeley's grocers 192
Blinds, Bobbins & Spools 196
Blomer, Charles 219
Blue Anchor Inn, Ongar 207
Blundell, John 143
Blyth, Tony 316
board of guardians, Hackney 179-186; Ongar 109, 110, 112, 133, 134, 135, 222
Bobbingworth, rector of 19

ASPECTS OF THE HISTORY OF ONGAR

Bolden, Flo Ethel 184; Pat 278
Bolton, Stephen 18
Bonder, Alexander 288
Boodle, John, surgeon 108, 220
boot & shoemakers/shops 138, 194, 196
Boram, Charles 143; James 143
Borough, The 120, 190
Bowes 114, 119, 311; farm 186, 310; field 310, 317; school 305
Bowman, Nurse 135
Boxford rectory, Suffolk 46
boxing 31, 309
Boyce, Francis 110
Boyd, William Henry 207
Boyer, bank agent 201; Francis 191; G P 16
Boydell, John (d. 1804) 60, 64
Boyland, Rev John 32
Brace, Bernard 282; Bernie 279
Bramham, Mr W 179, 180
Brassey, Lord 271; Thomas 231
Brassley, Paul 273
Brentwood, chapel riot 44; gasworks 164; grammar school 53, 57, 59, 98[16], 147; industrial school 179
Brentwood Road 293, 310, 314
Brett, Percy Edward 143
Bretton, Elizabeth 190; George 207, 255
breweries & brewing 152, 207, 208, 209, 211-212, 253
Brewery Cottages, Marden Ash 212
brick, mediaeval great 13; Roman 1, 3, 13
brickworks 202, 246, 249, 250, 256, 312
Bridge, Jeremiah 138
Bridge Motors 201, 299
Bright, George 134
Brighty family 253
Bright Freeman Partnership (Loughton) 267
Britannia & Clerical Life Offices 215
Brockes, Andrew 211; Joseph, grocer, 191
Brooke, Richard 44
Brooklands Garage 201, 202, 203
Broom, Alfred Edward 143; Rosina 312[2]
Brown, Inspector Arthur 140; Inspector Arthur Edward 140; Bob 279; Charles 191, 201; George 268; H E 250; Herbert Boyer 117, 191, 259; Miss Lieutenant 281; Percy Boyer 116, 191
Browning, Inspector Thomas 140
Brucesmith, Mrs L A 160, 167
Bryant, C 280, 281
Buchanan, Walter 25
Buckle, Miss, boarding school 149
Budworth, Captain Philip John 16, 140, 189, 260-262, 267; Rev Philip 260
Budworth Hall 53, 117, 118, 175, 202, 224, 250, 262-269, 283, 285, 290, 291, 316; ballroom 265; Memorial Committee 262; Memorial Fund 256; trustees 265
builders 115, 202-203, 216, 256, 293, 297
Bull Inn 206-207, 209
Bull, Richard 107
Bullock, Henry 275

bumby 252; see also privies
Bunhill Fields burial ground 55, 59
Burgess, Sarah 197
Burghley, Lord 45, 46
burial board 112, 116, 120, 121
Burrel, George, saddler, 200
Burrell, Inspector James William 140
buses 308; Greenline depot 310; rail bus 241; see also omnibus
Bushey Lea 2, 107, 112, 314
Butcher, Inspector Alfred 140
butchers 115, 190-191, 307, 308; butchers' boys 307
Buthers, drapers, 196
Butler, John William 170, 171
Butt, Mrs, sweet shop, 198
butter market; see Ongar market house
Buxton, D A J 226
Byles, Rev Thomas 31, 32, 308

Cadet corps 161, 162, 163, 164, 231
cage, old 111
Calamy, Edward 24
Calmet's *Dictionary of the Bible* 58
Camp, butchers 190; Mr 117, 119; Scout 280
Campe, John 15, 106; Thomas (d. 1719) 15
Camus, L 167
Capital brewery, Ongar 212
Capel-Cure, Major G 284; see also Cure, Capel
Carey, Richard 138
Carlick, Miss 296
Carlow, Councillor J W 169
Carman, Jane, milliner, 134
carpenters 138, 184
carpets 195
carriers 79, 205, 206, 207, 255
Carter, butchers 190, 291, 308; Elias 211; George 190; Mary 190; P J 190; Patrick 190; Peter 190, 308, 312[2]; William 190
Cartwright, Inspector Alan 140
Casford, William 154
Casson, Sir Hugh 10
Castle, Mr T 257
Castle Farm 119; House 37, 38, 47, 62, 74-79; see also Castle Street; Ongar castle; Saxon burgh
Castle Street 1, 3, 117, 119, 123, 125, 250, 290, 292, 306, 315; number ten, 74, 85-88
Catchpole, Supt Joseph 140
Cater, Gustavus George (d. 1945) 169, 170, 171
Caulfield, Rev John 32
Cecil, Rev Richard (d. 1863) 15, 100[55]; Robert 46; Mrs Salome (d. 1844) 93; Sir William 46
cedar 314, 316
cemetery, see Bunhill Fields, Nottingham General Cemetery, Ongar Cemetery
Central Essex Light Railway 245; House 151, 250, 253; Line 234, 236
Cerizay 315
Champness, Mrs 18

INDEX

Chancellor, Frederic, architect 10, 222
Chandler, George 143
Chanell's printers 192, 197, 259
Chapel cottages 307
Chaplin, P 188
Chapman, chemist 197; Richard James 215
Chase, The 120
Chelmsford Diocesan Education Committee 147; isolation hospital 227
chemists & druggists; see pharmacies
Cherry garden cottage 139
cherry tree 315, 316
Chevers Hall, High Ongar 151
Chief Constable of Essex 139, 141
Childs, Austin 255, 258; Emily Blanch 255, 257, 258; Mr H 280; Henry (d. 1920) 120, 195, 255-259; Jane (d. 1902) 255, 257; Janet 255, 258; Mary Ellen 255, 258; Mr 122; Samuel 212; William Henry 195, 250, 255, 256, 258
childbirth 304
Chipping Ongar; see under Ongar
Chocolate Box sweet shop 197, 198
cholera 223
Christie, Charles H F 114, 115, 116, 120, 258
Chrysanthemum Show 265
Church, butchers, 190
Churches; see under name of church, chapel, congregation or meeting house
Church fields 190
churchwardens 20-21, 108, 110, 127, 128, 131, 147, 156
circus 310
Clare, David 284, 288; Doreen 284
Clark, Emily, milliner, 255; family 311; Mr O W 158, 167; Dr W.C. (d. 1902) 114, 115, 116, 118, 120, 160, 161, 164, 166, 258
Clarke, Elizabeth 255; Samuel 25
Clayton, Rev John junior 50
Cleeve, Edward 293
Clerk of Peace for Essex 189; (see also parish clerk)
Clerke, John the (d. 1285) 21
Cliffe, Robert 145
clock, Budworth Hall 264; Mr Johnson's 275; St Martin's 110
Clockwork Mice, The 187
Cloverley Road 290, 293-301
coaches 205, 206, 233; builders 200; proprietors 152, 205
coal merchants 295, 306, 308
Cobbold, John Chevalier MP 231
Cochrane, Rev 135
Cock Tavern 208-209
Coe, Mr 120; William 109, 133
Colchester, Angel Lane 68, 72, 73, 75; Bucklersbury Lane chapel 68, 73; MP 44; Royal Grammar School 150; St Helen's Lane meeting house 26; St Martin's church 69; town clerk 44; West Stockwell Street 68
Cole, William 215
Coleclough & Palmer 212; James 212

Coles, Cliff 312[2]; gents outfitters 196; Jack 276; Laurie 279; Rob 279
College of Preceptors 155, 156, 167
Collier's Hatch 7
Collingridge, Rev Charles 32
Collins, Frank 279
Colston, Edward 19
Colvin, Brig Gen R E 225
Comber, R A W 280
Comerford, Hugh 143
Compton, Bishop (his survey) 24
Conder, family 77; Luck 75, 99[35]; Thomas 73, 99[34]
Coney Heath 7
Congregational church, Ongar 52, 53, 100[55], 203, 256, 259, 291, 308, 311; schoolroom 97[7], 263, 280; scout group 281; see also Independent church; nonconformity; Ongar chapel; Ongar meeting house; United Reformed church
Connor, Rev James 32
constable, murder of 142; Ongar hundred 138; parish 110, 111, 127, 133, 138-139; police 139-142; special 111, 142-143
Cook, Henry John 143; Nathan, coachbuilders, 200
Cooke, Rev Mr 66, 67
Cooper, John 110; Thomas 190
Co-operative Society 192, 195, 196, 197, 203; pharmacy 218
coopers 314
Coopers Hill 314, 316; see also Marden Ash Hill
Cordell sweetshop 198
cordwainers 195, 210
corn merchants/factors 192, 207, 211
Cornell, F 199; Herbert 143; ironmongers 199, 207; Jeames, blacksmith, 200
Costigan, Dee 286
Cottage Homes; see Ongar Cottage Homes
Cottis, Mr 271
Council offices 123
Court of Arches 19, 23
Cousins, Edward 110
Coward, Jill 176
Cowee, bakers 193; John Ellington 296; Thomas 114, 115, 116, 121, 122, 188, 190, 250; Thomas junior 190
Cozens farm, High Ongar 152
Crabb, John 128
Cracknell, Eddy & Mavis 296; Les 303, 312[2]; Leslie & Florence 295
Cracknoll, Joseph 215
Craigens drapers 195
Cranmer, Archbishop Thomas 35, 36, 40, 41
cricket 162, 217; see also Ongar Cricket Club
Cripsey Brook 1, 42, 118, 119, 124, 223, 251, 253, 293, 294, 308, 314, 316; viaduct 231
Crome, Dr Edward 39
Cromwell, Sir Oliver 14; Thomas 34, 35, 37
Crook, Rev Jacob 23
Cross, Rev Walter 25
Crossingham, John 138

Crown Inn, Ongar 23, 206, 208, 209
Cullum, Stuart 282
Cunliffe Smith, Sir Charles 263
Cure, Capel 85, 109, 133, 134
curriculum (school) 153, 159, 160, 161, 170, 172, 173, 175; National Award (1984) 174
Curtis, bakers 193
Cycling Club 309; Shelley speedway 290

dairy 295
Dapifer, Hamo 8
Darbey, Mr 129
Darby's Row, Marden Ash 212
Darlington, Joseph 139; Robert 139; Sophie 139
Darton & Harvey, publishers 71, 72
Davey, F E Ltd 184; Richard, grocer 191
David, Dr A S.227
Davies, Geoff 284
Dawkins, G J 160
Dawson, Mr & Mrs 158
Day, Dalley 45
Dearman, Jim 312[2]
Dedham, Essex 28
deer park; see Ongar Great Park
Dement newsagent 197
dentistry 215
derailment at North Weald 233
Derham, Edwin 210
Dick, Bob 279; Paul 279
Dicker, builder & undertaker 297; Frederick H (d. 1938) 143; Leslie 297, 298
Dickinson, John, wheelwright 200
diet (school) 152, 166
diphtheria 223, 227, 303; antitoxin 223, 227; immunisation 227
dissent, religious; see nonconformity
district nurses 304
doctors 107, 110, 217, 219-228, 304; parish 129, 220, 222
Doddridge, Rev Phillip 27, 28
Domesday Book 2, 9
Domino clothes shop 196
Donavon, Mrs 196
Downton, Wilts (MP for) 41
drainage 110, 118, 124, 222, 223, 252, 293
drapers 122, 194-196, 218, 255-259
Drea, Rev Brian 33
dressmakers 134, 194, 255
drill hall 198; see also yeomanry
Drum & Monkey Club 225, 226
Dyers, Marden Ash 53, 74, 92-93, 211

East, Christopher 282
Easter, Jean 312[2]
Eastern Counties Cooperative Dairy Assoc 271; Counties Railway 207, 230-231; Union Railway 231
Eastaugh & Wright 192
education; see curriculum; schools

Edwards, George, draper 256; Mike & Jean 299
egg packing station 306
electricity 250, 251, 266
Elizabeth I (Queen) planned visit to Ongar 46, 76
eleven plus exam 172
Elliott George Walter 154
Ellis, Ellen, dressmaker 255
Elms Estate 294, 300
Ely, Mr 122
Emberson, Roger 282
Emergency Hospital Scheme 226
employment 306
engraving 53, 54, 55, 56, 60, 63, 64, 69
Epping 27, 250; & Ongar Rail Users Committee 239; & Ongar Railway Ltd 240; & Ongar Rural District Council 125; Forest District Council (EFDC) 125, 176, 240, 315; Forest Railway Co 239; nonconformist minister 27; Ongar Railway Society 239; Railway Company 230; Union workhouse 31
Essex & Herts Community NHS Trust 227; County education committee 175-176; County court 272; House 123; Hunt 195, 265, 309
Eustace, Count of Boulogne 2
evacuees 266, 298, 311
Evans, Peter 285, 288; Thomas 249
Eve, Robert 133
Everett, Mr M 283; Martyn 282
Everyday Shoes 196
ex officio oath 45

Fairfield Road 202, 310
Fane, Rev F A S 262, 263, 267
Farm Life 272
farmers 115, 270-273, 306, 310
farriers 139
Faux, Mr & Mrs 297; Rene 297
fees (school) 150, 151, 159, 160
Fenchurch Street Station 230, 233, 237
Fenn, Gertrude 15, 264; John 15; John Patrick 143, 259, 265; May 15; Mr 117; Walter 15, 201
Ferguson, Dr R 227
Fetter Lane meeting house 59, 62
Fewell, Miss 146; sweetshop 197, 198
Finbow, George 279
Finch, John 139; Mary 139; Mr W A 183; William 139
Fippes, Mary 145
First World War 4, 142, 159, 163, 167, 205, 265, 297, 303, 309
Fisher, Mr A 280, 281; Bishop John of Rochester 34; Mr W 296
fire engine 110, 111, 124, 206, 256, 272; escape 256; hose 122; hydrants 122; insurance 110, 122; station 309; see also Ongar Voluntary Fire Brigade
fishmongers 210, 306
five parishes, the 175
Fleet, George 170
Flood, Supt Henry 139, 140, 141
florists 115

INDEX

Fogg, Miss Minnie 257
football 162
Footer, Kim 283
footpaths 119, 310
Fordham, Inspector Charles 140; John Porter 211
Forest Hall, High Ongar 195, 281
Foster, Charles & Son 202; Charles, auctioneer 256, 293; C H 250, 252, 259; Daniel 129
foster homes 179, 180, 181
Four Wantz 119, 317
Fox, Inspector Charles 140, 223; Rev Henry 32
Foxe, John 39, 40, 41, 45
Francesca clothes shop 196
Francis, George 145; John 292; Richard 145; William 145
fruiterers 193
Freeston, greengrocer 194
Frost, John 282
furniture brokers 30; shop 195, 199
Fyfield Academy 152; primary school 144; Road 185, 309; Queen's Head 190

Gables, The 203
Gallagher, Inspector Patrick 140
Galvin, Rev Brian 33
Gann, Mr 297
Garden, Frances 55
Gardiner, Bishop of Winchester 41
gas inspectors 110, 112; price 181; rates 112; supply 149, 184; see also Bishops Stortford Gas Co; lighting; Ongar Gas Co
Gassor, Graham 316
Gate Cottage, Marden Ash 211
Geary, Robert 282
Gemmill, Gilbert 312[2]
general practitioner; see doctor
George Inn, Ongar 190, 207-208
Getgood Graham 283; Rene 312[2]
Gibbs, F 116
Giblin, bakers 193; Richard 210
Gibson, Henry W 114, 115, 121, 189, 256, 262, 263, 264, 267, 295; Mrs 112
Gidley, Charley 139; Fanny 194
Giffen, bootmakers 194, 195
Giggins, Inspector Richard 140
Gilbert, Ann (d. 1866) 54, 62, 74, 77, 78, 80, 82, 85, 87, 91, 92; Annie (d. 1941) 101[63]; Isaac Charles (d. 1885) 52, 53, 97[7], 112, 263, 264; James Montgomery 51; Rev Joseph (d. 1852) 51, 77, 80, 82, 89, 97[4], 99[23]; Josiah (d. 1892) 1, 52, 53, 55, 74, 78, 80. 83, 84, 89, 92, 93, 263; Mary (d. 1925) 53, 98[8]; Susan (d. 1871) 53, 92, 93
Gillett, Messrs of Croydon 264
Gilmour, Edwyn & Dorreen 300
Gingell, John, estate agent 259, 291
Glascock, Thomas, schoolmaster 149
glebe 108, 112
glovers 24
Godfree, C 164

Godfrey, leather goods 200; William 219
Gold, Peter, gents outfitter 196
Gomer, John G 281
Goodhall, Rev A 259
Gould, Cyril 276; Frank 143
Graves, Rev Thomas 23
Gray, C S & Son, brewers 209
Great Burstead, Essex 19, 23
Great Eastern Railway 121, 122, 230-235, 242
Great Lawn 317
Great Stony Field 112; Park 317; School 146, 186-187, 281, 283, 284; see also Ongar Cottage Homes
Greatherd, Anne (d. 1683) 15
Green, David 287; Rev John 27; Inspector Rupert 140; Theophilus 27; Walk 290
greengrocers 193-194, 217, 307
Greensted 249; church (see St Andrew's church); farm 313; Hall 10, 260, 261, 262; House 295; Road 117, 249, 310, 313; villa (see Roman buildings)
Greyhound Inn, Ongar 138, 208
Greylands 190
Griffin, Mr 164
grocers 115, 191-192, 257, 296, 308
Gualco, Rev Michael 32
Guild of All Souls 19
Gutteridge, PC George 142
Guy, Richard 138

Hackney, Dr H C C 224, 225, 227
Hackney, children's homes 252, 295, 309, 311 London Borough 186, 187, 295; Union 146
Hackshaw, Jane (d. 1780) 55; Robert (d. 1722) 55; Robert (d. 1738) 55
Hadler Miss Mabel 170; Mr 296
Hadley, George 276
Hadsel(e)y, Mr 85
Hadsley, Bert 312[2]; Mr S 121
hairdresser 306
Hall, A C 164; Alfred 120, 143; Miss E 18
Hallsford Bridge 253; ind..estate 199
Hammond, Charles William 143
Hancock, Mr 17; W 116
harness makers 200
Harper, George 39
Harris, George 20
Harrop, Ray 279
Hart, John 282
Hartley, Sir Frank 216
Harvey, Marilyn 286; Thomas 293
Haslam, James 109, 133
Hatchard, Mrs 254
Hatfield, Dr Sylvia 312[2]; Dr Ted 226, 284, 285
hatters 115
Hatton Garden, Clerkenwell 57
Hawks Bird & Co, brewers 207
Hay, Lucy 93
Hayward, grocers 191-192; Henry 140; Robert 114, 115, 121, 191-192

ASPECTS OF THE HISTORY OF ONGAR

Hazel, Rev James 32
headmasters 160, 164, 169, 170, 173, 176, 184, 186
healthcare 107, 219-228, 304
Heard, John, workhouse governor 130
Hendey, Thomas 207
Henl(e)y, W 128
Herbert, Edith Haddon 53, 98[9]; Mr 197; Thomas 52, 89, 101[66], 197
heretics, burning of 39, 41, 42
Heron Court 251
Herts & Essex Waterworks Co 119, 251, 252, 256
Hewett, Cecil 3, 16
Hewitt, William 10
Hickman, Rev W 66, 68
High Ongar 249, 252, 253, 294, 317; parish council 314; railway 246; workhouse 133, 134
highways 117, 118, 119, 124; board 112; traffic 120
Hill, Ann (d. 1668) 15; Robert (d. 1648) 14
Hillman, Mrs 254
Hind, R, artist 189
Hinton, James 56; John Howard 57
Hocking, butchers 190; Mrs 196
Hodsoll, Abraham 138
Hoffman, Francis 285
Holborn, Dyers Buildings 57; Red Lion St 65
Holbrook, William 138, 208
Holder, George, drapery assistant 255
Holmlea 190, 203
Holt, Fred, greengrocer 193; Mrs, sweet shop 198; Susan 207; Thomas 207; W.E 14
Hooker, Rev Thomas 23
Hope, Jill 217
Horide, Mr 191
Horner, Thomas 133
horse chestnut 314, 316, 318, 319
horse stealing 141
horticulture 290-292
hospitals, Red Cross military 32, 224, 265; Savings Assoc 225; see also Chelmsford Isolation; infirmary; Ongar & District Cottage; Ongar Isolation; Ongar Smallpox; Ongar Union; Ongar War Memorial; Rush Green Isolation; workhouse infirmary
Hough, John 312[2]
Hubbard, D Ltd 197, 198; see also Senners
Hull, Fish Street Chapel 81
Humphreys, Lilian 297, 299; Mr T 283; Tommy 282
hunting see Essex Hunt
Hurd, Ann, workhouse matron 134; John, workhouse master 134
Hurley, Rev Andrew 33
Hurlock, Brook 20
Hutchings, Den 279
Hutchins, Rev Thomas 28

Ibbetson, Rt Hon Sir Henry Selwyn MP 264
Ilfracombe, Devon 77
Ince, Rev Hugh (or Hugo) 23
Independent Congregation, Ongar 50

infirmary, Cottage Homes 183; workhouse 221, 223, 224
Ingelow, Jean 90
Ingelric the priest 2
Ingrey, C, artist 26
innkeepers 205, 206
inspectors 112; gas 116, 120; rates 112; sanitary 222; weights & measures 141, 143[9]
insurance agents 115, 256; company 222
International Stores 191, 308
ironmongers/hardware 144, 198-199
Isaac, Anne 36; Edward 36, 40, 43; Thomas 40
Ives, James 26

Jackson, Ralph (d. 1556) 41; Walter 295, 296, 297, 298
Jamboree, International Scout 285, 288, 289
Jarvis, Mr 253
Jefferys, Josiah 55, 57; Sarah Hackshaw (d. 1809) 55, 56; Thomas (d. 1771) 55, 98[13]
Jenkins, Mr W W, printer 197
Jessup, Mr, workhouse governor 130
Johnson Bros shoe shop 196; Mr 275
Johnston, Henry Alexander 211, 293
Jones, Allen 300; Cynthia 299; Miss E.M 265; family 250; Rev Godfrey 149; Henry Edward ("Gassy") 250, 251, 263, 265, 293, 294, 295, 296, 297; Private J 256; Len 290, 292, 295; Mary 295; Stanley H 266; W 164
Joseph King cottages 195, 198; Educational Trust 144; Trust 15, 144-148, 149, 181, 192; see also King, Joseph; King's Trust school
Joslin, George 141
Joy, George Frost 210
Joyner, Rev Daniel 23
Jouanneau, Rev H Maria 32
Jubilee, diamond (1897) 122; golden (1887) 264, 265; silver (1977) 285
Jump, Henry 31
Justice of the Peace 24, 44
Juvenilia 71

Kauffmann, Angelica 57
Keane, Rev Stephen 33
Kellam, Charles & Ingrid 298
Kelly, Anna 273; James Milroy 273; Paul 278
Kelvedon Hall 30; Hatch 291
Kent, Henry William 143
Kerr, John, ironmonger 199, 259; of Ongar Park Hall 270
Kerridge, sweet shop 197
Keys, George, constable 133, 138; George, workhouse master 134; John 139
Kilnfield 202
King, Ann (d. 1668) 15; Bert 292; Elizabeth (d. 1651) 15; Floss 292; greengrocer 194, 217; John (d. 1679) 15; Joseph (d. 1679) 15, 144; Mary 300; Richard 299; Robert 299; Susanna (d. 1693) 207; William (d. 1694) 207
King's Head Inn, Ongar 30, 166, 189, 209, 210, 276, 294, 308, 309
King's Trust cottages 144; school 114, 115, 117, 144, 146, 147, 169, 181, 303

INDEX

Kinzett, Rodney 296, 312[2]
Kirby, John Henry 215; shop 197; T.H 116
Knapman, Reginald 297
Knollys, Sir Francis 45
Knowleton Hall 203
Korf, Hermann, ladies tailor 195, 259, 303, 307; Marie (Nellie) 53, 97[7], 259, 298, 303, 305, 307, 312[2]
Kyne, Rev Father 30

Lacey, Albert 195; blacksmith 200; bootmaker 195; chemist 195, 218; Charles 198; cubmaster 280; Ernest 195; E F 281; Henry 200; Hilda 312[2]; J E 281; Nathaniel 26; Peter 195, 197; Walter 121; William 195; William Edward 143, 195
Laggett, Alan 282
Lambert, Sarah 28; Thomas 28
Lane, James 152
Latimer, Bishop Hugh 36, 39
Latin, Warwick 283
laundry 184
Lavender, butchers 190; Mr 216; sweet shop 197; T.N 259
Lavenham, Arundel House 67, 68, 70, 73; Cooke's House 66; Guildhall 56; Independent congregation 60; parish church 60
Lawrence sweet shop 197
Lay, Mr, saddler 295; Mrs 295
Layer Marney, Essex 44
Leach, Michael 176
Lee, Joe 312[2]; Joseph 210; Mr 310; Zoe 312[2]
Leigh, Terry 279
Lenham, John 208, 214, 220, 221
Lewis, J stationers/printers 197
Library, school 167; Ongar 315
Liddle & Sons 192
lighting 118, 120, 121, 124, 311; electric 266; gas 112, 116, 140, 183, 264; inspectors 110; rate 112, 120
lime subsidy 290
Linney, Enid 312[2]
Lion Inn 26, 189, 205, 209, 309; yard 310; see also Red Lion Inn
Little Bansons 112
Liverpool Street station 233, 235, 236
Livingstone cottages 53, 195; David 15
Lloyds chemist 215, 218
local government 104-126, 222; Board 115, 116, 224
Locomotive Club of Gt Britain 238
London & North Eastern Railway 231, 236, 242; County Council 186; Passenger Transport Board 236; Transport 237, 238, 239, 240, 243; Underground Ltd 240, 241
Long Meadow 7; Walk 310
Longfields 293, 294, 299; allotments 290
Lorkin, Rev John 19, 23, 24; Rev Patrick 32
Loughton, Essex 230, 231, 233, 236
Louth, John 39
Love Lane 112, 275, 277; recreation & sports club 308-309, 316
Loveland, Rev William 32, 33

Low, Ellen, matron 256; Robert William, workhouse master 256
Lucy, Matilda de 6; Richard de 4, 13
Ludlow, Malcolm 282; Roger 282

McConnell, Agnes 270, 271; Anna 271, 273; Archibald 270, 271, 273; Katherine 271; Primrose 270-273; Primrose junior 271, 273
McCormick & Sons, builders 183, 184, 185
McCorquodale family 195
McCrindle, Robert MP 176
McInnes, Supt John 139, 140, 141

Mabon, Mrs, sweet & tea shop 198; Em 312[2]
magistrates 109, 114, 115
Mallett, James (hanged 1825) 141
maltsters 211, 212
Manchester Unity of Oddfellows 222
Manning, Archbishop 30; David 297
Manor House 202; see also Ongar manor
Maple, Thomas 36, 37
maple 314, 318
market; see Ongar market
Marazion, Cornwall 77, 82
Marchant, Peter & Jane 299
March's jewellers 192
Marden Ash 249, 252, 294; brewery 253; Hill 306, 310; House 250, 293
market garden 193-194, 307; House 188, 189, 197; see also Ongar market
Marles, Charlotte 309, 312[2]; Mrs 311
Marriage, Arthur & Dorothy 297
Martin, Beryl 312[2]; Herbert 134; Mary (née Plaxton) 63; Thomas 63
Maryon's bakers 193
Masborough, nr Rotherham 77, 94
Mason, Alice 216; Mr 216
matron, workhouse 221, 222
Matthews, & Barker, coachbuilder 200, 307, 311; Mr, blacksmith 199, 200; Mill 297
Mayor. Nymphas 145; widow 145
Mead, Albert Frederick 143; F 259; Harry 143; John 24; Thomas 193
Meadow View 310
measles 47, 223
medical officer of health 118, 223, 251, 252; practitioner; see doctor
Medland Elizabeth (d. 1861) 89; James (d. 1823) 89
Medley, Elizabeth 44; George (d. 1562) 44; Henry 44; Wiliam 46
Midland Bank 197, 202
midwife 219
Mid Essex Light Railway 246
Mihill, H W, grocer 192, 199. 296
Mikado Motor Cycle Works 201
milk 162, 165, 166, 244; milkman 308
Mill Field 112; Lane 202
Millbank Avenue 314

ASPECTS OF THE HISTORY OF ONGAR

Miller, Giles, weaver 194
millers 192
milliners 134, 194, 255
Milnthorpe, Dr Derek 276
Mimault, Bernard 315
Mission of St Mary & St Joseph 30, 32
Mitchell, John 138
Mitford, Sarah (d. 1776) 14
Moloney, Rev Michael 32
Mood, Edith 255
Moore, Maurice 279
Morant, Rev Philip 37, 38
Moreton Road 310
Morgan, O B 168
More, Sir Thomas 36, 39
Morice, Anne (née Isaac) 36, 43; Elizabeth (née Medley) 44, 46; Henry 43; Isaac 46; James (d. 1557) 34-35 43; James (d. 1597) 38, 43-47; John 46, 47; John (Poyntz) 47; Margaret 44; Philip 34, 43; Ralph 34, 35, 36, 39, 40, 41, 43; Richard 46; William (d. 1554) 34-44
Morrys, Rev Thomas 44
Moro, Duke de 32
Moseley's music shop 192
motor car 119, 120, 124, 293, 305, 317; trade 200-201
Mott, Ann 196; Mr C junior 37, 260 Charles, glass/china dealer 196; Frank, bookseller/stationer 143, 196, 197, 202; Fred ("Smasher"), newsagent 196
motte & bailey castles 3
mulberry 315
murder 141, 142, 143[14]
Mynto, John 45
Myson, Bob 199, 309; hardware/timber merchant 200; Heat Exchangers 199; Marine 199

Nagle, Eileen 312[2]
National Health Service 226, 227, 228
Natural History of Enthusiasm 50
Navestock 128
Neil, Terry 282
Ness sisters, tailors 306
Nettleton, Elizabeth 27; Rev John 25, 26, 27, 28
New House Farm 74, 78, 80-85, 92
Newcombe's hardware shop 199
newsagents 196-197
Nicholls, Colin 279; George, saddler 200
Nickelsons bakers 193; Mt T.V 281
Nicols, Rev David 32
nightwatch 111. 139; rate 112
Nightingale, Peter 176
Noble, Colonel Sir Arthur 258; Austin 258; Augustus (d. 1853) 154; builders 202, 296, 298; F H N 202; Frederick 16, 116, 121, 249, 258, 264; Frederick Harold 143; Frederick Miller 202, 256, 258, 299; Harriet 258; Maria 202; Messrs 225; Richard (d. 1853) 86, 88, 151, 152, 153, 154, 202, 211, 222; Richard 258
Noble & Taylor 202
Nollekins, Joseph 14
nonconformity (religious), in Abbess Roding 26, 28; in Ongar 23-29; in Pilgrims Hatch 26

North Weald station 231, 233, 236, 237, 241, 244
North Wycke 273
Northern & Eastern Railway 230
Nottingham general cemetery 53
nurserymen/seedsmen 194

oak 313, 314, 315, 317, 318, 319
Oakes, William 208
Offin, Abraham 190
Offley Mr & Mrs 298
Offord, Samuel 128
Old Rectory, Chipping Ongar 19; see also Rectory, Chipping Ongar
Oliver, Richard 139
omnibus 209; see also bus
Ongar Academy 149-168
Ongar Allotments Society 290
Ongar & District Agricultural Society 291; Community Assoc 267; Cottage Hospital 224-225, 304; Horticultural & Allotments Society 256, 290-292
Ongar & Epping Building Society 206
Ongar Assembly Rooms Ltd 265
Ongar Bakery 193
Ongar Book Society 60
Ongar Bowls Club 217
Ongar Brewery Co 211
Ongar Bridge 119, 311, 314
Ongar Castle 1-5, 13, 34, 36, 37, 76, 317; summerhouse 38; see also Saxon burgh
Ongar Cemetery 53, 112, 118, 121, 123, 124, 217, 222, 259, 316, chapel 112, 264
Ongar chapel 50, 52, 94; see also Congregational church; United Reformed church
Ongar Christian Fellowship 268
Ongar Civil parish 125
Ongar Classis 23
Ongar Community Association 267
Ongar Comprehensive School 173-178
Ongar Conservative Registration Assoc 261
Ongar Cottage Homes 179-186; Hospital 224-225, 304
Ongar Cricket Club 115, 261, 275-279
Ongar Dunmow & Yeldham Light Railway 121, 181, 234, 245
Ongar Fair 4, 142, 189, 261, 262
Ongar Flower Club 291
Ongar Gas Co 120, 141, 249-251, 256 261; works 202, 247, 250, 256
Ongar General Friendly Society 222, 227, 261
Ongar Glee Club 264
Ongar Grammar School 16, 115, 149-168, 202, 231, 253, 305; see also Ongar Academy
Ongar Great Park 7
Ongar Horticultural Society 256, 290-292
Ongar House 228
Ongar Hundred 1, 23, 24, 40, 138, 188, 206
Ongar Isolation Hospital 221, 223-224
Ongar Junior School 147, 148[11]
Ongar manor 19, 36, 37, 46, 149; court 26; lord of 19, 188, 256; steward of 24

INDEX

Ongar market 4, 149, 188, 194, 308; see also Market House
Ongar meeting house 26-27, 50; see also Ongar chapel
Ongar New Town 236
Ongar Parish Council 113-125, 176, 223, 240, 253, 256, 258, 259, 268, 315, 316
Ongar Park cottage 271; farm 270; Hall 7, 270, 271, 272; wood 1, 7, 224
Ongar Petty Sessional Division 256, 261
Ongar Photographic Club 291
Ongar Primary School 144, 316; see also King's Trust School
Ongar railway 7, 30, 32, 118, 121, 159, 165, 230-247, 303, 305, 306; milk train 306; Preservation Society 239; station 121, 181, 189, 236, 243, 244, 250, 253, 294; see also railways; name of railway company
Ongar Residential (Public Assistance) School 186
Ongar Rural District Council 113, 116, 118, 123, 124, 125, 223, 224, 227, 253, 266, 293, 298
Ongar Secondary School 147, 168, 169-173, 305, 311
Ongar Show 283, 291, 310, 316
Ongar Smallpox Hospital 224
Ongar Sports & Social Club 285
Ongar Stores 192
Ongar Tobacco Stores Co 197
Ongar Twinning Assoc 315
Ongar Union (Poor Law) 110, 112, 113, 132-137, 141; workhouse 30, 109, 110, 129, 131, 133-137, 221, 223, 224
Ongar Voluntary Fire Brigade 111, 115, 122, 256, 261, 309
Ongar War Memorial Hospital 202, 225-227, 304; League of Friends 226, 292
Ongar Waterworks Co 119, 122, 223, 251, 252, 256
Ongar Works, Birmingham 199
Ongarian, The 160, 163, 164, 165, 167, 168
open spaces 124
Ord, Major 293
Original Poems for Infant Minds 71
orphanage (Catholic) 31
Osborne, Jack 284, 288; John, overseer 130; Joseph 210
O'Sullivan, Mary 196; Rev Michael 32
ostler 310
outdoor relief 107
Overseas Food Gifts Board 226
overseers 107-110, 114, 116, 117, 118, 127, 128, 130, 131, 134, 155, 156
Owen, Thomas Arthur 160

Pace, Dean Richard 34
Padmore, butchers 190, 191
Page, Mrs 279; Philip 278, 279
Paget, Mr 25
Pallavicini, Horatio (d. 1648) 14; Jane (d. 1637) 14
Palmer, James 211; widow Joan 138; John, relieving officer 133; Jonathan 211
Pare, Rev Henry 30, 32
parish amalgamations 19, 20, 41-43; boundaries 313; clerk 14, 21, 107, 115, 116, 117, 119, 120, 121; council (see Ongar Parish Council); surgeon 129, 220 (see also doctor)
Parker, Rev H J 129; John 154, 155, 156; Mary 197; Miss 146; William 129
Parochial Inquisition at Ongar 206
Parson, Sarah, baker 193
Paslow Hall, High Ongar 39
Pateman's shoe shop 196
Paul, Frank, butcher 190
paupers 108, 128, 129, 179, 220; see also vagrants
paving 149
Pavitt, William 139
Pay, Benjamin Joseph 143
Payne, Inspector Ronald 140
Peacock, Edward 214
Peake, John, surgeon 220, 222
Peaked Farm; see New House Farm
Pearce bakers 193; Miss Lottie 298
Pearson, W 280
Peck, David 283
Pelly, Mr Leonard 114
Penningtons Meadow 7
Penson, J, ironmonger 199; William 138
Pensons Lane 313
Pepper, Jno 215
Perry, butchers 190; Jean & Jim 298
Pertwee, Alfred 154; Arthur 154; Edward 154; George 154; Henry 154; John 153; Joseph 153
Petre, 12th Lord 30
petrol stations 192, 201
pharmacies 214-218
Phillips, Mr H.G, surveyor 298
photography 216, 217
physicians & surgeons; see doctors
Piggot's tent factory 136, 221, 224
Pilot Developments Ltd 240, 241
pine 316, 319
plague 219
Plasto, Great & Little 7
platelayer, railway 303
Plaxton, Henry 63; Mary 63
Playl, Elizabeth 194; J, fruiterer 193
Playle, William 190
Pleasance, The 189, 315; see also Wilderness
Pledger, Rev Elias 23
plumber 210, 295
poaching 183
police 111, 120, 139-143; court 261; station 140, 261; see also constables
Pollard, George, draper 256; Mr 164, 165
Pont, Keith 277, 278, 279
poor rate 107, 108, 129; relief 107, 108, 109, 110, 127-137, 222
poorhouse 108, 156; see also workhouse
population 137[7], 160, 190, 230, 252
Porter, Matthew 221; Rev Richard 19, 20; William 219
Portman, Lisa 287
post office 191, 194, 195, 196, 201, 206, 207, 244, 253
Potter, Frank Dobson, surgeon 222; John, surgeon 220, 222; Mr 17

329

ASPECTS OF THE HISTORY OF ONGAR

Poulton, Inspector Percy 140
Powell, Fred 198, 205, 307, 312[2]; Hazel 279; Trevor 279
Poyntz, John (d. 1618) 47
Pratt, Mr 183
Price & Co, clothiers 195; Mr, horseman 297; Mrs 297
printers 192, 197, 279[2&3]
Prior, Miss V. M 282
privies 118, 252, 253, 310-311
publicans 207, 210, 306; see also innkeepers
Pullens, bakers 193
punishment (school) 161, 169, 170, 171

Quaker meeting house, Gracechurch St 19
Queen Anne's Bounty 19
Queen's Scout Award 284, 287
Queensway 317
Quennell, Dr J.C 118, 223, 252

Raby, Misses 135
Rachell, Nathaniel 190
Raggett, Colin 312[2]; family 308
Railton, Mrs 254
railways 230-248; see also under Ongar railway; name of railway company
Rainbird Mr H D 296
Raison, Clara 140; Emily 140; Asst Supt Jeremiah 139; Lydia 140; Phoebe 139
Ramball, James 208
Rand, William 249
rates 112; ORDC 125; parish 20, 116, 121, 123, 156; surveyor 117; see also under gas; lighting; nightwatch; poor
Ray, Brenda 286; Rev Philip 10, 275
Rayleigh, Rev William 32
Rayleigh, Essex 55
recreation ground 123
rectors, Chipping Ongar 18, 19, 23, 24, 44, 147, 149, 165; Greensted 10, 26, 44
Rectory, Chipping Ongar 19; Field 316
Red Cow Inn, Shelley 208, 291
Red Lion Inn, Ongar 205-206; see also Lion Inn
redwood 314, 316, 319
Reed, Alfred 134
Rees, Dr Abraham (d. 1825) 63; D J, chemist 217
Reeve, Rev E J 262; Matthew, greengrocer 194
refuse collection 124
relieving officer 141
retirement home 203
Reynolds, Ellen 194; Mrs, dressmaker 134; Thomas 30
Rich, Mary 43; Sir Richard (d. 1567) 37, 39, 40, 41, 43
Richardson, A 259; John 221; T S, printer 275
Richmond, Duke of 34, 57; Steven 288
Roberts, Michael 282
Rivers, Richard 6
roads fig. 1, 305
Robinson, Inspector Charles Foster 140
Roden House 203; school 158, 203
Roding, River 1, 251, 252, 253

Rogers, Colin 282, 283; Ian 283; Mr R C 282, 283
Rolfe, Clapton 16
Roman brick 1, 3, 13; buildings 1, 13; roads fig 1, 1
Root, John, greengrocer 194; Angela & John 296
Rom River Sand & Gravel Co 247
Rose, Charles 113, 116; Edward, tailor 194-195, 307; George, artist 265; Mr 166; Mr & Mrs 146; Mr F 18; Thomas 195; Thomas E 114, 115, 121
Ross, Rev Lachlan 26, 28; Thomas 26
Rowden, Charles 211
Rowes, Mr 25
Rowland, Rev Robert 44
Royal Academy 52, 54, 98[11]; Chaplain 19; Oak Inn, Ongar 209, 210
Roydon Hall, Essex 34, 43; Temple Roydon 34
Rush Green Isolation Hospital 304
Russell, Lady Elizabeth 46
Ryan, Rev Cornelius 32
Rye Mead 39

St Andrew's church, Greensted 8-10, 41-42, 262, 313; advowson 44
St Edmund, legend of 10-11; window 8
St Helen's church 30-33, 217
St James' church, Marden Ash 311-312
St Martin's church, Ongar 1, 3, 4, 13-22, 42-43, 77, 78, 106, 107, 108, 113, 115, 144, 165, 261, 308, 315; advowson 19, 37; amalgamation of parishes 43-45; church rooms 292; church yard 19, 21, 106, 112, 315
St Martin's Mews 19
saddlers 200, 295, 307
Sadler, Frances 106, 192, 206, 211
Sainsbury's supermarket 147, 316
Sally Lunn 203
Sammes, Bill 276; Frank 276; John 210
Sanders, Mrs (née Clark) 165
Sandwich, Borough of, Kent 260
Sanger, 2nd Lt. Edward 167
Sawkins, newsagent, 197, 202
Saxon burgh 1
scarlet fever 303-304; isolation hospital, Rush Green 304
Schaeffer, Father 31
school 304-305; boarding school for ladies 149; boarding school (nonconformist) 27, 149; industrial schools 179; private 158, 305; secondary 305; workhouse 135; see also Bowes School, Great Stony School, King's Trust School, Ongar Academy, Ongar Comprehensive School, Ongar Cottage Homes, Ongar Grammar School, Ongar Primary School, Ongar Residential (Public Assistance) School, Ongar Secondary School, Roden House School, Windsor House School.
School Gazette 164, 165
schoolmaster 45, 139, 145, 146, 149, 150, 154, 305
schoolmistress 145, 146, 305
Scott, Michael 283
scouting in Ongar 280-289; scout hut 283-284, 316
Scuto, Rev Adrian 32
Schweir, Ernest Frederick 143

INDEX

Scruby, Miss Maria (Anna), postmistress 196; William, postmaster & stationer, 196, 262, 264
Seager, J.W. 298
Searl, William 214
Searle, George 194; "Granny's" greengrocer's shop 307; Mary 194; Phyllis 312[2]; Robert 194; Samuel 194; Sarah 194
Second World War 170, 226, 266, 298, 299, 311-312; see also evacuees
seedsman 115
Senners 197
sequestration (fruits of living) 19
Sergeant, Rev E W 315
servants 41, 186, 221, 255, 306
Servite friars 30
sexton 21-22, 24, 144
Seymour, Sir Thomas 35
Shadrack, Elizabeth 152; Miss 112; Thomas 152, 153, 156
Shakletons 20, 190, 316; see also Church Fields, Rectory Fields
Shaw(e), builder & architect, 203, 216; Walter 210
Sheffield scheme 180
Shelley 249, 251, 252, 290, 291, 317; Hall 128; speedway track 290
Shenfield, Essex 53, 55, 57, 59
Shepherd's Dairy 192; Shepherd's Galleries 249
Shipman, John 153
shoemakers see boot & shoemakers
Shoppers Paradise 192
Shuttleworth, Arthur 290; Bernard 275[4]
Silcock, F 116, saddlers 200
Silver Acorn 284, 288
Silvercroft 112
Silwood, Inspector John 140
Simmons, Inspector Thomas, murder of, 141; Sidney Mainwaring 143
Simpkins, George 136
Simpson, Supt 142
Sims, Henry, drapery asst, 255
Sinclair, Mr 231; Robert 242
Sitch, Scout 280; Tom 299
Skingsley, Mrs 254
Slater, Mr, his waggon, 79
Slaughter, William 138
Small, William 20
smallpox 108, 219, 223, 224; arrest of contact 224; at workhouse 135; inoculations 214, 220; smallpox tents at Toot Hill 135
Smart, Mr 120
Smirke, Robert (d.1845), 57, 64
Smith, A 116; Doreen & Wilfred 279, 299; Henry, bakers, 192; Miss, toy shop, 198; Smith & Ransomes 200; wife of wheelwright 135
Smith's Brasserie 208; Environmental Products Ltd 199
Smitherman, John, miller, 110
Smullen, Rev William 32
Smyth, Helen 297; Jasper, blacksmith, 200; Mr & Mrs 297

Snelling, George, ironmonger & furnishings, 199
Society of Arts 59; for the Protection of Ancient Buildings 16, 17, 261
soldiers 207
Somerset, Rev John 28
Sourby, Will 129
South Essex Waterworks Co 251
South Woodham Ferrars 154, 199
Southminster, Congregational burial ground 273
Southwell, Richard 39
Sparkes, George 24
Sparrow, Tufnell & Co Bank 191, 201
Spearman, Roger, 286; & Sons 297, 300
Spells, Ernest George 143; John 208; Mr 206
Spencer, Mr 184
Spiers, H 255; Jane (d.1902) 255, 257
Springpond 112
Spurgin, Joseph Cakebread 215
stables 205, 206, 207, 208
Staffen, Mrs 90
Stafford, Edward, Duke of Buckingham 36
Stag Inn 210, 295; field 310
Stane, George 145; Katherine 145; Robert 205; Susannah (d.1750) 205
Stanford Gate 7
Stanford Rivers 109, 110, 131, 134, 221, 223, 224, 253, 304; House 50, 74, 88-91
Stannard, Mr 186; Mrs 186
Stanton, Edward 14
Star Supply 192, 257; hardware 199
Starkey, Charlotte 209; Frances (d.1884) 209; Henry 138; Mr 129
stationers 196-197
Stebbing, Benjamin 145, 149
Stephens, Francis 15; Col H F 245
Stocker, Mr F W B. 115
Stokes, Edward 149,152; Elizabeth (d.1868) 152, 157; G & Sons, saddlers, 200, 295; James 152; Jane 152; Joan 312[2]; Jonathan (d.1810) 149; Jonathan 151; Len 306-307, 312[2]; Mary Ann (later West) 151; Richard (d.1875) 149-157; Richard (son of Thomas) 151; Thomas, of Chevers Hall, 151; Wilf 290
Stondon Massey 128, 250; rector of 143
Stondon Road 203
Stratten, Rev James 50
Storey, Miss G A 169
Strype, John 39, 43
Sucklings, blacksmith, 200; Thomas 200
Sunday school 60, 68, 98[21]; Lavenham 60; outing 303
Superintendent, police, 139, 140
surgeon see doctor
Surridge, cycle shop 201, 309; John 143, 201, 259, 307; Victor 201, 307
surveyors 110, 124; parish council 119; roads 117; district council 253
Sutherland, Tony 176
Sutton, Daniel 220, 221; R. 283

ASPECTS OF THE HISTORY OF ONGAR

Swallow, Mr J P 173, 174, 176, 177
sweet shops 197-198, 308
swimming bath 162
Swinburne, Admiral 256; Sir John 188; Lady 19
Sworder, Son & Gingell 291

Tabor, Miss 169
Tabour, George 190
Taff, sweet shop, 197
Tagell, Signal Instructor E 280
tailors 115, 139, 194-195, 306, 307
Tait, Keith 315
tallow chandler 214
Tanner, Rev James 16, 18, 19, 114, 115, 118, 120, 181, 290; Miss L W 19
Tasker, Countess Helen 30
taxis 305, 307;Tucker's taxis 198
Taylor family of Ongar 50-103
Taylor, Albert 202; wife,Alice 202
Taylor, Ann (later Ann Gilbert, d.1866) 51-52, 55, 62, 65, 71, 72, 73, 74, 75, 77, 87; proposal of marriage 99[28]
Taylor, Ann (née Martin, d.1830) 52, 61, 63, 64, 65, 66, 68, 73, 75, 79, 81, 84; death & funeral 88
Taylor, Ann (later Ann Hinton, d.1832) 56
Taylor, Charles (d. 1823) 55, 56, 57-59, 64
Taylor, Decimus 69
Taylor, E M 299; Emily 202, 304, 312, 321[2]; Eric (d.1994) 202
Taylor, George Albert 143
Taylor, Isaac (d.1807) 54-57
Taylor, Rev Isaac (d.1829) 26, 28, 29, 50, 53, 56, 57, 59-88, 315; death & funeral 87-88; educational methods 70
Taylor, Isaac (of Stanford Rivers, d.1865) 50-51, 52, 57, 58, 67, 69, 71, 72, 73, 74, 77, 81, 83, 84, 85, 88-91
Taylor, Canon Isaac (d.1901) 50
Taylor, Jane (d.1824) 51, 52, 55, 65, 71, 72, 73, 74, 75, 76, 77, 80, 81, 82, 83, 84, 86; death & funeral 87; illness 82-83, 86-87
Taylor, Jefferys (d.1853) 52, 67, 69, 71, 72, 75, 83, 84
Taylor, Jemima (later Mrs Herbert d.1866) 52, 53, 71, 72, 75, 77, 83, 89, 90, 101[66]
Taylor, Josiah (d.1834) 56-57
Taylor, Martha 194
Taylor, Martin (d. 1867) 52, 67, 73, 82, 83, 84, 93
Taylor, Mary (née Forrest) 57
Taylor, Rosa (b.1835) 93
Taylor, Sarah (née Jefferys, d.1809) 56; Sarah (later Mrs Hooper, d.1845) 56-57
Taylor, William, of Worcester, 53-54
Taywood Homes 187
tea dealer 191
tea shop 198
telegraph service 253
telephone 303; exchange 253, 254
temperance movement 262, 264
tennis 162, 308, 309
Territorial Army 309

Tesco 192
Thames Water Authority 253
Thimlaby, Miss Elizabeth, draper, 256
Thomas, David & Wendy 299; Rev J. 135; Russell 10
Thomson, James, master of Stanford Rivers Union workhouse 134; Sarah, matron of Stanford Rivers workhouse, 134
Thornthwaite, Mr 153
Thorpe, Amy 294; Mr, butler to Mr Jones, 294; Mrs 294
Thresh, Dr J C 223
Thurgood, John 279
Thurley, Arthur 282
Thurogood, Elizabeth 219
Till, John 107
Tillingham church, Essex 40
Tilson, Mr, headmaster, 305
Timms, Roger 279
Timothy Toys 198
Titanic, sinking of the, 31, 308
tobacconist, 197
Tolpuddle martyrs 313
Tombs, Clive 187
Toot Hill 135; Road 313
Torrance, Mr & Mrs 299
town crier 231
Town Hall, Ongar 105, 109, 133, 142, 188, 275
toy shops 197-198
Toys Galore 198
trade 188-204
Trahearn, Philip 106
tramps, see poor relief; vagrants
Travell, Wm 128
Traveller, Jesse 143
Traveller's, clothes, 196
Travers, James 160
trees, landmark 313-319; town centre 201; wardens 313, 314; see also under individual tree names
Tren, Rev John 26, 28
Trimmer, Blanche (d.1862) 260
Trundle, Mr, groom 297; Peter, toy shop, 198
tuberculosis (consumption) 223, 303
Tudor Cottage 313; Rose, clothes shop, 196
Tuftes Feilde 40
Tuke, Brian 44; George 44; Margaret (née Morice, d.1590) 44
Tustin, Miss, toy shop, 198
Twinkle, Twinkle Little Star 51, 72, 315
Two Brewers, End 139; public house 110, 119, 190, 210, 309; Row 139
Tyler, Captain 231;Thomasine 45
Tynge, William 138
typhoid 67, 223, 252
typhus 219
Tyro, Mr 25

Uden, Mrs 186, 281, 282; Mr W 186, 281
undertakers 202, 203, 256, 297, 298
Underwood, Eliza 221

INDEX

unemployment office 306
uniform, school 166, 305
union of parishes, Chipping Ongar & Greensted 19, 41-43; Chipping Ongar, Greensted, Shelley & Bobbingworth 20; Chipping Ongar & Shelley 20
United Reformed Church, Ongar 50, 52, 53, 203; see also Congregational Church, Ongar
utilities 249-254, 310-311

vagrants 111, 128, 136; see also poor relief
Vaughan, Rev Richard 19
Vaughan Jones, Canon J 13, 19, 226, 282
Vdid, William (d. 1691) 209
Velley, Thomas 24; Rev Thomas 106
Venables, Mr 120
veterinary products 217
vestry 104, 105, 105-113, 118, 127, 128, 129, 131, 132, 135, 155, 156, 220, 221, 222
victuallers 207, 209, 210

waggon, see carrier
Walker, Dr Anthony 144; Flying officer L 282; Leonard R I 14; Lewis 281; Mike 279; Thomas 220; Rev W.H 282
Walkley, J C, newsagent 197
Waller, Geoff 321[2]
walnut 315, 317, 318; l'arbre d'amitié 315
Walsingham, Sir Francis 44
Walter, Colonel R L 14
Waltham Abbey, Essex 39
Wantz Farm 112
Ward, Basil J 160; Bernard, Bishop of Brentwood, 32; David 215, 216; Frank 296
Wardens Farm 270
Warr, butchers, 190
watchmaker 196
watch committee, see night watch
Waterend Farm 273
water supply 117, 118, 119, 149, 222, 251, 304, 310; mains 119; price 181; workhouse 135; see also Herts & Essex Waterworks Company; Ongar Waterworks Company; South East Essex Waterworks Company
Watson, Fothergill 263; Monsignor 31
Watts, Dr Isaac 55, 67
Waylett, John 145
Wayte, Rev Thomas 19
Weal, Emily 134
weaver 194
Weaver, Rev Simon 26, 28
Webb, Philip 16; Rev Mr 62; Roy 300
Webster, Gary 199; James 110; sweet shop, 197
Weeden, Inspector Charles 140
weighbridge 183
Weldon, John 44
Wels, John, whalebone body maker, 194
West, Henry 151; Jane 152; John 152, 206; Mary Ann 151; Sarah 152
Westlake, Herbert 143
whalebone body maker 194
Whaler, Jane 300

wheelwrights 135, 200
Whitbread, John 129; Joseph 134
White, D W 198, 211; Rev G F 259, 280; Henry 145; Mrs 297; Paul 176; Richard 20; Sarah 145; Tyndale 263, 265; widow 145
White Horse, Ongar 207; House, Chipping Ongar 20, 115, 189, 202, 261, 311
White's of Ongar 192, 201
Whitehead, Samuel, wheelwright, 200
Whiterod, Mrs 254
whitesmith 139
whooping cough 223
Wightman, drapers 195; Mr 122; N H 257
Wild, harness makers, 200
Wilderness, The 115, 225, 260, 261, 315; see also The Pleasance
Wildman, Albert Charles 143, 160
Willet, William 210
Williams, Adam 278; George 206; Rob 284
Williamson, John 219
Willingale 221; airfield 217
willow 313, 314, 317, 318
Wilmott, Mrs, sweet shop 198
Wilson, harnessmakers 200; Dr G R 100[61], 224, 227, 259, 276; Jessie (d. 1926) 100[61]; Joshua (d. 1874) 100[61]; Mrs 196, 253; Dr Peter 100[61]; Thomas (d. 1843) 100[61]; Thomas (d. 1915) 100[61]
Win Lane, Ongar 74, 85
Winch, Ernest 295; Mr, builder, 293; Richard 295; Walter 295
Windsor House School, Ongar 158
wine & spirit merchants 191, 215, 216
Wingar's cycle shop 200; Eric & Kath 294; Mr 309; Ron 312[2]
Witham, John, wheelwright, 200
Witt, John 312[2]
Women's Royal Voluntary Service 266
Wood, Mr 279; widow 129; William, master of the poor house, 130
Woodhead, Mr Robert 116
Woodward, John & Jean 300
woodyard 306
Woolner, Inspector Alex 140
Worcester, Worcs.53
workhouse 107, 108, 109, 110, 128, 129, 134, 179, 221; fire 129; infirmary 135, 221; isolation block 221; master/governor 109, 130-131, 156; rules 131; sale of 135; see also Ongar Union; poorhouse
Wray, J H, of Chelmsford 264
Wren House 198
Wright, John 138, 198; John junior 198, 199; William 196
Writtle College 272
Wroth, Sir Thomas 43
Wyatt, Francis 40; George 147; Sir Thomas (d.1554) 43

Yeomanry, 1st Volunteer Battalion 262; 6th Essex 198; drill hall 198; Rifle Volunteer Brigade 256
yew 313, 316, 318
Young, Emma 152; John 219